# The People's Game

Sport in East Germany is commonly associated with the systematic doping that helped to make the country an Olympic superpower. Football played little part in this controversial story. Yet, as a hugely popular activity that was deeply entwined in the social fabric, it exerted an influence that few institutions or pursuits could match. *The People's Game* examines the history of football from the inter-related perspectives of star players, fans, and ordinary citizens who played for fun. Using archival sources and interviews, it reveals football's fluid role in preserving and challenging communist hegemony. By repeatedly emphasising that GDR football was part of an international story, for example, through analysis of the 1974 World Cup finals, Alan McDougall shows how sport transcended the Iron Curtain. Through a study of the mass protests against the *Stasi* team, BFC, during the 1980s, he reveals football's role in foreshadowing the downfall of communism.

Alan McDougall is Associate Professor of Modern European History and European Studies at the University of Guelph.

# The People's Game

## *Football, State and Society in East Germany*

By Alan McDougall

*University of Guelph*

**CAMBRIDGE**
**UNIVERSITY PRESS**

University Printing House, Cambridge CB2 8BS, United Kingdom

Cambridge University Press is part of the University of Cambridge.

It furthers the University's mission by disseminating knowledge in the pursuit of education, learning and research at the highest international levels of excellence.

www.cambridge.org
Information on this title: www.cambridge.org/9781107649712



First published 2014
First paperback edition 2016

*A catalogue record for this publication is available from the British Library*

*Library of Congress Cataloguing in Publication data*
McDougall, Alan.
The people's game : football, state and society in East Germany / Alan McDougall.
pages cm
ISBN 978-1-107-05203-1 (Hardback)
1. Soccer–Germany (East)–History. 2. Soccer teams–Germany (East)–History. 3. Soccer–Social aspects–Germany (East) 4. Soccer fans–Germany (East) 5. Soccer–Political aspects–Germany (East) 6. Sports and state. I. Title.
GV944.G4M44 2014
796.334′6409431–dc23 2014000261

ISBN 978-1-107-05203-1 Hardback
ISBN 978-1-107-64971-2 Paperback

# Contents

# Illustrations

A football map of the GDR.

# Abbreviations

| | |
|---|---|
| ASK | Army Sports Club |
| BFC | Berliner FC Dynamo |
| BSG | Betriebssportgemeinschaft (factory/enterprise sports club) |
| CDU | Christian Democratic Union |
| DEFA | Deutsche Film-Aktiengesellschaft (East German state film company) |
| DFB | Deutscher Fußball-Bund (German Football Association) |
| DFF | Deutscher Fernsehfunk (East German state broadcaster) |
| DFV | Deutscher Fußball-Verband der DDR (East German Football Association) |
| DS | Deutscher Sportausschuß (German Sports Committee) |
| DSB | Deutscher Sportbund (West German sports federation) |
| DTSB | Deutscher Turn- und Sportbund (East German sports federation) |
| FA | Football association |
| FC | Football club |
| FCK | FC Karl-Marx-Stadt |
| FCM | FC Magdeburg |
| FDGB | Freier Deutscher Gewerkschaftsbund (Free Federation of German Trade Unions) |
| FDJ | Free German Youth |
| FIFA | International Federation of Football Associations |
| FRG | Federal Republic of Germany |
| FSV | Fansportverein (fan sports club) |
| GDR | German Democratic Republic |
| GST | Gesellschaft für Sport und Technik (Society for Sport and Technology) |
| HFC | Hallescher FC |
| IM | Inoffizieller Mitarbeiter (unofficial informer) |
| KJS | Kinder- und Jugendsportschule (children and youth sports school) |
| MfS | Ministry for State Security (*Stasi*) |

| | |
|---|---|
| NCAA | National Collegiate Athletic Association |
| NOFV | Nord-Ostdeutscher Fußball-Verband (North-East German Football Association) |
| NSA | Nichtsozialistisches Ausland (non-socialist foreign countries) |
| NSRL | National Socialist League for Physical Education |
| OND | Opera Nazionale Dopolavoro (National Organisation of Recreational Clubs) |
| PDS | Party of Democratic Socialism |
| SBZ | Soviet-Occupied Zone |
| SC | Sports club |
| SG | Sportgemeinschaft (sports community) |
| SED | Socialist Unity Party of Germany |
| SPD | German Social Democratic Party |
| Stako | State Committee for Physical Education and Sport |
| SV | Sportverein (sports association) |
| UEFA | Union of European Football Associations |
| VP | People's Police |
| VSG | Volkssportgemeinschaft (folk sports club) |
| ZIJ | Central Institute for Youth Research |
| ZK | Central Committee |
| ZSG | Central Sports Club |

# Acknowledgements

On my way into Berlin to begin work on this project, I told the taxi driver the subject of my research. His response was incredulous laughter: 'a history of Brazilian football, yes, but the GDR?!' That was the end of our conversation. Fortunately, many others have been more supportive of my interest in the strange history of East German football.

I would like to thank everyone who kindly agreed to be interviewed about their experiences of GDR football, as well as the staff at the archives where I undertook research: in particular Anette Marx at the BStU archive; Jürgen Kumberg and the reading room staff at the Bundesarchiv; and Franz Herz at the NOFV (formerly DFV) archive. For their assistance, I am very grateful to Andreas Gläser, Heiko Heerklotz, Gerard Karpa, Carina Linne, Christian Pankratz, Marie Puddister, and Olaf Strogies. I would also like to thank Ryan Stackhouse for his sterling work on my behalf with GDR sports newspapers.

This project was funded by a grant from the Social Science and Humanities Research Council of Canada (SSHRC). I am very grateful for the SSHRC's generous support, as I am for the additional funding provided by the College of Arts at the University of Guelph.

At Cambridge University Press, the two anonymous readers' reports were extremely helpful in showing me what worked, and what did not quite work, in early drafts of the manuscript. Sincere thanks go to Michael Watson for his support and advice in bringing this project to fruition.

Finally, I would like to thank the friends and family who have been mainstays of my football obsession, beginning with my parents, who gave me the football bug and continue to provide wonderful support in all of my pursuits (academic, sporting, and otherwise). Leon Quinn, my long-standing *Ostfußball* comrade, gave superb advice on my manuscript, equal parts supportive and critical. Erika Westman managed to comment incisively on various iterations of my work, while raising our two beautiful young daughters and writing her own book – a superhuman effort that she carried off with the kindness and wisdom of someone who, in Bob Dylan's words, 'knows too much to argue or to judge'. The births of Sophie

(2010) and Lotte (2013) coincided with the start and finish of the writing process, meaning that GDR football will always be bound up with two of the happiest moments of my life.

Albert Camus wrote that ‘all that I know most surely about morality and obligations, I owe to football’. The people of Liverpool have fought a long campaign for justice, against very difficult odds, since the Hillsborough disaster in 1989. I dedicate this book to the memory of the Hillsborough victims and to my two daughters. YNWA.

Alan McDougall, Toronto

# 1 Introduction

The socialism I believe in is everyone working for each other, everyone having a share of the rewards. It's the way I see football, the way I see life. (Bill Shankly)[1]

'*Männer! Fußball ist alles!*' (Thomas Brussig)[2]

## Past and present in East German football

On 25 October 2011, Dynamo Dresden, the most popular football club in the region that once comprised the German Democratic Republic (GDR), travelled to Borussia Dortmund, the reigning *Bundesliga* champions, for a second-round match in the German Cup. After years spent struggling in the lower divisions, Dynamo were resurgent, sitting in mid-table in the second tier of German football (*2. Bundesliga*). They were no match for their hosts, who won 2–0. But the real story happened off the pitch. The game was delayed for fifteen minutes, as 4,500 Dresden fans outside the stadium clashed with police, throwing bottles and incendiary devices. When it began, unrest continued. Dynamo fans tossed fireworks onto the pitch. The referee suspended play on several occasions. Toilets were set alight, vendor stands vandalised, and 200 seats destroyed. Seventeen people were injured, including two police officers. Fifteen Dresden fans were arrested. The cost of the evening's rioting was estimated at 150,000 Euros.[3]

A month later the disciplinary commission of the German Football Association (*Deutscher Fußball-Bund*, DFB) convened to discuss the events in Dortmund, the fifth time that season that Dynamo fans had been involved in trouble. It decided to ban Dynamo Dresden from the German Cup for the 2012/13 season. The draconian punishment, the commission

[1] www.philosophyfootball.com/new_win.html.

[2] Thomas Brussig, *Leben bis Männer* (Frankfurt/Main: Fischer Taschenbuch Verlag, 2001), p. 95.

[3] Jack-Pitt Brooke, 'A return to all riot on the east German front', *The Independent*, 30 November 2011: www.independent.co.uk/sport/football/news-and-comment/a-return-to-all-riot-on-the-east-german-front-6269683.html.

chairman argued, was justified in the circumstances: 'Never was violence in our football stadia greater than in this year. There have never been deaths in our stadia. But if it carries on like this, it's only a matter of time'.[4]

The story did not end there. The cup ban was overturned on appeal in February 2012. The DFB still imposed a 100,000 Euros fine, banned Dynamo fans from an away match against Eintracht Frankfurt on 16 March, and ordered the closure of Dynamo's ground for a match against Ingolstadt on 11 March.[5] The Ingolstadt match became the site of a remarkable act of defiance against the ruling. Dynamo fans purchased more than 32,000 *Geistertickets* ('ghost tickets') for a game in an empty stadium, thereby setting a new attendance record.[6]

More than twenty years after unification, East German football remains an unloved cousin of its affluent West German counterpart. Whereas the media at home and abroad laud the healthy state of German football, the acme of which was the presence of two *Bundesliga* clubs, Bayern Munich and Borussia Dortmund, in the 2013 Champions' League final, the game in the former GDR is associated with the kind of fan violence that, like communism, should have been left behind in the 1980s. A typical – and typically overstated – view comes from the football historian Hanns Leske. 'In the East', he avers, 'there is not a civilised fan culture as there is in the West'.[7] Lack of success has done little to counterbalance the perception that East German football is a hooligan's playground. Just as the region has struggled economically since the *Wende* ('turn') of 1989–90, so its football teams have struggled to compete. No ex-GDR club has graced the *Bundesliga* since 2009. The region continues to produce outstanding young players. But the only *Ostverein* to match the best of the West since 1989 has been Turbine Potsdam, a marquee club in the growing but still largely ignored world of women's football.

There is an alternative narrative. Its content reflects the ongoing divisions between Easterners and Westerners (*Ossis und Wessis*) – the so-called

[4] 'Dresden wird vom DFB-Pokal ausgeschlossen!', *kicker online*, 24 November 2011: www.kicker.de/news/fussball/dfbpokal/startseite/561125/artikel_dresden-wird-vom-dfb-pokal-ausgeschlossen.html.

[5] 'DFB hebt Pokal-Auschuss von Dynamo Dresden aus', *Welt Online*, 23 February 2012: www.welt.de/sport/fussball/article13884259/DFB-hebt-Pokal-Ausschluss-von-Dynamo-Dresden-auf.html.

[6] 'Geister-Ticket Aktion von Dynamo Dresden sprengt alle Grenzen', *LVZ Online*, 10 March 2011: www.lvz-online.de/sport/regionalsport/run-auf-geistertickets-bei-dynamo-dresden-haelt-an–stadion-schon-fast-ausverkauft/r-regionalsport-a-128739.html.

[7] 'Der Fußball-Osten wird eine öde Steppe werden', interview with Hanns Leske, *3 Ecken Ein Elfer*, 5 August 2009: http://cms.3eckeneinelfer.de/index.php?option=com_content&view=article&id=104%3A-interview-mit-dr-hanns-leske-der-fussball-osten-wird-eine-oede-steppe-werden-&Itemid=12.

'wall in the head' (*Mauer im Kopf*) – in reunited Germany. According to this perspective, Dynamo Dresden's initial explusion from the German Cup was just the latest example of what one fan called the DFB's 'permanent hatred of all East Germans'. The persecution complex was not unfounded. Fan unrest involving numerous West German clubs – Nuremberg, Mainz, St Pauli, and Eintracht Frankfurt – in the 2011/12 season did not lead to similar penalties.[8] The solidarity apparent in the subsequent *Geisterticket* campaign reflected a sense of embattlement that dated back to at least the mid 1990s, when the DFB demoted Dynamo Dresden to the amateur leagues due to financial irregularities. It also had roots in the late GDR, when Dresden's rivals, Berliner FC Dynamo (BFC), the team of *Stasi* boss Erich Mielke, won ten consecutive league titles amid rumours of shady practices involving bought referees.

Aggrieved by past injustices under communism and capitalism, Dynamo fans' conspiratorial theories about the cup ban fed into a wider sense of disenfranchisement. Some ex-GDR clubs – Energie Cottbus, Erzgebirge (formerly Wismut) Aue, Hansa Rostock, and Union Berlin – have enjoyed notable successes since 1991. But many of the biggest names have fallen further than Dresden, including BFC. Hard times have been the norm rather than exception in the post-*Wende* economy too. The unemployment rate in Hansa's home state, Mecklenburg-Vorpommern, in April 2011 stood at 13.2%. In affluent Bavaria, home to Bayern Munich, it was just 3.9%.[9]

In the circumstances, football in the East became an important means of asserting lost or vanishing identities, of fighting back against 'a general devaluation of East German histories since reunification'.[10] Just such a reclamation motivated BFC's 2004 campaign to display three gold stars on club shirts, in defiance of a DFB ruling that granted this mark of privilege to clubs that had won the *Bundesliga* at least ten times (Bayern Munich), but not to the ten-time GDR champions.[11] Since the end of the 1990s, *Ostalgie* ('nostalgia for the East') has been expressed in film, literature, and music. Discarded socialist artefacts attract the cultish attention of online and mail-order collectors.[12] Even the most private of human activities has

[8] Brooke, 'A return to all riot on the east German front'.

[9] Quentin Peel, 'German unemployment falls below 3m', ft.com, 28 April 2011: www.ft.com/cms/s/0/23d92cda-7185–11e0–9b7a-00144feabdc0.html#axzz2d5AvXfQu.

[10] Daphne Berdahl, 'Re-presenting the socialist modern: museums and memory in the former GDR', in Katherine Pence and Paul Betts (eds.), *Socialist Modern: East German Everyday Culture and Politics* (Ann Arbor, MI: University of Michigan Press, 2008), p. 354.

[11] Jutta Braun, '"Very nice, the enemies are gone!" Coming to terms with GDR sports since 1989/90', *Historical Social Research* vol. 32, no. 1 (2007), 181.

[12] Berdahl, 'Re-presenting the socialist modern', pp. 354–5.

been given GDR-specific attributes, with East Germans claiming that they had more and better sex than West Germans.[13] Football has played its part in the retroactive assertion of GDR identity. At various times the two most successful post-*Wende* clubs, Hansa and Energie Cottbus, have become vehicles for articulating Eastern solidarity.[14] This unity in the face of adversity was fleeting. But it illustrates one of the ways in which East German football retains powerful political and socio-cultural functions – and helps to explain why many *Ossis*, even if they were not from Dresden, criticised the DFB's decision to bar Dynamo from the German Cup.[15]

So: a violent, apparently untameable fan culture; a sense that the authorities are conspiring against certain clubs for political reasons; and a persistent struggle to compete against the best teams in West Germany – East German football in 2011, for all of the changes of the previous two decades, bore more than a passing resemblance to the game as it was played in the twilight years of communist dictatorship. The controversies surrounding Dynamo Dresden also highlight the multiple ways in which, even in an age when it has become a relentlessly marketed, multi-billion dollar branch of the entertainment industry, football remains a potentially discordant part of modern societies. The game is still played on a contested terrain that provides both a refuge from, and an articulation of, socio-economic ills – and a means for millions of people, as Eric Dunning argues, to assert 'a relatively high … degree of autonomy as far as their behaviour, identities, identifications, and relationships are concerned'.[16]

## Revising a history of failure?

Mediocrity and an inability to compete at the highest level were, by common consent, central features of football under East German communism. Officials invested considerable resources in 'performance sport' (*Leistungssport*), in order to produce champions whose victories would illustrate communism's superiority over capitalism. In the 1970s and 1980s, this policy, based on sophisticated talent identification and training

[13] Josie McLellan, *Love in the Time of Communism: Intimacy and Sexuality in the GDR* (Cambridge: Cambridge University Press, 2011), p. 1.

[14] Markus Hesselmann and Robert Ide, 'A tale of two Germanys: football culture and national identity in the German Democratic Republic', in Alan Tomlinson and Christopher Young (eds.), *German Football: History, Culture, Society* (London: Routledge, 2006), pp. 45–7.

[15] For a cross-section of opinion among fans in the East, the majority of which condemn the DFB's decision, see the forum discussion 'Dynamo Dresden vom DFB-Pokal 12/13 ausgeschlossen' at the *Nordostfussball* website: http://diskussionen.die-fans.de/nordostfussball/40551-dynamo-dresden-vom-dfb-pokal-2012–2013-ausgeschlossen.html.

[16] Eric Dunning, *Sport Matters: Sociological Studies of Sport, Violence and Civilisation* (London: Routledge, 1999), pp. 3–4.

programmes as well as systematic doping, turned the GDR, a country of seventeen million inhabitants, into an Olympic superpower.

Football played little part in the success story. The East German national team reached the World Cup finals once, in 1974. Qualifying campaigns were otherwise marked by a tendency to squander favourable positions at critical moments. East German clubs struggled in international competition too. Only FC Magdeburg won one of the three major European trophies, the Cup Winners' Cup, also in 1974. The domestic league (*Oberliga*) was small and only intermittently competitive – characteristics shaped not only by the GDR's size, and the region's relatively minor role in German football before 1945, but by communist policies. The result was an inward-looking football culture that struggled to reach the international standards that the GDR set in athletics and swimming.

West German observers and post-*Wende* historians were not alone in regarding East German football as second-rate. The same sentiment prevailed in the GDR, among supporters and functionaries alike. A 1969 report by the East German sports federation (*Deutscher Turn- und Sportbund*, DTSB) spoke witheringly, and typically, of 'the stagnation of GDR football in mediocrity'.[17] Fan petitions (*Eingaben*) to the authorities in the 1980s used similar language, discussing stagnation in the leadership of the East German Football Association (*Deutscher Fußball-Verband der DDR*, DFV), in the national team, and in club football.[18]

In fact, East German football was never as bad as the gloomy analyses suggested. Günter Schneider, the former DFV president, noted in an unpublished study that UEFA ranked the GDR seventh out of thirty-three European nations in club football in 1976. The national team was also ranked among the top third of European countries.[19] Ulrich Hesse-Lichtenberger's 2002 history of German football challenged the 'misconception' that the game in the GDR was 'awful and spectacularly unsuccessful'. He pointed to its accomplishments in youth football and victories by the national side and club teams against eminent West European and South American opponents.[20] Simon Kuper and Stefan Szymanski's *Soccernomics* averred that the GDR – relative to population, experience, and GDP – was not an under-achiever. The authors' 'European efficiency table', covering results between European countries in the

[17] Stiftung der Parteien und Massenorganisationen, Bundesarchiv (SAPMO-BArch), DY 30/IV A 2/18/7, Probleme des Leistungsstandes des DDR-Fußballsports, 9 January 1969.

[18] See e.g. Chapters 8 and 10.

[19] Archivgut des Deutschen Fußballverbandes der DDR (DFV), I/2, Günter Schneider, 'Dokumentation über 45 Jahre Fußball in der SBZ/DDR' (unpublished, *c.* 1996).

[20] Ulrich Hesse-Lichtenberger, *Tor! The Story of German Football* (London: WSC Books, 2002), pp. 222–3.

period 1980–2001, ranked the GDR nineteenth out of forty-nine countries with an 'over-achievement' rating of 0.096. This placed it just behind West Germany, but ahead of England, France, and Italy.[21] In other words, East German football was marginally better than one might have expected it to be.

Fans and officials, though, did not measure success against a rational, data-based yardstick. They measured it against how bad GDR football seemed to be in comparison, first, with other sports in East Germany, and, second, with West German football. The football achievements of similar-sized countries such as Czechoslovakia (1962 World Cup finalists and 1976 European champions) and the Netherlands (World Cup finalists in 1974 and 1978) would also not have gone unnoticed. The complex history of this perceived failure – and what it tells us about the relationships between football, state, and society in the GDR – is the subject of this book.

## GDR football in historiographical context

In 2002 Ulrich Hesse-Lichtenberger described the history of East German football as 'one of the game's most fascinating tales still waiting to be told properly'.[22] A large body of writing on GDR football exists. Rather like the subject matter, it is of patchy quality. There are encyclopaedias and histories of the *Oberliga*,[23] accounts focused on the national team,[24] biographies of star players,[25] and club histories.[26]

[21] Simon Kuper and Stefan Szymanski, *Soccernomics: Why England Loses, Why Germany and Brazil Win, and Why the U.S., Japan, Australia, Turkey – and Even Iraq – Are Destined to Become the Kings of the World's Most Popular Sport* (New York: Nation Books, 2009), pp. 284–6.

[22] Hesse-Lichtenberger, *Tor!*, p. 222.

[23] Hanns Leske, *Enzyklopädie der DDR-Fußballs* (Göttingen: Verlag Die Werkstatt, 2007); Andreas Baingo and Michael Horn, *Die Geschichte der DDR-Oberliga* (Göttingen: Verlag Die Werkstatt, 2004); Horst Friedemann (ed.), *Sparwasser und Mauerblümchen: Die Geschichte des Fußballs in der DDR 1949–1991* (Essen: Klartext, 1991); Michael Horn and Gottfried Weise, *Das große Lexikon des DDR-Fußballs* (Berlin: Schwarzkopf & Schwarzkopf, 2004); Frank Willmann (ed.), *Fußball-Land DDR: Anstoß, Abpfiff, Aus* (Berlin: Eulenspiel Verlag, 2004); Frank Willmann (ed.), *Zonenfußball: Von Wismut Aue bis Rotes Banner Trinwillershagen* (Berlin: Verlag Neues Leben, 2011).

[24] Uwe Karte and Jörg Röhrig, *Kabinengeflüster: Geschichten aus 40 Jahren DDR-Elf* (Kassel: Agon Sportverlag, 1997).

[25] See e.g. Thomas Stridde, *Die Peter-Ducke-Story* (Jena: Glaux Verlag Christine Jäger, 2006).

[26] Club histories consulted for this book include Jörn Luther and Frank Willmann, *BFC Dynamo: Der Meisterclub* (Berlin: Das Neue Berlin, 2003); Jens Fuge, *Leutzscher Legende: Von Britannia 1899 zum FC Sachsen* (Leipzig: Sachsenbuch Verlag, 1992); Markus Hesselmann and Michael Rosentritt, *Hansa Rostock: Der Osten lebt* (Göttingen: Verlag Die Werkstatt, 2000); Annett Gröschner, *Sieben Tränen muß ein Club-Fan weinen: 1. FC Magdeburg – eine Fußballegende* (Leipzig: Gustav Kiepenhauer, 1999); Jörn Luther and Frank Willmann, *Eisern Union!* (Berlin: BasisDruck Verlag, 2010).

Much of the work, written by journalists and fans, commemorates a forty-year history that has been swallowed up since 1990 by West German dominance and the rise of football as a lucrative global brand. The introduction to a 2011 collection of essays on GDR football is tinged with *Ostalgie*, but also suggests that things have changed, and not necessarily for the better, throughout Germany: 'What blessed times, when in East as in West you could meet honest footballers on the street and give them a piece of your mind. Today top-class football has degenerated into a bloated event'.[27] East Germans' almost mocking affection for GDR football, and distance from what has succeeded it, are not only microcosms of their mixed feelings about the GDR and reunited Germany. They also reflect the complex, sometimes contradictory feelings among fans in many countries (England, for example) about what has been won and lost since their game became an integral part of the global capitalist economy and post-modern consumer society.

Scholarly studies of East German football are relatively thin on the ground. In a field that was until recently 'uncharted territory' for GDR specialists,[28] most of the literature focuses on the political instrumentalisation of the game. The Ministry for State Security (MfS, or *Stasi*) developed an extensive network of informers that included leading coaches, players, and referees.[29] It monitored fans' and players' contacts with the West, in a game that was resolutely international in scope and popularity. If a player fell foul of the authorities, the consequences could be severe – witness the possible, though unproven, *Stasi* involvement in the suspicious death of Lutz Eigendorf, a BFC player who fled to West Germany in 1979 and died in a car crash there four years later.[30]

A central issue to arise from recent research is the dysfunctional nature of authority in GDR football. Tensions and rivalries abounded, with the various interested parties – individual clubs and their industry-based benefactors, the DFV, the DTSB, the ruling SED (Socialist Unity Party of Germany), and the *Stasi* – rarely able to sing from the same hymn sheet. 'The bitter and frequent conflicts over the running of football', Mike Dennis and Jonathan Grix argue, 'offer a prime

27 Frank Willmann, 'Vorwort', in Willmann (ed.), *Zonenfußball*, p. 7.

28 Mike Dennis, 'Behind the wall: East German football between state and society', *GFL-Journal* no. 2 (2007), 46.

29 See e.g. Hanns Leske, *Erich Mielke, die Stasi und das runde Leder: Der Einfluß der SED und des Ministeriums für Staatssicherheit auf dem Fußballsport in der DDR* (Göttingen: Verlag Die Werkstatt, 2004); Ingolf Pleil, *Mielke, Macht und Meisterschaft: Die "Bearbeitung" der Sportgemeinschaft Dynamo Dresden durch das MfS 1978–1989* (Berlin: Ch. Links Verlag, 2001).

30 The Eigendorf case is discussed in Chapter 6.

case study of the contested nature of sport' – and the 'contested' character of the SED dictatorship itself.[31]

Another strand of the literature emphasises the external corollary to the picture of internal discord: the subversive impact of West German football.[32] The popularity of West German teams raised uncomfortable questions about national identity, undercutting the GDR's attempts to forge a separate sense of socialist nationhood. East German fans were often 'football cross-dressers', with allegiances on both sides of the Berlin Wall.[33] A fruitful means of analysing the ambiguities of this dual identity has been the only match played between East and West Germany, in Hamburg at the 1974 World Cup finals.[34]

There is also a burgeoning literature on fan culture, with a particular emphasis, as in studies of fan culture in England, on hooliganism. Spectator unrest was common in the 1950s and 1960s. But it became a serious problem in the Honecker era, when a distinctive terrace subculture emerged that was youthful, disrespectful of authority, and prone to violence. Studies have largely focused on the (often ineffective) attempts of the *Stasi* and regular police to quell the upsurge in hooliganism in the 1980s.[35] The preoccupation with a minority of troublemakers, though, tends to obscure other aspects of fan culture. The ways in which football was embedded in popular culture are only just beginning to be explored.[36]

One area that has been largely neglected is recreational football. The SED trumpeted mass sport as the basis for the GDR's international successes. In reality, the pursuit of Olympic glory was not always

[31] Mike Dennis and Jonathan Grix, 'Behind the iron curtain: football as a site of contestation in the East German sports "miracle"', *Sport in History* vol. 30, no. 3 (September 2010), 449–50.

[32] See e.g. Christian Becker and Wolfgang Buss, 'Das "Wunder von Bern" und die DDR', *Deutschland Archiv* vol. 37, no. 3 (2004), 389–99; Jutta Braun and René Wiese, 'DDR-Fußball und gesamtdeutsche Identität im Kalten Krieg', *Historische Sozialforschung* vol. 4 (2005), 191–210; Hesselmann and Ide, 'A tale of two Germanys', pp. 36–51.

[33] Mike Dennis and Norman LaPorte, *State and Minorities in Communist East Germany* (New York and Oxford: Berghahn, 2011), p. 124.

[34] See e.g. Thomas Blees, *90 Minuten Klassenkampf: Das Länderspiel BRD–DDR 1974* (Frankfurt/Main: Fischer Taschenbuch Verlag, 1999); Elke Wittich (ed.), *Wo waren Sie, als das Sparwasser-Tor fiel?* (Hamburg: Konkret Literatur Verlag, 1998).

[35] See e.g. Mike Dennis, 'Soccer hooliganism in the German Democratic Republic', in Tomlinson and Young (eds.), *German Football*, pp. 52–72.

[36] See e.g. the essays on fan culture in Willmann (ed.), *Fußball-Land DDR*, pp. 93–117, as well as the recollections of BFC fan Andreas Gläser in *Der BFC war Schuld am Mauerbau: Ein stolzer Sohn des Proletariats erzählt* (Berlin: Aufbau Taschenbuch Verlag, 2003) and Jena fan Christoph Dieckmann in '"Nur ein Leutzscher ist ein Deutscher"', in Wolfgang Niersbach (ed.), *100 Jahre DFB: Die Geschichte des Deutschen Fußball-Bundes* (Berlin: Sportverlag Berlin, 1999), pp. 311–36.

compatible with grassroots needs. Historians have recently examined holes in the GDR's self-styled image as a *Sportland* ('sports nation'), particularly during the Honecker era.[37] Though the DFV was the GDR's largest individual sports association, football has not yet figured greatly in these discussions.[38] Overcoming the neglect of the everyday history of football – how it was played, organised, and enjoyed by ordinary East Germans – is an essential aspect of this study.

Scholarly literature on GDR football can be summarised as erratic and un-theoretical. Only occasional attempts have been made to provide over-arching conceptual frameworks that place the game in the context of the structures and social realities of the SED dictatorship.[39] The opposing poles of discussion – insider perspectives on the game and revelations about *Stasi* collusion – tend towards nostalgia and denunciation respectively. In this regard, football reflects the post-*Wende* historiography of GDR sport, which initially pitted defenders of the system against scholars, doctors, and ex-athletes bent on exposing the corruption at the heart of the *Sportswunder* ('sports miracle').[40] Blanket *Stasi* monitoring of performance sport and the extensive state-sponsored doping programme constituted the case for the prosecution.[41] Coaches and administrators went on trial for supplying athletes with performance-enhancing drugs from a young age in the country's elite sports schools. Being an unpredictable, skill-based game, football did not feature prominently in the doping debates. Though the national team received pharmaceutical assistance as early as 1965, and doping appears to have been widely practised when GDR teams played on the international stage, state resources were concentrated in other areas. In domestic football, doping was strictly forbidden.[42]

[37] Jutta Braun, 'The people's sport? Popular sport and fans in the later years of the German Democratic Republic', *German History* vol. 27, no. 3 (2009), 414–28; Jonathan Grix, 'The decline of mass sport provision in the German Democratic Republic', *The International Journal of the History of Sport* vol. 25, no. 4 (March 2008), 406–20.

[38] An exception is Alan McDougall, 'Playing the game: football and everyday life in the Honecker era', in Mary Fulbrook and Andrew Port (eds.), *Becoming East German: Socialist Structures and Sensibilities after Hitler* (New York and Oxford: Berghahn, 2013), pp. 257–76.

[39] See e.g. Dennis, 'Behind the wall'; Dennis and Grix, 'Behind the iron curtain'.

[40] Mike Dennis and Jonathan Grix, *Sport under Communism: Behind the East German 'Miracle'* (London: Palgrave Macmillan, 2012), pp. 6–9.

[41] On *Stasi* involvement in performance sport, see Giselher Spitzer, *Sicherungsvorgang Sport: Das Ministerium für Staatssicherheit und der DDR-Spitzensport* (Schorndorf: Verlag Hoffmann, 2005).

[42] Giselher Spitzer, *Fußball und Triathlon: Sportentwicklung in der DDR* (Aachen: Meyer & Meyer, 2004), pp. 54–69.

Recent work on GDR sport has branched out from the initial focus on doping and surveillance.[43] There is a growing literature on spectatorship, with football leading the way, and a similar accretion of new research on recreational sport, where football has figured less prominently.[44] Studies have increasingly placed GDR sport in an international context, particularly through the lens of the country's fraught sporting relations with West Germany.[45] The salience of this approach was borne out in 2013, with the revelations in a Humboldt University study that West Germany, like its much-vilified socialist counterpart, had engaged in the systematic doping of its performance athletes.[46] Cold War sport had its dark secrets on both sides of the Iron Curtain.

In Christiane Eisenberg's view, sport's 'multidimensionality' is its greatest asset, 'since it takes the historian to the so-called ligatures of society, to the contact zones and weaving and knitting of the dimensions that hold society together'.[47] In the GDR, these sporting ligatures brought together the political as well as the social and cultural. No social history of East German football can be written with the politics left out, given the highly politicised nature of SED rule. Equally, no political history of the game should neglect its deep roots in the GDR's social and cultural structures. This study incorporates both perspectives, providing an account that is 'political' not, or not only, in the sense of policy and administration, but also in its analysis of how social and cultural practices shape, and are shaped by, the political environment around them.[48] A paradoxical function of the game, and of sport more generally, is that it is at once a 'dependent and

43 A summary can be found in Kay Schiller and Christopher Young, 'The history and historiography of sport in Germany: social, cultural and political perspectives', *German History* vol. 27, no. 3 (2009), 326–7.

44 On mass sport, see e.g. Jochen Hinsching (ed.), *Alltagssport in der DDR* (Aachen: Meyer & Meyer Verlag, 1998); Molly Wilkinson Johnson, *Training Socialist Citizens: Sports and the State in East Germany* (Leiden and Boston: Brill, 2008); Uta Klaedtke, *Betriebssport in der DDR: Phänomene des Alltagssports* (Hamburg: Verlag Sport & Co, 2007); Dan Wilton, 'The "societalisation" of the state: sport for the masses and popular music in the GDR', in Mary Fulbrook (ed.), *Power and Society in the GDR, 1961–1979: The 'Normalisation' of Rule?* (New York and Oxford: Berghahn, 2009), pp. 102–29.

45 See e.g. Uta Balbier, *Kalter Krieg auf der Aschenbahn: Der deutsch–deutsche Sport 1950–1972. Eine politische Geschichte* (Paderborn, 2007); Jutta Braun and Hans Joachim Teichler (eds.), *Sportstadt Berlin im Kalten Krieg: Prestigekämpfe und Systemwettstreit* (Berlin: Ch. Links Verlag, 2006); Kay Schiller and Christopher Young, *The 1972 Munich Olympics and the Making of Modern Germany* (Berkeley, CA: University of California Press, 2010), ch. 6.

46 'Studie enthüllt systematisches Doping in der BRD', *Spiegel-Online*, 3 August 2013: www.spiegel.de/sport/sonst/studie-der-humboldt-universitaet-systematisches-doping-in-der-brd-a-914597.html.

47 Schiller and Young, 'The history and historiography of sport in Germany', 318–19.

48 Olaf Stieglitz, Jürgen Martschukat, and Kirsten Heinsohn, 'Sportreportage: Sportgeschichte als Kultur- und Sozialgeschichte', in *H-Soz-u-Kult*, 28 May 2009, 24–5: http://hsozkult.geschichte.hu-berlin.de/forum/2009-05-001.

regulated' aspect of human agency and at the same time an 'independent and spontaneous' aspect of it.[49] As the communist authorities discovered, football could be bent into many political shapes, sometimes with considerable success, but it retained an ungovernable core that allowed it to survive as a relatively free enclave of leisure activity.

Football's singular role is beginning to feature in more socially oriented histories of East German sport. A broader range of scholarly work exists on the game's contested role in the Third Reich, where (as in the GDR) it was hugely popular and often regarded with distrust by the authorities. Recent studies have covered all manner of subjects: the DFB, coaches such as Sepp Herberger and Otto Nerz, individual clubs, Jewish footballers, fans, the media, and star players.[50]

Not only the game itself, though, but also the way in which its history in the Third Reich is written, has been contested. Football's own *Historikerstreit* (historians' dispute) occurred following the 2005 publication of Nils Havemann's officially commissioned study of the DFB under Nazism, *Fußball unterm Hakenkreuz* ('Football under the Swastika'). Havemann argued that the football association 'did not try to spread any particular political worldview into society'. It was motivated by business rather than political principles – and the acquiescence of leading functionaries to Hitler's regime needed to be viewed in this light. 'Like the majority of the German population', Havemann asserted, the DFB's support for the Nazi dictatorship was based, at least in the early years, on the latter's compatibility with pre-existing goals rather than on ideological affinity. The attitude of DFB functionaries to Nazism 'often wavered . . . between convinced support and open opposition, between engaged cooperation and unenthusiastic refusal'.[51]

Many historians were sceptical. They attacked the essentially apolitical view of the DFB that Havemann presented, in which 'timeless' phenomena such as 'striving for power, careerism, desire for economic profit . . . fear, jealousy . . . opportunism . . . egocentricity, vanity, and ignorance'[52] effaced ideological motives for collaborating with National Socialism. To many

[49] Schiller and Young, 'The history and historiography of sport in Germany', 319.

[50] See e.g. Rudolf Oswald, *"Fußball-Volksgemeinschaft": Ideologie, Politik und Fanatismus im deutschen Fußball 1919–1964* (Frankfurt/Main: Campus Verlag, 2008); Lorenz Peiffer and Dietrich Schulze-Marmeling (eds.), *Hakenkreuz und rundes Leder: Fußball im Nationalsozialismus* (Göttingen: Verlag Die Werkstatt, 2008); Dietrich Schulze-Marmeling (ed.), *Davidstern und Lederball: Die Geschichte der Juden im deutschen und internationalen Fußball* (Göttingen: Verlag Die Werkstatt, 2003); Markwart Herzog (ed.), *Fußball zur Zeit des Nationalsozialismus: Alltag – Medien – Künste – Stars* (Stuttgart: Kohlhammer, 2008).

[51] Nils Havemann, *Fußball unterm Hakenkreuz: Der DFB zwischen Sport, Politik und Kommerz* (Frankfurt/Main: Campus Verlag, 2005), p. 24.

[52] *Ibid.*, p. 29

scholars, this was a troubling reaffirmation of an old idea, advanced by the DFB for the best part of sixty years, namely that football was essentially an innocent victim of Nazism. Havemann drew particular criticism for in effect exonerating DFB functionaries of the charge of 'genuine', racially based anti-Semitism in their pragmatic decision to ostracise Jewish players and administrators from as early as April 1933.[53]

The Havemann controversy, played out in the lead-up to Germany's hosting of the World Cup in 2006, provided a sharp reminder of the difficulties of disentangling sport and dictatorship in twentieth-century Germany. No similarly discordant debate on GDR football has emerged. Football was never the main story in East German sport. The DFV, moreover, was a communist creation. Whatever room for manoeuvre it sought or gained, it lacked the independent antecedents of the DFB, which predated Nazism by thirty-three years. But many of the questions raised by Havemann's study – how to assess football's collusion with, yet apparent distance from, the political system in which it operated – are relevant to the game's ambiguous role in the history of the GDR.

Sport's established role in the history of the Third Reich reflects a sense that sports history is 'on the advance'.[54] It is certainly taken more seriously by historians today than in the early 1960s, when C. L. R. James, in his pioneering account of cricket and colonialism, *Beyond a Boundary*, wrote of his astonishment that social histories of Victorian England could be written without reference to the era's 'best-known Englishman', the cricketer W. G. Grace.[55]

James was a Marxist who loved sport. This made him unusual. Given the importance that it assumed in communist regimes such as the GDR, it is instructive to note Marxist hostility to sport, a 'ritual', in Theodor Adorno's words, 'in which the subjected celebrate their subjection'.[56] Adorno's unsmiling attitude was brilliantly parodied in a Monty Python sketch in which Marx, appearing on a television game show alongside Mao, Lenin, and Che Guevara, effortlessly answers questions about the class struggle, but misses out on the big prize (a 'beautiful lounge suite') because he does not know who won the 1949 FA Cup final. (The answer, as any self-respecting Marxist should have known, was Wolverhampton

[53] *Ibid.*, pp. 155–72. A summary of the critical responses to Havemann's work is provided by Dietrich Schulze-Marmeling, 'Von Neuberger bis Zwanziger – der lange Marsch', in Peiffer and Schulze-Marmeling (eds.), *Hakenkreuz und rundes Leder*, pp. 579–85.

[54] Stieglitz, Martschukat, and Heinsohn, 'Sportreportage', 24.

[55] C. L. R. James, *Beyond a Boundary* (London: Yellow Jersey Press, 2005), p. 208.

[56] David Inglis, 'Theodor Adorno on sport: the *jeu d'esprit* of despair', in Richard Giulianotti (ed.), *Sport and Modern Social Theorists* (London: Palgrave Macmillan, 2004), p. 85.

Wanderers, who defeated Leicester City 3–1).[57] Though the GDR styled itself as 'the workers' and peasants' state', its concepts of leisure and culture were essentially petty bourgeois. Ulbricht wanted the workers to read *Faust* and listen to Beethoven,[58] rather than spend their time on the more proletarian pursuit of football.

Scholarly attitudes to football's place in modern European history are now more advanced. Even neo-Marxist critiques of the game as a means of maintaining social order have been posited with greater sophistication in the past thirty years.[59] Recent football histories have not only included politics, but also tied the game to social and cultural perspectives – belying, at least in part, the Uruguayan writer Eduardo Galeano's lament that 'contemporary history texts fail to mention [football], even in passing, in countries where it has been and continues to be a primordial symbol of collective identity'.[60] Simon Martin's history of Italian football under fascism emphasises how the sport not only 'manufactured consent' for Mussolini's regime, but also fostered local and regional identities.[61] Robert Edelman's study of Spartak Moscow highlights how the Soviet Union's most popular football club provided a rallying point for relatively free expression.[62] Taking a contemporary controversy as its starting point – the red card given to French captain Zinedine Zidane for butting an Italian defender in the chest during the 2006 World Cup final – Laurent Dubois's 2010 monograph examines the centrality of race and empire to the history of French football.[63] Each example suggests football's importance in reflecting and shaping social and political processes, and in providing a cultural framework for generations of European males. In football, Tony Mason wrote in 1989, 'one enthusiast need only utter two words to another to betray the vast amount of sharing

[57] Ben Carrington, 'Sport without final guarantees: Cultural Studies/Marxism/sport', in Carrington and Ian McDonald (eds.), *Marxism, Cultural Studies and Sport* (Abingdon: Routledge, 2007), pp. 20–1.

[58] Axel Körner, 'Culture', in Mary Fulbrook (ed.), *Europe since 1945* (Oxford: Oxford University Press, 2001), p. 157.

[59] Jeffrey Hill, 'Sport and Politics', *Journal of Contemporary History*, vol. 38, no. 3 (July 2003), 373–4. The work of John Hargreaves and Richard Gruneau in the 1980s departed from the more conventional neo-Marxist analysis of Bero Rigauer a decade earlier (in which he argued that sport was essentially a mirror of work in capitalist societies).

[60] Eduardo Galeano, *Soccer in Sun and Shadow*, trans. Mark Fried (London: Verso, 1998), p. 209.

[61] Simon Martin, *Football and Fascism: The National Game under Mussolini* (London: Berg, 2004).

[62] Robert Edelman, *Spartak Moscow: A History of the People's Team in the Workers' State* (Ithaca, NY: Cornell University Press, 2009).

[63] Laurent Dubois, *Soccer Empire: The World Cup and the Future of France* (Berkeley, CA: University of California Press, 2010).

that is possible for them both, the product of a long involvement of time, attention and money'.[64]

'Is it wise', asks David Goldblatt in his recent global history of the game, 'to recount the history of the modern world without some reference to [football]? Whether the historians like it or not, football cannot be taken out of the history of the modern world and the history of the modern world is unevenly, erratically, but indisputably etched into the history of football'.[65] East German football might not exist in quite the void that Galeano and Goldblatt describe, but it deserves closer attention than it has hitherto received. The social and political history of the people's game presented here attempts to address the deficit.

## German football before 1945: a brief history

Football arrived in Germany, as it arrived throughout the world in the late nineteenth century, via Britain's informal empire – the network of expatriates, from itinerant dockworkers to engineers, who spread and consolidated the commercial predominance of the country that invented the modern game. Football's origins in places as far flung as St Petersburg and Buenos Aires involved first sightings of 'the crazy Englishmen' with their stitched leather balls, playing a simple but unfamiliar game.[66]

In Germany, football was initially the preserve of a small number of middle-class Anglophiles. Working-class interest in the game, widespread in England and Scotland, was absent for a number of reasons, from the apparent lack of pre-industrial 'folk-football' traditions to the hostility of working-class organisations, such as the SPD (the German Social Democratic Party), to leisure-time pursuits that distracted the proletariat from revolution.[67] Most of the football clubs that emerged in the Wilhelmine era were founded by teachers, doctors, lawyers, architects, engineers, and university professors.[68]

Between 1890 and 1914, football established a foothold in German sports culture. The DFB was formed in Leipzig in 1900. Its founding goals included 'the creation of unified playing regulations, the establishment of

[64] Tony Mason, 'Football', in Mason (ed.), *Sport in Britain: A Social History* (Cambridge: Cambridge University Press, 1989), p. 182.

[65] David Goldblatt, *The Ball Is Round: A Global History of Football* (London: Penguin Books, 2006), pp. xii–xiii.

[66] *Ibid.*, ch. 5.

[67] On football's origins in Germany, see e.g. Hesse-Lichtenberger, *Tor!*, pp. 15–27; Christiane Eisenberg, 'Football in Germany: beginnings, 1890–1914', *International Journal of the History of Sport* vol. 8, no. 2 (1991), 205–20.

[68] Havemann, *Fußball unterm Hakenkreuz*, p. 33.

regional associations, the fixing of general German football rules as well as the elimination of English football expressions'.[69] The latter aim reflected the shadow cast over German sports by the *Turnen* (gymnastics) movement that emerged at the beginning of the nineteenth century in response to Prussian military losses to Napoleonic France. In the late Wilhelmine era, *Turnvereine* (gymnastic clubs) had more members than the SPD, Germany's largest political party. They were generally middle-class, conservative, and hostile to 'the English disease' of football.[70] The DFB's founders, keen to establish football's political *bona fides* in an era of strident yet insecure nationalism, took up the cause of Germanisation. A list of terms drawn up in 1902 replaced the English 'corner' with *Eckball*, 'goal' with *Tor*, 'captain' with *Führer*, and 'forward' with *Stürmer*.[71]

Football, though, was hardly an ideal representative of the German nation, any more than it was later an ideal representative of the socialist GDR. The British influence was strong, in everything from club names to coaching. Most importantly, the working class slowly made incursions into the game. The basis for football's growing appeal was, arguably, less its nationalist tendencies than its ability to articulate local and regional identities in a young country with strongly federal traditions.[72]

During the First World War, many Germans encountered the game for the first time. There were the famous matches between British and German soldiers during the Christmas 1914 truce on the Western Front. Behind the front line, troops played regularly, as football eclipsed *Turnen* in terms of cross-class popularity.[73] Football's post-war boom owed much to these wartime experiences. The game became part of a Weimar mass culture that also included cycling, boxing, cinema, and music.[74] In 1914, the DFB numbered 2,233 registered clubs and 189,294 registered members. By 1928, it boasted 6,879 clubs and 865,946 players.[75] The last pre-war national championship final between Fürth and VfB Leipzig drew a crowd of 6,000. The replay of the 1922 final between Nuremberg and Hamburg in Leipzig attracted 60,000 people to a stadium designed to hold 40,000.[76]

[69] Lorenz Peiffer and Dietrich Schulze-Marmeling, 'Der deutsche Fussball und die Politik 1900 bis 1954: Eine kleine Chronologie', in Peiffer and Schulze-Marmeling (eds.), *Hakenkreuz und rundes Leder*, p. 17.

[70] Goldblatt, *The Ball Is Round*, p. 161.

[71] *Ibid.*; Hesse-Lichtenberger, *Tor!*, p. 23.

[72] Wolfram Pyta, 'German football: a cultural history', in Tomlinson and Young (eds.), *German Football*, p. 5.

[73] Peiffer and Schulze-Marmeling, 'Der deutsche Fussball und die Politik', p. 20.

[74] See e.g. Eric Weitz, *Weimar Germany: Promise and Tragedy* (Princeton, NJ: Princeton University Press, 2007), ch. 7.

[75] Havemann, *Fußball unterm Hakenkreuz*, p. 62.

[76] Hesse-Lichtenberger, *Tor!*, pp. 42–3.

Football's newfound status as a mass spectator sport was reflected in, and reinforced by, the building of venues. The Weimar Republic facilitated 'Germany's golden era of stadium construction'.[77]

Expansion boosted the DFB's depleted coffers and allowed it to strengthen its organisational stranglehold on the game. But football's working-class popularity was deeply suspicious to the conservative, anti-communist DFB leadership, who continued to present the game as a healthy, selfless means of contributing to German nationalism. The organisation clung to the ideals of amateurism – a position that would later be adopted, with similar ambiguities, by Nazi and GDR sports functionaries. Chairman Felix Linnemann described professional football in 1927 as a 'symbol of the downfall of a nation'.[78]

The *Gleichschaltung* ('bringing into line') of sport did not proceed from a rigid blueprint after Hitler became Chancellor in January 1933. Though the Nazi Party criticised professionalism in football, cycling, and boxing (hence the ambivalent relationship between the regime and star heavyweight Max Schmeling), it adopted often flexible policies towards pre-existing associations and clubs.[79] The same applied to international sport. Transatlantic boxing contests, football friendlies, and Olympic competition, in Barbara Keys' words, 'offered the Nazis a way to assert national power, while also opening avenues for the infiltration of internationalist ideals and values'.[80]

Not everyone benefited from this relatively tolerant approach. Communist and SPD sports organisations were shut down in 1933, while Jews (initially at least) were ordered into separate clubs. Individual sports were often a step ahead, anticipating the regime's wishes before they became binding orders. In April 1933 the DFB used the pages of *kicker*, a magazine founded by Walter Bensemann, a Jew now exiled in Switzerland, to emphasise that 'members of the Jewish race as well as people who are members of the Marxist movement are no longer acceptable in leading positions of the regional [football] associations'. FC Nuremberg, the dominant force in German football during the 1920s, expelled its Jewish members in the same month.[81]

77 Simon Inglis, *The Football Grounds of Europe* (London: HarperCollinsWillow, 1990), p. 276.

78 Peiffer and Schulze-Marmeling, 'Der deutsche Fussball und die Politik', pp. 25–6.

79 For an overview of the Nazi organisation of sport, see Arnd Krüger, 'Strength through joy: the culture of consent under fascism, Nazism and Francoism', in Krüger and James Riordan (eds.), *The International Politics of Sport in the Twentieth Century* (London: E & FN Spon, 1999), pp. 69–76.

80 Barbara Keys, *Globalizing Sport: National Rivalry and International Community in the 1930s* (Cambridge, MA: Harvard University Press, 2006), p. 116.

81 Peiffer and Schulze-Marmeling, 'Der deutsche Fussball und die Politik', pp. 30–1; Hesse-Lichtenberger, *Tor!*, pp. 62–4.

Such willing conformity, combined with the Nazi leadership's disinterest in the everyday running of football, bought the DFB some breathing space. Football, at least until 1936, was granted what Havemann has called 'supervised autonomy'.[82] Nazi restructuring allowed the DFB to reassert its commitment to amateurism, a principle espoused by both parties, while quietly building up more professional structures. The *Gauligen* (regional leagues), which were introduced in the 1933/4 season, reduced the number of top-flight clubs in Germany from 559 to 133. As in the GDR, players had jobs, but trained and played like professionals.[83]

The chief aim was to improve the national team. Outsiders at the 1934 World Cup finals in Italy, Otto Nerz's squad surprised everyone by defeating Austria's 'wonder team' to finish third. At the 1936 Berlin Olympics, however, Germany was embarrassingly eliminated by Norway in front of a 'very agitated' *Führer* (as Joseph Goebbels, also in attendance, noted in his diary). Worse followed at the World Cup finals in France two years later. Under new coach Sepp Herberger, and with a squad bolstered by the post-*Anschluß* influx of outstanding Austrian players, Germany lost at the first hurdle to Switzerland. The crowd pelted the German players with rotten fruit. Divisions between the Austrians and Germans were blamed for the humiliating exit.[84] Football, as David Goldblatt notes, 'would not yield entirely to the Nazi Party'.[85]

The Second World War disrupted Herberger's plans for Germany's football rehabilitation. The 1942 World Cup finals, slated for Germany, were cancelled. League football, as in the First World War, continued. Long before the final national championship was contested in 1944, however, it was an organisational shambles, with players regularly called up to the front and teams representing the Luftwaffe or the SS making up the numbers.[86] By this time, the DFB no longer existed. The second *Gleichschaltung* of German sport in the mid 1930s reduced its influence, especially over youth football, responsibility for which was given to the Hitler Youth. In 1940, the rump DFB leadership dissolved the organisation and placed its assets in the hands of the sports federation, the National Socialist League for Physical Education (NSRL).[87]

The game survived, but it was subsumed in the compromises and tragedies of the war years. Footballers' experiences during this period embraced active support for the regime (the ex-player and concentration

[82] Havemann, *Fußball unterm Hakenkreuz*, p. 117.
[83] Peiffer and Schulze-Marmeling, 'Der deutsche Fussball und die Politik', p. 34.
[84] Hesse-Lichtenberger, *Tor!*, pp. 77–8, 82–5.
[85] Goldblatt, *The Ball Is Round*, p. 311.
[86] Hesse-Lichtenberger, *Tor!*, pp. 87–96.
[87] Havemann, *Fußball unterm Hakenkreuz*, pp. 173–213.

camp guard Otto Harder), a more neutral path of 'keeping one's head down' (as epitomised by Sepp Herberger), and racial victimhood. In March 1943, the Jewish national team player Julius Hirsch was deported from Karlsruhe to Auschwitz, where he was murdered.[88] When the war ended in May 1945, football – like much of Germany – lay in ruins.

## Football in East Germany before 1945

The region that constituted the GDR played a peripheral role in German football before 1945. The powerhouses were located in the West (teams such as Schalke in the Ruhr) and the affluent South (most notably Nuremberg). Between 1903 and 1945, only two clubs from what became East Germany were national champions: VfB Leipzig (1903, 1906, and 1913) and SC Dresden, who triumphed in the war-weakened contests of 1943 and 1944.[89] The most famous national team line-up of the pre-Herberger era, the 'Breslau XI' that thrashed Denmark in 1937, contained not a single player from the eastern *Gaue* of the Third Reich.[90] In a 2008 volume on football in the Third Reich, none of the thirteen essays on club football dealt with an East German club. Hamburg, Munich, Vienna, and Gelsenkirchen were among the venues visited. Leipzig, Dresden, and Chemnitz were nowhere to be found.[91]

The imbalance is understandable, but it is also somewhat misleading. Football was no less popular in eastern Germany than elsewhere. The English import, for example, attracted widespread middle-class interest in Leipzig. In 1896 VfB Leipzig was formed as a breakaway from a gymnastics club where football was barely tolerated as an intrusion on patriotic drills.[92] Britannia Leipzig, formed three years later, was the brainchild of fourteen young men who caught the football bug and, fearful of what their fathers might think, included a secret oath (renouncing, among other things, cigarettes and lemonade) in the club's founding statutes.[93] When the DFB came into existence in 1900, it did so, not insignificantly, in Leipzig. In this sense at least, East Germany can be viewed as 'the fount . . . of German football'.[94]

88 Hesse-Lichtenberger, *Tor!*, pp. 97–100; Werner Skretny, 'Julius Hirsch: der Nationalspieler, den die Nazis ermordeten', in Peiffer and Schulze-Marmeling (eds.), *Hakenkreuz und rundes Leder*, pp. 493–4.

89 Hesse-Lichtenberger, *Tor!*, p. 292.

90 *Ibid.*, pp. 79–81.

91 Peiffer and Schulze-Marmeling (eds.), *Hakenkreuz und rundes Leder*, pp. 342–472.

92 Hesse-Lichtenberger, *Tor!*, p. 24.

93 Fuge, *Leutzscher Legende*, p. 7.

94 Stephen Wagg, 'On the continent: football in the societies of North West Europe', in Wagg (ed.), *Giving the Game Away: Football, Politics & Culture on Five Continents* (London: Leicester University Press, 1995), p. 118.

Though less successful, the game in the East was subject to the political and socio-economic influences that shaped its ascent in other parts of Germany. Football's rising popularity in the inter-war period, for example, led to the state-supported construction of purpose-built stadia in Rostock, where the 20,000-capacity *Volksstadion* was built with the support of workers' organisations between 1923 and 1928,[95] and Halle, where a new stadium with a capacity of 35,000 was opened in 1936. Having been named in 1939 after the martyred Nazi Horst Wessel, it later became, after the war, the Kurt Wabbel Stadium (in honour of a local wrestler killed at Buchenwald) and, still bearing the hallmark features of Nazi stadium design, the home of *Oberliga* side Hallescher FC.[96]

In the Nazi era, as previously, football was centred on the vibrant club cultures of the West and the South. But the Saxon *Gauliga*, one of sixteen regional competitions created in 1933, was no less popular. As was the case elsewhere, it was weakened by the demands of the war, as players were called up to the Eastern Front, stadia fell into disrepair (or were appropriated for other purposes), and mismatches became common.[97] By this time, clubs and functionaries in the East, like their counterparts in other parts of the Third Reich, had eliminated all Jewish influences from the game. Schild Leipzig, for example, faced constant difficulties after 1933. Their ground was vandalised. Police informers spied on meetings and social events. During the nationwide pogrom *Kristallnacht* ('the night of broken glass') in November 1938, Nazi thugs broke into Schild's clubhouse and tried to set it on fire. A month later the club – like all others within the two major Jewish sports organisations, Schild and Makkabi – was dissolved on Gestapo orders.[98] Such persecution was hardly concealed from the DFB. In Leipzig and elsewhere, it triggered no protests. In their brief portraits of the Nazi era, GDR club histories generally make little or no reference to the fate of local Jewish players.[99]

The careers of the early stars of GDR football were shaped and disrupted by Hitler's dictatorship, war, and the post-war transition to communism. Their stories form part of the collective biography of the Hitler Youth (or 'reconstruction') generation, born between 1919 and 1931, that played

95 Hesselmann and Rosentritt, *Hansa Rostock*, pp. 18–19.

96 Werner Skretny, 'Die Stadionbauten der NS-Zeit: "Es wird schon bezahlt"', in Peiffer and Schulze-Marmeling (eds.), *Hakenkreuz und rundes Leder*, p. 147; Inglis, *The Football Grounds of Europe*, p. 97.

97 Jens Fuge, *Der Rest von Leipzig: BSG Chemie Leipzig* (Kassel: Agon Sportverlag, 2009), p. 13.

98 Havemann, *Fußball unterm Hakenkreuz*, pp. 168–70, 275–6.

99 See e.g. Fuge, *Leutzscher Legende*, pp. 8–10; Luther and Willmann, *Eisern Union!*, pp. 27–32.

a pivotal role in raising East and West Germany from the rubble after 1945.[100] Local idol Herbert Voigtlander (b. 1920) began his goalkeeping career at VfB Chemnitz in 1930, switched to handball in 1938, survived 'Hitler's mad war', and became an important figure in various Chemnitz teams after 1945. Heinz Satrapa (b. 1927) spent his formative years at VfL Zwickau, before becoming the leading scorer in the Horch Zwickau side that claimed the inaugural *Oberliga* title in 1950. Satrapa's clashes with the socialist authorities ensured that he never played for the national team. His more politically reliable contemporary, Günter 'Möppel' Schröter (b. 1927), played until 1944 for Brandenburger BC. He enjoyed an illustrious post-war career at Dynamo Dresden and Dynamo Berlin and captained the GDR between 1958 and 1962.[101]

Information about the formative years of such players is sparse. The silence reflects what W. G. Sebald called 'the individual and collective amnesia' about the Third Reich that characterised the Hitler Youth generation, who focused energies on the forward-looking task of 'systematically rebuild[ing] our badly destroyed homeland' (as Voigtlander put it in 1949),[102] rather than looking back on the discredited past.[103] Exceptions to the rule were those willing to construct an anti-fascist narrative out of their experiences under Nazism. Fritz Gödicke was a prominent and controversial figure in the early years of GDR football as a player, coach, and administrator.[104] Born in 1919 in Zeitz, he joined the workers' sports club, Freie Turnerschaft Zeitz, in 1931.[105] Between 1933 and 1938 Gödicke played for SV (sports association) Zeitz, a move that goes unremarked in his autobiographical writings, but must have been related to the dissolution of socialist and communist sports clubs after the Nazis came to power. In 1938 he moved from Zeitz to Leipzig 'in order to become a better footballer', joining Tura 1899. Gödicke's recollections of the

[100] On the Hitler Youth generation, see e.g. Alan McDougall, 'A duty to forget? The 'Hitler Youth generation' and the transition from Nazism to communism in post-war East Germany, *c.* 1945–49', *German History* vol. 26, no. 1 (2008), 24–46; Dorothee Wierling, 'The Hitler Youth generation in the GDR: insecurities, ambitions and dilemmas', in Konrad Jarausch (ed.), *Dictatorship as Experience: Towards a Socio-Cultural History of the GDR*, trans. Eve Duffy (New York and Oxford: Berghahn, 1999), pp. 307–24.

[101] Horn and Weise, *Das große Lexikon*, pp. 295–6 (Satrapa); Leske, *Enzyklopädie*, pp. 450–1 (Schröter), p. 509 (Voigtlander). See also the interview with Voigtlander, 'Torwächter lernen nie aus!', *Die Neue Fußball-Woche*, 11 November 1949, 16.

[102] 'Torwächter lernen nie aus!', 16.

[103] W. G. Sebald, *On the Natural History of Destruction* (Toronto: Knopf Canada, 2003), p. 10.

[104] Biographies of Gödicke can be found in Horn and Weise, *Das große Lexikon*, p. 130; Leske, *Enzyklopädie*, p. 162.

[105] Archivgut des DFV, XV/63/4/1 (Nachlaß Fritz Gödicke), Person. u. berufliche Entwicklung, n.d.

1938–45 period focus on Tura's role 'as a centre for former workers' sportsmen' and its clandestine function as a place for 'illegal meetings of the communists'.[106]

Called up in June 1943, Gödicke's unpublished notes give a detailed chronological overview of his stint in the Wehrmacht, but contain little reflection on what he saw – 'a curious blindness to experience' also apparent in accounts of the Allied air raids on German cities during the Second World War.[107] Wounded on the Eastern Front in January 1944, he fought in the rearguard action on the Western Front in late 1944 and early 1945. Gödicke was taken prisoner by the Americans near Leipzig in April 1945 and held in a camp where he reconnected with some of his Tura team-mates. He was released in late June, almost immediately joined the communist party, and became a leading figure in the rebuilding of sport in Leipzig.[108] A modest part of the Chemie Leipzig squad that won the league in 1951, Gödicke was by then better known as an administrator (he was the *de facto* head of GDR football between 1950 and 1952). His later career as a coach included a successful spell at Wismut Aue (1955–8) and a less fruitful stint as national team coach (1958–60).[109]

Gödicke's autobiographical sketches are those of a self-consciously anti-fascist footballer. They present a narrative in which uncomfortable aspects of the game's existence during the Third Reich (the persecution of Jews, for example) are absent and in which the post-war motif of selfless reconstruction, based on salvaging the workers' heritage of German sport, is to the fore. The necessity for an apparent fresh start, for wiping the historical slate clean at *Stunde null* ('zero hour'), was no less imperative in football than in other areas after 1945. Gödicke's story replicated the 'pragmatic pact of silence' that allowed the SED regime and the Hitler Youth generation to come together in unquestioning activism,[110] in the process 'obscuring a world that could no longer be presented in comprehensible terms'.[111]

## How football was (dis-)organised in the GDR

Football's post-war reorganisation was sluggish in the Soviet-Occupied Zone (SBZ). Matches were largely confined to the communal level until 1947. Only in 1948 did the Soviets sanction the creation of a zone-wide

[106] Archivgut des DFV, XV/63/4/3 (Nachlaß Fritz Gödicke), Erste Aktivitäten auf sportpolitischem Gebiet in Leipzig bis zur Gründung des FDJ-Sportes (1945–1948), n.d.
[107] Sebald, *Natural History*, p. 20.
[108] Archivgut des DFV, XV/63/4/1, Person. u. berufliche Entwicklung.
[109] Horn and Weise, *Das große Lexikon*, p. 130.
[110] McDougall, 'A duty to forget?', 27.
[111] Sebald, *Natural History*, p. 10.

sports body, the communist-led German Sports Committee (DS). The inaugural SBZ championship that year was a slapdash affair, with qualifying rules that varied from region to region. A football office (*Sparte Fußball*) was not formed within the DS until July 1949, the same month in which the DFB was re-founded in West Germany. One of the office's first actions was to introduce a league competition for the 1949/50 season. The opening matches took place in September, one month before the founding of the GDR.[112]

In December 1950 the DS football office was renamed the 'football section' (*Sektion Fußball*). In July 1952, it became a full member of FIFA, the international governing body of football.[113] Two years later, the football section was – along with the DFB and the Saarland FA – one of twenty-nine founder members of UEFA, the governing body of European football. In her study of the globalisation of sport in the 1930s, Barbara Keys argues that 'it was in elite sport . . . that modern states came to see the greatest political benefits to participation in international culture'.[114] This recognition underpinned the determination of GDR administrators to secure membership in international sports organisations during the 1950s. East Germany, despite its reputation, was never a 'closed society'.[115] However haltingly, the country was part of European football culture.

Despite signs of progress at home and abroad, the 'lawless state of affairs'[116] that prevailed in East German football after 1945 was not easily or quickly overcome. Administrative waters were muddied by the creation in 1952 of the State Committee for Physical Education and Sport (Stako), under the leadership of Manfred Ewald, an administrator with little sympathy for football. Between 1952 and 1957, the organisation of sport essentially passed from the DS to the Stako, though the former remained in existence. The dual structure did football little good. It coincided with a frenetic period of restructuring that culminated in 1954 in the creation of eight new *Oberliga* teams and the relocation of Dynamo Dresden to Berlin and Empor Lauter to Rostock.[117] As tensions between the DS and the Stako made clear, administrators tended towards polyphony rather than symphony when it came to football.

112 Football in the SBZ is discussed in Chapter 2.

113 Horn and Weise, *Das große Lexikon*, p. 385.

114 Keys, *Globalizing Sport*, p. 179.

115 Jan Palmowski, 'Between conformity and *Eigen-Sinn*: new approaches to GDR history', *German History* vol. 20, no. 4 (2002), 502.

116 SAPMO-BArch, DR 5/1276, letter from Ludwig L. to *Die Neue Fußball-Woche*, 5 February 1954.

117 The restructuring is discussed in Chapters 3 and 5.

Figure 1. In the Berlin stadium named after him, party leader Walter Ulbricht (left) shares a conversation with head of sport Manfred Ewald during the GDR's 1–0 win over Romania, November 1967. Both men regarded football with suspicion and preferred to focus resources elsewhere in mobilising sport for the construction of socialism. The Walter Ulbricht Stadium, renamed the World Youth Stadium after Ulbricht's fall from power, was torn down in 1992.

A resolution of sorts was reached with the creation of a national sports federation, the DTSB, in 1957. It replaced the DS and also took over many of the Stako's responsibilities for elite sport. In 1989 the DTSB had approximately 3.7 million members. They paid monthly contributions of 1.30 Marks (adults) or 0.20 Marks (children) to practice sport in one of more than 10,000 registered clubs.[118] The DTSB incorporated thirty-three individual sports associations. The largest were for angling, gymnastics, and football. The DFV, which was founded in May 1958, replaced the DS football section as the national organisation responsible for the game. Its highest organ, the *Verbandstag* (national assembly), convened every two years to elect a presidium, the organisation responsible for the day-to-day running of affairs. Authority in the GDR's fifteen counties (*Bezirke*)

[118] On the organisation and structure of the DTSB, see Andreas Herbst, Winfried Ranke, and Jürgen Winkler (eds.), *So funktionierte die DDR: Band 1* (Hamburg: Rowohlt Verlag, 1994), pp. 234–43.

was represented by the *Bezirksfachausschuß* (county technical committee), elected periodically by the county delegates' conference (*Bezirksdelegiertenkonferenz*). This structure was replicated at district level, where the local delegates' conference (*Kreisdelegiertenkonferenz*) elected a district technical committee (*Kreisfachausschuß*) to manage issues on a daily basis.[119]

The DTSB and the DFV agreed about the need to improve the GDR's international football reputation. But they often disagreed about how this should be achieved. In simple terms, the disagreement played the football-specific focus of the DFV against the DTSB's ambitions to build the GDR into an Olympic superpower – a project in which football, a team sport of minor importance to the Games, was accorded only a bit part. Many of the persistently unstable features of East German football – from the tinkering with league structures to the imposition of training methods from individual Olympic disciplines – arose from this tension, which peaked in the 1970s and 1980s, as officials such as Günter Schneider and Karl Zimmermann sought Politburo support for greater autonomy within the DTSB.[120] The DFV was not, or not always, a cipher. In 1964, it attacked the reforms of 1954 for creating 'a big hole in football's connection to workers in the factories'. '[T]housands of fans', the DFV argued, had been alienated from newly created teams in Dresden, Erfurt, Halle, and Leipzig.[121]

The contested nature of football did not just pit the DFV against the DTSB. It was further complicated by the divergent aims of other parties. The SED leadership took a sporadic interest in the game, primarily in the shape of the Central Committee (ZK) department for sport, headed by Rudi Hellmann between 1960 and 1989. Interest in football could be found in the trade union organisation (*Freier Deutscher Gewerkschaftsbund*, FDGB), which sponsored the national cup competition and was responsible for sport in the workplace. The long-standing FDGB chairman Herbert Warnke, for example, was a passionate fan of Union Berlin. He complained to the Stako in 1955 about the defensive football played in the GDR, the lack of publicity for the FDGB Cup, and the negligent treatment of clubs in East Berlin.[122]

Alongside Hellmann and Ewald, the third dominant figure in GDR sport was Erich Mielke, the Minister for State Security and (between

[119] Archivgut des DFV, I/1, Satzung des Deutschen-Fußball-Verbandes im Deutschen Turn- und Sportbund, 1958.

[120] For the DFV perspective, see Archivgut des DFV, I/2, 'Dokumentation über 45 Jahre Fußball'.

[121] Archivgut des DFV, I/1, Gliederung über Probleme des Fussballs in der DDR, 20 May 1964; Konzeption von Vorschlägen zur weiteren Verbesserung der Arbeit im DFV, 30 July 1964.

[122] Archivgut des DFV, XV/63/6, letter from Herbert Warnke to the Stako football section [*sic.*], 28 January 1955.

1953 and 1989) president of SV Dynamo. Mielke's interest in football was driven by his support for BFC (he rarely missed a home game) and came second only to his love of ice hockey, which was so great that he singlehandedly saved the sport from extinction as an elite sport in 1969, by bankrolling a league whose only two members were the teams of Dynamo Berlin and Dynamo Weißwasser.[123]

Mielke's approach was one example of the 'club egoism' (*Vereinsegoismus*) that pervaded GDR football, taking in regional party bosses, such as Harry Tisch in Rostock and Werner Eberlein in Magdeburg, and directors of factories that sponsored football teams, such as the head of the Carl Zeiss factories in Jena, Wolfgang Biermann, and the head of the Brandenburg steelworks, Hans-Joachim Lauck.[124] A successful team could put a town or region on the map. It could grant the SED a degree of popular legitimacy that was hard to find in other areas. Lothar Stammnitz, the deputy SED leader in *Bezirk* Dresden and a keen Dynamo Dresden supporter, was not the only politician to think that victory on Saturday would equate to increased work productivity on Monday. The game's magnetism, as journalist Klaus Ulrich related in 1990, ensured that some SED leaders spent more time talking to footballers than to local party officials.[125]

The narrow focus on one's own club was replicated at all levels of the football pyramid, from the *Oberliga* to competitions at county (*Bezirk*) and district (*Kreis*) level. 'Locality', as Jan Palmowski argues, 'was an arena of considerable negotiation between party and citizens'.[126] It reinforced ideas and patterns of behaviour that did not necessarily accord with communist expectations. Just as it was difficult for the SED to harness local festivals to a socialist festival culture, so it was hard for the regime to marry local football interests – similarly 'anti-structural' in their unpredictable departure from the set patterns of everyday life – to those of the game at the national level.[127] Nowhere was this more obvious than in the unruly behaviour of spectators. Football was one of many strands of youth culture – from Elvis and Beatles fans in the 1950s and 1960s to punks, Goths, and heavy metal fans in the 1980s – that constantly slipped through the state's hands.[128] It consistently

123 Leske, *Erich Mielke*, pp. 86–8.

124 On competing interests in football, see e.g. Dennis and Grix, 'Behind the iron curtain', 448–50; Leske, *Enzyklopädie*, pp. 15–17.

125 Leske, *Enzyklopädie*, p. 17.

126 Jan Palmowski, 'Regional identities and the limits of democratic centralism in the GDR', *Journal of Contemporary History* vol. 41, no. 3 (July 2006), 525.

127 Jan Palmowski, *Inventing a Socialist Nation: Heimat and the Politics of Everyday Life in the GDR 1945–90* (Cambridge: Cambridge University Press, 2009), pp. 78–9, 96.

128 On youth rebellion, see e.g. Mark Fenemore, *Sex, Thugs and Rock'n'Roll: Teenage Rebels in Cold-War East Germany* (Oxford: Berghahn, 2007); Marc-Dietrich Ohse, *Jugend nach dem Mauerbau: Anpassung, Protest und Eigensinn* (Berlin: Ch. Links Verlag, 2003).

played to its own tune in a country that valued harmony and the collective over discord and the individual.

The result was insularity, tortuous debate, and a chaotic mediocrity that left Manfred Ewald, among others, shaking his head. In 1974 the East German football team returned home from its greatest achievement, a sixth-place finish at the World Cup finals, to a reception hosted by Politburo member Paul Verner. The DTSB boss was not happy about having to attend. He allegedly remarked: 'I have never received a team that did not win any medals'.[129] In Ewald's view football was a pampered child, the recipient of resources out of proportion to its modest achievements. Many football administrators and coaches, in contrast, saw the game as the poor relation of GDR sport: much discussed but little understood, and frequently overlooked as a consequence of the state's Olympic fixation. The truth lies somewhere between these two assessments.[130] A blemish on the 'sports miracle', hugely popular as both spectacle and participatory activity: the people's game offers wide-ranging revelations about the complex interactions between state and society in the GDR.

## Sources, structures, and arguments

This book provides a social and political history of East German football 'in the round', examining people's experiences watching and playing the game, as well as the ways in which the state treated the game and its participants.[131] Research carried out at the Federal Archive (*Bundesarchiv*) in Berlin – home to the holdings of the SED, the FDGB, the DTSB, and many other organisations involved in football – underpins this study. Further work at a national level was carried out in the *Stasi* archives, where the material made available to me concentrated on fan surveillance during the 1970s and 1980s. The DFV archive contained rare finds, including the *Nachlaß* (personal effects) of Günter Schneider and Fritz Gödicke and reports on women's football.

To broaden my fields of enquiry, research was undertaken in four regional archives. The geographical areas covered incorporated football hotbeds (Dresden) and backwaters (Brandenburg) as well as places in between (Erfurt and Halle). Local perspectives became clearer, even if they were mediated through official bodies. Another valuable source was the club archive of Union Berlin. It contained material on the club's

[129] Archivgut des DFV, I/2, 'Dokumentation über 45 Jahre Fußball'.

[130] See Volker Kluge, *Das Sportbuch DDR* (Berlin: Eulenspiegel Verlag, 2004), p. 122.

[131] On writing GDR history 'in the round', see McLellan, *Love in the Time of Communism*, pp. 16–17.

outreach work with supporters in the 1970s and 1980s, spectator unrest, and players' off-field misdemeanours.

Printed primary sources were utilised, primarily in the form of the DFV's weekly newspaper, *Die Neue Fußball-Woche*. Editions of two other newspapers dating from 1947–8, *Junge Welt* (the official organ of the Free German Youth, FDJ) and *Deutsches Sport-Echo* (Germany's only post-war daily sports newspaper), were consulted to gain insights into football in the SBZ, a subject that left few archival traces. My desire to understand how football was experienced and represented led me to a range of other sources, including works of fiction, films (from fluffy musicals to revealing documentaries), and photographs. The work of Bernd Cramer, Harald Hauswald, and Werner Mahler – as shown in this book – provides fascinating glimpses into the vanished world of GDR football culture.

In order to get more directly at people's experiences, this book makes use of fourteen interviews. I was most interested in uncovering the grassroots perspectives on football that are often neglected in archives and newspapers. Like love and sex, football's presence was assumed. The SED might have controlled public discussions about sexuality, but it found it much harder to influence people's sexual preferences and habits.[132] Football, bridging more obviously the public/private sphere, was likewise something that a large part of the population experienced on a regular basis almost regardless of what the state said or did. Supporters watched *Oberliga* games every weekend. Armchair fans had their rituals in front of the television. Kids like goalkeeper Robert Enke in Jena built their weeks around training and matches. Not even reunification in October 1990, recalled one of his team-mates, interrupted these routines.[133]

The bulk of my interviewees are thus either fans (of BFC, Dynamo Dresden, Lokomotive Leipzig, and Union Berlin) or people who played the game at a recreational level. The material collected offers different perspectives, other than the published record(s), giving the reader a sense of 'coming closer to' (*Annäherung*)[134] how football was experienced as a regular, often unremarked part of an individual's life. From interviews conducted for her history of sexuality in the GDR, Josie McLellan concluded that many of her interlocutors 'saw their life histories as entirely unrelated to the political system they had lived under'.[135] In football,

[132] See McLellan, *Love in the Time of Communism.*

[133] Ronald Reng, *A Life Too Short: The Tragedy of Robert Enke*, trans. Shaun Whiteside (London: Yellow Jersey Press), p. 15.

[134] Alf Lüdtke (ed.), *The History of Everyday Life: Reconstructing Historical Experiences and Ways of Life*, trans. William Templer (Princeton, NJ: Princeton University Press, 1995), p. 313.

[135] McLellan, *Love in the Time of Communism*, p. 20.

a similar conclusion holds true. For fans and recreational players, the state was often a distant or irrelevant factor in their everyday enjoyment of the people's game.

The history presented here is arranged thematically, with chronological bookends examining, respectively, football in the SBZ between 1945 and 1949 (Chapter 2) and the end of GDR football between 1989 and 1991 (Chapter 15). In between, three parts (each with four chapters) deal with the three focal points of my work. Part I focuses on football as performance sport, as experienced by its central characters, the players. Chapters deal with the lives of elite footballers, the national team, club football, and *Stasi* surveillance. Part II switches attention to football as a spectator sport. Chapters tackle spectatorship in the Ulbricht era, the new fan culture of the Honecker years, the rise of hooliganism in the same period, and BFC's controversial dominance of the 1980s. Part III concentrates on football as a mass participatory activity. Its four chapters consider football and the 'history of everyday life' (*Alltagsgeschichte*), women's football, matches between East and West German amateur teams, and facilities.

My study posits three interlinked arguments about football's significance in communist East Germany. First, it contends that the game provided people with an eclectic and colourful means of preserving identities that were separate from, and often in collision with, identities endorsed by peers and by the state. The term *Eigen-Sinn* was coined by Alf Lüdtke in his study of workers' shop-floor behaviour during the Wilhelmine and Weimar eras to denote how individuals, through a 'self-assertive prankishness' that eschewed (direct) political engagement, carved out spaces from colleagues and bosses.[136] It has since been adopted by GDR historians, with a primary focus on 'vertical' *Eigen-Sinn* (i.e. separation from one's superiors, often taken to mean separation from the claims of the state).[137] *Eigen-Sinn* has thus become a shorthand for the ways in which citizens used, refused, and adapted to communist dictatorship. In football, Lüdtke's dual concept returns to the fore. The game was certainly a site of what Martin Broszat, in the context of the Third Reich, called *Resistenz* ('immunity') to state

136 Alf Lüdtke, *Eigensinn: Fabrikalltag, Arbeitererfahrungen und Politik vom Kaisserreich bis in den Faschismus* (Hamburg: Ergebnisse, 1993). See also the definition of *Eigen-Sinn* in Lüdtke (ed.), *The History of Everyday Life*, pp. 313–14.

137 See Thomas Lindenberger (ed.), *Herrschaft und Eigen-Sinn in der Diktatur: Studien zur Gesellschaftsgeschichte der DDR* (Cologne: Böhlau Verlag, 1999). On the evolving meaning of *Eigen-Sinn*, see Esther von Richthofen, *Bringing Culture to the Masses: Control, Compromise and Participation in the GDR* (New York and Oxford: Berghahn, 2009), pp. 10–12.

power.[138] It reinforced identities – individual, local, regional, national, and international – that sat awkwardly alongside socialist ideals. In the GDR, as in capitalist societies, the popular cultural activity of football overlapped with, and resisted, hegemonic structures.[139] But football, with its tribal characteristics, was also a form of 'horizontal' *Eigen-Sinn*, i.e. a means of differentiating oneself from one's peers. This was important in the GDR, where uniformity and collectivism were strongly emphasised.

The autonomous spaces that players and fans found and protected can be tied to the book's second major argument. Football exposed in unique ways the limits and dysfunctionality of the SED dictatorship. Recent scholarship has highlighted the fractured reality behind the GDR's Cold War image as a grey totalitarian monolith.[140] Rather it was a vast, unwieldy, and multi-layered creation. Citizens were often active participants in state initiatives, especially at the local level, where the line between state and society was unclear. Equally, their lives had dimensions outside or beyond the state's reach – dimensions that social historians are now beginning to unearth.[141]

Football revelled in a 'surprising degree of autonomy', indicative of both the 'fragmentary distribution of power' in the GDR and the multiple compromises that accompanied the application of authority.[142] Wherever one looks in the history of East German football, one is struck by the limits of the SED dictatorship. This was not for the want of trying in certain areas, as witnessed by the efforts to improve the national team or to combat hooliganism; but, in others, the limits were self-imposed. When it came, for example, to various aspects of recreational football, such as the women's game or the upkeep of facilities, the SED was like an absentee landlord with more important buildings to supervise. It was impossible even for a regime with the GDR's ambitions to regulate every sphere of cultural and social life. The limits on communist power, both willed and unwilled, remind us that football was about much more than interactions with a dictatorship.

[138] Martin Broszat, *Nach Hitler: Der schwierige Umgang mit unserer Geschichte* (Munich: Oldenbourg, 1986), pp. 68–91. On Broszat's discussion of *Widerstand* (active 'opposition') versus *Resistenz* (passive 'immunity') in a GDR context, see Corey Ross, *The East German Dictatorship: Problems and Perspectives in the Interpretation of the GDR* (London: Arnold, 2002), ch. 5.

[139] John Hargreaves, *Sport, Power and Culture: A Social and Historical Analysis of Popular Sports in Britain* (Cambridge: Polity Press, 1986), p. 136.

[140] See e.g. Fulbrook (ed.), *Power and Society in the GDR*; Fulbrook and Port (eds.), *Becoming East German.*

[141] See e.g. McLellan, *Love in the Time of Communism*; Palmowski, *Inventing a Socialist Nation.*

[142] Dennis, 'Behind the wall', 69.

Located in an ambiguous public/private sphere that was neither oppositional nor pro-regime, football was a liminal activity, at once dependent on the centralised state and detached from it. Football's 'betwixt and between' existence allowed practitioners to 'be themselves' in ways that were not possible in the more institutionalised and regulated areas of a small, relatively stable society such as the GDR.[143] East German 'rituals of reversal' such as football or local festivals were not merely means of letting off steam and thus reinforcing order. In euphemising the population's distance from state socialism, they also had a more subversive value.[144] The lives of those involved in football, I argue, were governed by a constrained autonomy that suggests that the GDR's social history was constantly yet fluidly shaped by the twin forces of *Eigen-Sinn* and conformity. Football was ultimately a contested space, where play and spectatorship illustrated the colourful ambiguities of everyday life under communism.

In Francis Spufford's novel *Red Plenty*, a fictionalised Nikita Khrushchev, en route to his meeting with US President Eisenhower in 1959, muses on communism's ability to offer 'a better life' than capitalism: 'better food, better clothes, better planes (like this one), better football games to watch and cards to play and beaches to sit on'.[145] The better life, including the better standard of football, was created no more successfully in the GDR than in the Soviet Union. But studying the East German attempt to bring communism to football (and football to communism) can illuminate a great deal, not only about state and society in the GDR, but also about football's importance in reflecting, and sometimes shaping, developments in modern industrial societies. For all of its insularity, East German football was part of a 'transnational system of relations',[146] one in which the local actors were aware of, and in dialogue with, the world beyond their tightly policed borders. Sometimes this flagged up the GDR's otherness. A DFV report from 1964, for example, devoted extensive space to the English club Arsenal's ultra-modern training facilities, with the unspoken aim of contrasting them with the spartan facilities available to GDR clubs.[147] Yet differences between the game under communism and capitalism were not always obvious. In the 1980s, leaving aside results in European club competition, GDR football – with its struggling national team,

[143] On liminality, see Victor Turner, *The Forest of Symbols: Aspects of Ndembu Ritual* (Ithaca, NY: Cornell University Press, 1967), pp. 93–111.
[144] Palmowski, *Inventing a Socialist Nation*, p. 254.
[145] Francis Spufford, *Red Plenty* (London: Faber and Faber, 2010), p. 21.
[146] Stieglitz, Martschukat, and Heinsohn, 'Sportreportage', 7.
[147] Archivgut des DFV, I/1, Analyse über den Stand der leistungsbestimmenden Faktoren im Fussball, 19 August 1964.

hooligan problems, run-down stadia, and unsympathetic government – bore a striking resemblance to its English counterpart.

A game with cross-class appeal but indubitably proletarian roots, football was one of the most authentic expressions of working-class experience in East Germany. It might not have been (even for men) 'everything', as the coach claims at the end of Thomas Brussig's play *Leben bis Männer*. But football was a powerful political force, as the public outcry against BFC's dominance in the 1980s in particular suggested, and a political force that – in the spirit of Bill Shankly's maxim – was often truer to socialism's collective and egalitarian values than the regime that ruled in socialism's name. The following history shows the often unconscious ways in which football subverted or eluded state control. Authoritarian attempts to mobilise, or marginalise, the game for political purposes – as the histories of the Soviet Union, Francoist Spain, fascist Italy, Nazi Germany, and apartheid South Africa attest – often backfire. This intractability is part of football's enduring appeal as a global cultural practice that, for all of its problems, retains a dramatic and democratic core.

# 2 Football reconstructed

## Football at 'zero hour'

When the Soviet military authorities in Leipzig authorised the resumption of sporting competition in the autumn of 1945, one of the new sports communities (*Sportgemeinschaften*) that came into existence was SG Thekla. Thekla's 'footballers of the first hour' were a motley crew of returning soldiers and PoWs. They had previously played for ATV Thekla or SV Leipzig, two of the local clubs that were dissolved as part of the initial post-war drive towards de-Nazification in occupied Germany.[1] Before the scale of the bureaucratic task in front of them became apparent, the occupiers sought sweeping purges of institutions and individuals tainted by complicity with Nazism. Law Number 2, passed by the Allied Control Commission in October 1945, liquidated the NSRL, the umbrella organisation for sport in the Third Reich, and banned all clubs that had been NSRL members. Directive 23 from December 1945 stipulated that 'non-military sporting organisations of a local character' were only permitted to compete in their district, subject to authorisation from the relevant occupying power.[2]

Facilities for the new club were, in the words of one founder member, 'truly catastrophic'. ATV Thekla's old ground in the north-east of the city was now a vegetable patch. The players relocated to a nearby facility that had survived the war partly intact. Changing rooms were situated in a restaurant 150 metres from the pitch. There was one bucket and cold water only for washing after training or matches. Meetings as well as social gatherings took place in local pubs.[3]

From modest beginnings, SG Thekla built a thriving football club. In the Leipzig district league, the first team finished second and third

[1] Günter Haase, 'Die Zeit vor der Vereinsgründung (1945–1950)', in Rolf Beyer, *Rotation Leipzig 1950: 50 Jahre* (Leipzig: Self-published, 2000), p. 7.

[2] Johnson, *Training Socialist Citizens*, pp. 48–9; René Wiese, 'Hertha BSC im Kalten Krieg (1945–1961)', in Braun and Teichler (eds.), *Sportstadt Berlin*, p. 99.

[3] Haase, 'Die Zeit vor der Vereinsgründung', p. 7.

respectively in the 1946/7 and 1947/8 seasons. By the time that it qualified for the Saxon regional league (*Landesliga*) in 1950, the name Thekla had been jettisoned in favour of something more suitable to the prevailing political climate, as the SED promoted factory-based clubs that broke with Germany's compromised sporting past. Thekla thus briefly became SG Union Leipzig, under the tutelage of a yeast factory, before settling on sponsorship from the printing industry and the name BSG Rotation Leipzig Nord.[4]

SG Thekla's story typified the early years of football in the SBZ. Amid political and economic devastation, sport was a low priority for military officials and administrators primarily concerned with existential issues. Conditions were primitive. Of Berlin's 426 gymnasia, 301 were destroyed in the war. Eleven of the twenty-three sports grounds in one Leipzig district met the same fate. The sporting amenities that survived were often turned into makeshift hospitals or gardens.[5]

Football's relative unimportance, though, made it important, as a welcome distraction in difficult times. 'Keeping up everyday routines, regardless of disaster', as W. G. Sebald sceptically noted, 'is a tried and trusted method of preserving what is thought of as healthy human reason'.[6] Sport, like going out to bars and dance halls, offered a stable and enjoyable activity that could be practised in essentially apolitical ways. Rebuilding football allowed both a distancing from politics past and present – in a period when, in Victor Klemperer's words, Germans were, or at least wanted to be, 'absolutely without history'[7] – and the survival of local identities and traditions. It required fierce volunteer commitment; a willingness to work within, and around, the strictures of Soviet occupation; and, in terms of facilities, the ability to make a silk purse from a sow's ear.

Grassroots activism, rather than central directives, drove football forward at *Stunde null*, foreshadowing the centrifugal tendencies that characterised the game's development in the GDR. A small group of friends founded SG Thekla. Various dedicated individuals – including the head of a local publishing house (and later prominent sports functionary), Heinz Schöbel – ensured that it survived and prospered.[8] Another example was at SG Leutzsch, the forerunner to Chemie Leipzig. Its chairman, Karl Plättner, just returned from an English PoW camp, oversaw the transfer of scarce building materials from

[4] *Ibid.*, pp. 7–12. [5] Johnson, *Training Socialist Citizens*, pp. 47–8.
[6] Sebald, *Natural History*, p. 42.
[7] Victor Klemperer, *Ich will Zeugnis ablegen bis zum letzten: Tagebücher, 1942–1945* (Berlin: Aufbau Verlag, 1999), p. 773 (diary entry from 11 May 1945).
[8] Beyer, *Rotation Leipzig*, p. 23.

crumbling regatta stands on the canal to the club's stadium in the west of the city in 1946, a painstaking process that took almost a year and relied on volunteer help from the players.[9] Particularly in rural areas such as Thuringia and Mecklenburg, the reinstitution of regular competition – despite a lack of public transport, a dearth of useable facilities, and the bitterly cold winter of 1946/7[10] – owed much to the ingrained and politically unquestioning work ethic of football-loving elements of the 'reconstruction generation'.[11]

Supporters flocked to matches. Forty thousand people attended the final of the first SBZ championship between SG Planitz and SG Freiimfelde Halle in Leipzig in July 1948.[12] It was a similar story throughout occupied Germany, as people sought diversion from the hardships of daily life. West German clubs such as Bayern Munich played 'calorie matches' (*Kalorienspiele*) in front of large crowds, after which the players – no less needy of sustenance than those watching – were paid by local entrepreneurs with food and drink rather than money.[13] Preoccupation with the bare necessities shaped football in its early post-war guises. The success of coaching courses in Leipzig, for example, depended on the presence of the Leutzsch striker Gerhard Hübler, not because of his football skills, but because his family business supplied vegetables to Soviet forces stationed in the city. A word in the right place from him ensured that participants would not go hungry.[14]

If food shortages were a common concern among players across partitioned Germany, the paths taken by the game that they played rapidly diverged. In the Western zones, official directives on de-Nazification notwithstanding, clubs quickly resumed former identities, allowing the likes of Bayern Munich and Schalke 04 to keep a direct line to traditions much older than the Nazi dictatorship. By 1946 regional leagues and organisations were in place, ensuring a standard of competition that, despite the vexed issue of amateurism, soon made West German football an international force.[15] In the SBZ, in contrast, most of the football

[9] Fuge, *Leutzscher Legende*, p. 12.

[10] See e.g. 'Fußball in Mecklenburg-Vorpommern', *Junge Welt* (*JW*), 5 March 1947, 4; 'Der Jugendfußball in Thüringen', *JW*, 16 April 1947, 4.

[11] On the 'reconstruction' (or Hitler Youth) generation, see e.g. McDougall, 'A duty to forget?'.

[12] Baingo and Horn, *Die Geschichte der DDR-Oberliga*, p. 10.

[13] Dirk Bitzer and Bernd Wilting, *Stürmen für Deutschland: Die Geschichte des deutschen Fußballs von 1933 bis 1954* (Frankfurt/Main: Campus Verlag, 2003), pp. 167–8.

[14] Archivgut des DFV, XV/63/4/3, Erinnerungen und Einschätzungen zum FDJ-Sport, n.d.

[15] Bitzer and Wilting, *Stürmen für Deutschland*, pp. 166–9, 171–2; Hans Joachim Teichler, 'Fußball in der DDR', *Aus Politik und Zeitgeschichte* 19 (2006), 26.

played before 1948 fell into the category of communal sport, as per the Allied directive of December 1945. Teams could only play opponents from the same town or city. Players were restricted to playing for clubs in the district in which they resided. The constraints, as the GDR's football newspaper *Die Neue Fußball-Woche* conceded in October 1949, caused a 'standstill'. Competitive matches were scarce. Standards dropped.[16]

Unlike the Western powers, the Soviets had no truck with resurrecting the tainted past. The upshot was a bewildering parade of club name changes, mergers, and even relocations. SG Leutzsch, for example, emerged in 1945 from the remnants of Tura 1899 Leipzig (formed in 1938 after a merger of two local clubs), but only kept the Leutzsch name for four years. In 1949 it was briefly renamed ZSG Industrie Leipzig; a year later it became BSG Chemie Leipzig.[17] The 'name salad' at the former SG Thekla did not end in 1950 when the club became Rotation Leipzig Nord. The following year it was renamed Rotation Leipzig Nordost. In 1955 it became Rotation Leipzig Südwest. Only in 1958 did the club adopt the more permanent name of BSG Rotation Leipzig 1950.[18]

A similarly confusing process took place elsewhere in Eastern Europe, one that reflected the shifting political sands of the late 1940s and 1950s. One of Hungary's leading pre-war teams, MTK Budapest, for example, was taken over by the secret police after the communists came to power. It underwent no fewer than four name changes – from Textiles to Bástya to Vörös Lobogó and finally back to MTK – between 1950 and 1957.[19] In Poland during the period of liberalisation bookended by Stalin's death in 1953 and Gomułka's coming to power three years later, twelve first division clubs dropped their socialist nomenclature in favour of names that predated communism.[20] Naming, and renaming, was an inherently political act.

## Early football competitions

Given the GDR's reputation as sponsor of the world's most ruthlessly concentrated sports system, it is instructive to note the disorder that governed sporting activities in the SBZ between 1945 and 1947. While the SED undoubtedly viewed sport as a means to a political

16 Archivgut des DFV, I/1, 'Dokumentation über 45 Jahre Fußball'.
17 Fuge, *Leutzscher Legende*, pp. 9–15, 18. 18 Beyer, *Rotation Leipzig*, pp. 13–15.
19 Jonathan Wilson, *Behind the Curtain: Travels in Eastern European Football* (London: Orion, 2006), pp. 73–4.
20 Vic Duke, 'Going to the market: football in the societies of Eastern Europe', in Wagg (ed.), *Giving the Game Away*, p. 93.

end, and sought to exert control on how and where it was played, the era of communal sport did not lend itself to a simple political narrative. The administrative influence of each of the SBZ's five states (*Länder*), not to mention the anomalous four-power occupation of Berlin, created a heterogeneous landscape. This was certainly the case in football.

In the immediate post-war period, footballers often came up with do-it-yourself solutions. Street football was a popular pastime in many rubble-strewn neighbourhoods – and remained so until at least the mid 1950s, when functionaries in the Berlin district of Weißensee, mindful of broken windows and held-up traffic, were still exhorting boys to play in more organised forms.[21] In the absence of footballs, children kicked around tennis balls or made balls from rolls of fabric.[22] As in any environment of privation, from the back alleys of industrial towns in northern England to the *favelas* (shanty towns) of Brazil, material shortages encouraged improvisation and a sense of autonomy. The schoolboy team established in 1946 at Eintracht Mahlsdorf on the outskirts of Berlin played in white gym shirts with home-made red strings affixed to them. Nets were made of fencing wire.[23] Such experiences forged the volunteer ethos that was integral to GDR sport. From the outset, it was encouraged by the financially pressed authorities – witness, for example, a 1947 call for 'self-help' (i.e. citizens' monetary and labour contributions) in rebuilding facilities in Berlin.[24]

In terms of competitive football, uniform structures and regulations came slowly. In September 1945, the Soviets authorised the first inter-city match, in which a Berlin XI defeated a team from Wittenberg 6–3 – an event that indicated that there were ways around the communal sport directive.[25] Such encounters relied on the discretion of local Soviet officers, some of whom were clearly football fans. Eight matches between Leipzig teams and teams from other cities, including Dessau and Dresden, took place in 1945 and 1946.[26]

In general, though, the football scene was fractured. The FDJ's attempts to organise an SBZ football championship in 1946 foundered on the differing structures in place in the *Länder*.[27] The regional

21 'Von der Straße auf den Fußballplatz', *Die Neue Fußball-Woche*, 14 February 1956, 11.
22 Johnson, *Training Socialist Citizens*, pp. 50–1.
23 www.bsv-eintracht-mahlsdorf.de/Verein/verein3.htm.
24 'Ein dringendes Gebot der Volksgesundheit – Baut Sportplätze!', *Deutsches Sport-Echo* (*DSE*), 16 June 1947, 3.
25 Archivgut des DFV, I/1, 'Dokumentation über 45 Jahre Fußball'.
26 Archivgut des DFV, XV/63/4/1, Fußballstädtespiele Leizpig, n.d.
27 Archivgut des DFV, I/1, 'Dokumentation über 45 Jahre Fußball'.

championships in Thuringia and Saxony in 1947/8 were played on a knock-out basis and bizarrely stopped at the semi-final stage. In Mecklenburg the regional authorities organised a two-division championship and saw their tournament through to its conclusion, with SG Schwerin emerging as champions.[28] At the same time, competitive leagues flourished in cities such as Leipzig, home to a twenty-six-team competition by 1949.[29] Owing to its four-power occupation, Berlin was a special case. A conflict played out there between the communal sport model favoured by the Soviets and the reintroduction of 'associational' sport (the *Verein* model) supported by the Western powers. Political tensions did not prevent a busy playing schedule. The 1945/6 all-Berlin championship was contested across four divisions; 20,000 people watched Wilmersdorf (from the West) defeat Prenzlauer Berg (from the East) in the final. In the following season a city league (*Stadtliga*) was created; the first Berlin cup final held; and the first inter-zonal match authorised, a 2–2 draw between Berlin and Düsseldorf representative teams at the Olympic Stadium in front of 55,000 fans. In Berlin, more than anywhere else, the impracticalities of the communal sport regulation, and popular attachments to pre-1945 traditions, were evident. During the Berlin blockade, the Soviets allowed a first East Berlin club to re-adopt its traditional name (VfB Pankow) and sanctioned a German championship contest between Berlin champions Oberschönweide and St Pauli from Hamburg.[30]

The match between Oberschönweide and St Pauli, which the latter won 5–1 in July 1948, was the subject of extensive press coverage. The FDJ newspaper *Junge Welt* issued a special edition to mark the occasion, containing profiles of the Oberschönweide squad, an interview with the St Pauli coach, and even a joke editorial that played on the hoariest football clichés ('the only thing that is certain in a football match is that the winner will be the team who scores a lot of goals in their opponent's net and prevents any going in their own').[31] In the SBZ, as later in the GDR, there was friction between football's enforced isolation and the desire of its participants to remain open to the outside world, and to West Germany in particular. *Junge Welt* devoted considerable space to football in the Western occupied zones.[32] It also looked further afield,

[28] Archivgut des DFV, XV/63/4/1, handwritten notes on '1947/8', n.d.

[29] Fuge, *Leutzscher Legende*, p. 12.

[30] Archivgut des DFV, XV/63/4/1, handwritten notes on Berlin football, 1945–8, n.d.; Wiese, 'Hertha BSC im Kalten Krieg', pp. 98–102.

[31] Sonder-Ausgabe zum Fußballkampf FC St. Pauli-Oberschöneweide, *JW*, 18 July 1948, 1–3.

[32] See e.g. 'Ein Blick in den deutschen Fußballsport', *JW*, 10 April 1947, 4.

whether it was to laud the fairplay of English players (in contrast to the 'serial moaners' in the East German game), or to offer amusing tidbits about a player in northern England who fell into a sinkhole during a game and a riot at a match in Kenya triggered by a medicine man burying a chicken's stomach beneath the pitch.[33] The internationalism belied the blinkered tendencies more commonly associated with football under Soviet occupation.

Communal restrictions were lifted in 1947/8, allowing teams to compete in regional championships for the first time. But vital time had been lost. National structures were re-established more rapidly in other European countries, including the future West Germany, where, as *Junge Welt* noted admiringly in April 1947, 'we find the old, familiar [club] names'.[34] It is interesting to speculate on the long-term effects of this 'false start' for East German football.[35] The 'club egoism' that complicated the DFV's attempts to bring GDR football up to world-class standards certainly had roots in the enforced localism of the 1945–8 period, when the first seeds of an inward-looking football culture were sown and the evident desire to be part of a German, and indeed international, football community was stymied.

## Football of the new type?

In 1948 football became more centralised. The first SBZ championship, though, was more indicative of the dysfunctional present than the communist-controlled future. With all Berlin teams barred on account of the city's special status, the knock-out tournament held that summer involved ten teams, two from each of the SBZ's five regions. Qualification rules varied. The champions and runners-up from Mecklenburg and Brandenburg were invited. The two leading teams from the other three *Länder*, where championship tournaments had not been played to a conclusion, made the cut. Particularly strange was the competition in Thuringia, where the teams that qualified were SG Sömmerda and SG Weimar Ost. After losing 2–1 at Weimar Ost, however, SG Meiningen protested that the hosts had fielded an ineligible player. As the case was not heard before Weimar's next match against SG Suhl, the Meiningen players took to the field for this match in their full kit – and were only persuaded to leave after lengthy discussions.[36]

[33] 'Auf dem Fußballfeld wird nicht gemeckert', *JW*, 18 August 1948, 5; 'Sportallerlei', *JW*, 17 March 1948, 7.

[34] 'Ein Blick in den deutschen Fußballsport', 4.

[35] Teichler, 'Fußball in der DDR', 26.

[36] Baingo and Horn, *Die Geschichte der DDR-Oberliga*, p. 10.

After a series of knock-out matches in late June and early July 1948, SG Planitz from the small Saxon town of Zwickau emerged as the first East German football champions, defeating SG Freiimfelde Halle 1–0 in the final in Leipzig. The chaos of the tournament was followed by a tightening of the political reins. The Soviet authorities, despite their concessions to club and inter-zonal football in Berlin at the time, vetoed Planitz from travelling to Stuttgart (in the French zone) for a quarter-final match in the German championship against FC Nuremberg. The Saxons exited the competition without playing in it.[37] This indicated a hard-line shift in the SED's sport policies at this time, one that corresponded to the more authoritarian and centralised precepts of the Leninist 'party of the new type' then being hammered into shape through purges and self-criticism.[38] The creation of the DS in October 1948 gave the communists the opportunity to enforce monopoly control over football's ragged structures. New sports clubs had to register with the police. Any clubs that failed to break with the associational model were to be dissolved. Favour was conferred on SGs with progressive names (and the right political credentials) or newly created factory sports clubs (*Betriebssportgemeinschaften*, BSGs).[39] Any notion of an independent sports movement, including the resurrection of workers' sports clubs disbanded by the Nazis after 1933, disappeared.[40]

Football was not transformed overnight. As late as August 1948, an article in *Junge Welt* suggested an ambivalent attitude to the *Berufssport* ('professional sport') prevalent in the Western zones, criticising not so much its existence as recent examples of professional athletes posing as amateurs.[41] Though regional championships were organised throughout the SBZ for the first time during the 1948/9 season, the tension between past and future visions of football was reflected in the fact that two cup competitions took place, one for older ('bourgeois') clubs and one for BSGs, sponsored by the FDGB and won by Waggonbau Dessau.[42] The introduction of the factory-based sports model was not always a change only, or entirely, for the worse. When SG Leutzsch was fused with four other local clubs to create ZSG (Central Sports Club) Industrie Leipzig in 1949, it received an influx of cash and new players. At the same time, day-to-day operations were left in the hands of functionaries

[37] *Ibid.*, p. 11.
[38] See e.g. Peter Grieder, *The East German Leadership, 1946–1973: Conflict and Crisis* (Manchester: Manchester University Press, 1999), ch. 1.
[39] Teichler, 'Fußball in der DDR', 26–7.
[40] Johnson, *Training Socialist Citizens*, pp. 55–9.
[41] 'Unsere Stellung zum Berufssport', *JW*, 11 August 1948, 5.
[42] Baingo and Horn, *Die Geschichte der DDR-Oberliga*, p. 11.

and coaches from the old SGs.[43] The GDR's most popular underdog club was itself the product, and at least partially the beneficiary, of the reconfiguration of East German football that began in earnest in 1948.

Amid the myriad name changes and mergers, which were reflective of a broader and unpopular SED campaign to root out autonomy in the cultural sphere,[44] many footballers and other sportspersons consciously maintained links to the past. Privately, they referred to their BSGs as *Vereine*.[45] *Stunde null* was more wish than reality. Cultural practices in sport and entertainment (amateur drama and folk music, for example) displayed distinctive continuities with the pre-1945 era.[46]

## Planitz versus the plan

The outcome of the second SBZ championship in 1949 at first sight suggested that football had stepped into political line. In the final in Dresden in June, 50,000 spectators watched the Saxony Anhalt champions ZSG Union Halle defeat Fortuna Erfurt 4–1 to claim the *Ostzone* title. A team representing the factory sports movement, newly created out of the Freiimfelde sports club that had lost to SG Planitz in the 1948 final, thus triumphed over one bearing a name (Fortuna) redolent of associational sport.[47]

The fate of the 1948 champions illustrated both the changing nature of East German football and the inability of the authorities to make a clean break with the past. Planitz, the DS leadership complained in May 1949, resisted plans to turn it into a BSG tied to the Horch car factories in Zwickau and instead 'allows itself to be led according to the old bases of bourgeois sport'. SG officials and local party members, including the mayor, hampered the changes necessary to create a factory-based 'democratic sports movement'.[48] Under political pressure, the team struggled to get its title defence off the ground, failing to qualify for the SBZ-wide knock-out competition from the Saxon championship.[49] The most controversial match was a 2–1 loss at home to ZSG Industrie Leipzig on 1 May 1949. When the referee disallowed two first-half goals by Planitz, there were angry mutterings among the crowd of 20,000. At half time,

43 Fuge, *Leutzscher Legende*, pp. 12–15; Haase, 'Die Zeit vor der Vereinsgründung', p. 9.
44 See e.g. Richthofen, *Bringing Culture to the Masses*, pp. 31–2.
45 Johnson, *Training Socialist Citizens*, pp. 97–8.
46 Palmowski, *Inventing a Socialist Nation*, p. 25.
47 Baingo and Horn, *Die Geschichte der DDR-Oberliga*, pp. 12–13.
48 SAPMO-BArch, DY 24/3405, letter from the DS to the SED leadership in Saxony, 4 May 1949.
49 Baingo and Horn, *Die Geschichte der DDR-Oberliga*, p. 12.

the stadium announcer, instead of calming the situation, 'threw more oil on the fire'. He accused the referee of being 'bought' by a factory team (i.e. ZSG Industrie). The mayor reinforced this viewpoint, telling the crowd that 'them up there' (*die da oben*) had fixed the game in advance. Four hundred fans occupied the stadium building to which match officials fled at the final whistle. Police units needed an hour to disperse them.[50] Watching dignitaries drew the obvious conclusion. The Planitz team was dissolved and its best players incorporated into a newly created BSG, Horch Zwickau.

Crowd trouble was not confined to supporters of politically suspect teams. In the middle of May 1949 SG Dresden Friedrichstadt met SG Meerane at the Leutzsch Stadium in Leipzig in a play-off match to determine the Saxon championship. Most of the 27,000 spectators in attendance were fans of ZSG Industrie Leipzig, who harboured faint hopes of qualifying for the SBZ championship in the event of a Meerane win. Friedrichstadt, however, won 3–2. When a Meerane goal was disallowed, there were angry protests, in which a policeman had the helmet struck from his head.[51] Leutzsch fury originated in Industrie's controversial loss to the Friedrichstadt team in Dresden a few days earlier. After a late penalty gave the hosts a 3–2 win, away supporters stormed the pitch. Players and officials required mounted police protection to reach the changing rooms.[52]

The incidents in May 1949 involving fans of both the old (Planitz) and the new (ZSG Industrie) suggested continuities with the 'club fanaticism' and terrace violence of the Weimar and Nazi eras.[53] They also pointed the way forward. The combustible nature of football crowds – and the space that stadia provided for the kind of unfettered and (in some cases) politically provocative behaviour that would have been unacceptable almost anywhere else – posed problems to which the SED, like the Nazi Party before it, never found satisfactory answers.

## Sealing football's division

By the time that Union Halle claimed the SBZ championship in June 1949, Germany's political division was all but sealed. Following the fusing of the three Western zones and the promulgation of the Basic Law in May 1949, the Federal Republic of Germany (FRG) came into

50 SAPMO-BArch, DY 24/3405, letter from the DS to the SED leadership, 4 May 1949.
51 Fuge, *Leutzscher Legende*, p. 16.
52 Archivgut des DFV, XV/63/4/3, Erinnerungen und Einschätzungen zum FDJ-Sport.
53 See e.g. Oswald, *"Fußball-Volksgemeinschaft"*, pp. 252–99.

existence, leaving the Soviets with little choice but to sanction a separate state in the East. The GDR was founded on 7 October. Football's division was an inevitable consequence of the creation of two Germanies. The DFB, dissolved in 1940, after playing an acquiescent role in the Nazification of football, was re-founded in July 1949 as West Germany's highest football authority. In the same month, the DS created an independent football office (*Sparte Fußball*).[54] The idea of a national championship, which had been strongly advocated ('the sooner the better') in *Deutsches Sport-Echo* two years earlier,[55] was dead in the water.

Berlin's football division took more permanent forms. A sport committee was founded in East Berlin in February 1949 and quickly joined the DS. Officials in West Berlin reacted by creating a separate sports organisation, which advocated the reconstitution of 'tradition clubs' such as the 1930 and 1931 German champions Hertha BSC (known since the end of the war as SG Gesundbrunnen). On 20 October an East Berlin FA was created. Five days later, the vast majority of clubs in the city's western sectors joined the newly formed football body there, which soon entered the DFB and went down the path of 'contract' (i.e. paid) football that East Germany now, and only now, began to denounce more forcefully.[56] The 1949/50 season, the last in which an all-Berlin football championship was contested, marked a farewell to regular matches between teams from East and West. Hertha, for example, played league games against Union Oberschönweide and VfB Pankow from the Soviet sector, as well as five friendlies against East German sides including cup holders Waggonbau Dessau and Horch Zwickau.[57] Games between teams from East and West Berlin continued across the open border in the 1950s. But reconstruction in football, as in other areas of post-war life, ultimately came at the cost of division.

## Between the lines: reflections on football in the SBZ

In May 1947, *Deutsches Sport-Echo* asserted that 'a German championship without the South German elite would be like a headless child'.[58] Little more than two years later, just such a headless child – shorn of the likes of Bayern Munich, FC Nuremberg, VfB Stuttgart, and VfR Mannheim – came into existence. On 3 September 1949 the first round

[54] Bitzer and Wilting, *Stürmen für Deutschland*, pp. 170–1; Archivgut des DFV, I/1, 'Dokumentation über 45 Jahre Fußball'.

[55] 'Der Anfang muß gemacht werden – ein Vorschlag für die Deutsche Fußballmeisterschaft 1947', *DSE*, 16 May 1947, 1.

[56] Wiese, 'Hertha BSC im Kalten Krieg', pp. 102–4.

[57] *Ibid.*, pp. 104–5.

[58] 'Der Anfang muß gemacht werden', 1.

of matches in the inaugural East German league championship began. Initially known as the *Zonenliga*, it had by the season's end adopted the name by which it would henceforth be known, the *Oberliga*. A month before the founding of the GDR, and fourteen years before the *Bundesliga* brought nationwide league competition to West Germany, East German fans could watch a national championship of their own. They did so in respectable numbers. Average attendance during the first season was 10,096. Sixty thousand spectators watched the title decider between Dresden Friedrichstadt and Horch Zwickau in April 1950.[59]

Between 1945 and 1949 East German football was only partly brought under the SED's control. To be sure, there was a trend towards centralisation from 1948 onwards, a process that favoured factory teams 'of the new type' over those that carried more obvious baggage from the past. This process was further institutionalised in April 1950, with the creation of eighteen central sports associations (SVs), which were based in various branches of the GDR's nascent command economy. Individual BSGs were now, in theory at least, beholden to the central leadership of the likes of SV Chemie (the chemicals industry), SV Fortschritt (textiles), or SV Stahl (steel). Political interventions multiplied. As across much of post-war Eastern Europe, tradition clubs were removed from the picture. The game, like East German society as a whole, was at the start of a radical transformation. Leading functionaries privately recognised the folly of this rupture. Banning all pre-1945 club names, Fritz Gödicke later conceded, was 'a serious, performance-hampering error that had to call up resistance'.[60]

Nonetheless, football under Soviet occupation was strikingly dissonant. Its development was uneven, with huge differences, for example, between the SBZ's football capital of Saxony, home of the winners and runners-up in the first *Oberliga* season, and the rural region of Mecklenburg in the north, which provided the two worst teams of the 1949/50 competition, including Vorwärts Schwerin, who won four of twenty-six games and had a goal difference of minus fifty-four.[61] Regional imbalances were exacerbated by an absence of zone-wide regulations on how football should be organised, itself a product of the Soviet directive on communal sport that held back teams and players before 1948. The result was a football culture that, whatever its international pretensions, encouraged the navel-gazing localism that the communists wanted to eradicate.

[59] Baingo and Horn, *Die Geschichte der DDR-Oberliga*, p. 15.
[60] Archivgut des DFV, XV/63/4/1, handwritten notes on 'Berliner Fußball', n.d.
[61] Baingo and Horn, *Die Geschichte der DDR-Oberliga*, p. 22.

SED interference in football did not always have the desired impact. Only two of the ten teams that contested the second SBZ championship in 1949 were factory sports clubs.[62] The SBZ's most popular team, SG Dresden Friedrichstadt, contained many of the players who had helped SC Dresden to win the last two German championships of the Nazi era. The inaugural SBZ champions, SG Planitz, initially resisted political pressure to turn the team into a BSG, serving instead as a site for 'selfish, tradition-bound sports policies'.[63] From very early on, football proved difficult to steer along communist lines. This was reflected in the spectator unrest that marred the 1949 SBZ championship, involving fans of both the politically suspect SG Planitz and the factory 'super club' ZSG Industrie Leipzig. In football, there was no *tabula rasa* when the Third Reich fell. The same was true of other cultural practices. In the FDJ's early years, as one founder member later remarked, the organisation 'borrow[ed] from the familiar musical heritage ... of the Nazi period. Much was carried over and in part further developed by the same people: campfires, devout spirit, midsummer celebrations, etc.'[64]

The limits of communist influence should come as no surprise. The DS created a football office only in July 1949. In the early days, it was a skeletal organisation, rarely staffed by politically suitable individuals, a problem that plagued organisations such as the FDJ and the party itself.[65] An investigation from 1953 revealed that many important positions in GDR football were occupied by 'petty bourgeois people, who were in large part [former] members of the Nazi Party and NCOs in the fascist army'. Only five of the nine leading officials were party comrades.[66]

Football's post-war reconstruction depended primarily on a grassroots activism that had little to do with what the SED did, or did not, want. The game was not a political priority. Qualified and reliable administrators were more urgently needed, and remained lacking, elsewhere. At the same time, people did not need the state's blessing or expertise to play the game, whether it was in the streets with a home-made ball or in the bombed wrecks of stadia that pockmarked the landscape. On the ground, those that counted were the likes of Günter Haase, founder

[62] *Ibid.*, p. 13.

[63] SAPMO-BArch, DY 24/3405, letter from the DS to the SED leadership, 4 May 1949.

[64] McDougall, 'A duty to forget?', 44.

[65] See e.g. Ulrich Mählert, *Die Freie Deutsche Jugend 1945–1949: Von den 'Anti-faschistischen Jugendauschüsse' zur SED-Massenorganisation* (Paderborn: Verlag Ferdinand Schöningh, 1995), pp. 282–91; Mary Fulbrook, *Anatomy of a Dictatorship: Inside the GDR 1949–1989* (Oxford: Oxford University Press, 1997), pp. 63–9.

[66] SAPMO-BArch, DY 30/IV 2/18/14, Einschätzung der Arbeitsweise der Sektion Fußball, 13 October 1953, fo. 2–8.

member of SG Thekla and active in the club as a player, children's coach, administrator, and referee over the following four decades; and Heinz Werner's favourite teacher, who introduced his pupils to football and other sports – and later told Werner the secret of survival amid the upheavals of the period: 'the most important rule in life is the rule of adaptation'.[67] There was from the outset an autonomous, localised feel to football in the East, despite the best efforts of the authorities, especially after 1948, to ensure control and compliance. These characteristics, as we shall see in the forthcoming chapters, were never entirely left behind.

Football's uneven development in the post-war years provided an early showcase of the limits of communist rule. It also embodied the tendency to secure one's own interests while cooperating at arm's length with structures of power that is characteristic of *Eigen-Sinn*. Players, coaches, and even politicians in towns such as Zwickau, home of SG Planitz, saw success as a means of safeguarding local identities against state incursions and regional rivals. Smaller clubs such as SG Thekla built teams that serviced local needs for competition, exercise, and social bonding. Football, like gardening, playing cards or going to church, was a popular activity that had been around much longer than the SED. It offered an established means of carving out autonomous, or partially autonomous, enclaves where the political climate of the day was of limited importance. As with the 'light cultural fare' of *Heimat* practices – comedies, amateur plays, local history talks, and choral singing[68] – the sport was a fitting pastime for a people who wanted to maintain customs of the past, while, like the eponymous heroine in Rainer Werner Fassbinder's *The Marriage of Maria Braun*, resolutely and pragmatically turning away from the political implications, and memories, of what had happened before 1945.

East German communists arguably made a cleaner break with the footballing past than did their counterparts in Czechoslovakia or Bulgaria, where popular pre-war clubs such as Sparta Prague and Levski Sofia survived in the new era.[69] There were no holdovers from the Nazi years in the *Oberliga* after Friedrichstadt's dissolution in 1950. But radical change was easier to decree than to enforce. Repeatedly changing a club's name did not necessarily change its identity, or make it any more socialist. The eventual successor to SG Planitz, BSG Sachsenring Zwickau, for example, became a repository in the 1970s and 1980s of

67 Interview with Heinz Werner, 24 May 2011; Beyer, *Rotation Leipzig*, p. 9.

68 Palmowski, *Inventing a Socialist Nation*, pp. 26–31. *Heimat* – meaning home, home town, or homeland – expresses a flexible sense of community and belonging that is central to understanding the history of modern Germany, including the GDR.

69 Duke, 'Going to market', p. 93.

the same kind of local patriotism that forced party officials to disband the original side in 1949. Functionaries in East Germany, like their counterparts in the People's Democracies of Eastern Europe or their Soviet role models of the 1920s and 1930s,[70] quickly discovered that they had 'to bend to the seemingly unshiftable popular preference for football', rather than (or, better put, as well as) bending football to their political needs.[71] This meant, for example, the creation of football teams under the auspices of powerful state institutions such as the police (Dynamo) and army (Vorwärts) – a concession to football's popularity that, at least in the case of Dynamo Dresden, bolstered regional pride, and anti-Berlin sentiments, in ways that, once more, ran counter to the SED's aims.[72]

There was not always an easy dividing line between the old and the new, between what was politically suspect and what was politically reliable, in football in the SBZ. This can be seen clearly in the early post-war history of BSG Chemie Leipzig. Under the name Tura 1899, it ended the Nazi era as Leipzig's leading club, enjoying strong working-class support in an area of the city where antipathy to Hitler was pronounced.[73] Tura was reconstituted after the war as SG Leutzsch, largely thanks to the volunteer efforts of officials and players, many of whom – including the later head of the DS football section Fritz Gödicke – played in Tura teams of the late 1930s and early 1940s. On the back of its working-class credentials (and high attendance figures), the club was then co-opted into the factory sports movement, first as ZSG Industrie in 1949 and then as BSG Chemie a year later, a move that initially brought material gains that offset any loss of autonomy. The team's raucous fans were hardly the respectful spectators favoured by socialist physical culture. But Chemie were *Oberliga* champions in 1950/1 and finished third the following year.[74] Its reputation as an underdog team only developed thereafter, as we shall see in Chapter 5. Initially, it benefited from the upheavals that made uncertainty the only certainty in the communist transformation of sport. A club with working-class traditions, prominent in Leipzig football during the Nazi era, first rebuilt as a popular SG and then incorporated into the factory sports movement, Chemie Leipzig embodied the mongrel identity of post-war East German football.

70 See e.g. Keys, *Globalizing Sport*, ch. 7.
71 Goldblatt, *The Ball Is Round*, p. 338.
72 On Dynamo Dresden, see e.g. Chapters 5, 6, 8, and 10.
73 Fuge, *Leutzscher Legende*, pp. 8–10; Archivgut des DFV, XV/63/4/3, Erinnerungen und Einschätzungen zum FDJ-Sport.
74 Fuge, *Leutzscher Legende*, pp. 19–30.

Football was an activity played and watched between the lines in East Germany – a contested space surrounded by, and subject to, both state and popular influence. The struggle, and overlap, between control and autonomy was already apparent in the SBZ, as the SED's sometimes disjointed attempts to bring football to heel ran into repeated difficulties. In these difficult years, football provided a source of entertainment and friendship that was almost certainly more important to its participants than the political restrictions that also shaped the game's development. By saving the traditions that they could, while working hard 'to build something new',[75] football's practitioners echoed the pragmatic ethos of the Hitler Youth generation. The people's game adapted to a new regime. But the new regime also adapted to the people's game. Football's reconstruction after 1945 owed a great deal more to grassroots fervour than it did to a communist masterplan.

[75] McDougall, 'A duty to forget?', 39. The quote is from a founder member of the FDJ.

# *Part I*

# Players

## Made in East Germany: football as *Leistungssport*

At around 10.30 p.m. on 8 May 1974, the jubilant footballers of FC Magdeburg embarked on a lap of honour at the Kuip Stadium in Rotterdam. They had just defeated Italian giants AC Milan 2–0 to win the European Cup Winners' Cup – the first and only time that a GDR team won one of the three European club competitions. Photographs of the celebrations are striking. Over their sweat-stained shirts, the players were bizarrely attired in hooded white dressing gowns provided by the East German textile manufacturer Malimo. Looking like a cross between boxers and schoolboys, they paraded around an almost empty stadium. A strictly vetted delegation of 288 people constituted the only East German presence in the stands.[1] Local indifference and the reluctance of Milan fans to travel to the Netherlands also contributed to an attendance figure of 5,000, the smallest crowd at any major European final. By 10.30, most of them had left. One of the great moments in East German football history went almost unnoticed.

FCM's triumph was an astonishing story. The team's average age was twenty-three. Each member of the starting line-up hailed from *Bezirk* Magdeburg, a region of 11,500 km² that contained little over one million inhabitants. Only Celtic, who won the European Cup in 1967, drew players from a similarly small catchment area.[2] FCM players came from villages and towns that people had never heard of, as journalist Heinz-Florian Oertel noted in an article that emphasised an achievement 'Made in Magdeburg'.[3] They began playing at small clubs with archetypal East German names such as Dynamo Stapelburg (captain Manfred Zapf), Einheit Burg (midfielder Wolfgang Seguin, scorer of the second goal in Rotterdam), and Lokomotive

[1] SAPMO-BArch, DY 30/J IV 2/3/2149, Entsendung einer Touristendelegation aus dem Bezirk Magdeburg zum Endspiel im Europapokal der Pokalsieger 1. FC Magdeburg–AC Mailand am 8.5.1974 in Rotterdam, fo. 14.

[2] Dirk Gieselmann and Philipp Köster, 'Ein Traum in Malimo', *11 Freunde Spezial: Die Siebziger* (2009), 52.

[3] 'Waterloo – 100 Kilometer nebenan', *Die Neue Fußball-Woche*, 14 May 1974, 9.

Halberstadt (striker Jürgen Sparwasser).[4] Many of the squad worked at the vast Ernst Thälmann heavy machinery factory (*Schwermaschinen-Kombinat Ernst Thälmann*), biking to training in the evenings and sharing a beer or two afterwards.[5]

In Magdeburg on 10 May, thousands of people gathered in the city centre to greet the 'heroes of Rotterdam' at the official reception. Celebrations ran late into the evening.[6] Belying the argument that the East German press never related praise from the Western media,[7] *Die Neue Fußball-Woche* proudly reported international acclaim for Magdeburg's attacking style of play, a welcome relief from the stifling defensive tactics of their Italian opponents.[8] The victory of the 'county XI' (*Bezirksauswahl*) opened GDR football's *annus mirabilis* – the year in which the national team played in the World Cup finals in West Germany and defeated the hosts, with a goal from FCM striker Sparwasser, and in which, as novelist Annett Gröschner later remarked, 'even girls became football fans'.[9]

Why, then, did Magdeburg's success fail to spark a long-term upturn? Several aspects of the communist response to the club's finest hour are instructive in answering this question. Rather than fans, those who boarded the four charter flights to Rotterdam on 8 May were hand-picked party dignitaries, some of whom apparently had no idea who FC Magdeburg were. As if to emphasise official distance from the topic on many people's minds, listings in the local SED newspaper did not confirm that the final would even be shown live on television until the day of the game.[10] Two days later, the story 'Bravo FCM' received less space on the same newspaper's front page than a report on the tenth congress of German–Soviet friendship.[11] The popular coach who masterminded the win over Milan, Heinz Krügel – long regarded with political suspicion by the party leadership – was sacked in 1977.[12] FCM were never the same force again.

As the aftermath of Magdeburg's victory illustrates, the East German leadership, in the words of David Goldblatt, 'never quite got it with football'.[13] Manfred Ewald, DTSB president from 1961 to 1988, had a

4 Gröschner, *Sieben Tränen*, pp. 165–6.
5 Gieselmann and Köster 'Ein Traum in Malimo', 51.
6 Gröschner, *Sieben Tränen*, pp. 79–80.
7 Sheldon Anderson, 'Soccer and the failure of East German sports policy', *Soccer & Society* vol. 12, no. 5 (September 2011), 659.
8 'ERFOLG der Offensive RUIN des Catenaccio!', *Die Neue Fußball-Woche*, 14 May 1974, 7–8.
9 Hesselmann and Ide, 'A tale of two Germanys', p. 40.
10 Gröschner, *Sieben Tränen*, pp. 74–5. 11 *Ibid.*, pp. 78–9. 12 *Ibid.*, pp. 119–23.
13 Goldblatt, *The Ball Is Round*, p. 596.

Figure 2. FC Magdeburg players celebrate victory over AC Milan in the 1974 European Cup Winners' Cup final. The two players holding the trophy, striker Jürgen Sparwasser (left) and captain Manfred Zapf, took very different paths after retiring from the game. Sparwasser defected to the West in 1988. Zapf became an establishment figure: FCM chairman, DFV functionary, and (briefly and disastrously) co-trainer of the national team.

notoriously low opinion of the game, with its emphasis on 'individualism and fanaticism' rather than 'discipline and rationalism'.[14] Under his watch, the GDR prioritised Olympic sports such as athletics and swimming, leaving limited resources and patience for the country's favourite game. Football suffered as a consequence of the state's Olympic fixation. Talented young sportsmen were channelled into sports that offered guarantees of a prominent position in the medal table. In the GDR, complained the FC Carl Zeiss Jena coach, Lothar Kurbjuweit, in 1986, 'the tall footballers become rowers!'.[15]

[14] Manfred Ewald, *Ich war der Sport* (Berlin: Elefanten Press, 1994), p. 66.
[15] Braun and Wiese, 'DDR-Fußball', 199.

Yet this was not the whole story. Shortly after the *Wende*, the double Olympic javelin champion Ruth Fuchs recalled a conversation with a footballer from Jena. He told her that 'I wouldn't put on my boots for the money that you got for your Olympic victory'. 'If the concept of privilege applied anywhere in the GDR', she concluded, 'then [it applied] in football'.[16] Mediocre players, Ewald recollected in 1994, received wages and perquisites disproportionate to their achievements, allowing them (by GDR norms) a very good standard of living.[17] Their demands were met by communist officials who, in contrast to Ewald, had plenty of time for football. In 1993, the former DTSB functionary Jürgen Heller spoke of the organisation's powerlessness in the face of football's unwillingness to submit to central directives. 'Earlier in Germany', Ewald once told him, 'there was small stateism (*Kleinstaaterei*) and every little prince kept his own ballet. Today they support football teams'.[18] The struggle against local patriotism (*Ortspatriotismus*) was a long and unrewarding one, creating divisions and rivalries rather than the unity sought by the centralising dictates of state socialism.

East German football was a site of neglect and privilege. An unresolved tension existed between doing everything to ensure that the GDR caught up to the international elite and distaste at the damage to socialist sporting norms to which this striving invariably led. Ewald may not have valued football highly. But he never imposed upon it the 'quick death' that befell basketball and ice hockey in 1969, swingeing cuts in funding that led most of the national team's basketball players to resign from the SED in protest and that farcically reduced the national ice hockey league from eight to two teams.[19] Football was too popular to be discarded in this way. Considerable time and energy was spent on raising standards. There were endless directives. A shortlist includes the reports that accompanied the major restructuring of 1954/5, when eight of the fourteen *Oberliga* clubs were converted into state-favoured sports clubs (SCs);[20] the preparations for the second major reform of 1965/6, when the football 'sections' were removed from existing SCs and turned into separate football clubs (FCs);[21] and the 'football resolutions' (*Fußballbeschlüsse*) of 1970, 1976, and 1983.

16 Leske, *Erich Mielke*, p. 92.

17 Ewald, *Ich war der Sport*, p. 57.

18 Leske, *Enzyklopädie*, p. 15.

19 Leske, *Erich Mielke*, pp. 87–8; Braun and Wiese, 'DDR-Fußball', pp. 193–4.

20 The eight new *Oberliga* SCs were Turbine Erfurt, Wismut Karl-Marx-Stadt, Rotation Leipzig, Einheit Dresden, Aktivist Brieske-Senftenberg, Dynamo Berlin, Empor Rostock, and Chemie Halle. See Leske, *Erich Mielke*, p. 132.

21 The nine new *Oberliga* FCs were Carl Zeiss Jena, Karl-Marx-Stadt, Vorwärts Berlin, BFC, Hansa Rostock, Lokomotive Leipzig, Hallescher FC Chemie, FC Magdeburg, and Rot–Weiß Erfurt. See Leske, *Erich Mielke*, p. 168.

Official assessments were as withering as they were unchanging. 'In terms of performance', asserted one 1960 report, 'we are in the bottom third of European national teams'.[22] The 1983 football resolution blamed the national team's failure to qualify for the finals of major international tournaments on the fact that 'other countries, including socialist countries' had more rapidly adopted new playing styles: 'World-class standards are set by the professional football of West European and South American national and club teams. With its teams the FRG has been part of the elite for years'.[23] As in many areas, from the availability of foodstuffs to the quality of their respective car industries, West Germany was in advance of East Germany on the football pitch. This created a self-perpetuating inferiority complex that obscured from its jaded participants many of GDR football's achievements.

Part I of this book examines the history of East German *Leistungssfußball* ('performance football'), focusing on the people at the heart of the story, the players. What was it like to play football under communism? Why was the game in the GDR perceived to be unsuccessful? What does this tell us about the regime that attempted, usually in vain, to bring it to heel? It is possible to place this narrative within a tripartite chronological framework: the experimental phase between 1949 and 1966; the stabilisation phase between 1966 and 1979; and the BFC era from 1979 to the *Wende*.[24] But the history of football in East Germany was marked by debates and problems that traversed these periods. A thematic approach, while not eschewing changes over time, allows a wider-ranging, more analytical treatment of important issues. The following four chapters examine footballers' lives in the GDR (Chapter 3), the national team (Chapter 4), club football (Chapter 5), and *Stasi* involvement in the game (Chapter 6).

Within the chapters, three central arguments are posited. First, that even beneath the stern gaze of the *Stasi*, and amid manifestations of conformity both large and small, players were capable of maintaining a strong sense of *Eigen-Sinn* in their lives and careers. Agency could be expressed in anything from disrespecting the sober dictates of a socialist lifestyle to, in extreme cases, leaving East Germany for the West. Players' attempts to safeguard a degree of independence interconnect with a second key point. Though guardians of a repressive police state, communist functionaries exerted remarkably little concerted influence on football. On a plethora of issues –

[22] SAPMO-BArch, DY 30/IV 2/18/14, Maßnahmen zur Erreichung hoher sportlichen Leistungen im Fußballsport der DDR, 10 February 1960, fo. 82.

[23] SAPMO-BArch, DY 30/IV 2/2.036/25, Beschluß zur weiteren Leistungsentwicklung im Fußballsport der DDR, February 1983, fo. 139.

[24] Leske, *Erich Mielke*, p. 107.

Figure 3. Lokomotive Leipzig midfielder Heiko Scholz in action against Dynamo Dresden, March 1988. Straddling the communist and post-communist eras, Scholz's eventful career included two landmark moments in the closing chapters of GDR football. His move from Leipzig to Dresden in the summer of 1990 marked the first one million Mark transfer deal between two East German clubs. He then played in the GDR's final international match against Belgium in September.

how the national team performed, how playing styles in the *Oberliga* evolved, whom players played for, how and what players were paid, how players trained and lived, and how football clubs were run – the game frequently gave the impression that it existed beyond SED control. The considerable autonomy that mass popularity earned for football's practitioners was, nonetheless, ring-fenced by the realities of one-party dictatorship. In the final reckoning, football and footballers existed in a contested space – between state control and local autonomy, between privilege and policing, and between professionalism and amateurism.

# 3 Footballers' lives

## Gilded elite? Playing football under communism

During Dynamo Dresden's run to the quarter finals of the 1985/6 UEFA Cup, the team's outstanding player was winger Frank Lippmann. The twenty-four-year-old scored five goals in six matches, including one in the 2–0 quarter-final first-leg victory over West German side Bayer Uerdingen in March 1986. He scored another in the return match, helping Dresden to a 3–1 half-time lead in Uerdingen and a seemingly unassailable 5–1 lead in the tie. It was Lippmann's last goal for his hometown club and one of his final acts as a GDR footballer. Hampered by an injury to their goalkeeper, Dynamo Dresden collapsed, conceding six goals in thirty minutes to lose the match 7–3. If East German football was a history of snatching defeat from the jaws of victory, the Uerdingen debacle was its nadir. 'Nothing excuses it', club officials angrily concluded.[1] Their mood was worsened by the news that on the morning after the game, Frank Lippmann – acting on the spur of the moment – absconded from the team hotel, thereby committing the treasonous act of *Republikflucht* ('flight from the Republic').[2] When GDR television replayed the Uerdingen game later that day, footage of him celebrating Dresden's second goal was cut from the programme.[3]

First approached to work as an informer (*Inoffizielle Mitarbeiter*, IM) in 1981, Lippmann consistently refused to cooperate with the *Stasi*, who gave him up as a hopeless case three years later.[4] Shortly after Christmas 1985, returning from a party under the influence of alcohol, he crashed his car into a police transport truck containing prisoners and fled the

1 Hauptstaatsarchiv (HStA) Dresden, 12456 SED Nachlässe V/2.39/046, Stellungnahme zur leitungsmäßigen Vorbereitung auf das Viertelfinale im EC-Wettbewerb gegen Bayer 05 Uerdingen am 05.03. und 19.03.1986, 21 March 1986.

2 Interview with Frank Lippmann in Jens Genschmar, *Mit Dynamo durch Europa: Die Europapokalspiele der SG Dynamo Dresden 1967–1991* (Dresden: Edition Sächsische Zeitung, 2011), p. 135.

3 Pleil, *Mielke, Macht und Meisterschaft*, p. 97.

4 *Ibid.*, pp. 178–9; Genschmar, *Mit Dynamo*, p. 135.

scene of the accident. Lippmann's decision to seek political asylum three months later was a logical escape from domestic troubles. For all of the vaunted power of the *Stasi*, there was little that the authorities could do about it – other than enforce a mandatory one-year suspension from football, pressurise his fiancée (who remained in East Germany until 1989), and take malicious pleasure in Lippmann's injury-plagued *Bundesliga* career.[5]

The Lippmann case fitted into the rich drama of GDR escapology between 1961 and 1989, exit stories that encompassed perilous swims, tunnels, hot-air balloons, home-made planes, shoot-outs, and false passports.[6] In step with popular retrospectives on the GDR – the tales of derring-do on display at the Checkpoint Charlie museum in Berlin – post-*Wende* literature on football has been drawn to such stories, where the narrative arc takes in secret police surveillance, individual acts of complicity and resistance, star players behaving badly, and an eventual flight to freedom, though not always to happy endings, in the West.[7]

Footballers' lives, though, did not usually follow this path. High-profile cases of *Republikflucht* were rare. The fortunes amassed by leading *Oberliga* players were, by Western standards, modest and atypical of the lesser earning potential of their peers. As in any country, a player's career was short and at risk of a premature end through injury or declining form. As in other authoritarian dictatorships, there was the risk of falling from political favour. The benefits notwithstanding, football was a precarious vocation, a world of popular adulation and foreign travel, but also of party interference, *Stasi* surveillance, and highly constrained freedom of movement.

What was it like to play football in East Germany? This chapter attempts to answer that question, focusing on players' experiences in the top three tiers of the football pyramid, the *Oberliga*, the *Liga* (second division), and the *Bezirksligen* (county leagues). It analyses players' biographical data, before discussing their political behaviour, for example during the June 1953 Uprising. Further sections examine the tensions between professionalism and amateurism (as illustrated through the vexed issue of money) and the careers of two leading players,

5 Genschmar, *Mit Dynamo*, p. 135; Leske, *Enzyklopädie*, p. 300; Horn and Weise, *Das große Lexikon*, pp. 220–1.

6 See e.g. Patrick Major, *Behind the Berlin Wall: East Germany and the Frontiers of Power* (Oxford: Oxford University Press, 2010), pp. 143–5.

7 See e.g. Leske, *Erich Mielke*; Pleil, *Mielke, Macht und Meisterschaft*; Heribert Schwan, *"Tod dem Verräter!" Der lange Arm der Stasi und der Fall Lutz Eigendorf* (Munich: Knaur, 2000); Ellen Thiemann, *Der Feind an meiner Seite: Die Spitzelkarriere eines Fussballers* (Munich: Herbig, 2005).

Dynamo Dresden striker Hans-Jürgen Kreische and FC Magdeburg midfielder Axel Tyll. Taken together, the material emphasises the limited ability of the SED regime to shape football and footballers according to its wishes, as well as the fluid and contested identities open to the latter, who existed in a liminal space between state demands and societal autonomy.

## Heroes like us: footballers in profile

No database provides a complete profile of the average East German footballer. Various sources, though, allow a composite picture to emerge. The state-run Office for the Support of Sport in the Factories (*Büro der Förderung des Sports in den Betrieben*) kept a record of the personal, family, and career histories of elite footballers with whom it made performance agreements in the 1970s and 1980s. A random sample of thirty-six files will be consulted here. In addition, individual squad profiles – taken from SC Frankfurt/Oder (1964) and three second- and third-division teams that played in West Germany in 1984 – are examined, in order to illustrate as fully as possible the personal, economic, and political status of those who were paid to play the people's game.

The thirty-six files cover a wide range of footballers at various clubs in the late 1980s, from talented youngsters, including three future members of the German national team, to current internationals and journeymen nearing the end of their careers. As is the case in most of the world, with the notable exception of North America, football was a largely working-class sport in the GDR.[8] In a state that unashamedly used the term for political purposes, defining who was 'working class' was difficult. As in Western Europe during the Cold War, it changed over time. By the 1980s, the 'unmaking of the German working class', a process that began under Nazism, was evident in the socialist East as well as the capitalist West, as economic diversification, divisive shop-floor practices, and increasingly individualised self-perceptions fractured working-class solidarity.[9] The individualist retreat of the Honecker era, as we shall see in subsequent chapters, impacted on footballers as well as brigade workers and collective farmers. But it is worth emphasising that the

[8] On the working-class backgrounds of English footballers, see Kuper and Szymanski, *Soccernomics*, pp. 18–23.

[9] See e.g. Mary Fulbrook, *The People's State: East German Society from Hitler to Honecker* (New Haven, CT and London: Yale University Press, 2005), pp. 215–20; Andrew Port, *Conflict and Stability in the German Democratic Republic* (New York: Cambridge University Press, 2007), pp. 215–16.

game's practitioners – from *Oberliga* stars to supporters and recreational players – maintained, and indeed articulated, a working-class identity that often overrode increased differentiation in the workforce.

At least twenty-three of the thirty-six players surveyed in the *Büro der Förderung* files came from working-class families. Their parents worked variously as machinists, cloakroom attendants, hairdressers, welders, truck drivers, and mechanics. Only rarely were players' parents from middle-class professions such as teaching, government service, or engineering. Conversely, a relatively low percentage of footballers – just five of the thirty-six (14 per cent) – were members of the self-styled party of the working class, the SED. Players, like supporters, were reluctant comrades.[10] The figure – notably lower than the nationwide figure for SED membership, one in five of the adult population (20 per cent), during the Honecker years[11] – suggests the ingrained apoliticism of elite athletes, in East Germany as elsewhere, and a *Resistenz* to communist rule that was more pronounced in the predominantly working-class *Oberliga* than among, for example, the intelligentsia, who were generally, and to the leadership's concern, over-represented in the party ranks.[12]

The files offer generally unadorned information about a player's educational background (not infrequently at one of the elite 'children and youth sport schools' – *Kinder- und Jugendsportschulen*, or KJS – that buttressed the GDR's 'sports miracle'),[13] any vocational courses that he took (most commonly to become a sports teacher), salary progression, and medical history. Of interest is the category 'ties to the West' (*westliche Verbindungen*). Like other public faces of the regime, such as the classical singer Theo Adam and the rock band The Puhdys,[14] elite footballers were granted travel visas more straightforwardly than the general public. But the privilege was always conditional. Suspicious ties to friends or family in the West could hamper travel opportunities and career prospects. It is thus striking that sixteen of the thirty-six players admitted having ties to 'non-socialist foreign countries' (*Nichtsozialistisches Ausland*, NSA). These were rarely as extensive as those of the

[10] See various files in SAPMO-BArch, DR 509/. To protect players' anonymity, the Bundesarchiv requires that no individual file numbers be cited. Twenty-six files were consulted in the survey of thirty-six players.

[11] Fulbrook, *The People's State*, p. 4.

[12] On the attempt in the 1970s to limit the intake of new party members from the intelligentsia, and thereby create space for additional working-class applicants, see e.g. Stefan Wolle, *Die heile Welt der Diktatur: Alltag und Herrschaft in der DDR 1971–1989* (Bonn: Bundeszentrale für politische Bildung, 1998), p. 107.

[13] On the KJS, see e.g. Dennis and Grix, *Sport under Communism*, pp. 61–3.

[14] Major, *Behind the Berlin Wall*, p. 201.

Sachsenring Zwickau player Michael G., who had seven relatives dotted across the Federal Republic, as well as an uncle in California. It was more common for players to list the odd relative or acquaintance in West Germany with whom they had little or no contact. As if to confirm SED paranoia, two of the three Wismut Aue players who undertook *Republikflucht* in Sweden in July 1989 are listed here as having contacts in the West.[15] Honecker's policy of *Abgrenzung* ('demarcation'), namely sealing off the GDR from unhealthy Western influences, was subject to all kinds of loopholes, from the Leipzig Trade Fair to the transit routes where East and West German drivers shared the same service station.[16] Many of them arose from the unsolvable tension between the GDR's quest for *Weltniveau* ('world-class standards') and its simultaneous desire to be inoculated from the class enemy. The contradiction made *Abgrenzung* all but impossible to enforce in football, where international competition ran throughout most of the year and standards were set by teams from Western Europe.

The files depict the underbelly of GDR football, the mundane reverse of tales of crashed cars and flights to the West. The career of journeyman goalkeeper Detlev Z., a sports teacher by trade, took in stops at four *Oberliga* clubs. After starting at FC Karl-Marx-Stadt, he was delegated to Wismut Aue in 1973 and then moved three years later to Carl Zeiss Jena. In 1981 he was forced to leave Jena, and barred from top-flight football for two years, after 'violating the norms of performance sport'. His offence was to have embarked on a relationship with a woman after he got divorced – a seemingly anachronistic complaint, given the state's increasingly laissez-faire attitude to marriage, and the subsequent increase in divorce rates, during the 1970s and 1980s,[17] but one that very much reflected the SED's ingrained 'petty bourgeois morality'.[18] A moralistic note was also struck in the file of Polish-born Bernhard K., who was sacked by Carl Zeiss Jena in 1978 for repeated curfew infractions at the club dormitory and excessive drinking.[19]

During the ban, Z. did his military service and played lower-league football at BSG Aktivist Kali Werra Tiefenort. In 1985 he returned to the elite with BSG Stahl Brandenburg, a well-funded club that had just been promoted to the *Oberliga*, and whose coach, Heinz Werner, specialised in rehabilitating disgraced players.[20] His contract with the DFV as a

15 Various files in SAPMO-BArch, DR 509/.
16 Major, *Behind the Berlin Wall*, pp. 188–9.
17 See e.g. Betts, *Within Walls*, pp. 108–15; McLellan, *Love in the Time of Communism*, pp. 77–81.
18 Major, *Behind the Berlin Wall*, p. 199.
19 File on Bernhard K. in SAPMO-BArch, DR 509/.
20 Interview with Heinz Werner.

performance sportsman was terminated in 1990, when Z. was thirty-seven years of age and earning just over 1,000 M per month as a welder in a Brandenburg factory.[21] Too old to jump on the *Bundesliga* gravy train rolling into the East, he would have departed from football in the GDR's dying days with uncertain prospects.

Z.'s case emphasises the precariousness that characterised the careers of many GDR footballers. Though political circumstances were different, they were not so dissimilar to the careers of journeyman footballers in the West before the game's renaissance in the 1990s and the greater financial clout accorded to players by the Bosman judgement, the 1995 European Court ruling that granted out-of-contract players freedom of movement: transfers that were undertaken with little or no regard for a player's wishes and salaries that were good, but not enough to retire on. Pressures that were partly or entirely absent in the West also existed: the potential complications arising from having contacts in West Germany; military service; secret-police surveillance; and the factory work and vocational training that players, as state-supported 'amateurs', squeezed in between training and matches. Heinz Werner, who played for Lokomotive Stendal during the 1950s, combined six training sessions a week with a job in the sales department of the team's sponsoring factory. Even the FCM players who won East Germany's sole European trophy in 1974 could not entirely neglect workplace or study commitments.[22] By GDR standards, footballers led privileged lives. But the level of privilege varied widely and was always subject to some form of political scrutiny, however inconsistently it was applied.

A good example of this scrutiny is provided by the 'short biography' (*Kurzbiographie*) that football teams submitted to the DTSB for every player selected to play in matches in West Germany. Football featured regularly in the approximately eighty annual encounters that the DTSB and its West German counterpart, the DSB (*Deutscher Sportbund*), agreed upon in 1974, as part of sport's contribution to East–West détente.[23] In 1984, three East German *Liga* and county league teams were granted permission to play in the West: TSG Bau Rostock, against Hertha 03 Zehlendorf in West Berlin; BSG Motor Grimma, against FC Olympia Lampertheim; and BSG Lokomotive Stendal, against SC Willingen.

Of the twenty-one-man party put forward for Bau Rostock's match in West Berlin, a relatively high number (five) were SED members, though

[21] File on Detlev Z. in SAPMO-BArch, DR 509/.

[22] Interview with Heinz Werner; Gröschner, *Sieben Tränen*, pp. 48–53.

[23] Braun and Wiese, 'DDR-Fußball', 203.

this included the delegation leader, always a comrade on such trips. Nine players had relations in the West, three of whom were in written contact with them. Those barred from making the trip included Uwe B., whose father and uncle lived in the Federal Republic, and Udo H., whose stepmother and aunt lived there. The equation between political and moral reliability in GDR sport – the need for the country's 'diplomats in tracksuits' to embody the best qualities of socialist personalities[24] – is re-emphasised by the fact that the delegation's four divorced members were all red-flagged. A question mark was raised in particular against Gerhard K., whose marital rupture was compounded by non-membership of the SED and having two relatives in the West, including one in the United States.[25]

The nineteen-man delegation selected for Motor Grimma's match in Lampertheim offered fewer headaches. The rosily formulaic comments appended to each player's biography – almost everyone is described as 'fair' and 'hard-working' on the pitch and in the workplace – suggest a sugar-coating of awkward issues to ensure that the trip could be made with the strongest team. Only one of the nineteen was listed as having a relative in the West; there were no divorcés (the four unmarried players are listed as 'single' and 'good family relations' are praised in several cases); and the delegation contained seven SED members.[26] Similarly uncritical assessments characterised the portraits of the twenty-five-man delegation put forward for Lokomotive Stendal's trip to Willingen. They hint at the *Schönfärberei* ('glossing things over') that typified Honecker-era reports, reflecting a retreat from the engaged socialist governance of the 1960s into something more pragmatic and less inquisitive about citizens' private opinions and behaviour.[27]

If the 1960s marked the key decade in the SED's attempts to reshape society according to its precepts, football proved no exception. Concern about educating players along socialist lines was strong at this time, as suggested by a 1964 survey of squad members at *Liga* side SC Frankfurt/Oder: Günter S. was described as having a positive attitude to the GDR, but also as a lazy trainer who 'tends towards arrogance and thinks himself intellectually superior'; Manfred F. was a good trainer, but one about whom there were 'moral concerns' including the break-up of his marriage and listening to Western radio stations; Herbert F. was described as politically hesitant, with a tendency towards excessive drinking partly related to separation from his family; and vice-captain Gerhard M. was

24 Dennis and Grix, *Sport under Communism*, p. 70.
25 SAPMO-BArch, DY 12/3101, Kurzbiographien, n.d., fo. 177–97.
26 *Ibid.*, Kurzbiographien, n.d., fo. 289–307.
27 Fulbrook, *Anatomy*, pp. 72–6.

a 'difficult' character ('very spontaneous') who trained on his own terms but played hard in matches.[28]

In contrast, Lok Stendal players, like their Grimma peers, were described in 1984 in the emptiest of clichés: sober, hard-working, and possessors of an unfailingly 'good attitude to our workers' and peasants' state'. Twelve of the delegation, including six players, were SED members. The high number of applicants with relatives in the West – ten in total, six of whom were in touch with various aunts, uncles, grandparents, and cousins – was unsurprising, given Stendal's proximity to the border with West Germany.[29] When Lok arrived in Willingen for the match on 14 October, relatives of one of the players, Manfred G., waited to greet him at the team hotel. Most likely for this very reason, G. had been pulled from the squad before it left East German soil.[30] Privileges such as foreign travel could be taken away as quickly as they were granted in the GDR's Kafkaesque bureaucratic edifice.[31] Footballers inhabited a liminal space, where sport met surveillance, and where *Eigen-Sinn* and conformity were anxious bedfellows.

### Footballers and politics

During the 1950s, functionaries complained repeatedly about athletes who focused solely on sporting endeavours. A 1953 report publicly criticised players at *Oberliga* team Motor Dessau for ducking out of political classes and refusing to support remilitarisation. The time for 'sport only' attitudes, it asserted, belonged in the past.[32] If most leading footballers were hardly political animals, it did not stop them from being deployed, like other socialist celebrities, in propaganda campaigns. *Eigen-Sinn* was not simply shorthand for subversion. It also embraced, with varying degrees of ideological enthusiasm, conformity.[33] In 1957, the squad of champions Wismut Karl-Marx-Stadt put their faces and signatures on a football-shaped advertisement exhorting people to vote for the SED in upcoming elections. Four years later,

[28] Brandenburgisches Landeshauptarchiv (BLHA), Rep. 730 Nr. 2350, Angaben und Einschätzung über die Spieler des DDR-Liga-Kollektivs des Sport-Clubs Frankfurt (Oder), n.d.

[29] SAPMO-BArch, DY 12/3104, Kurzbiographien, n.d., fo. 31–55.

[30] *Ibid.*, Reisebericht: Durchführung eines internationalen Fußballspieles in der BRD am 14.10.84 – SC Willingen-BSG Lok Stendal, 16 October 1984, fo. 5–7.

[31] Major, *Behind the Berlin Wall*, p. 201.

[32] 'Wie lange soll das noch so weitergehen?', *DSE*, 4 February 1953, 5.

[33] See Palmowski, 'Between conformity and *Eigen-Sinn*', 501–2.

players from the army team Vorwärts Berlin featured prominently in media reports depicting popular support for the construction of the Berlin Wall.[34]

Footballers' political activism, though, did not always proceed in ways that were so *linientreu* ('loyal to the party line'). In June 1953, the East German state was rocked by political unrest. Triggered by strikes and walkouts among construction workers in Berlin, it spread quickly to more than 350 towns and villages across the young republic. Five hundred thousand people took part in protests. Only the intervention of Soviet tanks saved the SED regime. Six thousand people were arrested and as many as 209 killed as order was restored.[35]

Little has been written about the role of footballers in the June Uprising. The limited evidence suggests, first, that football was one of the more problematic sections in various industry-sponsored sports clubs and, second, that footballers' behaviour largely reflected that of the general population: a small minority who defended the GDR against 'fascist' provocateurs, a somewhat larger minority who protested, and a majority who sat on the sidelines, neither endorsing nor attacking the discredited government. SV Chemie, for example, reported that most of its athletes adopted passive attitudes on 17 June, repeatedly citing the 'sport only' argument. The sections most heavily involved in the unrest were boxing, football, and wrestling. Certain Chemie players, including individuals from the *Oberliga* team in Leipzig, were praised for their partisan responses. But functionaries from Chemie teams in Halle and Jena were variously accused of being involved in the strike leadership and inciting workers to liberate fellow athletes from prison. The entire first team at Chemie Radebeul took part in demonstrations.[36]

A similar range of responses can be gleaned from other reports. Players from *Oberliga* side Lokomotive Stendal defended their factory against demonstrators. Others, such as the footballer at Empor Görlitz arrested as a strike ringleader and still in custody in early July, were on the other side of the barricades. Two players from a textiles industry (Fortschritt) team in Leipzig, one of whom was a party member, gave clearest voice to the 'wait and see' pragmatism of the majority of GDR citizens. They professed to have no opinions about the unrest ('yeah, and what should

[34] Archivgut des DFV, XV/63/4/7 (Nachlaß Fritz Gödicke), 'Klare Stellungnahme zu den aktuellen politischen Problemen – Aufruf zu den Wahlen!', n.d.; *Die Neue Fußball-Woche*, 22 August 1961, 1, 7.

[35] McDougall, *Youth Politics*, pp. 49–50.

[36] SAPMO-BArch, DY 34/3665, Auswertung der durchgeführten Instrukteureinsätze und Berichte aufgrund der Vorkommnisse am 16. und 17.6.1953, 6 July 1953.

we say about it then?').[37] Rarely radical, still less revolutionary by nature, East German footballers tended to hang back during the June unrest, focusing on training sessions or matches. Where footballers were involved in strikes, walkouts, and demonstrations, it was episodically – often on an individual basis and with no regime-toppling thoughts in mind. They were generally preoccupied with narrower concerns: the higher wages and preferential treatment given to army and police teams (a complaint voiced by Chemie Leipzig players); the seemingly annual structural changes in football; and the dearth of equipment, especially boots.[38] In this regard, they were little different from the wider population, whose grievances in June 1953 were often local and material, rather than national and ideological. Grouching about everyday frustrations, footballers occupied an uncertain middle ground: neither the socialist role models that the regime desired nor rallying points for anti-socialist subversion.

A similar tension was notable among the GDR's brightest young footballers. Youth football was an area in which the GDR excelled. Those selected at a young age to attend a KJS were identified as potential future *Oberliga* and national team players. Despite the privileged position, they were also ordinary young people, subject to the same influences as their peers – influences that were often as distasteful to the communist regime as they were difficult to curb. For the most part, young footballers were at the tamer end of a spectrum of youth misbehaviour that included many FDJ members and centred on alcohol-induced, lightly political pranks: using a picture of Honecker for air-rifle target practice, for example, or singing the West German national anthem in public.[39] Disciplinary measures against Union Berlin youth players in 1976 and 1977 focused on their breaking of dormitory curfews and contravention of training camp bans on alcohol.[40]

On occasion, non-conformity had darker undertones. The provocative use of fascist slogans – often, seemingly, to rile the dutifully anti-fascist East German state – was common during the 1960s. By the late 1970s, though, a minority of young East Germans had taken the rhetoric to heart. Secondary-school pupils watching the film *Naked among Wolves* at a Leipzig cinema in 1977 cheered when the SS attacked prisoners at Buchenwald, urging them to 'kick the Jewish swine to death'. In the same

[37] *Ibid.*, Situationsbericht, n.d.; Situationsbericht zur Arbeit unserer BSG'en in Verbindung mit den Unruhen des 17. Juni 1953, 7 July 1953.

[38] *Ibid.*, Auswertung der durchgeführten Instrukteureinsätze, 6 July 1953.

[39] Fulbrook, *Anatomy*, pp. 167–8.

[40] Union Berlin Archive, Verhandlungsprotokoll, 21 October 1977; Aktennotiz, 26 October 1976.

year, extremists at a school in Leibniz glorified Nazi genocide and urged that their teachers be sent to the gas chambers ('the men will be castrated, the women fucked to death').[41]

The neo-Nazi emphasis on masculinity and leadership found a small but sympathetic audience among young football supporters. Young players were not necessarily immune either. On 28 April 1978 the director of the Emil Wallner KJS in Karl-Marx-Stadt informed the local education authorities about disturbing incidents involving students from the school's football section. Four young players had founded a 'club for organised neo-Nazis' at a disco in the city a week earlier. The previous day, two of the quartet had stood for ten seconds at the start of class to honour Hitler's birthday. Further investigations revealed that another six pupils were involved in the two incidents, which were linked, in typical SED fashion, to general signs of Western-influenced misbehaviour. These included 'glorification' of professional football, especially in England and West Germany; listening to West German radio stations in the dormitories; and abusing 'progressive' pupils using anti-Semitic and anti-communist language. All ten pupils were expelled from the KJS and its sponsoring football club, FC Karl-Marx-Stadt, and returned to the local school system. The KJS director resigned. Others – including various dormitory staff, two teachers, and four FCK youth coaches – were dismissed.[42]

Repercussions were felt at other clubs. The chairman of Union Berlin organised two meetings with youth-team coaches to discuss the Karl-Marx-Stadt incident in May. His formulaic 'instruction' (*Belehrung*) focused on the external bogeyman, reiterating the need for 'a clear separation from professional football'. Home-grown factors in the growth of right-wing extremism were elided.[43] A similar unwillingness to grasp the nettle was evident in Karl-Marx-Stadt, even though what happened at the Emil Wallner KJS was one of 600 nationwide neo-fascist incidents involving teenage schoolchildren in the first five months of 1978 alone.[44] The usual suspects were mentioned: a lack of political vigilance; a neglect of FDJ work; and a focus only on sporting issues. Just as functionaries linked supporter interest in West European football with hooligan tendencies, so the tenuous connection was made between coaches allowing young footballers to watch an England–West Germany match on television and subsequent neo-Nazi manifestations among a

[41] Fenemore, *Sex, Thugs and Rock'n'Roll*, pp. 222–6.
[42] SAPMO-BArch, DY 12/3352, Abschlußinformation zum besonderen Vorkommnis an der Kinder- und Jugendsportschule "Emil Wallner" Karl-Marx-Stadt mit Schlußfolgerungen und Maßnahmen, n.d.
[43] Union Berlin Archive, Belehrung, 18 May 1978.
[44] Dennis and LaPorte, *State and Minorities*, p. 171.

handful of pupils.[45] This kind of reductionism emphasised the pervasive campaign of 'psychological warfare' being waged by the West against impressionable socialist youth.[46] It made little sense in football, which, alongside cinema, was one of East Germany's richest means of cultural exchange with the non-communist world.[47] The SED wanted the GDR to be a world leader, yet put obstacles in the way of young players who wanted to learn, as was natural enough, from countries (including West Germany) that were at the pinnacle. How was the SED to lead the political struggle against professional football when international standards were set by countries with professional structures? The contradictions inherent in the response to this conundrum were sharply exposed on the issue of players' wages.

## Paid to play: money and GDR football

In May 1968 Dynamo Dresden were relegated from the *Oberliga*. In the dressing room immediately after the decisive match against Chemie Leipzig, the players, led by star performers Klaus Sammer and Hans-Jürgen Kreische, promised to stay together to earn promotion back to the top flight. Anyone who left the club in such a situation, it was alleged, was a 'scoundrel' (*Lumpen*). The sense of unity, though, quickly broke down over a predictable subject – money. At a team dinner the same night, several players let slip propositions that they had received from other *Oberliga* clubs, offering wages higher than those paid by Dynamo Dresden, as well as cash bonuses of as much as 10,000 M. At a team meeting on 4 June, two players announced their intention to leave. Another complained that Dresden paid the worst of all *Oberliga* clubs. We play, he declared, for 'begging pennies'.[48]

The fundamental cause of this unsettled situation, the Dynamo Dresden leadership concluded, was the 'reigning anarchy' on the question of how and what players should be paid. Dynamo Dresden players, it was claimed, earned a maximum monthly wage of 1,450 M. Other clubs paid their stars as much as 2,500 M per month.[49] Despite the introduction of

[45] SAPMO-BArch, DY 12/3352, Abschlußinformation zum besonderen Vorkommnis.
[46] Fenemore, *Sex, Thugs and Rock'n'Roll*, pp. 74–8.
[47] On cinema and cultural exchange, see Ina Merkel, 'The GDR – a normal country in the centre of Europe', in Fulbrook (ed.), *Power and Society*, pp. 198–9.
[48] SAPMO-BArch, DO 101/1825/8, Bericht über eine Aussprache der Genossen Oberst Welz, Oberstleutenant Gasch und Hauptmann Hausner vom Büro der Zentralen Leitung der SV Dynamo mit Genossen des Vorstandes der SG Dynamo Dresden (Fußball), 6 June 1968.
[49] *Ibid.*

'performance wages' in factories in the 1960s, glaring discrepancies were unusual in the East German workplace, where incomes were generally levelled as much as possible and material rewards frowned upon.[50] The effect on Dynamo Dresden squad morale was profound. When one player was fined for being late for training during the 1967/8 season, his truculent response was as follows: 'first pay what is owing to me, then you can take it away'.[51]

Behind the image of disciplined and modest amateurs, the reality of life as a footballer in East Germany was shaped, as it was elsewhere in the world, by money. This had always been the case, despite repeated attempts to differentiate the fiction of football in the East, where players held regular jobs and played in their spare time, from the mercenary practices of football under capitalism – a formal commitment to amateurism that ironically echoed the DFB's resolute opposition to 'professional football' (*Berufsfußball*) during the Weimar era, as well as the stances of other unlikely allies, such as the English Football Association (FA) until the abolition of the maximum wage in 1961, and the National Collegiate Athletic Association (NCAA) in the United States today. One 1960 report bemoaned a playing culture in which the drive for money trumped the desire to excel.[52] Erich Loest's novel *Der elfte Mann*, published in 1969, charted the story of a young man torn between his football career and studies. The finely observed scenes were a product of the year that Loest spent shadowing players and officials at Lokomotive Leipzig. Reflecting on the book in 1992, the author noted that one theme had been taboo from the start:

> Once a month a man with a suitcase from Halle came over [to Leipzig], the players called him 'Uncle'. Individually they went to him in a room to receive their wages. There was no discussion among each other about how much. National players earned more, performance counted. The *Oberliga* players of the GDR were professionals, everyone knew it, and nobody talked about it.[53]

Material inducements made their way more subtly into the novel, in the scene where the ageing *Oberliga* striker Zöbl is visited by a functionary from an ambitious third division team and offered various perquisites, including access to two holiday homes and a new apartment, to join them.[54]

[50] Fulbrook, *The People's State*, pp. 229–30.

[51] SAPMO-BArch, DO 101/1933/1, Information über die mit dem Vorsitzenden der SG Dynamo Dresden – Gen. Oberstleutenant Lehmann geführte Aussprache, 8 February 1968.

[52] SAPMO-BArch, DY 30/IV 2/18/14, Gedanken zur Veröffentlichung des Präsidiums des DTSB – "Zur Situation im Fußballsport der DDR", 29 August 1960.

[53] Erich Loest, 'Zu dieser Ausgabe', *Der elfte Mann* (Munich: Deutscher Taschenbuch Verlag, 2006), p. 299.

[54] Loest, *Der elfte Mann*, pp. 190–2.

In the year that Loest's novel was published, the DTSB attempted to bring order to the 'reigning anarchy' that Dynamo Dresden bosses had complained about. A central feature of what became the 1970 football resolution (*Fußballbeschluß*) was regulation of club finances. All players, the DTSB declared, were to be paid only according to their vocational qualifications. Additional incentives were to be discontinued, with the exception of centrally approved bonuses payable to the likes of national team players. The DTSB was to direct the flow of money to football clubs, rather than letting them distribute it themselves, as had previously been the case. In adopting this harder line, football was to be returned to socialist principles and an end made to the practice of run-of-the-mill *Oberliga* players earning 1,500 M per month (the average monthly wage of factory workers in 1975 was 898 M),[55] having up to 30,000 M in their bank accounts, and owning cars and holiday homes.[56]

The regulations had some effect. BSG Stahl Eisenhüttenstadt, just relegated from the *Oberliga*, were demoted a further division in 1970 for making illegal payments to players, coaches, and administrators.[57] At the end of the following season, BSG Chemie Wolfen were demoted from the second to the third division after illegally spending 36,000 M of the sponsoring factory's money on bonuses.[58] Tellingly, only small teams fell foul of the new rules – and then only in the immediate aftermath of the 1970 directive. For bigger clubs with powerful backers, it was business as usual. An army of vested interests ensured that central control of football finances remained weak. A small sample of the infractions compiled by the DFV in 1986 included the 30,000 M in cash offered by Rot–Weiß Erfurt to two players that the club wanted to obtain from FCM and Wismut Aue, respectively; the 4,500 M bonus given to each player and the coach at *Liga* team Chemie Ilmenau for avoiding relegation; and the players earning as much as 2,200 M per month at county league team BSG Motor Ludwigsfelde.[59] During the 1987/8 season, seventeen of the twenty-nine-man squad at BSG Stahl Brandenburg earned more than

[55] Wolle, *Die heile Welt*, p. 49.

[56] SAPMO-BArch, DY 30/IV A 2/18/7, Probleme des Leistungsstandes, 9 January 1969.

[57] Jörn Luther, 'So rollte der Ball im Osten', in Willmann (ed.), *Fußball-Land DDR*, p. 15.

[58] SAPMO-BArch, DY 12/3326, letter from the DFV to Paul Verner, 6 August 1971, fo. 267–8.

[59] SAPMO-BArch, DY 30/IV 2/2.039/251, Beispiele und Fakten für die unzureichende Einheitlichkeit und Geschlossenheit der am Prozeß der Durchsetzung des Fußballbeschlusses von 1983 beteiligten staats- und wirtschaftsleitenden Organe, 18 June 1986, fo. 126–9.

4,000 M per month. The average monthly wage was supposed to be between 800 and 1,100 M.[60]

To the very end, the DFV grappled with the contradiction between the desire to make GDR football competitive – one 1964 report noted the correlation between paying players well and international success[61] – and socialist distaste for spendthrift excess on a sport that brought more trouble than rewards. The contract system for *Oberliga* players announced in 1989 was a tentative nod towards the *de facto* professionalism that had been introduced in communist countries such as Hungary, Poland, and the Soviet Union.[62] Players were obliged, under the terms of their contract, not to seek financial recompense beyond its stipulations on wages and bonuses.[63] At the same time, perhaps as a concession to the GDR's parlous financial state and in a vain attempt to salvage a semblance of socialism's amateur ethos, the DFV introduced measures to cut financial support, reduce squad sizes, and shorten training hours at *Liga* and county league clubs.[64] The incoherence at the heart of GDR football is clear here. The mantra of raising standards and modernising, epitomised by the contract system, was undermined by a downgrading of the second and third divisions that, if carried through, would have made it harder for talented players to reach their potential. The collapse of the SED dictatorship rendered the reforms moot, shoving East German football into a world of free-market competition for which, as we shall see in Chapter 15, it was woefully unprepared.

Belying older descriptions of totalitarian rule, imperviousness to central directives appears to have been a key component of East German communism, as studies of organisations such as the FDJ and the *Kulturbund* (Cultural Association), as well as contentious issues such as nudism, have amply demonstrated.[65] In football, this ensured that players moved for large sums of money, despite the ban on transfers, and received cash bonuses and other material benefits,

60 *Ibid.*, letter from Höfner to Günter Mittag, 8 September 1988, fo. 200–1; Information über die Spielervergütungen der Fußballoberligamannschaft "BSG Stahl Brandenburg", 2 September 1988, fo. 202–4.

61 Archivgut des DFV, I/1, Analyse über den Stand der leistungsbestimmenden Faktoren, 19 August 1964.

62 SAPMO-BArch, DY 30/4966, Zu einigen Fragen des Kommerzes und der Professionalisierung im Sport der UdSSR und anderer sozialistischer Länder, n.d., fo. 54–70; Information zum ungarischen Leistungssport, 31 March 1987, fo. 86–7.

63 SAPMO-BArch, DY 30/IV 2/2.039/251, sample contract (*Vertrag*), n.d., fo. 213–18.

64 *Ibid.*, Begründung für die Neufassung der Richtlinie für die II. Fußball-Leistungsklasse Liga, n.d., fo. 219.

65 See e.g. Fenemore, *Sex, Thugs and Rock'n'Roll*; McDougall, *Youth Politics* (on the FDJ); Palmowski, *Inventing a Socialist Nation*; Richthofen, *Bringing Culture to the Masses* (on the *Kulturbund*); McLellan, *Love in the Time of Communism* (on nudism).

despite the illegality of such practices. In this unchanging, and seemingly unchangeable, landscape, the central authorities exuded an air of helplessness. Their directives were only so much white noise, quickly tuned out by functionaries and players with their own interests to protect. *Eigen-Sinn* here was less about non-conformity than it was about non-compliance.

Considerable power and influence in football lay not at the centre, but at the periphery, among local party bosses and factory directors. Numerous scholars have noted the important role of intermediary actors in the functioning of social and cultural activities in the GDR.[66] Sometimes these figures were ordinary citizens 'with a bit more at stake in the system than everybody else'.[67] At other times, they were powerful figures. In 1975 Hansa Rostock's patron, FDGB boss Harry Tisch – a heavy drinker – infamously sacked coach Heinz Werner twenty minutes into a game against Carl Zeiss Jena.[68] Werner later had a more positive experience of local patronage as coach of Stahl Brandenburg, where the head of the town's steelworks, Hans-Joachim Lauck, gave him unlimited resources for players and facilities.[69]

It was men like Lauck and Tisch who sanctioned, or turned a blind eye to, the perquisites that clubs used to attract or keep players. Their actions were not directed against communist rule, but nonetheless made impossible a transparent and united administration of the game. In 1988 Wolfgang Biermann wrote to Rudi Hellmann about the declining fortunes of the club that his internationally renowned optics factories sponsored, FC Carl Zeiss Jena. Identifying various causes for this decline – from the 'incestuous' practice of employing ex-players to the loss of players to rival teams – Biermann appealed to the central authorities for help. If things did not change, he warned, Carl Zeiss would remove its name, and all financial support, from the club.[70] Yet the same individual, as the DFV's 1986 report on illegal payments noted, undermined the system from which he now wanted assistance, giving Jena players weekly bonuses of 1,000 M for a win and 600 M for a draw.[71] Less than a year after Biermann's letter to Hellmann, Jena functionaries were accused of poaching Marcus Wuckel from FCM, with

66 See e.g. Palmowski, *Inventing a Socialist Nation*; Richthofen, *Bringing Culture to the Masses*; Wilton, 'Regime versus people?'.

67 Richthofen, *Bringing Culture to the Masses*, p. 45.

68 Interview with Heinz Werner; Leske, *Erich Mielke*, p. 387.

69 Interview with Heinz Werner.

70 SAPMO-BArch, DY 30/4967, letter from Wolfgang Biermann to Rudi Hellmann, 30 March 1988, fo. 84–8.

71 SAPMO-BArch, DY 30/IV 2/2.039/251, Beispiele und Fakten, 18 June 1986, fo. 127.

a lucrative offer that included a four-room flat, a holiday bungalow, and a car.[72] Localism to the last subverted attempts to rationalise and centralise East German football.

Money, finally, was emblematic of the uncertain status of GDR footballers, namely the constrained autonomy under which they lived. On the one hand, many of them enjoyed a lifestyle that ordinary East Germans would have regarded as privileged. Even young *Oberliga* players, the DFV complained in 1986, owned single-family houses, garages, allotments, and cars. Players at county league side BSG Motor Hennigsdorf earned monthly wages of 1,700–1,800 M for doing twenty hours of factory work per week.[73] Money, in some cases at least, fostered a political conformity that reminds us that football was a site of control as well as *Eigen-Sinn* – witness the enthusiasm with which, for example, national team players Reinhard Lauck and Bernd Bransch endorsed communist candidates in the 1974 national elections.[74]

Yet the apparent riches, modest by *Bundesliga* standards, were unevenly distributed. Of the twenty-man squad that helped Dynamo Berlin finish eighth in the *Oberliga* during the 1963/4 season, eight lived either with their parents or in the club's dormitory block.[75] Moreover, earning potential came with strings attached. Marcus Wuckel may have been offered various inducements to move from Magdeburg to Jena in 1989, but he was not allowed to go. Players, as the file of the peripatetic journeyman Detlev Z. illustrates, were rarely masters of their own destiny. Power in East German football may have been diffuse and disputed, but it was not in their hands. This was true even of those who reached the summit of the game.

## Life at the top: Hans-Jürgen Kreische and Axel Tyll

When Rangers hosted Dynamo Dresden in the first round of the Fairs' Cup in October 1967, the programme notes described twenty-year-old striker Hans-Jürgen Kreische as 'one of the most difficult forwards to dispossess that our defenders have met. He covers the ball as he speeds in, and in his physical power, apart from his natural ability, can drain the

[72] SAPMO-BArch, DY 30/4969, Standpunkt des DFV der DDR zu den Versuchen von Funktionären des FC Carl Zeiss Jena, Marcus Wuckel zum Gemeinschaftswechsel zu bewegen, 26 January 1989, fo. 52.

[73] SAPMO-BArch, DY 30/IV 2/2.039/251, Beispiele und Fakten, 18 June 1986, fo. 128–9.

[74] 'Eindeutiges Bekenntnis', *Die Neue Fußball-Woche,* 21 May 1974, 1–2. On Bransch's work with the MfS, see Leske, *Enzyklopädie*, pp. 80–4.

[75] SAPMO-BArch, DO 101/1825/8, Einschätzungen der Spielerkader der Sektion Fußball, 2 June 1964.

challenger of any advantage he may appear to hold'.[76] An exceptional young player, whose goal ensured victory for the GDR in the final of the UEFA junior tournament against England in 1965 (the country's first major international success), Kreische became '*the* Dresden idol'[77] – the focal point, captain, and chief goalscorer in the outstanding Dynamo team of the 1970s that won five league titles and two cup finals. Winner of the golden boot, as the *Oberliga*'s top scorer, on four occasions and the GDR player of the year in 1973, Kreische scored twenty-five goals in fifty appearances for the national team, taking part in its sixth-place finish at the 1974 World Cup finals.[78] His cult status, confirmed in fan mail sent to Dynamo Dresden during its golden decade,[79] was reinforced by family history. Kreische's father, Hans, was part of the Dresden Friedrichstadt side that controversially lost the league championship to Horch Zwickau in 1950 and departed en masse for West Germany. A homesick Kreische senior returned to the GDR in 1954 and closed out his career with Dynamo Dresden.[80]

'Hansi' Kreische was the kind of star player that the GDR sports authorities had trouble handling. As was the case with the Jena striker Peter Ducke, another brilliant goalscorer, natural talent conferred suspicion rather than admiration on him.[81] Though not as ill-disciplined as 'Black Peter', Kreische frequently ran foul of coaches and administrators, most notably the Dresden coach, Walter Fritzsch.[82] Following national team games against Wales and Italy, club officials reminded Kreische in 1969 'for the umpteenth time' of the need to work on his long-standing 'athletic and moral' weaknesses.[83] During the following season, he was subject to no fewer than nineteen meetings along similar lines, but still did not perform to the expected standards. The causes, a 1970 report concluded, were under-developed fighting qualities, inflated self-worth, and excessive drinking.[84] Reading the in-house evaluations of Kreische, one is hard-pressed to remember that he was the side's most lauded

[76] SAPMO-BArch, DO 101/078, programme from Rangers vs. Dynamo Dresden, 4 October 1967.
[77] Horn and Weise, *Das große Lexikon*, p. 196.
[78] For biographical information on Kreische, see Horn and Weise, *Das große Lexikon*, pp. 196–8; Leske, *Enzyklopädie*, p. 275.
[79] The fan mail is examined in Chapter 8.
[80] The Friedrichstadt–Horch match is discussed in Chapter 7.
[81] On Ducke, see Stridde, *Die Peter-Ducke-Story*.
[82] Interview with Hans-Jürgen Kreische in Genschmar, *Mit Dynamo*, p. 30.
[83] SAPMO-BArch, DO 101/043/1, Bericht über Sportfreund Hans-Jürgen Kreische, 21 May 1969.
[84] SAPMO-BArch, DO 101/074, Einschätzung des Spieljahres 1969/70 der Deutschen Fußballmeisterschaft der DDR, 10 July 1970.

Figure 4. Dynamo Dresden striker Hans-Jürgen Kreische signing autographs for fans, March 1974. One of the stars of GDR football, 'Hansi' Kreische was a hugely popular figure, who had his share of run-ins with the authorities. The photograph shows that players' hair got longer on both sides of the Iron Curtain during the 1970s.

player, a striker who was respected throughout Europe and feted by GDR media and fans alike. Though an SED member, Kreische apparently displayed little interest in acquiring the 'political knowledge' that might have made him a more palatable figure to those who ran football.[85]

Clashes that pit headstrong and talented footballers against equally bull-headed coaches and unsympathetic administrators are not the preserve of football behind the Iron Curtain. The premature end to Kreische's career, however, might have been avoided in a less stifling and more supportive environment. Following a European Cup defeat to Liverpool in December 1977, the striker retired at the age of thirty-one, after having scored a total of thirty-seven goals in Dresden's title-winning campaigns during the previous two seasons. The official reasons cited were his age, a desire to give young players more first-team opportunities, and the intention to ease the coaching transition from Fritzsch to Gerhard Prautzsch – a switch that had been much delayed and was eventually made, against Fritzsch's wishes, in September 1978. But privately Kreische made it clear that he felt capable of playing top-flight football for another couple of years. It was the endless quarrels with Fritzsch, he claimed, that forced his hand. They were exemplified by the coach's decision to leave him as an unused substitute for the home game against Liverpool after he had warmed up for twenty minutes, thereby making him look 'ridiculous' in front of his adoring crowd. Characteristically, the Dynamo leadership welcomed the opportunity to be rid of a 'very weak character, [who] tended to bitch, and often tried to avoid hard training' – and seemed most concerned about how to explain Kreische's sudden departure to the media and fans.[86] For the young Martin in Steffen Pockart's novel, *Das Leuchten der Giraffen* ('The Giraffes' Lights'), this was the moment when 'the first small shadow fell over [his] Dynamo world'. Martin's father watched Kreische's final appearance in tears.[87] But there was no attempt to dissuade 'Hansi'. Dynamo Dresden's golden period ended, coincidentally or not, with the retirement of their talisman. After winning their fifth league title in eight years in 1978, the team did not reclaim the *Oberliga* crown until 1989.

The career of Kreische's contemporary, the midfielder Axel Tyll, was less dramatic, but no less storied. A star, like Kreische, of GDR youth teams, he was an integral component of the other outstanding East

85 *Ibid.*, Jahresanalyse des Fußballschwerpunktes der SG Dynamo Dresden für das Spieljahr 1971/72, 9 June 1972.

86 SAPMO-BArch, DO 101/043/1, Aktennotiz zur Kaderangelegenheit Hans-Jürgen Kreische, 29 December 1977.

87 Steffen Pockart, *Das Leuchten der Giraffe: Kotte ... Cocker ... Kaffee-Mix* (Norderstedt: Books on Demand, 2010), pp. 15–16.

Figure 5. Axel Tyll celebrates FC Magdeburg's 2–0 victory over AC Milan in the 1974 European Cup Winners' Cup final. The triumph of the *Bezirksauswahl* ('county XI') in Rotterdam was a remarkable achievement. Tyll, who set up the second goal for his midfield colleague, Wolfgang Seguin, was more local than most, having started his career at BSG Motor Mitte Magdeburg.

German side of the 1970s, FC Magdeburg. With FCM, he won three league titles and three FDGB Cups between 1972 and 1979. He was part of the team that stunned AC Milan to win the European Cup Winners' Cup in 1974. Club success contrasted with Tyll's international career. He played only four times for the national team.[88]

By 1982, Tyll's time at FCM was approaching its end. Informed by the club that he was surplus to requirements, the twenty-nine-year-old sought alternatives. He wanted to continue playing top-level football for another team, BSG Wismut Aue. But sports functionaries in Magdeburg, supported by FCM officials, had other ideas. They rejected Tyll's request in December, granting him permission to move only to a lower-division team in *Bezirk* Magdeburg. At this point the player wrote a petition to the DTSB, in which he argued that his long years of service to FCM had earned him the 'gesture of fairness' that would allow him to continue his *Oberliga* career at another club. Tyll framed his complaint

[88] Horn and Weise, *Das große Lexikon*, p. 350.

within acceptable legal and rhetorical boundaries, melding individual concerns, increasingly prominent under consumer socialism during the 1970s, with state-friendly reassurances. He cited sections of the DTSB statute and the GDR constitution to support his right to be re-deployed at a club suitable to his talent and experience, a solution, he argued, that met his needs and those of socialist society.[89]

Tyll's petition never got off the ground. Whether this was a result of outside pressure, or further personal reflection, is unclear. But within a week of the petition being sent, the FCM chairman Manfred Zapf – Tyll's former team-mate and the captain of the side that lifted the Cup Winners' Cup in 1974 – reported that, 'after several discussions with our club leadership', Tyll had withdrawn his request to move to Aue. He instead joined county league side Einheit Wernigerode. The player confirmed Zapf's statement, citing 'mature reflection and a consultation with the doctor' as the decisive factors in ending his *Oberliga* career.[90]

The solution appears to have worked out well. Tyll and his family put down roots in Wernigerode. He helped Einheit to win the county league title in 1988 and worked as a sports teacher at a local school.[91] But the initial decision on what to do and where to go had not been Tyll's, or at least not his alone. Workplace constraints limited freedom of movement for footballers, just as they did for other citizens, especially in a period (the 1970s) when career mobility declined markedly in the GDR.[92] While some players, as we shall see in Chapter 6, refused to accept the constraints and departed for West Germany, the vast majority, like Kreische and Tyll, accepted their lot, building their careers and lives in the socialist East, even as they distanced themselves from its political practices. They represented the 'grumbling and conformity' that may have constituted the default position of East Germans living under communism.[93]

Kreische and Tyll provide interesting case studies of the liminal status of GDR footballers, practitioners of a profession that at once granted autonomy and imposed restrictions. Though Kreische in particular clashed with the authorities on a regular basis and only nominally fulfilled his duties as a party comrade, both men could ultimately be

[89] SAPMO-BArch, DY 12/3357, petition from Axel Tyll to the DTSB leadership, 22 December 1982.

[90] *Ibid.*, letter from Manfred Zapf to the *Bezirk* Magdeburg performance sport commission, 29 December 1982; letter from Tyll to the DTSB leadership, 11 January 1983.

[91] Horn and Weise, *Das große Lexikon*, p. 350; Leske, *Enzyklopädie*, p. 497.

[92] Ralph Jessen, 'Mobility and blockage during the 1970s', in Jarausch (ed.), *Dictatorship as Experience*, pp. 341–60.

[93] Fulbrook, *Anatomy*, p. 139.

regarded as loyal citizens, who continued to serve East German football, and thus the East German state, after their retirement in coaching and educational capacities. Both enjoyed great successes, earned good money, and travelled the world with their clubs and the national team. Few GDR citizens got Kreische's opportunities to go Christmas shopping in Hamburg, or to drink port with work colleagues in a Portuguese hotel.[94] He and Tyll were part of a gilded sporting elite. They were also popular icons, symbols of local patriotic pride in Dresden and Magdeburg respectively – and, as such, less easily set in the regime's image than successful Olympic weightlifters, swimmers, or javelin throwers. This was especially true of the idolised Kreische. But Tyll too inspired starstruck responses. The young FCM supporter Kathrin Gaebel later recalled how she found out where Tyll and Jürgen Pommerenke lived, but never plucked up the courage to ring on the former's doorbell.[95]

In the final reckoning, though, the adulation of the crowd, league titles, and cup triumphs brought only a constrained form of autonomy. Neither Kreische nor Tyll ended their careers in a manner of their own choosing. Both left top-level football reluctantly and prematurely. Both went to less exalted places in the football pyramid according to the state's wishes, playing out the rest of their lives in the GDR in relatively modest surroundings. Privilege then became the privilege of memory. The professionals, one might say, returned to the ranks of the amateurs.

[94] Genschmar, *Mit Dynamo*, p. 31. [95] Gröschner, *Sieben Tränen*, p. 132.

# 4 The national team

## Beautiful losers

In September 1952, three months after the East German football association (*Sektion Fußball*) had been granted FIFA membership, the GDR played its first official international fixture against Poland. Thrown initially by the early kick-off time in chilly Warsaw, the visitors soon dictated matters, dominating the match for seventy minutes. They created numerous chances, but failed to score. Against the run of play, the Poles took the lead. As the East Germans pushed forward looking for an equaliser, the hosts added two further goals in the last five minutes, for a final score of 3–0. 'We lacked a bit of luck', concluded the head of the delegation, Helmut Behrendt, in his match report. When the team arrived home two days later, much to Behrendt's chagrin, only one person was there to greet it.[1] It would be another three years, six matches, and two coaches before the GDR won a game, recording a 3–2 victory over Romania in Bucharest in September 1955.

The trip to Warsaw in many ways anticipated the ill-starred history of East Germany's national team. Hard-luck stories abounded, so often that they could not always be explained away by invoking misfiring strikers and inspired goalkeepers. An unmistakable pattern of snatching defeat from the jaws of victory defined the GDR's performances on the international stage. 'Whenever there was a qualifying campaign', concluded Ulrich Hesse-Lichtenberger, 'you could bet the GDR would end up one point short'.[2] Glorious opportunities to reach the quadrennial finals of the World Cup were passed up in the elimination rounds ahead of the 1966 tournament in England and the 1982 tournament in Spain. Things were worse in the other major international tournament, the European Championship, which was first held in 1960. In campaigns to reach the

[1] SAPMO-BArch, DR 5/19, Bericht über die Delegation zum Fussball-Länderspiel Volkspolen–DDR am 21.9.1952 in Warschau, n.d.

[2] Hesse-Lichtenberger, *Tor!*, p. 223.

1964, 1976, 1980, and 1988 finals, the GDR blew winning positions through a mixture of ill fortune and nervy play.[3]

The end result was that the national team qualified only once for the finals of the World Cup (in West Germany in 1974) and never made it to the finals of the European Championship. This modest record earned it the unkind, though not inaccurate, moniker 'world champion in friendlies'.[4] The coach who narrates Thomas Brussig's play *Leben bis Männer* – assured by his local party boss after 1974 that he will be allowed to travel to watch the GDR in the next international tournament – waits in vain for his moment in the sun: 'I tell you, I had a lot of time to learn to hate this team'. The GDR, he concluded, were 'notorious qualification losers' (*Qualifikationsversager*).[5] Helmut Klopfleisch, an outspoken follower of West German football who attracted the attention of the *Stasi*, was blunter: 'Look, East Germany were rubbish! They only got 5,000 people watching the national team, and even then they had to bus in kids who would have watched anything'.[6] Klopfleisch's conclusion was greatly exaggerated. As we saw in Chapter 1, the GDR's stereotypical awfulness at football does not stand up to close scrutiny. Perception, though, was everything. Klopfleisch was not alone, either at home or abroad, in viewing the East German team in a negative light.

This chapter examines the chequered history of the national team, from its unheralded beginnings in 1952 to its unlamented demise in 1990. Why were the officials and coaches who turned the GDR into an Olympic superpower unable to do the same in the world's most popular sport? What do the national team's failures, and successes, tell us about the sport's role in shaping East German identity? Focusing on the GDR's twin relations with Soviet bloc and West European football – and paying particular heed to the encounter between East and West Germany at the 1974 World Cup finals – the chapter emphasises the complexities and ambiguities that governed the self-image(s) of GDR football. The national team, it is argued, showcased the multiple ways in which, for players and fans alike, sporting *Eigen-Sinn* could both include and exclude official socialist narratives. Unable to consolidate public support gained during fleeting moments of success, it was a microcosm of the rootlessness that the East German state never overcame. With football, as

[3] Hence Christoph Dieckmann's description of the GDR national team as 'beautiful losers' in '"Nur ein Leutzscher ist ein Deutscher"', p. 323.

[4] Matthias Koch, '"Weltmeister der Freundschaftspiele"', in Willmann (ed.), *Fußball-Land DDR*, pp. 139–41.

[5] Brussig, *Leben bis Männer*, pp. 42–6.

[6] Kuper, *Football against the Enemy*, p. 24.

with the concept of *Heimat*, a forum for popular identification with the communist regime ultimately had the opposite effect, serving as a flexible space in which citizens could 'develop subjectivities and engage in practices that were distinct from the party's ideas of patriotism and nationhood'.[7]

## Learning to win? GDR football between East and West

There is no single reason why GDR football struggled to make an international splash. But a major part of the problem, as in many areas of East German life, was politics. The GDR began playing competitive fixtures at the height of Cold War tensions, when both sides – to borrow from a British journalist writing before England's seminal encounter with Hungary in November 1953 – 'regard[ed] a sporting triumph as a justification for their "superior" way of life'.[8] The climate ensured that, in terms of coaching models and playing schedules, the focus was placed firmly on learning from one's socialist allies.

This policy was not entirely illogical. The best football team in the world between 1950 and 1956 was indisputably Hungary's *Aranycsapat* ('golden squad'). Led by the likes of Puskás, Hidegkuti, and Kocsis, it flourished at the height of the brutal Stalinist dictatorship of Mátyás Rákosi. Olympic champions in Helsinki in 1952, and World Cup finalists two years later, Hungary was at the vanguard of world football. Its coaches instituted a tactical revolution that rendered obsolete the previously dominant, and highly rigid, 'W–M' formation, pioneered in the 1930s by the English coach Walter Winterbottom, and replaced it with a more fluid 4–2–4 structure that was quickly adopted by the world's leading teams.[9] This fact was not lost on GDR players and coaches. As the national junior team prepared for a tournament in West Germany in 1954, comrades at BSG Rotation Naumburg urged it to take inspiration from Hungary's sensational 6–3 win over the 'motherland' of football, England, at Wembley Stadium the previous autumn.[10] As early as 1950, the football authorities urged closer contacts with Hungary, as it was 'the nearest country where the best football is being played and where the best

[7] Palmowski, *Inventing a Socialist Nation*, p. 110.

[8] Ronnie Kowalski and Dilwyn Porter, 'Cold War football: British–European encounters in the 1940s and 1950s', in Stephen Wagg and David L. Andrews (eds.), *East Plays West: Sport and the Cold War* (London: Routledge, 2007), p. 71.

[9] Wilson, *Behind the Curtain*, pp. 72–3.

[10] SAPMO-BArch, DR 5/1275, letter from BSG Rotation Naumburg to the GDR junior team, 2 April 1954. On this match, and Hungary's 7–1 win in the return game in Budapest, see Wilson, *Behind the Curtain*, pp. 68–79.

coaches are to be found'.[11] The two most successful national team coaches before the appointment of Georg Buschner in 1970 were Hungarians, János Gyarmati (1955–7) and Károly Soós (1961–7) – rare foreign presences in the insular world of GDR football.[12]

It made less sporting sense to take the Soviet Union as a role model, but political necessity elevated it to a position alongside, and even above, Hungary. There were elements of wishful thinking in this policy, insofar as the Soviet Union was not then or later one of the world's football superpowers. Progress was undoubtedly made in the early post-war years, as illustrated by Dynamo Moscow's successful tour of Britain in late 1945.[13] But the Soviets had no formally organised national team until the 1952 Olympics. Between 1948 and 1953, various club sides and select XIs defeated a series of hand-picked opponents but none of Western Europe's best teams.[14] At a conference in 1955, though, the GDR coach Gyarmati rather absurdly placed the Soviets above his homeland in terms of conditioning, tactics, and technique (more accurately, he rated the GDR poorly in the latter category).[15] The schedule for a football conference the previous December talked about the 'good improvement' in Soviet football, while the game in the West had supposedly gone backwards[16] – in the year that West Germany won the World Cup and the Soviets did not enter the tournament. Coaches who espoused the ideas of the victorious West German coach Sepp Herberger, such as Chemie Leipzig's Otto Westphal, did not last long. Shortly after the sacking of Westphal in 1953, his colleagues were urged to discard 'pseudo-scientific Western' thinking in the field of sports science and to read up instead on Soviet football theory, most notably Boris Arkadiev's 'The tactics of a football match'.[17]

The orientation towards the Soviet bloc was reflected in the national team's schedule, which studiously avoided encounters with the world's

11 SAPMO-BArch, DY 12/281, 1. Trainerausbildung mit Hilfe der Sowjetunion und Ungarn, 1 August 1950, fo. 36.

12 Horn and Weise, *Das große Lexikon*, p. 406.

13 See David Downing, *Passovotchka: Moscow Dynamo in Britain, 1945* (London: Bloomsbury, 2000).

14 Robert Edelman, *Serious Fun: A History of Spectator Sports in the USSR* (Oxford: Oxford University Press, 1993), pp. 87–95.

15 SAPMO-BArch, DY 12/308, Protokoll über die Trainerrats-Tagung am 14.10.1955 in Berlin Deutsche Sporthalle, n.d., fos. 33–9.

16 SAPMO-BArch, DR 5/137, Durchführung des I. Fußball-Kongresses der DDR, 14 December 1954.

17 'Wie lange soll das noch so weitergehen?', *DSE*, 11 February 1953; 'Leistungssteigerung – das "A und O"', *DSE*, 25 March 1953. Arkadiev, the coach of army team TsDKA Moscow, forcefully argued the superiority of Soviet football in the journal *Sovietskii Sport*. See Edelman, *Serious Fun*, pp. 93–4.

leading West European and South American teams. Between 1955 and 1965, East Germany played fifty-six international matches, of which twenty-nine were against fellow communist states in Eastern Europe, eleven were against newly independent Asian and African states (such as Ghana, Guinea, and Indonesia), one was against South American opposition, and fifteen were against West European nations.[18] In those fifteen games, however, there was arguably only one top-tier opponent, England, who defeated the GDR 2–1 in Leipzig in 1963. The match was an anomaly, the product of DFV general secretary Kurt Michalski's good relationship with English officials, rather than any shift in the pattern of international fixtures.[19] In its history, the GDR played Poland nineteen times and Bulgaria and Romania eighteen times apiece, but only contested four matches against each of England, Brazil, and Italy – and just a solitary fixture against West Germany.[20]

A letter to *Die Neue Fußball-Woche* in February 1956 asked the following question: 'Why [are we] still not playing international matches against capitalist countries?'[21] Part of the answer could be attributed to the *de facto* boycott of matches against the GDR by NATO states. Between 1955 and 1969, the Hallstein Doctrine stipulated that West Germany would break off diplomatic ties with any state, save the Soviet Union, that established formal relations with the GDR. In the international world of sport, the policy was hard to enforce. The GDR flag and other insignia were the subject of 'cat and mouse' games between the East and West German authorities, with Cold War posturing on both sides, but this did not necessarily impede the participation of GDR athletes in international events.[22] Bonn periodically flexed its muscles, as, for example, when the intervention of the West German embassy led to the cancellation of a friendly match between Turkey and the GDR in 1957. The fact that the East Germans instead arranged a game against English club Luton Town suggests that, in football as in other sports, there were ways around the West German embargo.[23] The Hallstein Doctrine was thus not the whole story. As in the Soviet case, East German reluctance to play the world's top nations was driven by fear of embarrassment at the hands of the class enemy. The editorial response to the question posed in *Die Neue Fußball-Woche* admitted as much,

[18] Karte and Röhrig, *Kabinengeflüster*, pp. 189–94. [19] *Ibid.*, pp. 60–1.

[20] Horn and Weise, *Das große Lexikon*, pp. 401–2.

[21] 'Warum noch keine Länderspiele mit kapitalistischen Staaten?', *Die Neue Fußball-Woche*, 7 February 1956, 2.

[22] Schiller and Young, *The 1972 Munich Olympics*, pp. 157–9.

[23] Archivgut des DFV, I/1, 'Dokumentation über 45 Jahre Fußball'.

suggesting that the national team's 'constant string of defeats' made encounters with Western nations inadvisable.[24]

The consequences of the unchallenging schedule went largely unaddressed. Other scapegoats – poor coaching, lack of ideological preparation, and local patriotism – were more commonly blamed for the national team's failings. Without suitably competitive preparation, though, the GDR was more often than not unable to defeat the world's best teams when it mattered. East German football, as one DFV official later noted, 'stewed in its own juices'.[25] Among coaches and players alike, an inferiority complex developed. Their West German counterparts were not necessarily better trained or educated, but they had, in Heinz Werner's words, a 'self-confidence' that was absent in the hermetic world of GDR football.[26]

Werner's comparison is telling. Mediocrity was made worse by West Germany's emergence as a global football power. In Sönke Wortmann's 2003 film about the West German triumph at the 1954 World Cup finals, *The Miracle of Berne*, uniformed FDJ members, including the protagonist's brother, Bruno, who has left the FRG to experience socialism first hand, watch the final against Hungary on television. The scene tacitly endorses West German claims to the *Alleinvertretung* ('sole representation') of the German nation, while suggesting sport's powerful role in the survival of cross-border German identities in the 1950s.[27] East German reactions were mixed, but tended to stress the latter point. The SED newspaper *Neues Deutschland* strove for a neutral tone during the tournament, as did Wolfgang Hempel's radio commentary on the final. In the excitement of the last few minutes, though, Hempel broke protocol by referring to the 'West German team' as 'the German team' and 'the Germans'.[28] West Germany's unexpected 3–2 victory left the SED in an awkward position. Credit had to be given to Sepp Herberger's team, but political ground could not be lost on the back of nationalistic euphoria that, at times, troublingly recalled the recent past. DFB President Peco Bauwens' invocation of the '*Führer* principle' at post-match celebrations in Munich suggests that Rainer Werner Fassbinder's scepticism about the 'self-discovery' of West German democracy in July 1954, as displayed in the famous closing scene of *The Marriage of Maria Braun*, was not misplaced.[29] Some of the excitement of the moment, however,

[24] 'Warum noch keine Länderspiele?', 2.
[25] Interview with Holger Fuchs, 23 May 2011. [26] Interview with Heinz Werner.
[27] *Das Wunder von Bern* (dir. Sönke Wortmann, 2003).
[28] Becker and Buss, 'Das "Wunder von Bern"', 392–9.
[29] In the closing scene, Maria and her husband are killed in an explosion at their home at the very moment that radio commentator Herbert Zimmermann proclaims victory in

made it into communist publications. *Junge Welt* called the 'miracle of Berne' 'the greatest triumph in the history of German football'.[30]

While East–West solidarity clearly still existed, formal cooperation was difficult, as Bonn and East Berlin fought battles big and small about how Germany was to be represented on the international stage. This could be seen in the tortuous negotiations to send a joint football team to the 1956 Olympics in Melbourne. Back-and-forth discussions about coaches (the reluctance of GDR officials to support Herberger's appointment), players (the East Germans proposed that seven of the starting XI should come from the GDR, as West Germany had 'no better options' in the named positions), and the team kit (possibly blue, without the 'federal eagle' that adorned West German shirts) ended without agreement.[31] A German side containing only West German players departed for Australia that autumn under Herberger's leadership, but was eliminated in the first round by the Soviet Union. Ahead of each of the following two Olympics, in Rome in 1960 and Tokyo in 1964, the winner of a play-off match between East and West Germany represented Germany in the football tournament. West Germany earned the honour for the Rome Games. The GDR turned the tables four years later and won the bronze medal. From 1968, when the International Olympic Committee granted equal recognition to the National Olympic Committees of the two halves of divided Germany, both countries participated independently in the football tournament and the rest of the Olympic competition.[32]

The East German football team enjoyed its greatest success in the Olympic Games. The bronze medal in Tokyo was repeated in Munich in 1972; a silver medal was won in 1980 in Moscow; and, in 1976 in Montreal, the GDR XI defeated Poland 3–1 to win Olympic gold. The results, though not without a degree of prestige, fooled no-one. Amateur rules forbade all professional footballers from taking part in the Olympics before 1988. The field was left open to teams from the socialist bloc, where players, nominally at least, enjoyed amateur status. Communist states dominated Olympic football competition between 1952 and 1980. The insignificance of such victories was bluntly conceded in the

Berne. For a positive reading of West Germany's win, see Arthur Heinrich, 'The 1954 Soccer World Cup and the Federal Republic of Germany's self-discovery', *American Behavioral Scientist* vol. 46, no. 11 (July 2003), 1491–505.

30 Becker and Buss, 'Das "Wunder von Bern"', 393–5.

31 On the negotiations, see SAPMO-BArch, DR 5/167, Verhandlungskonzeption mit den westdeutschen DFB und Vorbereitungsplan der Olympia-Kandidaten, 24 October 1955; and various correspondence, primarily between DFB boss Peco Bauwens and the president of the GDR's National Olympic Committee Heinz Schöbel, in SAPMO-BArch, DY 12/5331, fo. 1–47.

32 Schiller and Young, *The 1972 Munich Olympics*, pp. 158–64.

1983 football resolution. The gold and silver medals at the previous two Olympiads, it reported, had been achieved in the absence of the world's best teams. When they were thrown into the equation – at the World Cup and the European Championship – the GDR foundered.[33] As the international reputation of East German sport soared in the 1970s and 1980s, one sore spot remained. 'East Germany', a British journalist concluded in 1974, 'are probably the best (or worst) example [of] how not to run football successfully'.[34] In the same year, ironically, the national team provided a rare moment of optimism – and, in the process, a test case of the complex relationship between state and nation in the GDR.

## Us against us? The 'Sparwasser goal'

The goal was simple. In the seventy-eighth minute of a tense and scoreless match, a long ball from the right flank by the substitute falls into the path of the striker. He heads it into a yawning gap that has opened up in the penalty area, and then sends a close-range, right-foot shot over the goalkeeper's despairing lunge. In celebration he executes an ungainly forward roll, before being engulfed by jubilant team-mates.

Jürgen Sparwasser's winning goal in the 1974 World Cup match between East and West Germany in Hamburg was the highpoint in the history of GDR football. A book has been written about the responses of various people (players, coaches, journalists, politicians, and fans) to the question 'Where were you when the Sparwasser goal went in?'[35] 'You'd only have to write "Hamburg '74" on my gravestone and everyone would know who it is', the player himself concluded.[36] Coming six weeks after FC Magdeburg's triumph over AC Milan in the European Cup Winners' Cup final, a game in which Sparwasser also played, and amid encouraging performances from the GDR's junior teams, the unexpected victory over the hosts and reigning European Champions suggested a new dawn for East German football. For once, in November 1974, the DFV opened a report on the national team on a cautiously upbeat note. With a sixth place finish at the World Cup, it had reached the 'performance target', as measured in sporting and political terms, for the year.[37]

[33] SAPMO-BArch, DY 30/IV 2/2.036/25, Beschluß zur weiteren Leistungsentwicklung, fo. 139.

[34] John Moynihan, *Football Fever* (London: Quartet Books, 1974), p. 98.

[35] Wittich (ed.), *Wo waren Sie*. [36] *Ibid*., p. 126.

[37] SAPMO-BArch, DY 12/1243, Schlussfolgerungen für die weitere Arbeit im DFV der DDR im Ergebnis der Einschätzung des Abschneidens der Weltmeisterschaft 1974, 25 November 1974, fo. 96.

Figure 6. Jürgen Sparwasser and Erich Hamann celebrate the GDR's win over West Germany in Hamburg at the World Cup finals, June 1974. Defensive midfielder 'Ete' Hamann was the unheralded substitute who set up the Sparwasser goal that gave the GDR its most famous victory. This was one of only three international appearances that he made in a career played largely in football outposts such as Neubrandenburg, Eisenhüttenstadt, and Frankfurt/Oder.

On-field improvement coincided with a period of stability and openness. Honecker replaced Ulbricht as party leader in May 1971. A more youthful and optimistic era appeared to be at hand. At the eighth party congress in June, Honecker announced a lavish programme of welfare spending ('the unity of economic and social policy') that aimed at creating a prosperous socialist society. Cultural policies and attitudes were relaxed. The SED 'made its peace with jeans and long hair',[38] a concession that created space in 1973 alone for socialism's Woodstock, the World Youth Festival in East Berlin; the Levi's-loving anti-hero of Ulrich Plenzdorf's novella, *The New Sorrows of Young W.*; and the franker depiction of sexual and gender relations in Heiner Carow's popular film, *The Legend of Paul and Paula*. In the previous year, relations with West Germany had been normalised with the signing of the Basic Treaty. The GDR was released from more than twenty years of international

[38] McLellan, *Love in the Time of Communism*, p. 28.

isolation, joining the UN and taking up diplomatic relations with the Western world. In the changing domestic and international circumstances, Sparwasser's goal, argued Günter Gaus, West Germany's first diplomatic representative in East Berlin, 'temporarily created a self-confidence out of the GDR's existence'.[39] It also tallied with the regime's attempts to cultivate a separate GDR identity – a process reflected in the 1974 constitution, which replaced the designation of the GDR as a 'socialist state of the German nation' with the de-nationalised description of a 'socialist state of workers and peasants'.[40]

The new dawn never arrived. Early hopes for the Honecker regime were disabused by spiralling debts, a renewed clampdown on artists (as epitomised by the expulsion of poet and songwriter Wolf Biermann in 1976), increased *Stasi* surveillance, and a tightly policed relationship with West Germany that aimed at *Abgrenzung* ('demarcation') rather than opening up. On the field too, the increased self-confidence of the early 1970s did not last. After victory against West Germany, the GDR failed to win another game at the 1974 World Cup finals, albeit against very difficult opponents. After losses to Brazil and the Netherlands, and a draw with Argentina, it was eliminated in the second round. Despite the progress that had been made, the DFV's November report concluded, GDR football ranked among the 'international middle class', deficient in terms of technical and tactical skills, speed, heading, tackling, and world-class individuals.[41] East Germany never again qualified for a major international tournament. Chastened by the embarrassing defeat at the hands of the 'so-called "GDR"' – the headline on the front page of the *Bild* tabloid newspaper the day after the game famously screamed 'Not like that, Mr Schön'[42] – the West German team regrouped and, under the guidance of a coach (the aforementioned Helmut Schön) who had left the GDR in 1950, won the World Cup, defeating the Netherlands 2–1 in the final. It remained one of the world's football superpowers throughout the rest of the GDR's existence.

What about East Germany's hero that night in Hamburg? Jürgen Sparwasser's winning goal arguably did him more harm than good. He became a liminal figure, both the 'good comrade' who had defeated the class enemy and the epitome of 'East German robot football' (in the words of West German midfielder Günter Netzer) who had struck a blow for the wrong side.[43] Sparwasser finished his illustrious playing career in 1979.

[39] Wittich (ed.), *Wo waren Sie*, p. 37. [40] Wolle, *Die heile Welt*, pp. 63–4.

[41] SAPMO-BArch, DY 12/1243, Schlussfolgerungen für die weitere Arbeit, 25 November 1974, fo. 96–7.

[42] Wittich (ed.), *Wo waren Sie*, p. 10. [43] Gröschner, *Sieben Tränen*, pp. 89–90.

Nine years later, during a trip to West Germany for a veterans' tournament in Saarbrücken, he disappeared from sight in a department store and committed *Republikflucht*. All that he left behind in his hotel room was an FCM tracksuit and a note of apology to his team-mates: 'It is difficult . . . to separate from you, but there was no other possibility'.[44]

The repercussions of the Sparwasser goal remind us ultimately of the SED regime's inability to create a national team, or indeed a national identity, that could compete with the West or win the lasting affections of GDR citizens. This was not necessarily clear at the time. The 1–0 win in the 'comparison of systems' (*Systemvergleich*) on 22 June 1974 may have been a Pyrrhic victory. But it was a victory nonetheless, one that revealed how, in football at least, a sense of ethnic German nationalism and a GDR-specific sense of nationhood were not mutually exclusive categories.

The match against West Germany appeared to be a rare example of GDR football going to plan. East Germany entered the World Cup finals on a sixteen-game unbeaten run, the longest in its history. It had a talented core of players, starting from the back with goalkeeper Jürgen Croy and libero (sweeper) Hans-Jürgen Dörner, continuing through midfield with the likes of Wolfgang Seguin, and rounded off with forwards such as Sparwasser, Joachim Streich, and Hans-Jürgen Kreische. Under Georg Buschner, new standards were set. Buschner coached the Carl Zeiss Jena team that won three *Oberliga* titles between 1963 and 1971. The ex-defender was a loyal communist and strict disciplinarian ('for the proper footballer there are no late nights, no lunchtime drinks, and no cigarettes'). His teams were fit and well-organised, if lacking in flair on occasion.[45]

An advisory pamphlet issued to SED functionaries in January 1974 claimed that 'the FRG team is a foreign opponent just like the teams from Chile and Australia',[46] the GDR's other group-stage opponents. The disingenuousness of this argument was laid bare by the screening that accompanied the selection of 'tourist delegations' to the matches in West Germany. Genuine supporters had no chance of obtaining tickets. Those allowed to attend were overwhelmingly SED members. Potsdam county's World Cup delegation of 141 individuals, for example, contained 123 comrades, 82 of whom had been to party school and 27 of whom were party functionaries. SED dominance of the

[44] SAPMO-BArch, DY 30/IV 2/2.039/251, Gesamtbericht über die Teilnahme der Altherrmannschaft des 1. FCM am Hallenturnier des 1. FC Saarbrücken in der Zeit vom 8–10.1.1988, fo. 188–91. Sparwasser's note is on fo. 192.

[45] Horn and Weise, *Das große Lexikon*, pp. 66–8; Leske, *Enzyklopädie*, pp. 94–5.

[46] BLHA, Rep 530 Nr. 5377, Antworten auf Fragen zur Fußball-Weltmeisterschaft 1974, January 1974, fo. 1–2.

Halle county delegation was even greater.[47] Directives emphasised that GDR tourists were 'normal people', acting in an 'unforced manner', who could be funny and 'never scorn a beer'.[48] The strict vetting, detailed instructions, and military-style preparations told a different story, one that reflected the GDR's paranoid dependence on West Germany for its own identity and sense of worth.

The team opened with a 2–0 win over fellow debutants Australia, drew 1–1 with Chile in West Berlin, and then defeated West Germany to qualify for the second round as group winners – a result that earned Buschner praise ('the cool-headed tactician') even from the strenuously anti-communist *Bild*.[49] East German media coverage evinced measured pride in the coach's preparations ('Buschner's tactics fit like a tailor-made suit' was the headline in *Die Neue Fußball-Woche*) and the players' contributions to a deserved victory.[50] The hand-picked tourist delegations, unsurprisingly, represented the GDR with equal discipline and success. The Halle delegation's report, for example, claimed that they had encountered no 'special problems'. Individuals followed the chain of organisational command and condemned the arrogance and increased nationalism of the West Germans. Victory against the hosts triggered 'particular joy' and was evaluated in the 'correct, class-based' manner – but the GDR team received strong support in its other matches too.[51]

Back home, the response of GDR citizens to the national team's unexpected success was more complex and ambivalent than such formulaic conclusions suggest. It revealed an *Eigen-Sinn* that included feelings of GDR national pride, but not necessarily at the expense of broader national sympathies. Citizens, in other words, cheered for East Germany on their own terms, rejecting the either/or response that communist functionaries demanded in Cold War sport. An SED report from the district of Calau on 21 June 1974, a day before the all-German clash in Hamburg, gave a generally upbeat assessment of the popular mood. The performances of the GDR team were widely praised, as was the extended television coverage – a subject that attracted 70,000 (mostly

[47] *Ibid.*, Statistischer Angaben über die Teilnehmer, n.d., fo. 39; Landeshauptarchiv Sachsen-Anhalt, Abteilung Merseburg (LHASA, MER), SED Bezirksleitung-Halle, IV/C-2/16/557, Statistische Angaben über die Teilnehmer, n.d.

[48] BLHA, Rep. 730 Nr. 4736, Für die Schulung zu den 10. Fußballweltmeisterschaften vom 13. Jun bis 7. Juli in der BRD, n.d., fo. 114–55.

[49] Horn and Weise, *Das große Lexikon*, p. 64.

[50] 'Buschners Taktik paßte wie ein Maßanzug', *Die Neue Fußball-Woche*, 25 June 1974, 4–5.

[51] LHASA, MER, SED Bezirksleitung-Halle, IV/C-2/16/557, Abschlußeinschätzung der Reiseleitung des Bezirkes Halle zur 10. Fußballweltmeisterschaft in der BRD und Westberlin, 8 July 1974, fo. 191–4.

complimentary) readers' letters to *Die Neue Fußball-Woche* during and immediately after the tournament.[52] Work discipline remained good 'despite the great levels of football enthusiasm'. But there were cracks in the façade. Young workers at a factory in Vetschau asked about the selection process for the tourist delegations and why only 'such a small circle of participants' was permitted to travel to West Germany. At a factory in Lübbenau, there were still workers who supported the West German team.[53]

Post-match reaction brought opinions into sharper focus. A minority, like exiled Hertha Berlin fan Helmut Klopfleisch, expressed angry disbelief: 'It was a day of mourning in our house'.[54] A more common response, though, was quiet delight in seeing the East German underdogs defeat their heavily favoured neighbours. As one BFC fan recalled, it was always nice to give West Germany 'a bloody nose' in sport.[55] Sandra Dassler, a thirteen-year-old Bayern Munich fan in 1974, remembered holidays in Hungary 'and those boastful West Germans with their Mercedes and our Trabant standing next to them' – and joined in the celebrations when the 1–0 win was announced during the handball tournament that she was attending in Thuringia.[56] Rudi Hellmann's wife reported 'an atmosphere otherwise only found on New Year's Eve' in Berlin's Mitte district after the game – a joyous mood also remembered, albeit more grudgingly, by Helmut Klopfleisch after the GDR's 'lucky win'.[57] The grassroots impact was significant. The coach in Brussig's *Leben bis Männer*, based in *Bezirk* Magdeburg, proudly noted an upsurge of interest in football after June 1974: 'We were overrun then by kids who wanted to be Sparwasser'.[58]

For the exiled writer Gerhard Zwerenz, living in Cologne in 1974, and the reform-minded André Brie, the GDR's win was a bittersweet moment, but still to be welcomed as a victory for the 'right' team (and, despite its many faults, the 'right' country). Ten-year-old Veit Spiegel, later a fan of Hansa Rostock, spent the game playing in the garden, but was happy when he heard his father and his friends 'screaming' to celebrate Sparwasser's strike. The fact that the match was against West Germany, he recalled, 'didn't matter to me, for me West Germany was a country like any other' – an unwitting internalisation of the party line that

52 'Genug vom Fußball', *Die Neue Fußball-Woche*, 23 July 1974, 4.

53 BLHA, Rep. 931 Calau Nr. 379, Information über Stimmung und Meinungen zur Fußballweltmeisterschaft, 21 June 1974.

54 Kuper, *Football against the Enemy*, pp. 20–1.

55 Interview with Olaf S., 29 May 2011.

56 Hesselmann and Ide, 'A tale of two Germanys', p. 44.

57 Blees, *90 Minuten Klassenkampf*, p. 66; Kuper, *Football against the Enemy*, p. 21.

58 Brussig, *Leben bis Männer*, pp. 35–7.

this was 'a game like any other'. Thirteen-year-old Marion Spröte's attention span was greater. She watched the match with friends at a holiday camp in Usedom ('I don't believe there was anyone who wasn't interested') and joined in the celebrations of the GDR's victory, even though her favourite player was the West German captain, Franz Beckenbauer.[59]

This kind of dual loyalty was typical, undercutting exclusive notions of GDR nationhood even in the moment of socialist victory. For young East Germans growing up in the 1970s and 1980s, the GDR was very much their country, whatever its faults. Yet West Germany remained a salient presence. Like Marion Spröte in the summer of 1974, nine-year-old Frank L. cheered Sparwasser's winning goal ('I can't deny it'), but was just as happy when the West Germans beat the Netherlands a few weeks later to become world champions.[60] Many East Germans seem to have quite happily supported two national teams, rejecting both the *Abgrenzung* of the Honecker regime and the older West German claim to *Alleinvertretung*.[61] The 1974 match undoubtedly showed what Thomas Brussig termed a 'disposition for identification' with the GDR: 'that is my country and I am for it'.[62] But it was a GDR identity that was to be found alongside, rather than instead of, German national identity. Television was important here. By the 1970s, football lovers could get regular fixes of *Oberliga* and *Bundesliga* games in the comfort of their living rooms, feeding the dual allegiances on display in 1974. Responses to the sole encounter between East and West Germany reinforce Eduardo Archetti's argument that identity in football 'is highly dependent upon multiplicity'.[63] They reveal a GDR football culture that stubbornly existed between East and West. They showcase too the limited ability of the East German state to mould identity, in football or elsewhere, solely around GDR-specific values and entities.

There seems to have been a surprising degree of happy unanimity among GDR citizens in their recollections of the Sparwasser goal. Yet, as André Brie recalls, this joy 'didn't go very far'.[64] GDR football's golden moment passed quickly, despite the Olympic victory in Montreal in 1976. After failing to qualify for the 1978 World Cup finals

[59] Wittich (ed.), *Wo waren Sie*, pp. 51–2, 90–1, 102, 115–16.
[60] Interview with Frank L., 25 May 2011.
[61] See e.g. interview with Sven S., 24 May 2011; interview with Rainer, 29 May 2011.
[62] Hesselman and Ide, 'A tale of two Germanys', p. 44.
[63] Eduardo Archetti, 'The spectacle of identities: football in Latin America', in Stephen Hart and Richard Young (eds.), *Contemporary Latin American Studies* (London: Arnold, 2003), p. 121.
[64] Wittich (ed.), *Wo waren Sie*, p. 90.

in Argentina, the national team closed the 1970s with a vital match against the Netherlands in Leipzig. Victory would have ensured qualification for the 1980 European Championship. But it lost 3–2 after squandering a 2–0 lead, perhaps the most painful of the GDR's many qualification near misses.[65]

In fascist Italy during the 1930s, when the *Azzurri* won the World Cup twice in succession, and even for a time in Franco's Spain (when the national team won the 1964 European Championship), success on the football pitch conferred a degree of legitimacy on dictatorships that were otherwise not universally popular.[66] The same may have applied in Poland after the country's third-place finish at the 1974 World Cup finals, a performance that excited national pride rather than pride in socialism.[67] No such luxury was afforded the GDR, even in its finest hour. 'We were an unpopular team', Georg Buschner ruefully concluded.[68] This was an overly harsh assessment. But it is suggestive of how the *Auswahl* ('selection'), however unwittingly, embodied the ambiguities and incompleteness at the heart of GDR identity.

## Decline in the individualist age? The national team in the 1980s

Domestically and on the international stage, the final decade of East German football mirrored the political climate. The false optimism of the 1970s gave way to pessimism, anger, and a palpable sense of decline. BFC dominated the *Oberliga* by fair means and foul, while East German clubs, with odd exceptions, struggled in European competition. The national team meanwhile stumbled from one qualifying campaign to another. Georg Buschner was sacked as head coach in 1981, after defeat at home to a strong Poland side had ensured that the GDR could not reach the 1982 World Cup finals. Deteriorating relations with the squad and the DTSB leadership, both of which (albeit for different reasons) resented his authoritarian idiosyncrasies, sealed his fate. He apparently learned of his dismissal on West German television.[69]

[65] Karte and Röhrig, *Kabinengeflüster*, pp. 123–4.

[66] On the mobilisation of public support for the Italian team during the 1934 World Cup finals (hosted by Italy), see Martin, *Football and Fascism*, pp. 183–94. Spain's 1964 European Championship win is discussed in Phil Ball, *Morbo: The Story of Spanish Football* (London: WSC Books, 2001), ch. 10.

[67] Anderson, 'Soccer and the failure of East German sports policy', pp. 657–8.

[68] Koch, '"Weltmeister"', p. 139.

[69] Horn and Weise, *Das große Lexikon*, p. 68; Leske, *Enzyklopädie*, p. 95.

Buschner was never adequately replaced. Rudolf Krause, a pedagogue whose methods worked better in youth football than with the senior team, stacked the squad with defenders ('five liberos', as one fan recalled)[70] and drove supporters away. His successor in 1983, the ex-Jena head coach Bernd Stange, survived for five years, but was unable to turn around the team's fortunes. 'I can try for the French playing style', he reportedly said in 1985, 'but if the players aren't there, it remains a dream'.[71]

When Stange was replaced in the autumn of 1988, it was with a disastrously conceived triumvirate of ex-FCM player and chairman Manfred Zapf (who had never before coached a team), FCK coach Heinz Werner, and long-time DFV youth trainer Frank Engel. Werner's recollections illustrate the constrained autonomy that shaped the careers of top-level coaches and shed light too on the crisis of leadership that had engulfed the GDR by the late 1980s. He did not want to coach the national team, especially not as part of an 'unworkable' trio, but the newly appointed DFV general secretary, Wolfgang Spitzner, closed off all other avenues and even suggested that Werner's only remaining option would be to emigrate to West Germany. In order to safeguard his sons' careers, and possibly to fulfil a long-held ambition of coaching at the World Cup finals, Werner took the job.[72]

His ambition, though, was never realised. After taking one point from three qualification matches for the 1990 World Cup finals in Italy, a run that included an embarrassing 2–0 home defeat to Turkey, both the dressing room and public opinion were lost. Crisis talks organised in May and June 1989 by Rudi Hellmann offered fascinating insights into the chaos and dissension that had gripped GDR football. They also reflected the increasingly individualistic preoccupations of citizens in the late Honecker era, as private motivations effaced collective ones. Players, Heinz Werner later noted, were no longer prepared 'to give everything for the cause', focusing instead – in the words of BFC striker Thomas Doll – on getting 'the right [amount of] money' for their endeavours.[73] The national team's breakdown spoke to the wider breakdown of the SED regime's social contract with its citizens.

At the talks, the players pulled no punches. Wearing the national team's colours, they reported, was no fun at all: 'Other players at our

[70] Interview with Frank L.

[71] SAPMO-BArch, DY 30/IV 2/2.039/251, Einige Gesichtspunkte zur Einschätzung des Wettkampfjahres 1984/85 durch den Deutschen Fußballverband der DDR, n.d., fo. 109–12.

[72] Interview with Heinz Werner. [73] *Ibid.*

clubs laugh at us if we're called up to the national team'. Players from Dresden, Karl-Marx-Stadt, and Leipzig asserted that there were better training plans at their clubs: 'In the national team, we don't know how we should play'. The most telling indicator of the bankruptcy of GDR football, and of the unravelling of the communist dictatorship in a summer when East German citizens escaped in droves to the West via the unguarded border in Hungary, was the players' final plea, unthinkable even six months earlier: 'Let us play abroad, then we can learn and that would benefit the national team too'.[74]

The national team's days, though, were numbered. It played only twelve more fixtures under the guidance of Eduard Geyer, before its 293rd and final game, a 2–0 win against Belgium in Brussels on 12 September 1990. Just over three weeks later, Germany was reunited and the GDR ceased to exist. The DFV was dissolved on 20 November and incorporated into the DFB. The *Auswahl*'s undistinguished history was over.

## Unqualified failure? Conclusions on the *Auswahl*

In Roberto Bolaño's novel *The Third Reich*, set in a Spanish resort town during the 1980s, the protagonist Udo and some friends end up one evening in a bar where a football match between Germany and Spain is being shown on television. Excitement gives way to disappointment, as the vacationing Germans realise that it is the East German team, rather than the West German one, that will be playing. 'Naturally', Udo writes, 'we paid no attention to the match'. Later that evening at a club, when the group find out that the East Germans lost the match 2–0, Udo recalls the moment as 'something strange … a turning point, as if from that moment on all the clamour of the club might turn into something else entirely, a horror show'.[75]

As Simon Kuper and Stefan Szymanski have argued, given its wealth and size, the GDR in fact over-achieved (albeit marginally) in football.[76] The national team recorded victories over French, Dutch, and West German teams at the peak of their powers – and also drew with Argentina, England, and Brazil.[77] Four Olympic medals counted for less in football than in other sports, but required winning performances against strong teams from the socialist bloc. The GDR excelled in youth

[74] SAPMO-BArch, DY 30/4969, memo from Hellmann to Krenz, 7 June 1989, fo. 148–52.
[75] Roberto Bolaño, *The Third Reich*, trans. Natasha Wimmer (New York: Farrar, Strauss and Giroux, 2011), pp. 35–7.
[76] Kuper and Szymanski, *Soccernomics*, pp. 284–6.
[77] Hesse-Lichtenberger, *Tor!*, p. 222.

football, winning UEFA's under-18 tournament in 1965, 1970, and 1986, and finishing third in the 1987 World Youth Cup. The DFV created a system that consistently produced talented young players. Those who came through that system in its twilight years, including Matthias Sammer and Michael Ballack, played a major role in the successes of the post-unification national team.[78] As Heinz Werner later noted, 'we never knew how strong we were'.[79] The line between success and failure in elite sport can be thin: the *Auswahl*, as the qualification near misses suggested, was an unlucky team more often than it was a bad one.

Yet the uneasy sense of mediocrity that hung over GDR football, obliquely referenced in Bolaño's novel, is hard to ignore. Given East Germany's stunning success in other sports, the substantial resources invested in football, and the performances of other, similar-sized nations during the period (Hungary in the 1950s and Czechoslovakia and the Netherlands two decades later), it is easy to understand the widespread perception of the *Auswahl* as a failure. It is simpler to narrate the story of under-achievement than to pinpoint why it happened. A variety of factors – local and universal, sporting and political – must be considered. Football was, and remains, the most world's most competitive and widely professionalised sport. It was much harder for the GDR, a small country with finite resources, to win the World Cup (or even to qualify for the finals) than it was to win global events in rowing, speed-skating, or weightlifting – hence the Politburo's decision in 1969 to focus on precisely those kinds of sports at football's expense. A similar dynamic explained the football struggles of the much larger Soviet Union, where officials were wary of international competition in the professionalised arena of football and focused primarily on winning Olympic medals, thereby (as was the case in the GDR) spreading talent more thinly across a wider range of sports.[80] The fact that the Soviet Union's Cold War adversary, the United States, was not a football-playing nation made this point of sporting emphasis all the more obvious.[81]

In other ways too, football did not fit easily into the communist system. *Stasi* files reveal that leading clubs such as BFC and Dynamo Dresden gave anabolic steroids to their players during the 1980s. But the intensity and impact of doping in football, an unpredictable, skill-based sport, was less dramatic than in sports where simpler, more controllable factors (speed or endurance, for example) were paramount.

[78] *Ibid.*, 223; Dennis, 'Behind the wall', p. 59.
[79] Interview with Heinz Werner. [80] Edelman, *Serious Fun*, pp. 129–30.
[81] Kowalski and Porter, 'Cold War football', p. 79.

Pharmaceutical resources were applied in a more concerted fashion elsewhere.[82] The Bayern Munich player Paul Breitner speculated on the drug-induced behaviour of GDR footballers, while newspapers such as the *Bild* reported on the 'white pills' given to players in the East before international matches.[83] But West Germany's state-sponsored doping programme appears to have promoted football more successfully than the GDR's did. Though the main focus, as in the GDR, was on the athletes (and drugs) that would boost the country's Olympic medal haul, West German footballers – according to a 2013 Humboldt University study – were given amphetamines such as Pervitin at three World Cup finals.[84]

A stereotype has persisted that East European teams of the communist era possessed talented but mentally brittle players, who were cowed by a philosophy that encouraged unthinking collectivism – in Günter Netzer's words, 'robot football' – over spontaneous individualism.[85] There is no hard and fast rule to confirm that political systems, or the prevailing political conditions, predetermine football results. The Hungarian golden squad of the 1950s, forged at the height of Stalinist dictatorship, married a collective philosophy to individual talent to create one of the greatest teams in football history. Czechoslovakia won the 1976 European Championship (defeating West Germany in the final) during the grim period of normalisation that followed the crushing of the Prague Spring. Amid popular unrest and state repression back home, Poland finished third in the 1974 and 1982 World Cup finals.

The East German national team came closer to the communist stereotype, regularly choking on the big occasion. As DFV reports consistently lamented, it lacked individuals who could take a game by the scruff of its neck. This was partly a consequence of the party's ideologically rooted distrust of star players such as Peter Ducke and 'Hansi' Kreische. Matthias Sammer, who led Germany to the European Championship and won the prestigious European Footballer of the Year award in 1996, tells an instructive story, from his days as an outstanding young player at Dynamo Dresden: 'One day, the squad players were given new boots. Mine were the only ones that didn't fit. They were three sizes too large. It was pure harassment, as individualism wasn't tolerated'.[86] The 'deadly' lack of initiative repeatedly shown by players

82 See e.g. Dennis and Grix, *Sport under Communism*, pp. 116–17, 154–5.
83 Spitzer, *Fußball und Triathlon*, pp. 60–2.
84 'Studie enthüllt systematisches Doping in der BRD'.
85 Gröschner, *Sieben Tränen*, p. 89; Hesse-Lichtenberger, *Tor!*, p. 223.
86 Hesse-Lichtenberger, *Tor!*, p. 223.

on the international stage was also psychological, a 'mental frailty' born of GDR football's inferiority complex.[87]

Distrust of the individual and faith in a tightly controlled collective were socialist values that fell on stony ground in football. The SED tried to rectify the situation by imposing greater control, most notably through a network of secret-police surveillance of players, coaches, and officials that will be discussed in Chapter 6. It is hard to know the extent to which *Stasi* involvement in football impacted the national team's performance. The fact that Buschner and Stange, among many others, worked for long periods as informers did not come to light until after the *Wende*.[88] But such activities certainly contributed to an atmosphere, however vague and unspoken, of suspicion and fear that undermined attempts to build a world-class football team.

At the same time, a different kind of political interference also had a deleterious effect. Local patriotism was an anarchic force in GDR football, fuelling a running battle between the central authorities – themselves often not on the same page about football matters – and factory or other sponsors about where priorities lay. In contrast to Hungary in the 1950s, where the army team of Honvéd formed the core of a highly successful national team, the club–country symbiosis in the GDR foundered repeatedly on the disconnections between centre and periphery. Even when one dominant club, BFC during the 1980s, seemed like an obvious candidate to replicate the Honvéd role, its methods were so controversial and the team so unpopular that it proved impossible. BFC's players were booed, not fêted, at international games around the GDR, as the national team, like the national economy, went from bad to worse.

Politics played a multifarious role in GDR football. The importance of individual components may be hard to weigh, but the cumulative effect of outside pressures on the national team was not a positive one. Here the autonomous space that football carved out for itself was at its most constrained. Internationals earned good money and travelled the world – you are unlikely to see pictures of many other GDR citizens relaxing in their swimming trunks on Rio's Copacabana beach.[89] But, as leading representatives of 'the world's most authoritarian and monitored sports system',[90] they were subject to scrutiny that ordinary *Oberliga* players largely evaded. The fact that football failed to illustrate the superiority of socialist sport only added to the pressures upon those selected to play for

[87] Interview with Theo Körner, 26 May 2011; interview with Sven S.
[88] Leske, *Enzyklopädie*, pp. 95–6, 463–6.
[89] See Horn and Weise, *Das große Lexikon*, p. 60.
[90] Schiller and Young, 'The history and historiography of sport in Germany', 326–7.

their country. Political interference made international success less attainable and players less likely to perform to their capabilities at key moments, thereby reinforcing the game's outsider status. The record of the East German national team, modest rather than poor, reminds us of the sporting spaces that were beyond the reach of the GDR's medal-winning machine. A symbol of the complex, multi-layered nature of identity in East Germany, the *Auswahl* revealed more about the limits, than the extent, of communist power.

# 5 Club football at home and away

## Thinking local, acting local

In the autumn of 1955, county league team BSG Motor West Karl-Marx-Stadt faced a goalkeeping crisis. The first-team regular had left the club in the middle of the season. Motor West's trainer turned to local rivals BSG Motor Germania Karl-Marx-Stadt for a replacement. On 18 October he and another Motor West representative met the Germania goalkeeper at a local café. Motor West offered to match the goalkeeper's earnings at the Germania machine factory without any night shifts or having to work too hard ('you can practically do nothing, you just have to turn up') and to pay match-day expenses of up to 50 M. At away games, the Motor West coach promised, 'you'll get so much to eat that you'll have to send it back'. After plying him with alcohol, the coach took his prospective signing to a dance bar and paid for his taxi home. The inducements, though, failed to work. The goalkeeper decided to stay where he was. Furious Germania officials reported the incident to the football authorities and demanded punishment according to the rules that forbade player transfers. Should our sportsmen, they asked, be role models for other workers, or just 'men turning up for money'?[1]

The quarrel provides a small and revealing window into the world of club football. Here were two teams from the same sports club (Motor, representative of the machine and motor-vehicle construction industries), playing in the third tier of GDR football, at bitter odds over one goalkeeper. Such internecine rivalries were the curse of functionaries seeking to build a rational league structure that would benefit the national team. Whereas the central authorities sometimes encouraged local patriotism in industry – as a means of recruiting workers to major factories in otherwise undesirable small towns such as Schwedt and

1 SAPMO-BArch, DY 12/308, letter from BSG Motor Germania to the Sektion Fußball, 1 November 1955, fo. 4–5.

Frankfurt/Oder[2] – there was no centrifugal policy in sport. Football pulled away from the centre regardless. The phenomenon was not confined to the *Oberliga*. Competition for resources could be fierce within the same city and the same organisation, as coaches and officials at all levels sought the extra player who could help them to win promotion or avoid relegation. There was no other sport, or indeed cultural activity, in which the communists faced the same depth and complexity of local interests.

The entrenched and multi-layered nature of football localism was very much reflective of global practices. From the *campanilismo* (provincialism) that compromised fascist attempts to nationalise Italian football in the 1930s to the regional resistance to Kwame Nkrumah's authoritarian reorganisation of Ghanaian football in the 1960s,[3] football's role as a lightning rod for channelling and expressing local identities has been a constant feature of its growth and appeal. In East Germany, football was an important means of 'imagining the local sphere', reappropriating socialist transformation for smaller stages and thereby undercutting the premise of a monolithic GDR national culture.[4] Local patriotism was not confined to football, infiltrating everything from travel guidebooks and festivals to workplace productivity. But it found some of its most vivid expression there.

GDR football was a war of attrition, pitting the dictatorial (but often frustrated) aims of the centre against the wilfulness of the periphery, in the form of clubs, players, and officials who obstinately refused to sacrifice local interests to the greater good of socialism. The conflict should not be posited schematically. The aims of the centre were often inconsistent and subject to rival interpretations. The DFV's interests, for example, were not always compatible with those of the DTSB. The SED leadership frequently criticised both organisations. Clubs benefited from state largesse even as they ignored state directives – and were capable of invoking suitably outraged socialist rhetoric when they suffered the consequences of a rival team breaking rules that everyone else broke. East German football was a site of co-option and collusion, as well as resistance and autonomy. Inter- and intra-city (or regional) enmity was often the key issue, rather than conscious defiance of the authorities in Berlin. Nonetheless, a constant thread running through this history is the back-and-forth between political interventions and localised *Resistenz* to such interventions.

[2] Jeanette Madarász, 'Economic politics and company culture: the problem of routinisation', in Fulbrook (ed.), *Power and Society*, pp. 61–2.

[3] Martin, *Football and Fascism*, pp. 165–71; Peter Alegi, *African Soccerscapes: How a Continent Changed the World's Game* (Athens, OH: Ohio University Press, 2010), pp. 58–9.

[4] Palmowski, *Inventing a Socialist Nation*, pp. 96–105.

This chapter examines East German club football in light of the tensions that existed among local, national, and international interests and experiences. Attention is first centred on the domestic game. The thorny issue of player delegations (i.e. transfers) and the case study of BSG Chemie Leipzig are used to showcase the pervasiveness and self-replicating nature of football *Eigen-Sinn*; the restricted ability, and at times willingness, of the SED regime to cauterise regional ambitions and rivalries; and the liminal space in which most clubs operated, as representatives of the socialist state and the local community. The chapter's final section shifts to the international arena, examining the experiences of GDR teams in European club competition. Drawing on the records of Dynamo Dresden and BFC, the argument here reinforces the dichotomy at the heart of the East German game between comforting insularity and risky internationalism. In the process, it highlights the external as well as the internal limits on the SED's socialist remaking of football.

## Delegating power: transfers and local politics

As part of the reforms of 1954, which parachuted eight state-favoured sports clubs into the *Oberliga*, the 1952 league champions BSG Turbine Halle, which was then under a cloud of suspicion since many of the team's players had left the GDR after the June 1953 Uprising, were subsumed into the newly formed SC Chemie Halle. It quickly became apparent that the ex-Turbine players had no interest in their new team. At private gatherings for birthday parties and bowling evenings, they recalled happy days at the BSG and promised to guard the 'old Turbine traditions'. Many of them rejoined Turbine Halle at the first opportunity, leaving SC Chemie in the midst of a relegation struggle. Those who refused to return to their roots were labelled 'traitors'. A civil war of sorts broke out between the two organisations, one that pitted the working-class appeal of the BSG against the elitist concerns of the SC. Turbine coaches tried to win back players from Chemie's youth team ('you'll soon be playing again under the Turbine flag'), an SC coach was barred from Turbine's sports ground, and an afternoon friendly between Turbine and *Oberliga* side Motor Zwickau, attended by 5,000 people, was organised to clash with Chemie's league match against Rotation Babelsberg. Those watching were heard to remark on the 'old Turbine spirit' and to deride the rootless and relegation-bound SC.[5]

[5] SAPMO-BArch, DY 34/3800, Bericht über die Situation im Halleschen Fußballsport nach der Aufstellung der jungen SC Chemie-Mannschaft in der Stadt Halle, August 1955.

The fierce desire to keep or reclaim players was tied to populist resentment of state-sponsored attempts to create a football elite via the SCs (and later, in 1965/6, via the FCs). When comrades at BSG Motor Zwickau rejected the proposal to become a sports club in 1960, they did so by citing the Zwickau team's view of the current league champions, ASK (Army Sports Club) Vorwärts Berlin: 'ASK Vorwärts are a solid "professional team" that provides high achievement. We, though, are a real workers' team and want to stay that way'.[6] The pejorative use of the word 'professional' is instructive. Among the players at Motor Zwickau and Turbine Halle, where a similar appeal to working-class values was made, we see emerging the invention of socialist tradition, an attempt to put down politically acceptable, yet distinctive, roots in a football culture, and indeed society, that was characterised during the 1950s by upheaval. Turbine Halle, after all, had been founded only in 1950, so the 'old Turbine traditions' idealised by players did not stretch back far. Motor Zwickau had started life, as Horch Zwickau, the year before. In accounts of the controversial championship decider during the first *Oberliga* season in 1949/50, the Horch team is commonly portrayed as the new, unloved challenger to the true 'tradition club', SG Dresden Friedrichstadt.[7]

It is fascinating to see how players and officials at such BSGs appropriated working-class 'traditions' that were less than a decade old, couching their protests against the new SCs in unimpeachably socialist language. This suggests an *Eigen-Sinn* that was capable of taking the funding and rhetoric that it needed from the regime, while at the same time drawing on older, local loyalties to carve out, or safeguard, community interests – a duality on display too in festivals such as the *Sommergewinn* ('onset of summer') in Eisenach, where residents used generous state resources to put on a deeply local production.[8] Football traditions, even when dressed in socialist clothing, could express multiple identities. Above all, though, these identities were embedded in the local, confirming the game's flexible role as an expression of *Heimat.*

The political complexities that could surround transfers were evident in the contest to secure the services of the highly rated Sachsenring Zwickau player Hans-Uwe Pilz. In the autumn of 1981, Pilz requested a transfer to Dynamo Dresden in order to improve his prospects of getting into the national team. The DFV supported his request. However, officials at Sachsenring Zwickau – a club with a long history

6 SAPMO-BArch, DY 30/IV 2/18/19, Bericht über die Aussprache über die Perspektiven der BSG Motor Zwickau am 17.11.1960 in Zwickau, 24 November 1960, fo. 82–3.

7 The Friedrichstadt–Horch game is discussed in Chapter 7.

8 Palmowski, *Inventing a Socialist Nation*, pp. 138–41.

of resisting central directives[9] – refused to sanction Pilz's departure until the end of the season, hoping to buy time to talk him out of the move.[10] When the player made a second request to leave in early 1982, a third party got involved. Having again approved Pilz's move to Dresden on 12 January, the DFV learned the following day that the county DTSB leadership in Karl-Marx-Stadt had authorised a delegation to FC Karl-Marx-Stadt instead. Unbeknown to the SED county leadership, FCK officials dispatched a petition to Honecker a week later, in which complaints were made about the DFV's neglect of football there and willingness to support the delegation of talents such as Pilz away from the region. After wrangling that lasted into February, and involved both Hellmann and Ewald, the DFV's original decision was upheld.[11] Pilz enjoyed a successful career in Dresden, winning the league title twice and the cup on four occasions, and earned thirty-five caps for his country.

The Pilz case was instructive on a number of levels. The player's experience exemplified the liminal space between dependence and autonomy in which leading footballers worked. Pilz's wishes were granted, but not without a struggle. During the initial delegation to Dresden in September 1981, Pilz lived in a dormitory at the edge of town while his wife remained in Zwickau, where she was abused on the streets and subjected to late-night rings on the doorbell. The carrot and the stick were then used to persuade him to remain in Zwickau. Factory functionaries and the mayor offered support, in the form of a new car, while threatening their coveted star with disciplinary measures if he decided to go.[12]

Equally striking was the lack of coordination among the institutions and individuals involved in the transfer. The right hand appeared to have no idea what the left was doing. The DFV's decision to send Pilz to Dresden was resisted by officials in Zwickau and then gazumped by the DTSB leadership in Karl-Marx-Stadt, which decided (seemingly against the wishes of the SED leadership there) to have the player delegated to its own flagship club, FCK. Order was restored only after Ewald and Hellmann intervened. In recounting the rather confusing story to

[9] See Chapters 2 and 7.

[10] SAPMO-BArch, DY 30/4946, Information über die Vorbereitung und Durchführung der Delegierung des Sportsfreundes Hans-Uwe Pilz von der BSG Sachsenring Zwickau zur SG Dynamo Dresden, 26 January 1982, fo. 53–4; Abschrift des Berichtes des Sportfreundes Hans-Uwe Pilz zu seinem Wechsel von der BSG Sachsenring Zwickau zu Dynamo Dresden, 8 January 1982, fo. 55–7.

[11] *Ibid.*, petition from the FCK leadership to Honecker, 21 January 1982, fo. 40–2; letter from Hellmann to Honecker, 1 February 1982, fo. 50–1; Stellungnahme zum Brief aus Karl-Marx-Stadt, 1 February 1982, fo. 58–60.

[12] *Ibid.*, Abschrift des Berichtes, 8 January 1982, fo. 55–7.

Honecker, Hellmann criticised both 'narrow-minded' BSG interests that stood in the way of transfers to elite clubs and the failings of FCK, languishing in tenth place in the *Oberliga* and an unattractive destination for ambitious players.[13]

Pilz's protracted transfer went to the heart of the local patriotism that made football so appealing to fans, in East Germany and elsewhere, and so exasperating to officials. Sachsenring Zwickau and FCK were eager to ward off the outside claims of Dynamo Dresden, but, situated barely twenty miles apart in *Bezirk* Karl-Marx-Stadt, were equally concerned with outdoing each other. The county's deputy SED leader, Lothar Weber, informed Hellmann of the 'decades-long' strained relationship between the two clubs. It went so far that some young players from Zwickau, with the support of their parents, apparently preferred to give up any hope of an international career rather than attend the sports school sponsored by FCK in Karl-Marx-Stadt.[14]

Finally, Pilz's move to Dresden highlighted the inadequacy and hypocrisy of the GDR's system for moving players. Abhorring the word 'transfer' and mindful of the ideological need to differentiate East German football from the mercenary practices of its West German neighbour, both Ewald and Hellmann emphasised the rarity of delegations. In reality, the outlawing of transfers except in centrally decreed exceptional circumstances only fed multiple resentments at the arbitrary use of power by the DFV and certain leading clubs, while inevitably encouraging practices not dissimilar to those in the West. 'Wheeling and dealing', as Matthias Koch concluded, 'was ubiquitous'.[15]

The result was a fragmented and murky system, shaped by a see-saw struggle between fiercely defended local interests and sporadic central interventions. On the one hand, the DFV or a powerful football patron ensured on occasion that top players moved according to their wishes. BFC pushed through the transfer of HFC striker Frank Pastor to East Berlin in 1984, despite the angry response in Halle. He was taken away, anonymous petitioners complained to Hellmann two years later, and now the team plays in front of empty terraces and young people watch only West German football.[16] On the other hand, though, such cases

13 SAPMO-BArch, DY 30/4946, letter from Hellmann to Honecker, 1 February 1982, fo. 50–1.

14 SAPMO-BArch, DY 30/4959, letter from Hellmann to Honecker, 19 February 1982, fo. 55–6.

15 Matthias Koch, 'Rasen-Rivalen – und alle gegen den BFC', in Willmann (ed.), *Fußball-Land DDR*, p. 59.

16 Leske, *Enzyklopädie*, p. 16; SAPMO-BArch, DY 30/4980, anonymous petition to Hellmann, 26 May 1986, fo. 4.

were rare. Clubs at all levels used whatever means necessary to procure or safeguard their players. These included, as we have seen, a variety of unauthorised practices, such as offering large signing-on fees, bigger apartments and new cars, and monthly wages in excess of factory pay scales.

The authorities were unable, and often, it seems, unwilling, to take a firm stand against this widespread abuse of socialist principles. The outraged rhetoric sounded less convincing as the years went by, reflecting perhaps the increasingly 'live and let live' approach of the Honecker government to cultural and social activities that, like football and music, gave people pleasure and administrators headaches. The international ground shifted too. By the time of the Pilz furore in 1982, the GDR – prefiguring its role as lead critic of Gorbachev's reform programmes after 1985 – was almost a lone voice of opposition within the socialist bloc to the evils of commercialism and professionalism in sport. The Soviet Union, Bulgaria, Czechoslovakia, Hungary, and Poland had all recently allowed older sports stars, including footballers, to move to the West.[17] The pretence of amateurism, and the accompanying long-standing opposition to transfers, was crumbling, even as Hellmann claimed defiantly in 1987 that 'another, professional path will not be taken in GDR football'.[18] In the same year, the DFV general secretary, Karl Zimmermann, proposed the introduction of a three-week transfer window at the end of each season.[19] In May 1989, the DFV introduced a transfer system.[20] Just as the Honecker regime decided in the early 1970s effectively to give up the ideological struggle against citizens who wanted to watch West German television or purchase Levi's jeans (and allowed the sale of colour TVs and Levi's), so it now tacitly admitted that the struggle against professionalism in sports could not be won. 'There is in fact professional sport (*Berufssport*) here too', Erich Honecker told a Politburo meeting in February 1989. 'We don't need to get agitated

[17] SAPMO-BArch, DY 30/4946, Niederschrift über ein Gespräch beim Botschafter der UdSSR in der DDR, Genossen Pjotr Abrassimow, am 27. April 1981, 28 April 1981, fo. 6–7; Information zu Problemen der Kommerzialisierung und Professionalisierung des internationalen Sports und deren Auswirkungen auf sozialistische Länder, 10 September 1981, fo. 20–6.

[18] SAPMO-BArch, DY 30/4966, Information über eine Beratung der Abteilung Sport und des Generalsekretariats des Deutschen Fußball-Verbandes der DDR mit den Vorsitzenden der Fußballclubs, Sektionleitern der Oberliga-Mannschaften und Trainern der Oberliga-Mannschaften sowie den [illegible] für Sportfragen der Bezirksleitungen der SED am 5. [Juni] 1987, fo. 136.

[19] Leske, *Erich Mielke*, pp. 223–4.

[20] SAPMO-BArch, DY 30/IV 2/2.039/251, Begründung für die Neuregelung der Klub- und Gemeinschaftszugehörigkeit, 1989, fo. 211–12.

about it. Footballers are being sold. *Oberliga* players are therefore professional sportsmen'.[21] The May directive gave a more realistic picture of GDR football. It was quickly rendered obsolete, though, by the 'gentle revolution' that brought down the SED dictatorship and gave footballers, like the rest of the population, a freedom of movement that was exercised in a westward direction.

## A case study in *Resistenz*: Chemie Leipzig

The GDR was a small country, a place where a self-proclaimed socialist internationalism existed uncomfortably alongside a self-imposed insularity. Turned in on themselves after the building of the Berlin Wall in 1961, and subject to the smothering attentions of a police state, East Germans sought refuge in small, local comforts: family and friends, the allotment (archetypal site of Günter Gaus's 'niche society'), and football. In places such as Cottbus, Frankfurt/Oder, Leipzig, Magdeburg, and Rostock, party bosses – like their counterparts in fascist Italy during the 1930s – saw competitive teams as a means of winning political legitimacy and supported them accordingly. Popular clubs, moreover, sometimes survived and prospered even without powerful patrons – as the fascinating history of Chemie Leipzig reveals.

On 10 May 1964, in the description of reporter Werner Eberhardt, 'the motorways between Jena and Erfurt were a single caravan of green and white along the entire 150-kilometre stretch'. The motorcade, bedecked in flags and slogans, contained thousands of supporters of BSG Chemie Leipzig, en route to Erfurt for a match against relegation-threatened Turbine that would determine the destination of the league title. Backed by this raucous support (the Erfurt players, one Chemie player later recalled, 'were scared shitless'), two early goals ensured victory for the visitors from the working-class Leutzsch district of the GDR's *Messestadt* ('trade fair city'). With it, Chemie won the *Oberliga* ahead of Empor Rostock and SC Leipzig. At the final whistle, there was a pitch invasion, in which players were divested of boots and shirts and carried around on the shoulders of joyous fans.[22] 'I'm not sure', concludes Ulrich Hesse-Lichtenberger, 'if there's ever been a more sensational and unexpected outcome to a season anywhere in Europe in the past century. (If so, I'd like to hear about it)'.[23]

Founded in 1950, BSG Chemie Leipzig was the successor, via various post-war name changes, to Tura 1899 Leipzig, one of the city's

[21] Braun and Wiese, 'DDR-Fußball', 199. [22] Fuge, *Leutzscher Legende*, p. 57, 70–2.
[23] Hesse-Lichtenberger, *Tor!*, pp. 227–8.

best-supported clubs during the Nazi era.[24] Chemie became one of the leading forces in the nascent *Oberliga*, winning the title in 1950/1 and finishing third the following season. Halfway through the 1952/3 season, the Chemie team was stripped of many of its best players, who were moved to the newly created army team, Vorwärts Leipzig. This first act of political interference was unsuccessful. Vorwärts garnered little popular support in Leipzig and were quickly relocated to Berlin, part of the musical chairs that made club football so unstable in the GDR's early years. At Chemie, meanwhile, young players replaced departed internationals. The team drew crowds of over 40,000 to its home games, the beginnings of the 'legend of Leutzsch', which would become an enduring part of East German football culture.[25] Chemie offered a team anchored in a distinctive neighbourhood – like the original Spartak team in Moscow's working-class Presnya district,[26] Boca Juniors in the Buenos Aires neighbourhood of La Boca, or Liverpool FC in the city's L4 district – and traditions that predated communism's arrival. State-imposed additions to the Leipzig football scene found it difficult to compete.

When the first major restructuring of football took place in 1954, Chemie Leipzig was one of the biggest casualties. Under the proviso of concentrating efforts on the newly created SCs, the resources of the chemical industry were focused on SC Chemie Halle. In Leipzig, precedence, and a place in the *Oberliga*, was given to sports clubs representing the railway and printing industries, Lokomotive and Rotation. There was no room in the new set-up for Leipzig's most successful side. Almost the entire Chemie Leipzig team was delegated to SC Lok. The rump BSG was demoted to the fourth tier of East German football (the *Bezirksklasse*) and renamed Chemie Leipzig-West.[27]

For the next nine years, a period left undiscussed in official publications celebrating the club's twentieth anniversary in 1970,[28] Chemie Leipzig was sponsored by a local lacquer and paint factory that occasionally provided money for equipment such as boots. It was kept going by volunteers, including a bookkeeper at the factory, who served as *de facto* club chairman, and various youth team coaches (Chemie's juniors, not insignificantly, remained a national force during this difficult period). The first team, a motley crew of ex-*Oberliga* players, reserves, juniors, and students, never made it out of the district leagues to which it had

[24] The pre-1945 and early post-war history of the club that became Chemie is discussed in Chapters 1 and 2.

[25] Fuge, *Der Rest von Leipzig*, pp. 14–15.

[26] Edelman, *Spartak Moscow*, pp. 10–42.

[27] Fuge, *Der Rest von Leipzig*, p. 15.

[28] Archivgut des DFV, XV/63/4/6 (Nachlaß Fritz Gödicke), Zwanzig Jahre BSG Chemie Leipzig, 1970.

been condemned in 1954, though it could still draw crowds of 5,000 for matches against local rivals.[29]

Grassroots commitment ensured that Chemie Leipzig did not disappear from the map. But it required another of the SED's periodic interventions to return the team to the top flight. In a neat reminder of the multi-layered nature of local patriotism, the forgotten BSG was the inadvertent beneficiary of the frustrated ambitions of Leipzig sports functionaries. Neither of the SCs, Lokomotive or Rotation, had drawn consistently large crowds since their creation in 1954. Neither had been successful. Lok's cup victory over Empor Rostock in 1957 was the only trophy that came to the GDR's second-largest city during this nine-year period.[30] Aware of the political capital that could be gained from success on the pitch, local politicians concluded that a further concentration of resources was required. In 1963, the county DTSB leadership sanctioned the merger of Lok and Rotation into SC Leipzig. The *Oberliga* place freed up by the union was given to BSG Chemie Leipzig. The new hierarchy was clear. The best players in Leipzig were to be delegated to the new super club. The rest were dispatched to Leutzsch to play for Chemie.[31] For all of the discussion about football's relative autonomy, Chemie's experiences in 1954 and 1963 served as a reminder of the dictatorial caprice that shaped club histories. How and why decisions were made, as Günter Schneider later observed, 'was and remained incomprehensible' to the football-going public.[32]

By any standards, the results of the restructuring were unexpected. Chemie, absent from the *Oberliga* for nine years, offered a mishmash of second-string players from Lokomotive, Rotation, and elsewhere. The press dismissed the team as relegation fodder ahead of the 1963/4 season. 'The interest of Leipzig football supporters is focused above all on SC Leipzig', declared the local SED newspaper.[33] Chemie's outsider status was reiterated by the identity of its head coach. Alfred Kunze was respected as a theoretician of the game, but – like Heinz Krügel at FCM in the 1970s – he was too outspoken for the DFV's liking. At a meeting in November 1953, he gave an astonishingly frank assessment of the East German state in the wake of 17 June. The uprising, he stated, showed that the GDR was not built on 'a clear moral basis of law'. Here 'people are just numbers'; the country was governed by 'sledgehammer

[29] Fuge, *Leutzscher Legende*, pp. 54–6.
[30] *Ibid.*, p. 57; Fuge, *Der Rest von Leipzig*, pp. 16–19.
[31] Fuge, *Der Rest von Leipzig*, pp. 20–4.
[32] Archivgut des DFV, I/1, 'Dokumentation über 45 Jahre Fußball'.
[33] Fuge, *Leutzscher Legende*, p. 59.

politics'. At the same meeting, he criticised the unthinking lionisation of Soviet football and the 'victory at any price' ethos that permeated the domestic game.[34] With such political views, it is little wonder that Kunze's stint at Vorwärts Leipzig was a short one.[35] Chemie Leipzig, whom he first coached during the 1953/4 season, seemed to be a more natural fit. Yet Kunze returned to Leutzsch only in 1963, after a five-year stint at another establishment club, Lok Leipzig. His career trajectory was typical of the compromises that even more independent-minded coaches made in order to prosper, or at least to survive, in their profession. *Eigen-Sinn* and conformity were mutually reinforcing, rather than opposite tendencies.

Reading Jens Fuge's blow-by-blow accounts of Chemie's march to the 1963/4 *Oberliga* title, a sense that something sensational is happening is almost hidden by the proficiency of the 'rest of Leizpig'.[36] Chemie were at or near the top of the table for the whole season. Backed by fanatical support at the picturesque Georg-Schwarz Sportpark – a stadium, from Simon Inglis's approving late-1980s perspective, with '[n]o lights, no modernity, only a few party slogans, but heaps of green and white charm'[37] – the team put the elite to the sword. A home win over Vorwärts Berlin in the penultimate round of matches ensured that Chemie needed only a draw in the final game in Erfurt to claim the title. The 2–0 win on 10 May, as noted, triggered delirious scenes of celebration among Chemie's large away following. *Die Neue Fußball-Woche* was moved to comment that 'seldom was a German champion so fêted as Chemie!'[38]

Chemie's victory was primarily a local rather than a national embarrassment to the authorities. Red-faced comrades in Leipzig were left to ponder how their unloved 'town-hall team' had ended up in third place, while the cast-offs from Leutzsch celebrated a second *Oberliga* title. But it highlighted football's volatility, a trait that the SED regime could never embrace or understand. In Ulrich Hesse-Lichtenberger's words, 'you could almost see Manfred Ewald tearing out his hair over this unruly sport'.[39] The 1963/4 season was in some respects a watershed in the history of GDR football. Never again did a BSG win the league title. The formation of football clubs the following year, including FC Lokomotive Leipzig (the former SC Leipzig), and the 1970 football resolution created

34 SAPMO-BArch, DY 12/2695, Bericht, 26 November 1953, fo. 30–1.
35 Fuge, *Der Rest von Leipzig*, p. 126.
36 See Fuge, *Leutzscher Legende*, pp. 57–72; Fuge, *Der Rest von Leipzig*, pp. 30–82.
37 Inglis, *The Football Grounds of Europe*, p. 96.
38 Fuge, *Der Rest von Leipzig*, p. 76.
39 Hesse-Lichtenberger, *Tor!*, p. 228.

a more settled elite. Teams found it difficult to replicate the surprises of the 1950s and early 1960s. Under Kunze's guidance, Chemie finished third in the *Oberliga* in the 1964/5 season, again ahead of SC Leipzig, and won the FDGB Cup the following year, defeating Lokomotive Stendal 1–0 in the final. Decline then set in. The 1970s and 1980s were spent mostly in the *Liga*. Chemie's unruly young fans attracted more attention than the team. Older supporters meanwhile lamented the passing of the good old days, when players had the character lacking in modern footballers, and criticised the regular delegation of players from Leutzsch to Lokomotive.[40]

The story of Chemie Leipzig aptly illustrates the constrained autonomy under which players, coaches, and supporters operated in GDR football. Few BSGs experienced the vicissitudes of communist state power – its arbitrariness and indifference to popular demands – more readily than Chemie, as the experiences of 1954 and 1963 testify. Teams could be made or unmade on party orders, even if the results of such interventions could not be guaranteed. There was no easy or long-term means of winning against the odds. Indeed, it became harder over time. BSGs such as Chemie were increasingly marginalised in the Honecker era, as state-approved FCs, most notably BFC, swept up the domestic honours.

Yet, for all of the restrictions that it faced, Chemie Leipzig was a persistent symbol of the *Resistenz* to dictatorship that made football an untrustworthy partner for the communists. In assessing the place of another underdog club, Union Berlin, in the history of GDR football, Theo Körner described it as emblematic of 'not letting things get you down ... [of] not conforming boundlessly to the system', and of 'consciously trying to maintain traditions and keep connections' – both to the club's pre-GDR history and to its sister club in West Berlin, Union 06. Tellingly, Körner compared Union to Chemie Leipzig. In both cases, club history mixed conformity and defiance to create an invented socialist tradition that honoured the victories, and defeats, of 'the common man'.[41] Whether it was the trumping of Vorwärts Leipzig in 1953, the outspokenness of Kunze, the miraculous *Oberliga* triumph of 1964, or the loud and distinctive fan culture, the team from Leutzsch, like Union, provided 'a small departure from the dreary everyday life of socialism'[42] – and a means, deliberate or otherwise, of destabilising communist sport.

[40] SAPMO-BArch, DY 30/4982, petition from Hans H. to Hellmann, 22 April 1983, fo. 141–5.

[41] Interview with Theo Körner.

[42] Fuge, *Leutzscher Legende*, p. 161.

## East Germany and a Europe of football

In the autumn of 1957, champions Wismut Karl-Marx-Stadt became the first East German team to enter the European Cup, UEFA's flagship competition, which had first been contested two years earlier. In the second round, Wismut played the Dutch champions, Ajax Amsterdam. The first leg in East Germany ended in a 3–1 victory for the visitors. En route to the return match in the Netherlands, the GDR team missed a connection and got stuck in West Germany, with barely any money to its name. To pay for bed and board for his players, the Wismut coach Fritz Gödicke pawned his watch. That night, team members ate a frugal meal and slept three to a bed. Perhaps unsurprisingly, they lost 1–0 in Amsterdam the following day. In the meantime, Ajax officials picked up the tab for the hotel rooms and rescued Gödicke's watch from hock.[43]

Wismut Karl-Marx-Stadt's trip to Amsterdam is interesting for a number of reasons. On the pitch, the defeat pointed to the gap that separated top GDR teams from their West European counterparts, a gap that remained in place for much of the next thirty years. Off the pitch, the fact that the Wismut squad ended up stranded and broke in West Germany reflected the GDR's straitened economic circumstances more than ten years after the end of the Second World War. In a country where rationing continued until 1958, the purse strings for sports-related travel, especially travel that required Western currencies, were tightly held. Finally, Wismut's adventure – for all of its difficulties – reminds us that, at the height of Cold War hostilities, football remained a vibrant site of cultural transfer between East and West, cutting a sporting swathe through the political divide of the Iron Curtain.

This point is worth emphasising. The GDR's first forays into European competition took place in a period (1955–60) when it experimented with a Soviet-style calendar-year season, running from February to November. What made sense in the colder climes of the Soviet Union was illogical in the more temperate GDR. It threw the *Oberliga* out of sync with the rest of Europe, which continued to follow the traditional August–May scheduling, leaving teams at their peak in the summer months when everyone else rested. Arguments that players would get fewer injuries, that better pitches would improve standards, and that warmer spectators would drink less alcohol failed to hide the transparent political motivations for the change.[44]

[43] Archivgut des DFV, XV/63/4/1, Bemerkungen zur Reise nach Amsterdam für das Spiel gegen Ajax am 20.11.57, n.d.
[44] SAPMO-BArch, DR 5/1277, Änderung der Spielzeit – Ja oder Nein?, 1953.

The DFV quickly abandoned the experiment with the calendar-year season, returning the championship in 1960/1 to its usual late-summer–spring cycle. 'Learning from the Soviet Union', and reducing football to a summer sport, ran into local difficulties, such as declining attendance figures during July and August, when many fans went on holiday.[45] The decision, though, was ultimately shaped by the GDR's desire to be part of what Henri Delaunay, the Frenchman behind the creation of UEFA, called 'a footballing Europe'.[46] Whereas the other European institutions of the 1950s, such as the European Economic Community, were narrowly West European, UEFA was a broad church that, through its three club competitions, created regular and genuinely pan-continental encounters. In football, as in music and cinema, the GDR often found itself positioned, somewhat uneasily, between East and West, and between the insularity and internationalism that represented the opposing poles of East German socialism. That tension was never overcome. But the Europeanisation of football in the mid 1950s – a glamorous mid-week product played from September to May in floodlit stadia and watched by vast, multinational audiences – provided a sporting dialogue that at least partly elided the diplomatic isolation that the GDR faced until the 1970s. Football's ability to work as a mutable space, capable of housing multiple identities, ensured that local, national, and international needs could be met through tentative engagement with a Europe that included NATO as well as Warsaw Pact member states.

## Not for export? GDR clubs in European competition

Opening up to Europe, though, created as many problems as it solved. Wismut Karl-Marx-Stadt were not the only East German club to experience a truncated European campaign. The GDR's record in UEFA's three club competitions – the European Cup, the UEFA Cup (known until 1971 as the Fairs' Cup), and the Cup Winners' Cup – was modest. Fifteen teams represented the country between 1957 and 1991. Only one, FC Magdeburg, won a European trophy, the 1974 Cup Winners' Cup. Two more sides, Carl Zeiss Jena in 1981 and Lok Leipzig in 1987, lost in the final of the same tournament. Dynamo Dresden and BFC never advanced beyond the semi-final stages of the UEFA Cup and Cup Winners' Cup respectively. Most tellingly, the East German record in UEFA's premier competition, the European Cup, was poor. No team ever made it past the quarter finals.[47] East German clubs were

[45] Leske, *Erich Mielke*, p. 150. [46] Goldblatt, *The Ball Is Round*, pp. 398–9.
[47] Horn and Weise, *Das große Lexikon*, p. 102, 411–15.

competitive against strong West European teams. Dynamo Dresden and Hansa Rostock, for example, variously won at least one leg of European ties against the likes of Juventus, Leeds, Inter Milan, Porto, and Barcelona.[48] But, like the national team, club sides tended to blink at the vital moment, more often than not losing such prestigious matches on aggregate.

Second only to the national team's misfortunes, the weak showing of clubs in Europe was the major source of the SED's long-running dissatisfaction with football. The third football resolution (*Fußballbeschluß*) in 1983 was largely inspired by embarrassing performances on the continental stage during the 1982/3 season, when all five East German clubs were eliminated in the first round of competition, a clean sweep that was matched only, as the *Berliner Zeitung* gloomily noted, by the representatives of Cyprus, Luxemburg, and Malta.[49] Much of the popular anger at BFC's domestic hegemony in this period was fuelled by their underwhelming record in the European Cup. The international success of leading teams from other small European leagues – between 1986 and 1988, the European Cup was won by Steaua Bucharest (Romania), Porto (Portugal), and PSV Eindhoven (the Netherlands) – suggested that something was wrong with the *Oberliga*. In Europe, fans argued with no small degree of *Schadenfreude*, the *Stasi* team was unable to handpick friendly referees and thus came to grief.[50] Like the GDR's iconic car, the Trabant, BFC dominated the domestic market (*faute de mieux*), but travelled badly.

As with the national team, the struggles of clubs in Europe should not be overstated. Czechoslovakia, a communist state of similar size to the GDR, had a worse record, producing one European Cup Winners' Cup winner, Slovan Bratislava (in 1969), and no other European finalists. But the perception of under-performance was undeniable. Many of the reasons for it are familiar from the agonised debates about the *Auswahl*: the competitiveness of European football, which made it harder to win the European Cup than the equivalent prize in volleyball or water polo; the lack of star performers in a system that discouraged individualism; and the oppressive political production (from ideological schooling to *Stasi* surveillance) that accompanied each international appearance of a GDR team. It is hard to imagine that preparations for Dynamo Dresden's European debut against Scottish side Rangers in 1967 were helped by a pre-match test on the subject of 'the economic system of

48 Hesse-Lichtenberger, *Tor!*, p. 222. 49 Leske, *Erich Mielke*, pp. 211–12.

50 See e.g. SAPMO-BArch, DY 30/4980, anonymous petition to the ZK, 27 October 1985, fo. 2–3; SAPMO-BArch, DY 30/4982, petition from Jens G. to Krenz, 22 March 1986, fo. 40–2.

socialism in the GDR'.[51] On trips to the West, in the words of one Dynamo fan, 'players were not free in the head'.[52]

Reports in the 1960s and 1970s assigned much of the blame for poor international performances to the local patriotism that made football competitive but self-absorbed. In putting the case for a further concentration of resources in 1975, Rudi Hellmann argued that 'there are neither in friendly socialist nor in Western countries renowned football clubs that draw talent and elite players from so small a territory as a county'[53] (as was common practice in the GDR). Framed by the idea of extending the catchment areas of leading clubs, the 1976 football resolution was a typically confused mixture of open-mindedness (coaches were to be sent on study trips to the Netherlands and England) and dogmatic refusal to recognise that football was any different from other Olympic sports, an approach that was reinforced by the appointment of a rowing coach, Werner Lempert, as DFV general secretary.[54] The policy of concentration introduced on Lempert's watch did more harm than good, creating an uncompetitive league where the gulf between top sides such as BFC and the bottom-feeding BSGs widened appreciably. It is no coincidence that the records both of the national team and of club teams in European competition were, with odd exceptions, disappointing during the BFC era. Even BFC fans, prickly about claims of perceived favouritism towards their team, admitted that the *Oberliga* procession was a major cause of their team's problems outside East Germany. Against most domestic opponents, as Olaf S. argued, BFC could win at '80%' of its best performance. Suddenly finding the extra 20% against Europe's elite was not easy.[55] In the struggle between internationalism and isolationism that characterised football, the *Oberliga* – a small league in a small country, populated by self-interested clubs and unambitious players – acted as a brake on European aspirations.

Match reports submitted by club officials after Dynamo Dresden's European matches in the 1970s reinforce the sense of GDR football's inferiority complex against Western opposition. After losing 2–0 in the first leg of the first round of the 1971/2 European Cup to Ajax, the Dynamo Dresden chairman Wolfgang Hänel conceded that the match

51 SAPMO-BArch, DO 101/078, Vorbereitungsplan für die Messestädte-Cup-Spiele am 20.9. und 4.10.67 gegen Glasgow Rangers, n.d.

52 Interview with Jens Genschmar, 18 May 2011.

53 SAPMO-BArch, DY 30/IV 2/2.036/25, Kurze Einschätzung der Lage im Spitzenfußball der DDR und einige Probleme für die Aussprache der Genossen der Parteiführung mit Leitungskadern des DTSB der DDR und des DFV der DDR, 14 March 1975, fo. 6–15.

54 *Ibid.*, Beschluß zur weiteren Leistungsentwicklung im Fußballsport der DDR, 7 April 1976, fo. 29–50.

55 Interview with Olaf S.

'clearly showed the differences that still exist between the current level of GDR football and our hosts'. In front of 60,000 passionate fans, the defending European champions attacked from the outset, scoring twice in nineteen minutes and playing 'football of the most modern style', a fluid system that the team's many admirers called 'total football'.[56] To escape with only a 2–0 defeat was, in the circumstances, not a bad result, leading Hänel to assert with no apparent irony that Dresden had 'real chances' to reach the second round if they raised their performance level 'by 100%' in the second leg.[57] The match ended in a 0–0 draw, after which Hänel conceded more realistically that Dynamo's opportunity had disappeared in Amsterdam.[58]

Hänel's reports often inferred, rather disingenuously, that GDR teams played with one hand behind their back – the honest amateurs of the socialist bloc against the seasoned professionals from the West. The idea of the jejune East Germans, isolated and unprepared for what they faced, does not exactly square with what we know about the communist sports system – and certainly would not explain why Ajax apparently drew inspiration in the early 1970s from Dynamo Dresden's sophisticated scouting and coaching structures.[59] But it does speak to the defensiveness and uncertainty at the heart of GDR football identity. When Dynamo Dresden were eliminated in the second round of the 1970/1 Fairs' Cup by Leeds United, Hänel's report emphasised how 'the English professionals proved their strength in all areas, were extremely good on the ball, and mastered all the tricks that were needed to come through the tie'.[60] The step-up in class from the *Oberliga* often found teams wanting. Hänel's report on Dresden's 2–0 away defeat to Liverpool in the quarter finals of the UEFA Cup in 1973 admitted that the 'nervousness' of the injury-hampered visitors could not be overcome and led players to miss important goal-scoring opportunities. Liverpool, 'an embodiment of the European and world elite in football', won the return leg in the GDR 1–0 to progress comfortably to the semi-finals.[61]

[56] On total football, see David Winner, *Brilliant Orange: The Neurotic Genius of Dutch Football* (London: Bloomsbury, 2000).

[57] SAPMO-BArch, DO 101/079, Kurzbericht über die Durchführung von internationalen Sportveranstaltungen in der DDR, 20 September 1971; report on the Ajax–Dynamo Dresden match, 21 September 1971.

[58] *Ibid.*, Kurzbericht über die Durchführung von internationalen Sportveranstaltungen in der DDR, 29 September 1971.

[59] Interview with Jens Genschmar.

[60] SAPMO-BArch, DO 101/078, Kurzbericht über die Durchführung von internationalen Sportveranstaltungen in der DDR, 6 November 1970.

[61] SAPMO-BArch, DO 101/079, report on the Liverpool–Dynamo Dresden match, 9 March 1973; report on the Dynamo Dresden–Liverpool match, 23 March 1973.

## Bitter cup: encounters with West Germany

Defeats against West European teams might have been less painful to SED functionaries if the tormentors had not included *Bundesliga* clubs. Of the five first-round losses in Europe in September 1982 that sparked the following year's *Fußballbeschluß*, two were against West German sides. Whereas the national teams of East and West Germany met only once, their clubs played on a more regular basis. The results were one-sided. In sixteen encounters in UEFA's three showcase tournaments, the West German team progressed to the next round on thirteen occasions. Only Lokomotive Leipzig, twice in the UEFA Cup (against Fortuna Düsseldorf in 1973/4 and Werder Bremen ten years later), and FC Magdeburg, against Schalke 04 in the same tournament during the 1977/8 season, secured wins for the GDR.[62]

Preparations for all-German clashes were extensive, resembling plans for a military campaign more than plans for a football match. When Dynamo Dresden played Bayern Munich in the autumn of 1973, in the first and most memorable of the East–West match-ups, a recent 'mega-event' template sprang readily to the authorities' mind. For the World Youth Festival – the GDR's ten-day statement of open-mindedness (*Weltoffenheit*), held that summer in East Berlin – the *Stasi* ran its largest-ever operation. *Aktion Banner* involved the pre-emptive screening of 30,000 young people, who – like the student Michael in Reiner Kunze's *Die Wunderbaren Jahren*[63] – were regarded as potential trouble-makers. Sixty thousand security staff, including 27,000 *Stasi* officers, were on duty during the event, ensuring that the festival-goers sang and danced through the night under watchful eyes.[64]

With the ink barely dry on the Basic Treaty, the Dynamo–Bayern clash appeared to offer an opportunity for sporting détente. There was, briefly, even a suggestion that the West German politician Egon Bahr, a key figure in the *Ostpolitik* negotiations of the early 1970s, might attend the second leg in Dresden (in the end, he apparently concluded that 'his interest in sport is not that great, especially in November').[65] Yet preparations on both sides were replete with Cold War paranoia. Fearful

[62] Horn and Weise, *Das große Lexikon*, p. 77.

[63] Reiner Kunze, *Die wunderbaren Jahren* (Frankfurt/Main: S. Fischer Verlag, 1976).

[64] Kay Schiller, 'Communism, youth and sport: the 1973 World Youth Festival in East Berlin', in Alan Tomlinson, Christopher Young, and Richard Holt (eds.), *Sport and the Transformation of Modern Europe: States, Media and Markets, 1950–2010* (Abingdon: Routledge, 2011), p. 55.

[65] SAPMO-BArch, DY 30/11336, Niederschrift aus dem Gedächtnis über persönliche Unterredungen mit Minister Bahr am 23. Oktober 1973 (Michael Kohl).

of being poisoned or spied upon, Bayern officials came up with a spurious argument to avoid spending the night before the match, as per UEFA regulations, in the host city. The difference in altitude between Munich and Dresden, the club president explained, 'might turn out to be detrimental to our performance'. The Bayern squad arrived in Dresden only a few hours before kick-off, incensing East German officials and disappointing their many fans in the East.[66]

Bayern's arrogance was not groundless. The two-leg match was placed under a blanket of *Stasi* surveillance. *Aktion Vorstoß* covered the selection process for a 'tourist delegation' to Munich for the first leg on 24 October, ticket distribution for the return leg in Dresden on 7 November, match-day security in and around Dresden's Rudolf Harbig Stadium (involving 3,110 *Stasi* officers), and extensive policing of the hotel where around 400 fans awaited Bayern's arrival. In the perfect image of *Abgrenzung*, a photograph (Figure 7) shows these fans, looking resigned rather than agitated, cordoned off from the Western objects of their attention by a line of policemen. The Bayern team's pre-match meal was not poisoned. But *Stasi* operatives apparently ensured that Dynamo coach Walter Fritzsch gained advance notice of Bayern's line-up and formation.[67] As with the World Youth Festival, a vast security apparatus was successfully mobilised 'to suggest to the world the façade of a stable GDR'.[68]

Even with help from the secret police, however, the balance of power could not be shifted the GDR's way. The thrilling tie epitomised the defeat from the jaws of victory mentality that afflicted East German football and that prevented the talented Dresden sides of the 1970s from making it past the quarter finals of any European competition. The first leg in Munich ended in a 4–3 victory for the hosts, after Dynamo had twice been in front. The return match in Dresden ended in a 3–3 draw, after the hosts had come back from an early 2–0 deficit to lead 3–2, before conceding the decisive goal (as in the first leg) to Bayern's prolific striker Gerd Müller.[69] The following season in the same competition, Bayern eliminated FC Magdeburg in another tie characterised by extensive *Stasi* operations and West German fears of poisoning. Bayern caused local outrage by refusing to eat at their hotel on the night before the

[66] Hesse-Lichtenberger, *Tor!*, p. 230; SAPMO-BArch, DO 101/078, note by Hänel, 8 November 1973.

[67] Leske, *Erich Mielke*, pp. 402–8; SAPMO-BArch, DO 101/078, Trainingsruhe am Tag des Europa-Cup-Spieles gegen den FC Bayern München, 1 November 1973; Spiel am 7.11.73, n.d.

[68] Wolle, *Die heile Welt*, pp. 166–7.

[69] Genschmar, *Mit Dynamo*, pp. 46–7.

Figure 7. Fans gathered outside Bayern Munich's hotel in Dresden, November 1973. There was huge anticipation in the city ahead of the European Cup clash between Dynamo and Bayern, the first time that East played West in one of UEFA's three club competitions. The size of the crowd suggests Bayern's popularity behind the Berlin Wall. The police cordon shows that the concept of *Abgrenzung*, the 'demarcation' of citizens from unhealthy Western influences, was sometimes taken literally.

return leg in Magdeburg. FCM lost 5–3 on aggregate, after letting slip a 2–0 lead in West Germany.[70]

There was no disgrace in such defeats. Hänel's post-match report on the loss to Bayern in November 1973 noted 'the real progress in GDR club football' shown by Dynamo's exciting displays.[71] The performances of both Dynamo and FCM against the West German champions inspired local patriotism even as supporters queued up for autographs of Beckenbauer and Müller. The silver lining was harder to find in the 1980s, when the gulf between East and West German football, as in other areas of competition between the two countries, widened. The most notorious example was Dynamo Dresden's loss to Bayer Uerdingen in the quarter finals of the 1985/6 UEFA Cup. The match provided the

[70] Gröschner, *Sieben Tränen*, pp. 98–115.
[71] SAPMO-BArch, DO 101/078, untitled report (Hänel), 8 November 1973.

backdrop for Dynamo winger Frank Lippmann's flight to the West. Even without a high-profile case of *Republikflucht*, though, it would have been astonishing. After sixty minutes of the return leg in West Germany, Dresden held a 5–1 aggregate lead over a modest *Bundesliga* outfit. Thirty minutes later, the visitors were out of the competition, having conceded six goals to improbably lose the tie 7–5.

Like an eyewitness at the scene of a car crash, the *Stasi* collected jubilant West German newspaper articles on the 'miracle at the Grotenburg Stadium'.[72] The defeat marked the beginning of the end of the career of popular Dynamo libero Hans-Jürgen Dörner. Lippmann's room-mate on the ill-fated trip to Uerdingen was stripped of the club captaincy the following year and pushed hastily towards retirement.[73] Head coach Klaus Sammer was also on borrowed time. The post-match report by Sammer's assistant Dieter Riedel noted the familiar element of bad luck (Dynamo had to change goalkeepers at half time because of injury) but did not gloss over the calamitous loss. It echoed many of the analyses that were produced over the years about the inability of East German footballers to get it right on the international stage: 'nervousness, a tendency to panic, and disorganisation' in pressure situations, an insufficient number of high-quality players (as exemplified by the Dynamo substitutes in Uerdingen), and the fact that 'we possessed no player who was in the position to have a mobilising impact on the team'.[74] This lack of leadership was a feature of football under East German communism. Sammer was an exception during his playing days, as was his talented son, Matthias, who was compared to tennis star Boris Becker on a trip to West Germany in the mid 1980s. The relative independent-mindedness which Sammer senior carried into his coaching career (as shown, for example, in his criticism of refereeing performances in BFC games) was not to the liking of the *Stasi*, which wanted him sacked before the Uerdingen debacle. At the end of the 1985/6 season, he was dispatched to train young players at Dynamo Meißen.[75]

BFC epitomised the weak record of GDR clubs in Europe. Many East German goods had limited export value. The same was true of the country's most successful and least popular team. During the ten consecutive seasons in which it represented the GDR in the European Cup,

72 For West German newspaper reports on the match, see Bundesbeauftragte für die Unterlagen des Staatssicherheitsdienstes der ehemaligen Deutschen Demokratischen Republik (BStU), MfS, HA XX/221, fos. 46–51.

73 Hesse-Lichtenberger, *Tor!*, p. 223; Horn and Weise, *Das große Lexikon*, pp. 81–2.

74 HStA Dresden, 12456 SED Nachlässe V/2.39/046, Einige Ursachen der blamablen Niederlage gegen Bayer Uerdingen, 21 March 1986.

75 Pleil, *Mielke, Macht und Meisterschaft*, pp. 99–105.

BFC reached the quarter-finals only twice, in 1979/80 and 1983/4. The other eight campaigns ended in first- or second-round exits, unacceptable for a club whose founding goals in 1965 included the development of 'a team that embodies the European elite'.[76] In a few cases, BFC could take comfort in losing to the team that went on to win the European Cup: Nottingham Forest in 1978/9, Aston Villa in 1981/2, and Hamburg the following season.[77] Often, though, early exits came at the hands of teams that BFC expected to beat: Czechoslovakian champions Baník Ostrava in 1980/1, Austria Vienna in two consecutive seasons in the mid 1980s, and the Danish side Brøndby in 1986/7.[78]

The nadir was reached in the team's final tilt at the European Cup in the autumn of 1988, when signs of a changing of the guard in football were as faint as they were in the Politburo. The *Stasi* prepared for the arrival of West German champions Werder Bremen for the first leg of a first-round tie against BFC in time-honoured fashion: exhaustive security measures around the team hotel, tightly policed ticket distribution, the shadowing of seventy West German journalists by DTSB and BFC officials, and a weighty *Stasi* presence at the match, where guests included former West German chancellor Willy Brandt and the mayor of West Berlin, Eberhard Diepgen.[79] The GDR champions responded in style, winning 3–0.

In equally time-honoured fashion, the wheels then came off. BFC were thrashed 5–0 in the return leg by a highly motivated Werder team – a result celebrated loudly by Dynamo Dresden fan Jens G. and his army friends.[80] Giselher Spitzer has suggested that the turnaround can be traced to the fact that the BFC team was doped in the first leg, but not in the second.[81] More convincing, though, was the ex-Jena player Jürgen Raab's comment in 2001 that the humiliating loss sprang from BFC's inability to cope with 'the enormous media pressure' that followed its first-leg victory. In the end, as BFC goalkeeper Bodo Rudwaleit conceded, 'it was a mental thing'.[82] In an apt reminder of the economic disparity between East and West, the visiting players were apparently distracted from their match-day preparations by the opportunity to cheaply procure West German goods in their hotel – a sale organised with some psychological acuity by the Werder general manager,

[76] Leske, *Erich Mielke*, p. 471. [77] Interview with BFC fans, 29 May 2011.

[78] Horn and Weise, *Das große Lexikon*, p. 413.

[79] BStU, MfS HA XX/10313, Information zum Stand über die eingeleiteten Sicherungsmaßnahmen anläßlich des Europapokalspieles des BFC Dynamo gegen SV Werder Bremen am 6.9.1988, 2 September 1988, fo. 45–54.

[80] Interview with Jens Genschmar. [81] Spitzer, *Fußball und Triathlon*, p. 60.

[82] Leske, *Erich Mielke*, p. 476.

Willi Lemke. 'That here', said coach Jürgen Bogs after the match, 'was a load of crap'.[83] It was BFC's last appearance in the European Cup. As exit music, it could hardly have been more appropriate.

## Three stripes good, two stripes better?

Ahead of Vorwärts Berlin's game against Wolves in the 1959 European Cup, army officials, aware of the poor quality of GDR sports footwear, authorised the purchase of Adidas football boots for the players due to represent the socialist fatherland in England. In order to avoid any unwelcome association between a West German sports company and the GDR military, black boot polish was bought on the day before the game. When the Vorwärts players stepped onto the pitch in the Midlands in front of 56,000 spectators, the three stripes on the side of their boots had been reduced to two.[84]

The anecdote reveals much about the GDR's fragile sense of self-identity and wary relationship with European football. Like its engagement with Western pop music in the 1960s, or the supervised freedom that it granted at the 1973 World Youth Festival, the GDR's forays into European football competition after the mid 1950s were simultaneously characterised by paranoia and openness. Strenuous efforts were made to control the environments in which teams operated, especially outside the Soviet bloc. But involvement in UEFA tournaments inevitably meant compromises, compromises that exposed the ambiguities – the intersection of local, national, and international influences – at the heart of East German football. Klaus Sammer, the Dynamo Dresden captain, recalled how he and his team-mates first watched a James Bond film during their trip to Scotland to play Rangers in the 1967/8 Fairs' Cup.[85] Ahead of Bayern Munich's game in Magdeburg in 1974, police reports noted nervously that a small number of FCM fans had got together with visiting Bayern supporters to drink beer and make bets on the outcome of the clash between the East and West German champions.[86] Football's fluidity – the fact that FCM supporters could express outrage at the Bayern team's refusal to eat East German food, yet happily seek out Bayern fans for drinks or Bayern players for autographs – meant that there was no fixed narrative upon which the communists, or indeed their political opponents, could rely. Cracks appeared faster than they could

83 Luther and Willmann, *BFC*, pp. 191–3.
84 Jürgen Nöldner, 'FC Vorwärts Berlin, Meister 1958, 60, 62, 65, 66, 69', in Friedemann (ed.), *Sparwasser und Mauerblümchen*, p. 61.
85 Genschmar, *Mit Dynamo*, p. 11. 86 Gröschner, *Sieben Tränen*, p. 114.

be filled. The SED regime constantly sought tighter security, but shortfalls were inherent in the very act of engaging with the class enemy on, and around, the football pitch.

The cracks widened in the 1970s and 1980s. These were decades in which West Germany helped to set the European football standard; in which televised exposure to West German football became almost universal; and in which West German clubs regularly beat their GDR counterparts. If club football at home – with its narrow vistas and intense local rivalries – undermined SED control from within, club football abroad, with its regular access to international travel and competition, undermined SED control from without. European football exposed players and fans alike to the shortcomings of the domestic game, in much the same way that exposure to Western consumer lifestyles (through television or tourism, for example) laid bare the shabbiness and bottlenecks in the GDR's shortage economy. If East German football teams stood for a ragged kind of domestic charm, West German teams stood for a successful cosmopolitanism that represented the Europe outside the GDR's gates. Participation in European competition conferred legitimacy on the game in East Germany, but only at a cost, leaving it vulnerable to assertions of *Eigen-Sinn* that could take myriad forms (including, as we shall see in Chapter 6, flight to West Germany). The SED's repeated failure to strengthen its authority through club football showcased the game's ability to resist the designs of a dictatorship that elsewhere established a model of elite sport development still in use today.[87]

[87] On the GDR sports model in Australia, Britain, and China, see Dennis and Grix, *Sport under Communism*, pp. 171–86.

# 6 Football and the *Stasi*

## 'Death to the traitor!'

Late in the evening on 5 March 1983, a black Alfa Romeo driven by the Eintracht Braunschweig footballer Lutz Eigendorf skidded off a road in the West German town and crashed into a tree. He was taken to hospital with severe head and chest injuries. The accident report showed that no other vehicle was involved. The car had no mechanical faults and the driver was not wearing his seat belt. Eigendorf's blood alcohol level was far over the legal limit. Two days later, he died in hospital at the age of twenty-six. Police and coroners concluded that this was a tragic accident, caused by the driver's alcohol-impaired judgement.[1]

Not everyone was convinced. Eigendorf, after all, was no ordinary *Bundesliga* player. During the 1970s, he was one of the brightest stars of GDR football. A product of the elite Werner Seelenbinder sports school in Berlin, the midfielder joined BFC in 1970 and was a first-team regular by the middle of the decade. In 1978, he made his national team debut against Bulgaria, scoring both goals in a 2–2 draw. In the same year, his three-year stint in the MfS's Felix Dzierzynski Guard Regiment ended and Eigendorf became a candidate member of the SED.[2] His exemplary path to the top of the East German game, though, ended abruptly in March 1979. On the way back from a match in Kaiserslautern, Eigendorf disappeared at a rest stop. Instead of returning to his wife and daughter in East Berlin, he took a taxi back to Kaiserslautern and claimed political asylum in the West.[3]

Eigendorf's talent and careful upbringing at BFC ensured that Erich Mielke took his defection as a 'personal defeat'.[4] *Stasi* operations were quickly begun to ensure that Eigendorf's wife and daughter did not join him in the West and to monitor his uncooperative parents in

[1] Schwan, *"Tod dem Verräter!"*, pp. 13–14.
[2] *Ibid.*, pp. 111–15; Leske, *Erich Mielke*, p. 351.
[3] Leske, *Erich Mielke*, pp. 353–4. [4] Luther and Willmann, *BFC*, p. 84.

Brandenburg. No stone was left unturned in the campaign against the departed player, which deployed a total of fifty officers.[5] Eigendorf's wife was persuaded to divorce her husband, having fallen for a 'Romeo' agent planted by the secret police. Agents in West Germany reported in detail on Eigendorf's struggles to become a first-team regular at Kaiserslautern, his new relationship with a young student, and his transfer to fellow *Bundesliga* outfit Eintracht Braunschweig in 1982.[6]

In 2000, in a book entitled *Tod dem Verräter!* ('Death to the traitor!'), the journalist Heribert Schwan advanced the thesis that Eigendorf was murdered by *Stasi* operatives. Schwan reconstructed a scenario in which the player was kidnapped in his car and forced to drink alcohol containing a poisonous substance, after which he was chased to his death in the fatal crash.[7] Suspicions about the circumstances of Eigendorf's death are justified. The blood alcohol level found in his body after the crash was the equivalent of 4.3 litres of beer or 2 litres of wine, an unlikely Saturday night session for a person described by friends and family as a modest drinker.[8] But the murder thesis, the idea that an angry Mielke arranged to have Eigendorf killed, is based on speculation rather than hard facts. Conclusive evidence is lacking.

## Football's tyranny of intimacy

What happened to Eigendorf on the night of 5 March 1983 may never be known. His story, though, highlights the tenacity with which the East German state pursued traitors to the socialist cause. In the GDR's 'tyranny of intimacy',[9] there appeared to be few hiding places, even on the other side of the Iron Curtain. Eigendorf's case, the subject of both a book and a television film in 2000, offers a microcosm of wider popular (and, to a certain degree, scholarly) images of the GDR since reunification. This is the East Germany familiar to readers of Anna Funder's *Stasiland* (2003) and viewers of Florian Henckel von Donnersmarck's Oscar-winning *The Lives of Others* (2006), a grey and sinister world in which the *Stasi* exerted a malign and ubiquitous influence.[10] Public obsession with the *Stasi* after 1990, ironically echoing the organisation's obsession with public opinion, was rooted in the shocking disclosures of the *Wende*. *Stasi* offices were stormed quicker than panicky

[5] Thiemann, *Der Feind an meiner Seite*, p. 230. [6] Leske, *Erich Mielke*, pp. 355–61.
[7] Schwan, *"Tod dem Verräter!"*, pp. 260–70. Ellen Thiemann supports the murder thesis in *Der Feind an meiner Seite*. See pp. 233–6.
[8] Schwan, *"Tod dem Verräter!"*, pp. 260–1. [9] Betts, *Within Walls*, p. 23.
[10] Anna Funder, *Stasiland: Stories from behind the Berlin Wall* (London: Granta Books, 2003).

employees could destroy incriminating evidence, most famously at the mammoth East Berlin headquarters of the organisation on 15 January 1990. The scale of secret police operations became clear in the millions of files that were discovered and in subsequent revelations about high-profile informers, including sports stars. A vast machinery was set up to enable the reunified German state to make good on the popular demand 'I want my file!' By 1997 3.7 million applications for this personal reckoning with the past had been submitted to the Gauck Authority, the body charged with overseeing the MfS's bureaucratic war chest, which included 180,000 km of files, one million pictures, and 200,000 tapes.[11] In scholarly literature, the *Stasi*, largely absent from pre-1989 studies of the GDR, was now front and centre, a lightning rod for discussions about the dictatorship that it served and protected.[12] Fascination with 'The Firm' remains widespread, though recent studies have branched out from organisational history to examine, for example, its misguided 'spy-tech' preoccupations or its grassroots impact.[13]

The *Stasi*-centric view is amply reflected in football's post-*Wende* historiography. Hanns Leske has published exhaustively documented books that expose the dark underbelly of the game in the GDR. His research reveals a list of luminaries who worked for the *Stasi* as informers. It includes national team coaches Georg Buschner, Eduard Geyer, and Bernd Stange; players such as HFC star Bernd Bransch; and referees such as Bernd Stumpf and Adolf Prokop.[14] Leske concludes that one-third of a typical *Oberliga* squad (i.e. six out of eighteen players) were IMs – a far higher rate of collaboration than the GDR average, estimated (with the inclusion of part-time spies) at roughly one in every 6.5 citizens.[15]

Leske's work has been complemented by Ingolf Pleil's research into secret-police infiltration at Dynamo Dresden. It reveals that eighteen of the seventy-two players who represented the club between 1978 and 1989 were *Stasi* informants. Their number included national team players such as Gerd Weber, Ulf Kirsten, and Torsten Gütschow.[16] Pleil's study illustrates the refined tactics that the MfS used to recruit

[11] Betts, *Within Walls*, pp. 22, 233–4.

[12] See e.g. David Childs and Richard Popplewell, *The Stasi: The East German Intelligence and Security Service* (London: MacMillan, 1996); Mike Dennis, *The Stasi: Myth and Reality* (London: Pearson, 2003).

[13] See respectively Kristie Macrakis, *Seduced by Secrets: Inside the Stasi's Spy-Tech World* (Cambridge: Cambridge University Press, 2008) and Gary Bruce, *The Firm: The Inside Story of the Stasi* (Oxford: Oxford University Press, 2010).

[14] See e.g. Leske, *Erich Mielke*, pp. 281–323 (on Stange, Geyer, Bransch, and Buschner); Leske, *Enzyklopädie*, pp. 370 (on Prokop), 479–80 (on Stumpf).

[15] Leske, *Enzyklopädie*, p. 34; Betts, *Within Walls*, p. 45.

[16] Pleil, *Mielke, Macht und Meisterschaft*, pp. 12, 64–9, 72–7.

footballers, as well as the detailed tracking of players' behaviour, even long after their playing days were over. As Dynamo star Reinhard Häfner later observed, 'you were under observation the whole day long, regardless of whether you were in the stadium or the disco'.[17]

Such scholarly research, supplemented by popular accounts of the corrosive influence of the *Stasi* on the lives of players and their families,[18] serves as a counterpoint to the uncritical accounts of the game that have been penned by numerous ex-GDR journalists and writers since 1989. In several club and general histories, issues such as IM activity have been skated over, encouraging, in Leske's forthright words, 'an amnesia regarding the repressive arsenal of a totalitarian regime and unavoidable *Ostalgie* [that] leads to a whitewashing of the SED state'.[19] A particular target of his ire is Jorn Luther and Frank Willmann's 2003 history of BFC, which implausibly downplays *Stasi* influence, reducing Mielke and his colleagues (in Leske's words) to 'regrettable minor parts' in the club's pre-1989 history.[20]

Leske's work contains valuable research and irrefutable arguments. But it also tends to set up a simplistic binary relationship between collaborators and resisters and to betray limited understanding of the complex problems, and range of possible responses, that footballers faced under East German socialism. There were regional differences, for example. Players faced less pressure from the secret police in smaller cities such as Rostock and Zwickau than they did in Dresden and Berlin.[21] Many were recruited at a young age and provided intelligence that was more banal than incriminating, a relatively common evasion tactic among low-level informants throughout society.[22] No Dynamo Dresden IM, it has been claimed, ever ended the top-flight career of a fellow player through his reports to the *Stasi*.[23] Ex-players such as Ulf Kirsten who worked with the MfS are today revered as club heroes.

Motives for secret-police collaboration were complex and varied. They could include commitment to socialism, vanity, coercion, and material inducements. The diary entries of the writer Brigitte Reimann show how an approach from The Firm, in her case in 1957, was at once tempting and deeply troubling.[24] In Leske's monograph on the *Stasi* and football, these nuances are either absent or not taken up for discussion. Those who undertook years of IM activity are dealt with in a separate

[17] *Ibid.*, p. 28.
[18] Most obviously Schwan, *"Tod dem Verräter!"*; Thiemann, *Der Feind an meiner Seite*.
[19] Leske, *Enzyklopädie*, pp. 36–8.
[20] Leske, *Erich Mielke*, pp. 9–11; Luther and Willmann, *BFC*, pp. 70–1.
[21] See the interview with Gerd Kische in Leske, *Erich Mielke*, p. 372.
[22] Fulbrook, *The People's State*, p. 245.
[23] Interview with Jens Genschmar.
[24] Fulbrook, *The People's State*, pp. 241–4.

section from those such as the Hansa Rostock defender Gerd Kische (himself an IM), the Lok Leipzig goalkeeper René Müller, and Jürgen Sparwasser, who managed, one way or another, to evade the secret police.[25] Whether intentionally or otherwise, there is an undercurrent of moral judgement here that is as problematic as the *Ostalgie* that Leske criticises. He notes, for example, that when Georg Buschner died in 2007, the media were largely silent about the fact that this 'loyal party comrade' was a *Stasi* informant between 1966 and 1981. But, as Leske concedes, the value of the material that Buschner submitted to the authorities was questionable. He never denounced individual players and he was reported on by other IMs. The Jena *Stasi* office described him in 1959 as 'a careerist and individualist'. Towards the end of his coaching career, Buschner clashed with Ewald over the DTSB's dictatorial and ineffective management of football.[26] He was also known to be 'no friend' of the establishment team BFC, rarely selecting its players for the *Auswahl*, even after the club had started to dominate the *Oberliga* in the late 1970s.[27] Buschner's relationship to the communist state was a complex one, a mixture of loyalism and independent-mindedness that reflected the constrained autonomy open to those at the top of GDR football.

On the question of *Stasi* involvement in the game, it is useful to avoid either/or approaches, where condemnation and whitewashing are the only options, where the secret-police presence is everywhere or nowhere. The truth lies somewhere between the two extremes. As we shall see in this chapter, the limits to *Stasi* influence on football were just as instructive as its apparent magnitude, highlighting again the complexities of the communist dictatorship. The extent of the SED state, it becomes clear, made the effective policing of citizens more, rather than less, difficult. Even heavily scrutinised *Oberliga* stars found ways in which to defend their *Eigen-Sinn* against state incursions.

## Footballers and the West in the 1950s

When Honecker came to power in 1971, the total *Stasi* staff numbered 48,786. By 1989, the 'People's Own Listen and Look Company' (*VEB Horch und Guck*) had 91,015 full-time employees, or roughly one operative for every 180 GDR citizens. The figures in the Soviet Union and communist Poland were one per 595 and one per 1,574 citizens

25 Leske, *Erich Mielke*, pp. 281–335, 368–90.
26 *Ibid.*, pp. 320–3; Leske, *Enzyklopädie*, pp. 94–6.
27 Karte and Röhrig, *Kabinengeflüster*, p. 120.

respectively. Even Romania's feared Securitate had only one officer for every 1,553 citizens.[28] The number of IMs also mushroomed, from approximately 100,000 in 1968 to an annual average of between 170,000 and 180,000 from 1975 onwards.[29] In this heavily policed environment, *Republikflucht* was a difficult and dramatic act. Though the figures are not wholly reliable, it appears that only twenty footballers, plus the coach Jörg Berger, illegally left the GDR for the West between 1961 and 1989. Eight of them departed via newly opened cracks in the Iron Curtain in the summer and autumn of 1989.[30]

Before 1961, the picture was very different – and the state's ability to prevent defection far more constrained. Widely blamed for the intelligence failings that contributed to the June 1953 Uprising, the *Stasi* numbered only 9,000 staff in 1955. The most powerful organ of state repression in this decade was the People's Police (*Volkspolizei*, VP).[31] These organisations, moreover, worked in a geo-political climate that lacked the hermetic stability of the 1970s. Until the creation of the *Sperrzone* ('restricted area') along the internal border between East and West Germany in May 1952, human traffic between the two German states was largely unencumbered. From then until the construction of the Berlin Wall nine years later, sportspersons (like all other citizens) could still cross to the West, either temporarily or permanently, via the unguarded exits in the divided city. East Germans made 13.5 million trips to the FRG, and West Germans 9 million trips in the opposite direction, between 1950 and 1961.[32] Open borders encouraged regular sporting contact. There were almost 400 fixtures between teams from East and West Berlin in the first five months of 1952. As late as May 1955 an all-Berlin XI, comprising seven players from the East and four from the West, played a friendly match against a team from Prague.[33]

Berlin's unresolved status created a fluid situation for East German footballers, particularly before the international crisis surrounding it heated up from 1958 onwards. Entire teams decamped to the West in the early 1950s. The most prominent case involved eighteen players from SG Dresden Friedrichstadt, led by the later West German national team coach Helmut Schön, who departed for West Berlin in June 1950 following the controversial title decider against Horch

[28] Dennis, *The Stasi*, pp. 78–9. [29] Fulbrook, *The People's State*, pp. 241–2.

[30] Leske, *Erich Mielke*, pp. 258. [31] Betts, *Within Walls*, pp. 26–7.

[32] Patrick Major, 'Going west: the open border and the problem of *Republikflucht*', in Major and Jonathan Osmond (eds.), *The Workers' and Peasants' State: Communism and Society in East Germany under Ulbricht 1945–71* (Manchester: Manchester University Press, 2002), p. 193.

[33] Wiese, 'Hertha BSC im Kalten Krieg', pp. 116–17, 123–8.

Zwickau.[34] In the same year, another player exodus caused the division of East Berlin club Union Oberschönweide into two newly constituted East and West parts, BSG Motor Oberschönweide and SC Union 06 respectively.[35] Disentangling the personal, economic, and political factors that motivated people to leave the GDR for good was not an easy task, as one British observer noted at a West German refugee camp in 1961.[36] In the cases of Union and Friedrichstadt, political pressures, combined with the greater financial and footballing pull of the West, appear to have caused irrevocable breaches.

Those who went to the West were often, like Friedrichstadt's Hans Kreische, able to come back to the GDR with few complications – part of the 428,964 'returnees' who at least partially offset the wave of departures in the 1950s.[37] The authorities made great propaganda play of such returnees. A press release in 1950, entitled '"Even worse than under the Nazis ..." – A sportsman who got to know the "golden West"', recounted the story of Karl Langethal, a talented player from Thuringia. Langethal had, in his own words, 'allowed myself to be talked into signing a contract for a club in West Berlin'. But the lack of jobs there and other broken promises caused him to quickly come back to the GDR, where he had steady employment and played for his local team in Weimar.[38] The BSG Fortschritt Hartha player Theo Reichelt recounted a similar story three years later, pitying the exploited 'contract player in the prettiest colours' that he encountered during his unhappy spell at clubs in the Bremen area.[39] Personal redemption in both cases was tied to socialist reconstruction, in idealised accounts that illustrated the GDR's moral and political superiority over its West German counterpart. Reichelt spoke of his return to the GDR as a 'return to my *Heimat*', an indicator of the SED's early attempts to link socio-economic and sporting improvements to traditional ideas of German community and belonging.[40]

Happy endings, though, occurred less regularly than the SED regime would have liked. The overwhelming demographic trend was westward. An estimated 2.7 million people left the GDR for West Germany between 1949 and 1961. It was the only country in Europe with a shrinking

[34] *Ibid.*, pp. 106–11; Archivgut des DFV, XV 63/4/1, 'Zur Flucht von Dresdener Spielern', n.d.

[35] Luther and Willmann, *Eisern Union!*, pp. 36–8.

[36] Major, *Behind the Berlin Wall*, p. 82. [37] Major, 'Going west', p. 191.

[38] SAPMO-BArch, DY 12/281, "Noch ungünstiger als in der Nazizeit ..." – Ein Sportler lernte den "goldenen West" kennen, 9 November 1950, fo. 63.

[39] 'Die Vereine brauchen Geld – Meine Eindrücke in Westdeutschland und in der DDR', *Die Neue Fußball-Woche*, 6 January 1953, 13.

[40] *Ibid.* On *Heimat*, see Palmowski, *Inventing a Socialist Nation*, pp. 3–7, 37–8.

Figure 8. Helmut Schön at the sports school in Cologne, January 1950. Born in 1915, Schön played sixteen times for Germany during the Nazi era and was part of the SC Dresden team that won the national championship in 1943 and 1944. The Dresden native remained in the city after the Second World War, becoming player-coach at the renamed (and now politically suspect) SG Dresden Friedrichstadt. Four months after completing his coaching exams in Cologne under the tutelage of Sepp Herberger, Schön fled the GDR with most of his Friedrichstadt team-mates. He became West Germany's most successful coach, masterminding victory in the 1972 European Championship and the 1974 World Cup.

population.[41] In sport as elsewhere, a tougher line was adopted to counter the devastating migratory pattern in 1957 and 1958, a shift that coincided with the escalating Berlin crisis, Ulbricht's ousting of reform-minded Politburo rivals such as Karl Schirdewan, and Erich Mielke's appointment as *Stasi* boss.[42] In 1957 the DTSB banned all sporting interaction with West Berlin. When the DFV was formed a year later, it followed the party line, supporting matches with West German teams only after thorough ideological and sporting preparations had been

[41] Major, 'Going west', p. 191.

[42] Jens Gieseke, 'Ulbricht's secret police: the Ministry of State Security', in Major and Osmond (eds.), *The Workers' and Peasants' State*, pp. 50–2.

made.[43] The idea of *Republikflucht* as a publicly condemned act of treason became part of regime discourse several years before the Berlin Wall went up.[44] The first cases of it among elite footballers likewise predated the city's division. In September 1959 two players from champions Vorwärts Berlin, Horst Assmy and Rolf Fritzsche, crossed into West Berlin to join the city's then leading team, Tennis Borussia. The defection of two army footballers, particularly the talented winger Assmy, was a blow to East German football. As in the case of 'renegade' writer Alfred Kantorowicz, who had left for the West two years earlier,[45] it triggered a concerted media campaign to blacken the names of the departed. Emphasis was placed on the players' ingratitude to the socialist state that had trained and educated them. Former team-mates were brought forward to express, with what degree of conviction it is hard to say, their indignation at the 'false path' that Assmy and Fritzsche had chosen.[46]

## Footballers and *Republikflucht* after 1961

The decision to build the Wall caused a radical rupture in all areas of East German life. Football was no different. Overnight on 12–13 August 1961, the escape route to the West became immeasurably more difficult. The relative frequency with which footballers travelled abroad gave them more exit opportunities than the average citizen. Yet only two *Oberliga* players defected between 1961 and 1976, both in 1966: the young Carl Zeiss Jena winger Michael Polywka and the Chemie Leipzig goalkeeper Klaus Günther. Günther left his team-mates at Amsterdam airport as they returned from a European Cup Winners' Cup game against Standard Liège in Belgium in December. Regarded as a security risk because of an uncle living in Baden Württemberg, he made the trip to Liège after promising team-mates that he would not abscond. Only on the plane home was Günther's absence noticed. Attempts to persuade him to return to the GDR, including a plea from Chemie coach Alfred Kunze and the dispatching of his father to his uncle's home, were in vain. Günther emigrated for many of the reasons that other players, and indeed citizens, frustrated by the GDR's narrow horizons, made the same decision: 'I didn't want to be caged in, wanted to travel freely, and wanted to play in the *Bundesliga*'.[47]

[43] Wiese, 'Hertha BSC im Kalten Krieg', pp. 129–31.
[44] Major, 'Going west', p. 204. [45] Major, *Behind the Berlin Wall*, p. 99.
[46] Leske, *Erich Mielke*, pp. 264–8.
[47] On Günther's *Republikflucht*, see Fuge, *Leutzscher Legende*, pp. 83–4; Fuge, *Der Rest von Leipzig*, p. 98.

The small number of players who committed *Republikflucht* during this period cannot be explained solely by secret-police surveillance. The *Stasi* was not omniscient. It had a staff of 32,912 by 1967, but did not devote many resources to football.[48] Klaus Günther's flight illustrated this point. Before his eventual departure from the team in Amsterdam, he attempted to escape in Liège itself: 'I sat in the subway train, but it didn't go and didn't go. So I got out again and unnoticed rejoined the team'. Chemie's lax supervisory methods were reiterated at Amsterdam airport, where Günther's disappearance went unremarked until the plane was almost in the air.[49] *Stasi* officers were apparently nowhere in sight. If the organisation's goal, in Mielke's famous formulation, was 'to know everything and to report everything worth knowing',[50] the reality on the ground was often very different.

*Republikflucht* was a major risk, but factors other than the long arm of the *Stasi* must be considered. The fact that no-one followed in the footsteps of Polywka and Günther for ten years suggests that the vast majority of footballers were happy with their lot and recognised their relatively privileged status: 'It was enough to taste the western world every now and then when on European duty'.[51] Like intellectuals, doctors, and other *Reisekader* ('travel cadres'), footballers were on the upside of a two-tier travel system. Leading players frequently received enticing offers from West European clubs, including Jürgen Sparwasser (from Bayern Munich in 1974) and Dynamo Dresden midfielder Reinhard Häfner (from Swiss side Grasshopper Club Zürich in 1977 and from VfB Stuttgart two years later).[52] But these offers, often made in shadowy circumstances, were rarely taken up. Amid the one-for-all ethos that permeates team sport, not wanting to leave team-mates in the lurch played a part in the reluctance to take flight. More importantly, domestic ties kept players in the GDR far more often than they induced them to head west. As Stefan Wolle notes, the decision to commit *Republikflucht* had 'mental consequences' that went far beyond changing one's address, separating would-be emigrants from friends and family, possessions, and the rhythms of life as they knew them. It was an isolating experience, one that could leave individuals feeling doubly exiled. Wolf Biermann captured this sense of 'torn biographies' in lines from a poem written

[48] Dennis, *The Stasi*, p. 78. [49] Fuge, *Leutzscher Legende*, p. 84.

[50] Norman Naimark, *The Russians in Germany: A History of the Soviet Zone of Occupation, 1945–1949* (Cambridge, MA: Harvard University Press, 1995), p. 366. The quote comes from a speech that Mielke made in November 1947.

[51] Hesse-Lichtenberger, *Tor!*, p. 230.

[52] Gröschner, *Sieben Tränen*, p. 89; Genschmar, *Mit Dynamo*, p. 50.

shortly before his own enforced departure in 1976: 'I'd most like to be gone/And most like to stay'.[53]

When Lutz Eigendorf sought refuge at Kaiserslautern in 1979, he left behind his parents, wife, and young daughter, all of whom were interrogated and tailed by *Stasi* officers and informants. After Klaus Günther's abortive meeting with his father in 1966, he did not see him again for twenty years.[54] Emigration meant turning your back on your family and a secure living for an uncertain future in a different country. In a society where the public sphere had broken down in the face of communist repression, family solidarity was an asset to be zealously guarded, a sanctuary that grew in value as the communist regime gave greater latitude to the private sphere in the 1970s.[55] The risks of leaving, in the eyes of many players, outweighed the rewards.

The MfS embarked upon a policy of 'continuous expansion' from 1968 onwards, cementing its place at the heart of the state apparatus.[56] At the same time, East German sport underwent important transformations. At the 1968 Olympics in Mexico City, the GDR competed for the first time as a separate country and finished fifth in the medal table, ahead of West Germany. The following year, a Politburo directive created a two-tier system that focused resources on Olympic sports. The GDR's development into a sporting powerhouse meant more work for the *Stasi*. It was responsible for preventing defections to the West, guarding the secrets of state doping and training programmes, and monitoring athletes through a network of informants.[57] The dual strategy now at play in sport – increased competition with the West alongside increased surveillance of the GDR's 'diplomats in tracksuits' – reflected the wider dualism of the Honecker years, which saw the rapid growth of the *Stasi* alongside increasingly accomodationist attitudes to Western cultural influence.[58]

Ahead of two major sporting events in West Germany, the 1972 Olympics in Munich and the 1974 World Cup finals, the *Stasi* leadership issued 'Instruction 4/71' (*Dienstanweisung Nr. 4/71*), a document that formed the basis for saturation coverage of all elite sports, including football, in the 1970s and 1980s. It extended the range and number of IMs and set out strict guidelines for teams and individuals competing in the West, including much closer observation of those with contacts in West Germany.[59] In theory at least, blanket surveillance was now in

[53] Wolle, *Die heile Welt*, pp. 283–4. [54] Fuge, *Leutzscher Legende*, p. 84.
[55] Betts, *Within Walls*, pp. 49–50, 109. [56] Gieseke, 'Ulbricht's secret police', p. 54.
[57] Dennis, *The Stasi*, p. 133. [58] Betts, *Within Walls*, p. 146.
[59] Leske, *Erich Mielke*, pp. 275–81.

place. At the 1980 Winter Olympics in Lake Placid, the 176-strong party of athletes, coaches, officials, and journalists included 35 IMs.[60]

Yet eighteen of the twenty footballers who committed *Republikflucht* after August 1961 did so after Instruction 4/71 came into circulation. This suggests that the decision to leave the GDR was not solely conditioned by what the *Stasi* did or did not do. Gaps remained in the socialist system – and, from the late 1970s onwards, GDR citizens increasingly regarded that system as beyond repair. This reflected trends across Eastern Europe, as the growing influence of Western consumerism (through television in particular) and the gradual 'de-legitimation of the institutions of the socialist public sphere' created less patient, more individualised societies.[61] The year 1979 marked the pre-*Wende* highpoint for sporting *Republikflucht*. Apart from Eigendorf and Jörg Berger, defections that year included the coach of the national athletics team, the national wrestling team's doctor, and an internationally renowned swimmer.[62] For a minority of the sports elite, exit became the only viable option.

Between 1976 and the summer of 1989, footballers left for West Germany on a more regular basis, if still in small numbers. The ball was set rolling by two young HFC players, Norbert Nachtweih and Jürgen Pahl, who used a match in Turkey in November 1976 to seek asylum in the West. In contrast to peers such as Eigendorf, who struggled in the *Bundesliga*, Pahl became the first-choice goalkeeper at Eintracht Frankfurt for the next decade, while Nachtweih was indisputably the GDR's most successful export. He joined Bayern Munich from Frankfurt in 1982 and collected a host of honours with West Germany's top team. In a 1986 interview, Nachtweih provided interesting insights into what drove him to leave the GDR. Despite the excellent support for young sporting talent there, he argued, 'everything ran according to plan, individualism counted for nothing'.[63] Nachtweih's sentiments were shared by other emigration seekers – witness the petitioner who applied to leave in 1983 for 'purely personal and private [reasons] . . . We – that is my wife and I – are individualists and cannot identify with this state any longer'.[64]

In high-profile cases of *Republikflucht*, there was often a sense of shutting the stable door after the horse had bolted. The BFC

[60] Dennis, *The Stasi*, p. 134.

[61] Mark Pittaway, *Eastern Europe 1939–2000* (London: Arnold, 2004), pp. 130–1, 185.

[62] Leske, *Erich Mielke*, p. 259.

[63] See BStU, MfS, HA XX/221, fos. 44–5 for Nachtweih's interview with the *Berliner Morgenpost*, 2 March 1986.

[64] Major, *Behind the Berlin Wall*, p. 210.

coach Jürgen Bogs sardonically noted that the only consequence of the Eigendorf case was a directive banning players from staying anywhere below the third floor in Western hotels, so that they would not be tempted to jump out of the window to freedom.[65] Considering the rigorous guidelines in place, extraordinary security lapses were permitted. In November 1983, two BFC players, Falko Götz and Dirk Schlegel, committed *Republikflucht* during their club's visit to Yugoslavia for a European Cup match against Partizan Belgrade. Officials pointed the finger at Jörg Berger as one of the culprits involved in wooing the duo.[66] But Götz had extensive family ties in West Germany and was in regular contact with them. The decision to grant him *Reisekader* status was as risky as allowing Frank Lippmann to play in Dynamo Dresden's European away games during the 1985/6 season, despite various disciplinary infractions, including drunkenly fleeing the scene of a traffic accident, and long-standing knowledge of his numerous contacts in West Germany.[67] In the relatively independent domain of football, where a club's interest in securing the next victory often overrode political considerations, even the extensive powers of the *Stasi* could not preclude every possibility that a player might take flight. To understand life in the GDR, Jan Palmowski has written, 'we can neither ignore the workings of the *Stasi* nor privilege it above other forms of power'.[68] In football, other forms of power, whether in the hands of fans, adminstrators, or players, were myriad. They undercut *Stasi* attempts to shape the game's narrative.

## The Weber and Müller cases

At East Berlin's Schönefeld airport on 24 January 1981, three members of the national squad about to depart for a tournament in South America were arrested on suspicion of intending to commit *Republikflucht.* All three were Dynamo Dresden players: the defensive midfielder Gerd Weber, the full-back Matthias Müller, and the striker Peter Kotte. *Stasi* intelligence indicated that the trio planned to use their club's next visit to West Germany to defect.[69]

The case epitomised the complexity of the *Stasi* infiltration of football. Weber had been an IM since 1975, delivering more than seventy reports

[65] Leske, *Erich Mielke*, p. 368.
[66] SAPMO-BArch, DY 30/5040, letter from Pommer (SV Dynamo) to Ewald, 8 December 1983, fo. 8–9.
[67] Leske, *Erich Mielke*, pp. 269–71. [68] Palmowski, *Inventing a Socialist Nation*, p. 309.
[69] Pleil, *Mielke, Macht und Meisterschaft*, pp. 154–6.

on his team-mates. Reluctance to continue in this role was one of the factors that persuaded him to leave the GDR. In October 1980, when Dynamo Dresden were in the Netherlands for a UEFA Cup tie against Twente Enschede, Weber had a meeting with purported representatives of FC Cologne (in reality Dynamo Dresden fans who had left the GDR six months earlier), who offered him an annual salary of 200,000 M to join the *Bundesliga* side. They extended similar deals to Müller and Kotte. In contrast to Weber, neither was tempted. Critically, however, Kotte and Müller failed to inform the authorities about what they knew of Weber's intentions.[70]

The punishments meted out to the three players were severe. Weber was sentenced to twenty-seven months in prison. He was expelled from the SED and the police force, stripped of all state honours and educational privileges, barred from playing football at any level, forbidden from having contact with his former team-mates, and given a six-month ban on travel to fellow Soviet-bloc states.[71] After serving nine months, Weber was released from prison in December 1981. Though it abandoned work with him in 1982, the *Stasi* kept close tabs on their long-time informant and tried various means of returning him to the socialist fold. The carrot of revived career prospects as a coach was combined with the stick of steadfastly refusing Weber's applications for an exit visa to the West. The player finally left via the opened border between Hungary and Austria in August 1989.[72]

Müller and Kotte left prison after only five days and avoided most of the penalties that Weber faced. But they were expelled from the police and given lifetime bans from the top two divisions of GDR football. Barely a month after having boarded a plane to Argentina as players in the national team, the pair were delegated to county league outfits TSC Meißen and BSG Fortschritt Neustadt respectively, returned to the work force as manual labourers, and made eligible for six months of military service.[73] The swiftness of their fall from grace was hardly mitigated by

[70] The minutiae of the case are discussed in Leske, *Erich Mielke*, pp. 338–46. For Kotte's perspective, see the interview in Genschmar, *Mit Dynamo*, pp. 101–2.

[71] Pleil, *Mielke, Macht und Meisterschaft*, p. 159; HStA Dresden, 11857 SED – Bezirksleitung Dresden Nr. IV D – 2/16/748, Information über große Verletzungen der Gesetze der sozialistischen Sportbewegung und der Regeln des sozialistischen Gemeinschaftslebens und die sich daraus ergebenden führungspolitischen Schlußfolgerungen und Festlegungen in der SG Dynamo Dresden, 4 February 1981.

[72] Pleil, *Mielke, Macht und Meisterschaft*, pp. 164–72.

[73] *Ibid.*, p. 159; HStA Dresden, 11857 SED-Bezirksleitung Dresden Nr. IV E – 2/16/719, Aktennotiz über die abgeschlossene Eingliederung von M. Müller und P. Kotte in den Arbeitsprozeß und in Mannschaftskollektive der Bezirksliga, 27 February 1981.

Figure 9. Dynamo Dresden players Gerd Weber (wearing 5) and Peter Kotte (11) at a UEFA cup match against Hamburg, November 1974. The 1981 scandal, involving the pair and team-mate Matthias Müller, cost all three players their *Oberliga* careers. Weber, who had played thirty-five times for the GDR and was the youngest player in the team that won gold at the 1976 Olympics, never played again and became a mechanic. Kotte played for third-division side Fortschritt Neustadt until serious injury ended his career in 1984.

the hazy possibility of rehabilitation, especially given the scope of *Stasi* surveillance to which they were now subjected.[74]

Müller and Kotte clung to the idea that they could prove themselves as citizens as a means of returning to their former careers. In the process, they invoked notions of socialist justice that were integral to the GDR's self-image as well as common tropes in citizens' appeals for assistance in Stalinist Russia during the 1930s.[75] In July 1981, while undergoing military service in Rostock, Müller sent a petition to Mielke, requesting permission to play top-flight football again. The inability to play at a level

74 Pleil, *Mielke, Macht und Meisterschaft*, pp. 159–60.

75 Sheila Fitzpatrick, 'Supplicants and citizens: public letter-writing in Soviet Russia in the 1930s', *Slavic Review* vol. 55, no. 1 (Spring 1996), 91–2.

'that accords with my abilities', Müller wrote, 'has caused me many painful hours'. 'Long breaks' from the game were causing him to fall behind his *Oberliga* peers.[76] The petition was rejected. Müller was informed that he could play football at county league level and study to become a sports teacher, but that his career as an elite footballer was over.[77] The finality of the decision took time to sink in. In April 1983, the ZK sports department received a petition, this time from both Müller and Kotte, on the same subject – and responded in the same fashion.[78] Kotte's career ended after a serious injury in 1984. Müller played in the *Liga* for BSG Aktivist Brieske-Senftenberg between 1986 and 1989, but never any higher than that.[79]

The official statement about Weber, Müller, and Kotte in February 1981 made terse reference to 'gross violation of the principles of the socialist sports movement and the rules of socialist community life'.[80] Media silence was deafening. Newspapers omitted the trio's names from reports on the South American tour and from subsequent coverage of games involving a weakened Dynamo Dresden team. Kotte was removed from the list of leading *Oberliga* goalscorers. When BSG Fortschritt Neustadt gained promotion to the *Liga* in 1982, his face was even replaced by that of a team-mate in the team photograph published in *Deutsches Sport-Echo*.[81]

Public reaction betrayed exasperation with the SED's stern reticence. Here, as so often in football, compliance with the 'public transcript' of socialism (i.e. what the regime wanted to hear), a key factor in maintaining social peace, was threatened by an upsurge of the 'hidden transcript' (i.e. what people really thought).[82] The party leadership in Dresden reported in late February 1981 that discussion about the three Dynamo players was ongoing, fed by 'rumours and presumptions'. While some workers welcomed the punishment of the three 'traitors', many people

[76] SAPMO-BArch, DO 101/027/5, petition from Matthias Müller to Mielke, 7 July 1981.

[77] *Ibid.*, Stellungnahme zur Eingabe Müller, Matthias vom 7.7.1981 an den Minister für Staatssicherheit und 1. Vorsitzenden der Sportvereinigung Dynamo, Genossen Armeegeneral Mielke, n.d.; Bericht über das abschließende Gespräch zur Klärung der Eingabe des Müller, Matthias vom 7.7.1981 an den Minister für Staatssicherheit und 1. Vorsitzenden der Sportvereinigung Dynamo, Genossen Armeegeneral Mielke, 21 August 1981.

[78] SAPMO-BArch, DY 30/4984, letter from Gröger to Matthias Müller and Peter Kotte, 21 April 1983, fo. 92. The petition is not in this file.

[79] Leske, *Erich Mielke*, p. 348.

[80] HStA Dresden, 11857 SED – Bezirksleitung Dresden Nr. IV D – 2/16/748, Information über große Verletzungen, 4 February 1981.

[81] Leske, *Erich Mielke*, pp. 337–8, 346–7. The doctored photo is shown in Pleil, *Mielke, Macht und Meisterschaft*, p. 249.

[82] Palmowski, *Inventing a Socialist Nation*, pp. 12–14.

demanded further information. 'If it was really *Republikflucht*', one reader wrote to the local newspaper, 'then they should be condemned. But as our media tell us nothing precise, we have to take what we hear on West German radio'. There were open signs of dissent. Pupils at one Dresden secondary school collected forty signatures demanding the release of Weber, Müller, and Kotte before the headmaster confiscated the list. Young Dynamo fans wore black ribbons en route to their team's game in Aue on 21 February, in apparent commemoration of the three lost players. At the match, isolated pockets of supporters chanted Weber's name.[83]

Fans generally had unsentimental attitudes to players who left for the West. The departure of Frank Lippmann, 'good but no Dörner or Kirsten', from Dynamo Dresden in 1986 was overshadowed by the team's humiliating loss to Bayer Uerdingen. BFC fans might have been 'hurt' by the exits of Götz and Schlegel three years earlier, but the emergence of Andreas Thom, one of the club's greatest players, soon provided consolation.[84] But Weber, Kotte, and Müller were bigger losses. None of them had left the GDR. The circumstances surrounding their expulsion from top-flight football were never publicly explained. Moreover, they were popular players, particularly Kotte, and key components of the team that was BFC's nearest rival. Dresden fans unsurprisingly saw the lifetime bans as 'an order from Mielke', designed to prevent their team from reprising its successes of the 1970s.[85] Local patriotism and anti-Berlin sentiments were here given a conspiratorial shot in the arm, feeding attitudes that the regime wanted to stamp out.

The Weber case demonstrated the power of the *Stasi*: the extensive reach of its network of informants, as well as its ability to make high-profile individuals who stepped out of line disappear, destroying careers and lives almost overnight. That the *Stasi* could inflict such damage, effacing boundaries between the public and private sphere in ruthless fashion, was illustrated with similar force by the case of Klaus Thiemann. As IM 'Mathias', the *Deutsches Sport-Echo* journalist was one of The Firm's most reliable informants, reporting on the great and good of East German football – including fellow journalists, referees, officials, coaches, and players – between 1973 and 1989. When he was exposed in 1999, while working for the *Bild* newspaper, it emerged that his ex-wife

[83] SAPMO-BArch, DY 30/IV 2/2.036/25, Information der Bezirksleitung Dresden über Stimmen und Meinungen zu den Vorkommnissen bei der SG Dynamo Dresden, 26 February 1981, fo. 59–63.

[84] Interview with Jens Genschmar; interview with BFC fans.

[85] Interview with Jens Genschmar.

had been one of his unwitting victims. Ellen Thiemann spent three years in prison in the mid 1970s for attempted *Republikflucht*, after Thiemann had confirmed their initial escape plan to a suspicious *Stasi* officer.[86] As in the famous case of the dissident Vera Wollenberger, whose husband was outed as an IM after the *Wende*, Ellen Thiemann's experiences speak to the MfS's complicity in destroying the 'moral foundation' of social relations in the GDR.[87]

The Weber case also highlighted the cynicism about the SED regime that characterised public opinion during the 1980s, when interaction with the state generally became angrier and less respectful.[88] Workers discussing the doctored Fortschritt Neustadt team photo at a Dresden factory in August 1982 complained that such practices 'treat us like idiots'. One worker at a factory in Bischofswerda responded in jocular fashion, pinning the retouched team photo to a notice board with a pair of darts, above which stood the caption: 'picture puzzle – who can find Kotte?' Most of his colleagues, the reporting IM noted, read it and laughed.[89] Jokes took aim at all kinds of targets during the Honecker era, from leading Politburo figures and consumer goods shortages to the *Republikflucht* of footballers such as Eigendorf, Götz, and Schlegel: 'if you want to scarper to the West/being a BFC striker is best'.[90] They offered an unmistakeable sign of the SED's lack of popular legitimacy.

The vast *Stasi* network paid off in the dramatic events of 1981. It did not function as effectively three years later. In July 1984 the national team was in Sweden, playing a series of friendly matches in preparation for qualification matches for the 1986 World Cup. After a game on 7 July, officials from the GDR embassy informed the delegation leader Dieter Fuchs that there were 'clear signs' that the team's goalkeeper, René Müller, intended to commit *Republikflucht* during the trip. The player was immediately sent home for questioning. To hide the true nature of his return, Müller was accompanied by the two fellow Lokomotive Leipzig players, Hans Richter and Gerd Liebers. The trio were informed that they were needed in Lok's squad for a tour of Iran.[91]

86 See Thiemann, *Der Feind an meiner Seite*, especially Teil II; Leske, *Enzyklopädie*, pp. 489–91.

87 Betts, *Within Walls*, p. 48.

88 *Ibid.*, pp. 190–1.

89 BStU, MfS HA XX/2698, Information über Diskussionen zu Veröffentlichungen in "Die neue Fußball-Woche" Nr. 32/82 und "Deutsches Sportecho", Ausgabe A vom 29.07.1982 über die 1. Fußballmannschaft der BSG Fortschritt Neustadt, 27 August 1982, fo. 60–2.

90 Reinhard Wagner (ed.), *DDR-Witze Teil 2* (Berlin: Dietz Verlag, 1997), p. 139: 'Willst du in den Westen türmen, mußt du beim BFC stürmen'.

91 SAPMO-BArch, DY 30/4962, Bericht Dr. Fuchs, 9 July 1984, fo. 98–9.

Müller was an unlikely candidate for *Republikflucht*. A model professional, he had been the Lok goalkeeper since 1980, was a recent debutant in the national team, and had no relatives in the West. Even when Werder Bremen expressed interest in signing him in 1983, following an impressive performance in Lok's UEFA Cup victory over the West German side, Müller's ambitions did not countenance illegal departure.[92] Fuchs' report emphasised the DFV's surprise at the intelligence rumours. Müller's behaviour had always been 'trouble-free'. On the return trip to East Germany, he spoke to Fuchs at length about the national team's prospects and the house that he was building in Leipzig.[93]

The MfS claimed that it had 'secure information' about Müller's alleged plans, from an anonymous source who also suggested that Richter intended to defect.[94] The tip-off appears to have been groundless. *Stasi* operations often led to arrests and the successful *Zersetzen* ('subversion') of enemy targets. But they often ended in failure. *Stasi* officers in the county of Schwerin, for example, spent seven fruitless years investigating the provenance of a home-made submarine designed for *Republikflucht* that a passer-by spotted in the river in Perleberg in the early 1980s.[95] The dearth of reliable intelligence in the Müller case was exposed far more rapidly. Interviews with an angry Müller, whom the *Stasi* had never approached about IM work, and his parents brought no results.[96] Neither the DTSB nor the DFV was happy with the MfS's zealous conduct. When Ewald was informed of the incident on 8 July, the players were already on the ferry back to the GDR and he saw no point in correcting on the telephone 'what appeared to me from the outset a doubtful story'. The DTSB counselled a damage-limitation exercise, in which the false alarm was ascribed to the machinations of the never-sleeping class enemy. The three Lok players were immediately made available for the national team again.[97]

Müller subsequently earned a reputation as one of Europe's best goalkeepers. He won the GDR Footballer of the Year award in 1986 and 1987 and led Lok to the final of the 1987 European Cup Winners' Cup, where they lost 1–0 to Ajax. Müller remained in the GDR for family reasons. Like many of his fellow citizens, though, he became increasingly disillusioned by the stagnation around him and

92 Horn and Weise, *Das große Lexikon*, pp. 248–9; Leske, *Erich Mielke*, pp. 382–3.
93 SAPMO-BArch, DY 30/4962, Bericht Dr. Fuchs, fo. 98–9.
94 *Ibid.*, Leitungsinformation, 9 July 1984, fo. 100; Leske, *Erich Mielke*, p. 383.
95 Bruce, *The Firm*, p. 134.
96 Leske, *Erich Mielke*, pp. 383–4.
97 SAPMO-BArch, DY 30/4962, letter from Ewald to Krenz, 9 July 1984, fos. 94–5.

retreated, whenever possible, to the safety and relative freedom of the private sphere: it is not insignificant that, apart from football, the other thing that Müller discussed with Fuchs en route back to the GDR in 1984 was the home that he was building. In arguably the greatest year of his career (1987), he recalled in 2001, 'I saw that achievement isn't worth it. I already wanted to stop playing football. I knew [I'd] never go to a World Cup or European Championship, that there would not be another European cup final for a GDR team. That was the swan song for me'.[98] Müller's private disenchantment, echoed by many ambitious footballers in the 1980s, found a public outlet sooner than anyone could have imagined.

## The uncoupling of football and the *Stasi*

On 2 October 1989 Rudi Hellmann sent a memo to Egon Krenz about the *Republikflucht* of the FCK player Hans Richter. As Leske notes, there is an air of resignation in the brief missive.[99] Hellmann provided a short biography of Richter, the former Lok Leipzig star who accompanied René Müller home from Sweden five years earlier, noting his delegation to Karl-Marx-Stadt in 1987 and poor form in the current season.[100] There was no hint of the ritual discourse on traitors and class-enemy inducements that usually accompanied reports on high-profile cases of *Republikflucht*.

Richter was the last national team player to illegally leave the GDR. He escaped to Frankfurt am Main via Prague on 1 October, using the border with the West that Czechoslovakia had recently opened. As the rudderless SED dictatorship clung to power in the face of mounting popular discontent, player moves from East to West were already so normal that the West German magazine *kicker* barely paid attention to the political aspect of Richter's flight, concentrating on his debut for *Bundesliga* side Eintracht Frankfurt.[101] Eight of the twenty cases of footballing *Republikflucht* after 1961 occurred in the summer and autumn of 1989, part of a mass migration among athletes that decimated sports such as Nordic skiing, cycling, handball, rowing, and boxing.[102]

[98] Leske, *Erich Mielke*, p. 386. [99] *Ibid*., p. 274.
[100] SAPMO-BArch, DY 30/4969, memo from Hellmann to Krenz, 2 October 1989, fo. 276.
[101] Leske, *Erich Mielke*, pp. 274–5.
[102] Jutta Braun, 'Sport frei! – Der Weg in die Sporteinheit', in Braun and Teichler (eds.), *Sportstadt Berlin*, pp. 354–6.

The declining effectiveness of the *Stasi* policing of sport coincided with the beginning of the end of communist rule. In rapidly changing political circumstances, the private desire to migrate to West Germany became a very public demand, as illustrated by the mass occupation of Dresden railway station by frustrated would-be emigrants (*Ausreiser*) in November 1989.[103] Football and East German communism spent the best part of forty years in a mutual embrace. In 1989 they uncoupled, as the SED dictatorship headed quietly towards history's scrapheap and the game into the open-armed embrace of capitalism. Hellmann's passive response to Richter's act of defiance offered a small preview of a defining feature of the 'gentle revolution': the ready acquiescence of the party and state apparatus in the face of mass protests. As Mielke asked in angry bemusement in 1992: 'how did it come about that we simply gave up our GDR, just like that?'[104]

The speed and ease with which the GDR collapsed illustrates that the mightiest structures are often built on sand. Something of this analogy applied to the *Stasi* surveillance of football. At least during the 1970s and 1980s, the game was heavily policed by paid and unpaid observers. One-third of the players in an average *Oberliga* squad were IMs, with the number higher at clubs that participated regularly in European competition. Most of them were not known to their colleagues at the time. Some are still unidentified today.[105] Klaus Sammer spoke of three categories of IM: 'the idiots, those in an emergency situation, and those who wanted to make a career'.[106] The third category, in Leske's view, included coaches such as Meyer, Geyer, and Stange. The latter apparently once complained that the *Stasi* office in Gera had barely contacted him in two years.[107]

Even if one does not always agree with Leske's stern retrospective judgements, the corrosive impact of secret-police influence cannot be gainsaid. The *Stasi* took an interest in everything that happened at Dynamo Dresden, from the political attitudes and leisure-time habits of players to analyses of dressing-room cliques, as well as larger security issues such as screening individuals for travel outside the Soviet bloc.[108] To this end, the first-team squad was saturated with informants, including not only players such as Weber, but also the head coach (Geyer), the team doctor, and the team physiotherapist.[109] The accretion of detail, both banal and salacious, about leading figures in football circles was

[103] Betts, *Within Walls*, pp. 230–1. [104] Fulbrook, *Anatomy*, p. 252.
[105] Leske, *Enzyklopädie*, pp. 33–4. [106] Pleil, *Mielke, Macht und Meisterschaft*, p. 102.
[107] Leske, *Erich Mielke*, p. 565. [108] Pleil, *Mielke, Macht und Meisterschaft*, pp. 279, 281.
[109] A list of Dynamo Dresden IMs can be found in Leske, *Erich Mielke*, p. 328.

likewise apparent in Klaus Thiemann's reports to the *Stasi*, from the DFV official who showed more interest in sunbathing and watching girls on a French beach than an upcoming match to the hotel room and meal demands of an 'arrogant' BFC star.[110]

Identifying the scale of *Stasi* infiltration is a simpler task than identifying what such smothering surveillance meant. There seems to be a contradiction, or at least a tension, between the organisation's coercive power and its cognitive weakness, between the fear that it engendered and its relative inability to shape football according to its wishes. This contradiction was partly rooted in problems common to all intelligence-gathering services, but it was profoundly shaped by the unpopularity and insecurity of the SED regime, particularly in the period (the 1970s and 1980s) when the MfS changed from a classic secret-police apparatus into an 'all-embracing societal mission'.[111] Prior to the construction of the Berlin Wall, and arguably until the promulgation of Instruction 4/71, *Stasi* coverage of football was patchy. After Honecker's accession to power, there was a huge increase in the surveillance of performance sport, to the point where (from 1981 onwards) an office in *Stasi* headquarters, Main Department XX/3, dealt solely with sporting matters.[112] Yet cracks in the façade remained and indeed widened. The *Stasi* stretched itself too thin, unwittingly revealing the limits of dictatorship. Even Leske argues that the relatively small number of footballers who left the GDR for greener pastures was not due primarily to 'the watchful eyes of state security'.[113] If somebody was set on it, *Republikflucht* was difficult to prevent. 'Whoever wanted to go', argues one BFC fan, 'would have gone'.[114] The fact that so few footballers went suggests that, as in the case of René Müller, they recognised their privileged status, whatever its restrictions, and were loath to uproot their families for an uncertain future. The fact that many ex-GDR footballers, with exceptions such as Nachtweih, struggled in the *Bundesliga* was not lost on those who stayed behind.

Despite the resources that it poured into observing the game, the *Stasi* was as vulnerable as any interested party to football's resistance to order and planning, its complex web of competing interests, and the seeming irrationality of its local patriotism. As the false alarm of René Müller's rumoured *Republikflucht* illustrated, the secret police and other powerful organs (the SED, the DTSB, and the DFV) did not always work as a team. For leading clubs, even when they were infiltrated with informants,

110 Thiemann, *Der Feind an meiner Seite*, pp. 258, 285–6.
111 Dennis, *The Stasi*, pp. 242–6.
112 *Ibid.*, p. 133.
113 Leske, *Erich Mielke*, p. 564.
114 Interview with BFC fans.

getting results took precedence over guaranteeing security – hence Chemie Leipzig's decision to include Klaus Günther in its squad for a European match in Belgium in 1966 and BFC's decision to do likewise with Falko Götz for their European Cup tie in Yugoslavia seventeen years later. Lower down the football ladder it was a similar story. The chairman of BSG Fortschritt Neustadt wrote to Mielke in the summer of 1982 to request authorisation for Peter Kotte, the team's leading scorer as it won the Dresden county league during the previous season, to play in the *Liga* during the upcoming campaign. He and his colleagues also refused to cooperate in providing the *Deutsches Sport-Echo* with a team photo from which Kotte's face was removed.[115] Kotte's ban was not overturned and the airbrushed picture was published. But functionaries at Fortschritt Neustadt, like colleagues at football sections across the republic, sought wherever possible to question directives from above that damaged their interests. In the process they asserted an *Eigen-Sinn* that made football, in Simon Kuper's words, a 'slippery tool' in the hands of dictatorships.[116]

*Stasi* surveillance of football, like *Stasi* surveillance generally, fed the disharmony and dissension that it was meant to eradicate, undermining socialist cohesion and creating more problems than over-matched officers could monitor or solve.[117] Writing about youthful dissenters such as the swing youth and the Edelweiß Pirates during the final years of the Nazi regime, Detlev Peukert observed that 'parts of society increasingly slipped from its grasp, the more it perfected its formal armoury of methods of organisation and repression'.[118] Something similar occurred in the GDR. As more IMs were deployed after 1971, many of whom provided little intelligence of value, incidents of *Republikflucht* among footballers increased. Greater control did not prevent clubs from prioritising their interests over those of the national team, any more than it prevented supporters from following West German teams or behaving badly at away games. BFC's dominance of the *Oberliga* during the 1980s – built at least partly on a network of reliable 'sports friends' among referees – angered not only fans, but also the game's administrators and leading party functionaries such as Hellmann and Krenz, who were embarrassed by the favouritism shown towards the *Stasi* team. The interests of the MfS, the party, the sports authorities,

115 BStU, MfS HA XX/2698, Information über Diskussionen zu Veröffentlichungen, 27 August 1982, fo. 61.

116 Quoted in Edelman, *Spartak Moscow*, p. 3.

117 Betts, *Within Walls*, p. 49.

118 Detlev Peukert, *Inside Nazi Germany: Conformity, Opposition and Racism in Everyday Life*, trans. Richard Deveson (London: Batsford, 1987), p. 175.

and the football clubs rarely coalesced into a united vision of how the game should be run. On this contested terrain, the secret police was both ubiquitous and strangely ineffective, supplying the hidden dimensions of the constrained autonomy that governed footballers' lives under East German communism.

*Part II*

# Fans

## Watching football under socialism

On 12 May 1968, 7,000 spectators packed into the Sportpark Paulshöhe to watch a second division match between SG Dynamo Schwerin and BFC. They were incensed by the referee's performance in the visitors' 2–1 victory. During the game Dynamo Schwerin fans booed, whistled, and tossed bottles onto the pitch. At full time, a BFC player was struck and injured by a stone thrown from the stands. Eight hundred fans then chased the referee to the dressing rooms, shouting 'strike him dead' and 'string him up'. Order was not restored until an hour after the match. Twenty people were arrested and a police van escorted the referee to the edge of town.[1]

The DFV investigated the unrest later that month and heard two very different stories. BFC's report condemned the unsporting behaviour of 'hundreds of fanatical supporters', the easy availability of alcohol, and the lax security measures.[2] The Dynamo Schwerin report emphasised the disciplined behaviour of the majority of fans, the club's previously unblemished record, and various technical and situational issues – the failure of the PA system in rainy conditions and the ninety-metre walk from the pitch to the changing rooms – that exacerbated a tense atmosphere. The chief cause of the unrest, it argued, was an 'inadequate and one-sided refereeing performance'.[3] Local media at least partially agreed. Whereas *Die Neue Fußball-Woche* mentioned neither the unrest nor the referee's performance

[1] SAPMO-BArch D0 101/1825/8, Bericht über die Verhandlung vor der Rechtskommission des Deutschen Fußball-Verbandes – Punktspiel SG Dynamo Schwerin gegen BFC Dynamo am 12. Mai 1968 in Schwerin, 29 May 1968; Bericht über das Fußballpunktspiel zwischen SG Dynamo Schwerin und BFC Dynamo am 12. Mai 1968 auf dem Sportpark Paulshöhe, 15 May 1968.

[2] *Ibid.*, Bericht über das Punktspiel SG Dynamo Schwerin–BFC Dynamo am 12. Mai 1968 in Schwerin, 14 May 1968.

[3] *Ibid.*, Bericht über das Fußballpunktspiel, 15 May 1968.

Figure 10. Union Berlin fans watching a home game against BFC, 1980. The crowd at Union's An der Alten Försterei ground had a raucous reputation. Werner Mahler's photograph, though, captures the many faces of fandom: supporters here variously look bored, excited, nervous, and cold. Note the almost uniform dress code of parka jackets and home-made scarves.

in its match report, the *Schweriner Volkszeitung*, the regional SED newspaper, spoke of the official's role in 'not always … bringing calm to the game'.[4]

The DFV investigation displayed little sympathy for the hosts. It highlighted the unrestricted sale of alcohol at the match (2,700 bottles of beer), which resulted in 70–80 per cent of 'rampaging' Schwerin fans being drunk. It criticised Dynamo Schwerin's self-serving report, which blamed the unrest on everyone but the club itself. As punishment, the DFV ordered the closure of the Paulshöhe ground for three months. Dynamo Schwerin's first four home games in the following season were to be played at venues outside Schwerin.[5] Players and staff issued a public statement condemning the disturbances and promising to work to prevent their repetition.[6]

Spectator unrest occurred throughout the history of East German football, from protests at regional championship games in the late 1940s

[4] Leske, *Erich Mielke*, pp. 481–2.
[5] SAPMO-BArch D0 101/1825/8, Bericht über die Verhandlung, 29 May 1968.
[6] Leske, *Erich Mielke*, pp. 485–6.

to the hooligan violence of the GDR's twilight years. The Dynamo Schwerin case was not unusual, even in 1968 – witness the fighting among rival fans after an *Oberliga* match between Chemie Leipzig and Union Berlin on 21 September.[7] It crystallises, though, themes that are central to understanding what it meant to be a football fan in the GDR. The Schwerin–BFC clash showed how matches could provide supporters, outraged by refereeing incompetence and fortified by alcohol, with a relatively low-risk means of rejecting communist behavioural norms. It foreshadowed the issue that dominated fan discourse in the 1980s: perceived favouritism from match officials towards the *Stasi* team, BFC. It showcased too a permanent feature of the football landscape: local patriotism. Dynamo Schwerin may have been a junior partner within the Dynamo organisation, but neither its fans nor its officials intended to allow the flagship team, BFC, an easy victory in May 1968. Tensions between the two clubs dated back to the mid 1960s, when functionaries complained about Dynamo Schwerin's reduction to the status of a feeder club for BFC through the delegation of its best players to the capital. Their ambition was to turn the Dynamo club into a performance centre for the county of Schwerin and to gain promotion to the *Oberliga*.[8] The fallout from the match on 12 May showed that not only local Dynamo officials, but also the local press and the Schwerin branch of the *Stasi*, failed to grasp the seriousness of the unrest.[9] Regional identities clashed here with the centralising ethos of the GDR sports system, with its desire to concentrate resources in a small number of elite clubs. The trouble at the Sportpark Paulshöhe illustrated football's singular potential to at least temporarily upset this system.

The traditional focus of football histories, in Germany and across much of the world, has been institutions, clubs, and players. Little was written about football as a spectator sport. The situation has altered radically in the last thirty years, on the back of scholarly research, particularly into the hooliganism that blighted European football in the 1980s, and a revival in football's popularity, indeed modishness, since the early 1990s. The literary catalyst of the latter tendency was Nick Hornby's *Fever Pitch*, an intelligent, humorous reflection on the pleasure and pain of supporting his boyhood team, Arsenal. Hornby's book captured a shifting *Zeitgeist* in its insistence that 'most football fans do not have a

[7] Union Berlin Archive, Stellungnahme des 1. FC Union Berlin zu den Vorkommnissen beim Oberliga-Punktspiel BSG Chemie Leipzig gegen den 1. FC Union am 21.9.1968, 25 October 1968.

[8] SAPMO-BArch D0 101/1825/8, Aktennotiz zum Instrukteureinsatz Schwerin, 11 June 1965.

[9] Leske, *Erich Mielke*, pp. 482–3.

criminal record, or carry knives, or urinate in pockets, or get up to any of the things that they are all supposed to'.[10] It sparked a cottage industry of books detailing fans' experiences of being fans that quickly spread beyond the UK, as a cursory examination of literature on GDR football confirms.[11]

Socialist spectatorship was meant to reflect the character of the socialist system. It was not merely to be, in the words of Robert Edelman, 'a pleasurable way of passing time'.[12] Rather, as Soviet *fizkultura* (physical culture) experts argued in the late 1920s, the new spectator should eschew passive consumption, conveying instead a sober, disciplined identification with the state.[13] The reality was very different. In communist regimes, where alternative identities and means of expression were restricted, football spectatorship came to stand for values almost diametrically opposed to the idealised official version. Social historians have increasingly come to recognise the importance of place – both private space (the home) and public space, including parks, pubs, railway stations, and recreational areas – in uncovering the history of everyday life: how people interacted with each other and how they interacted with structures of power.[14] The football stadium is exemplary in this regard. It offered an autonomous enclave that allowed people to temporarily escape the political rules that constrained many areas of their existence.[15] At a match, Peter Handke wrote in 1965, 'the laws of daily life are to some extent repealed'.[16]

'To be a fan', stated the Armenian anthropologist Levon Abramian, 'is to be gathered with others and to be free'.[17] The sentiment was as applicable to the GDR as it was to the Soviet Union. Football, in the words of one Union Berlin fan, provided a 'free space', where, in the comfort of a crowd, you could 'go underground'.[18] A football ground was contested terrain, an ambiguous public/private sphere that brought people together ephemerally, in ways that were neither radically dissenting nor regime-endorsing.

[10] Nick Hornby, *Fever Pitch* (London: Victor Gollancz, 1992), p. 96.

[11] See e.g. Gläser, *Der BFC war schuld*; Pätzug, *Was wir niemals waren*; Willmann (ed.), *Zonenfussball*.

[12] Edelman, *Serious Fun*, p. 6.

[13] Mike O'Mahony, *Sport in the USSR: Physical Culture – Visual Culture* (London: Reaktion, 2006), pp. 63–5.

[14] Paul Steege, Andrew Stuart Bergerson, Maureen Healy, and Pamela E. Swett, 'The history of everyday life: a second chapter', *Journal of Modern History* vol. 80, no. 2 (June 2008), 363–8.

[15] Dunning, *Sport Matters*, pp. 3–4.

[16] Peter Handke, 'Die Welt im Fußball', in *Ich bin ein Bewohner des Elfenbeinturms* (Frankfurt: Suhrkamp, 1972), p. 138.

[17] Kuper, *Football against the Enemy*, p. 46.

[18] Interview with Tino C., 25 May 2011. A Dynamo Dresden fan likewise described the stadium as a 'very free space'. Interview with Jens Genschmar.

Football's importance as a liminal activity, one which allowed people to 'be themselves' in otherwise highly regulated social conditions, is exemplified by the experience of spectatorship in the GDR.[19]

Part II of this book offers an in-depth study of fans and fan culture, using a range of archival sources, including fan mail, petitions, and *Stasi* reports, as well as interviews with people who went to watch the game. It begins, in Chapter 7, with an examination of spectatorship during the Ulbricht era (1949–71), when football, at least as a live experience, was at its peak of popularity. The chapters which follow investigate various aspects of fandom during the Honecker years (1971–89): the emergence of a loud, youthful, and independent fan culture (Chapter 8); the growth of hooliganism (Chapter 9); and the public mutiny against BFC's dominance (Chapter 10).

The book's three central arguments underpin the material presented in Part II. The game, first, provided a means by which fans, like players, could preserve or develop an *Eigen-Sinn* that allowed them to posit identities – individual, local, class, national, and transnational – that did not conform to communist ideals. It was, to use the words of one Soviet sports historian, 'a small way of saying "no"'.[20] The autonomous enclaves that fans attempted to carve out for themselves, from their peers as well as from the state, point to a second major conclusion: the limits and even dysfunctionality of the SED dictatorship, which consistently failed to keep a lid on spectator unrest or other manifestations of a stubbornly self-regulating fan culture. Football proved to be a slippery customer – a place of multi-layered rival interests, not to mention drinking, obscene chanting, and pitch invasions, that ran counter to the party's vision of spectatorship. Equally, though, fans were never able to operate entirely beyond state influences. Football's public spaces were ultimately sites of give and take, indicative of the blurred boundaries between state and society, and between protest and conformity, that characterised the East German dictatorship.

[19] Turner, *The Forest of Symbols*, pp. 93–111.

[20] Robert Edelman, 'A small way of saying "no": Moscow working men, Spartak soccer, and the Communist Party, 1900–1945', *The American Historical Review* vol. 107, no. 5 (December 2002), 1442.

# 7 Spectatorship in the Ulbricht era

## Football and the Stalinist aesthetic

The 100,000-capacity Zentralstadion in Leipzig was the jewel in the GDR's sporting crown. Begun in March 1955, and completed with the help of volunteer labour in time for the showpiece Gymnastics and Sports Festival in August 1956, the imposing structure was a source of civic pride in Leipzig and drew admiring comments from people on both sides of the German border.[1] Like the Stadionul 23 August in Bucharest, the Népstadion in Budapest, the Lenin Stadium in Moscow, and the Stadion Dziesięciolecia in Warsaw, it embodied the Stalinist aesthetic that characterised stadium design behind the Iron Curtain during the 1950s: 'a vast, serious, open bowl, formed by earth banking and lined with benched seats divided into forty blocks'.[2] On 6 October 1956, the Zentralstadion hosted a football match between the East German champions, Wismut Karl-Marx-Stadt, and the West German champions, Kaiserslautern. The latter featured five players from the West German team that had defeated Hungary in the 1954 World Cup final. A crowd of 110,000 people crammed in, 10,000 of whom stood in the stairway entrances. They witnessed a 5–3 win for the visitors that was immortalised by Fritz Walter's 'forgotten goal of the century', a back-heel volley, struck from fifteen yards out as he fell forward to meet a cross that arrived behind him.[3]

The media coverage of Kaiserslautern's visit reminds us how strong the sense of shared German sporting identity was in the 1950s, despite the political impasse between Bonn and East Berlin. Writing in *Die Neue Fußball-Woche* three days after the game, Heinz-Florian Oertel spoke in awed terms of the 'European super team' from the Palatinate: 'Kaiserslautern was a magnet, Fritz Walter its nucleus'. Here was an international sports star, he wrote, on a par with the Hungarian footballer

1 Johnson, *Training Socialist Citizens*, pp. 113–24.
2 Inglis, *The Football Grounds of Europe*, p. 161.
3 Bröder-Jürgen Trede, 'Das vergessene Jahrhunderttor', *Spiegel-Online*, 6 October 2006: www.spiegel.de/sport/fussball/0,1518,440986,00.html.

Figure 11. Football in the 1950s: a scene from a match between Turbine Erfurt and Vorwärts Berlin, 1955. Vorwärts defender Werner Eilitz (left) – who played in the GDR's first official match against Poland in 1952 – challenges Turbine's star striker, Siegfried Vollrath. The packed stands, muddy pitch, and heavy-looking ball are typical of the period.

Ferenc Puskás and the Czechoslovakian distance runner Emil Zátopek.[4] Newspapers noted proudly the scale of interest in the game. The *Deutsches Sport-Echo* reported that more than 300,000 orders were placed within hours of tickets going on sale to the public.[5]

Despite the upheaval that characterised GDR football in the 1950s, spectators came to matches in large numbers. A crowd of 100,000 fans watched the *Oberliga* match at the Zentralstadion between local rivals Rotation Leipzig and Lokomotive Leipzig in September 1956, still the record attendance for a domestic fixture in Germany. The *Oberliga* attendance record was set in the 1951/2 season, when 3.6 million spectators came through the turnstiles.[6] Elsewhere, it was a similar story.

[4] '"Rote Teufel" brachten Fieber', *Die Neue Fußball-Woche*, 9 October 1956, 4.

[5] "Stadion der Hunderttausend noch zu klein", *DSE* article, n.d., in Archivgut des DFV, XV/63/4/7.

[6] Horn and Weise, *Das große Lexikon*, p. 379, 419.

During the 1953 season, more than 3.9 million people attended the 110 matches in the Soviet league (an average gate of 35,000). In England aggregate attendance reached a peak of 41 million in 1949 and remained above 30 million until the early 1960s.[7] In an age when televised coverage of sport was in its infancy, football spectatorship essentially meant the live consumption of matches.

This chapter investigates the experiences of fans during the Ulbricht years, focusing on two themes central to understanding the game's contested status in the GDR: supporters' resistant attitudes to the restructuring of football (most notably club relocations) and incidents of spectator unrest. They affirm the fraught and fluid relationship between fans, obstinate (*eigensinnig*) in defence of their limited sporting autonomy, and the state, fractured and often ineffective in its attempts to put football's unruly house in order. The chapter concludes by examining the evolution of spectatorship, from the predominance of live attendance at matches in the 1950s to the various armchair options widely available by the end of the following decade. The evolution reflected wider shifts in society, as the Ulbricht regime moved from the neo-Stalinist austerity of its early years to a cautious embrace of socio-economic reform and cultural diversification after 1961.

## (Re-)location: defending local interests in the 1950s

For most of the twentieth century, a 'conservative tendency' towards localism was an important feature of global football culture.[8] In Germany, local patriotism, and attempts to combat it, long predated the GDR. Plans to streamline Saxon football in 1919/20 and 1922/3 broke down in the face of resistance from individual clubs, and their supporters, in Chemnitz, Dresden, and Leipzig. What Rudolf Oswald calls 'the regionalisation of local identity', a reduction of the number of elite teams in a given city or region, was an ongoing process between 1930 and 1950.[9] Just like its predecessors, the SED regime struggled to enforce its will on recalcitrant football cultures. In East Germany, local identities – as expressed through football teams, carnivals, or Mayday festivals – were flexible and robust, in stark contrast to the static, party-imposed construct of GDR national identity.[10]

In the autumn of 1951, rumours swirled around the Saxon town of Zwickau that Heinz Satrapa, the local team's star player, had been

7 Edelman, *Serious Fun*, pp. 160–1; Goldblatt, *The Ball Is Round*, p. 333.
8 Hargreaves, *Sport, Power and Culture*, pp. 106–9.
9 Oswald, *"Fußball-Volksgemeinschaft"*, pp. 247–52.
10 Palmowski, *Inventing a Socialist Nation*, pp. 303–4.

offered substantial sums of money to move to SG Volkspolizei Dresden. The indignant response of local workers, many of whom were employed at the Horch automobile factory that sponsored BSG Motor Zwickau, made clear their sense of ownership. 'Satrapa has been developed first by Zwickau', asserted one woman, 'and belongs to Motor Zwickau'.[11] The player's move to Dresden was apparently called off at the last minute, after a taxi driver overheard Satrapa in conversation with visiting Dresden players. Showing commendable civic pride, he told Motor Zwickau officials about the rendez-vous. They arrived early the following morning at Satrapa's flat to make sure that he did not go anywhere.[12]

An indicator of how football could quickly stray into hazardous political territory, the 'Satrapa matter' was taken very seriously by the party leadership, including Ulbricht himself. The People's Police (VP) was at the heart of the GDR's nascent, and highly unpopular, remilitarisation campaign. The authorities quickly engaged in a damage-limitation exercise in Zwickau, framing Satrapa as the villain of the piece and attempting to dampen the anti-VP sentiments inflamed by Volkspolizei Dresden's underhand tactics.[13] The regime's sensitivity to local politics may have been reinforced by recent history. Motor (previously Horch) Zwickau was a workers' team that had evolved from a merger of three clubs, including SG Planitz, who (as we saw in Chapter 2) resisted incorporation into the communist-led sports movement in the late 1940s. Names changed in GDR football, but patterns of behaviour did not. In the 1970s and 1980s, the same club, known after 1968 as Sachsenring Zwickau, became a focal point for complaints about the neglect of factory teams and concomitant favouring of elite sides such as BFC and Dynamo Dresden, both of which were sponsored by the police state.

Local concerns, to the frustration of those charged with raising standards, were fiercely defended against the greater good. 'Everyone', as Fritz Gödicke later noted, 'wanted top-class football'.[14] Fans seldom prevented transfers, at best delaying them. Denied a move to Dresden in 1951, Satrapa joined Wismut Aue a year later. Nonetheless, the uproar among Zwickau fans had to be kept in mind. It was risky to ignore local or regional interests, as the issue of club relocations soon showed with greater force.

[11] SAPMO-BArch DY 12/2695, Mißstimmung über Machenschaften im Fußballsport, 23 October 1951, fo. 10–12.

[12] *Ibid.*, statement from Heinz Satrapa, 4 November 1951, fo. 17.

[13] *Ibid.*, letter from Fritz Gödicke to Edith Baumann, 15 November 1951, fo. 6; Stellungnahme der Sportvereinigung Deutsche Volkspolizei zu der Angelegenheit Satrapa, Motor Zwickau, 17 September 1951, fo. 18–20

[14] Archivgut des DFV, XV/63/4/1, notes on 'DDR-Fußball', n.d.

Jan Palmowski has noted how, in the GDR's foundational period, 'a tension developed between the preservation of tradition implicit in the ideal of heimat, and the socialist emphasis on reconstruction and transformation'.[15] A similar tension was apparent in football. A golden rule of football culture stipulates that a team's identity is fixed in the town or even neighbourhood in which it plays. The SED had no truck with such traditionalism. The result was a glut of name changes and relocations, echoing similar processes in Soviet and Hungarian football.[16] In the most extreme example, the army team founded as VP Vorwärts Leipzig in 1951 underwent no fewer than thirteen name changes and two relocations (to Berlin in 1953 and then to Frankfurt/Oder in 1971) over the course of the following forty years, ending up with the post-*Wende* name Frankfurter FC Viktoria 91.[17] Though remaining in one place, a further eight *Oberliga* clubs underwent either six or seven name changes during the same period.[18]

Interesting case studies of relocation, or attempted relocation, emerge from the restructuring of 1954, when eight of the fourteen *Oberliga* clubs were re-designated as elite sports clubs. Three of them were instructed to move in the middle of the season: SG Dynamo Dresden to Berlin (to become SC Dynamo Berlin – discussed in Chapter 10), BSG Empor Lauter to Rostock (to become SC Empor Rostock), and BSG Wismut Aue to Karl-Marx-Stadt (to become SC Wismut Karl-Marx-Stadt).[19]

At the time of their last game, a 1–0 win against Rotation Babelsberg on 24 October 1954, Empor Lauter occupied first place in the *Oberliga*. For a recently promoted team from a town of 8,000 inhabitants, this was a sensational achievement. The Cinderella story, however, did not sit well with the communist desire to develop a select number of football centres. Lauter were the smallest of no fewer than four *Oberliga* teams in Saxony, the hotbed of football in the East. In contrast, northern regions of the republic such as Mecklenburg lacked leading clubs. A plan was conceived to move Empor Lauter to the Baltic port city of Rostock, home to a new stadium and home base for the trade-union boss and passionate football fan Harry Tisch.[20]

15 Palmowski, *Inventing a Socialist Nation*, p. 63.

16 Edelman, *Serious Fun*, pp. 102–9; Viktor Karády and Miklós Hadas, 'Soccer and Antisemitism in Hungary', in Michael Brenner and Gideon Reuveni (eds.), *Emancipation through Muscles: Jews and Sport in Europe* (Lincoln and London: University of Nebraska Press, 2006), pp. 217–22.

17 Leske, *Erich Mielke*, p. 122.

18 Willmann (ed.), *Zonenfussball*, pp. 212–13.

19 Leske, *Erich Mielke*, pp. 132–3.

20 On the move from Lauter to Rostock, see Hesselmann and Rosentritt, *Hansa Rostock*, pp. 21–32; Leske, *Erich Mielke*, pp. 132–6.

On 26 October, Lauter's forthcoming match against Motor Zwickau was cancelled.[21] Two days later, at three o'clock in the morning, the Lauter squad left for Rostock via train. The departure time indicated the fear of public reprisals that governed the thinking of Empor officials. Rumours had circulated in the town for several weeks, however, and the railway station was occupied by Lauter fans even at that early hour. The show of strength apparently persuaded four of the fifteen players to stay behind. Removal vans took the players' possessions north a day earlier. Only police intervention prevented angry fans from overturning the vehicles as they were being loaded up. Relatives of the 'traitors', a number of whom had grown up in the Lauter area, were shunned. They were not served in shops or even spoken to.[22] The four players who refused to move included captain and playmaker Walter Espig. In a subsequent letter protesting against Empor Rostock's attempts to prevent them from joining local *Oberliga* side Motor Zwickau, Espig reminded functionaries of the 'great indignation' triggered among fans in the Erzgebirge (Ore Mountains) by recent events. He warned that 'another mistake' should not be added to those committed by SV Empor in engineering the move to Rostock.[23]

Fans in Lauter were powerless to prevent relocation. The move to Rostock gave players wider employment opportunities, better flats, and higher wages. It was a different story in the case of Lauter's near neighbours, BSG Wismut Aue, 'the team of the Erzgebirge'.[24] Aue's planned move to the *Bezirk* capital Karl-Marx-Stadt in 1954 collapsed in the face of local resistance. Miners working in the prestigious, Soviet-backed Wismut uranium industry threatened to down tools if their team was moved an hour down the road. Football in Aue was anchored in an organisation of great political and economic importance. Wismut *Kumpels* (mates), working in dangerous and unhealthy conditions, knew their value: 'We are Wismut', they boasted, 'we are invulnerable'.[25] They also had a reputation for political volatility. The GDR's 'first strike', involving 3,000 Wismut miners and civilians, took place in Saalfeld in August 1951.[26] Given the circumstances, the authorities backed down – a striking admission of football's importance as a symbol of working-class identity. In a bizarre compromise, Aue took the new

[21] SAPMO-BArch, DR 5/129, Absetzung der nächsten Oberliga-Spiele der Mannschaft Empor Lauter, 26 October 1954.

[22] Hesselmann and Rosentritt, *Hansa Rostock*, pp. 24–7.

[23] SAPMO-BArch, DY 34/3800, Beschwerde gegen die SV "Empor" wegen Freigabe der Oberligaspieler Espig, Vogel und Hertsch, 24 November 1954.

[24] Archivgut des DFV, XV/63/4/1, notes on 'DDR-Fußball', n.d.

[25] Port, *Conflict and Stability*, p. 56. [26] *Ibid.*, pp. 46–69.

appellation SC Wismut Karl-Marx-Stadt in November 1954, but continued to play in Aue.[27] The players themselves, also prepared to strike to prevent relocation, apparently regarded the fudged solution as the 'lesser evil'.[28]

Fans, then, were not passive recipients of party orders. Local teams, even local teams of recent, socialist provenance, could engender intense loyalty, particularly in Saxony. In the decade of socialist reconstruction, which was characterised by long working hours, rationing, ubiquitous propaganda, a scarcity of consumer goods, and limited leisure-time entertainment, watching football provided an affordable and regular diversion from the drudgery of everyday life. To have it suddenly and arbitrarily removed – as happened in Lauter and Dresden, and nearly happened in Aue, in 1954 – caused great, and festering, resentment. Fans did not forget. When Empor Rostock played in Saxony, even years later, their players were booed and abused as 'fish heads' (*Fischköppe*) by Aue and Zwickau fans.[29] Dynamo Dresden, even as they tumbled down the football pyramid in the late 1950s, maintained a loyal fan base that their successor Dynamo Berlin, resettled in the capital in November 1954, struggled to match. A bitter rivalry, shaped by durable stereotypes about Prussians and Saxons, developed between supporters of the two Dynamo teams as they fought for domestic supremacy in the 1970s and 1980s. Local and regional identities possessed a dynamism and immediacy that the national project of building socialism lacked, in sport and elsewhere.

The Lauter and Aue cases illustrate the give and take characteristic of GDR football, namely the ways in which it made uniform problem-solving impossible and drew the SED, however reluctantly, into consideration of local politics. The authorities were prepared to be flexible when faced with fan unrest in a key economic centre such as Aue. But they were prepared to be ruthless in moving a small-town team to an important regional hub (Rostock), where inhabitants enthusiastically welcomed a transplanted *Oberliga* outfit. Fans of Empor Lauter were not so lucky. Their decimated team, left to play in the county and district leagues, never recovered from the events of 1954. The independent spaces that supporters made for themselves could easily be taken away in the GDR. Theirs was a constrained autonomy, played out on a muddled and highly politicised template.

[27] Leske, *Erich Mielke*, pp. 144–5.

[28] Dennis and Grix, *Sport under Communism*, p. 140; Archivgut des DFV, XV/63/4/7, untitled notes, n.d.

[29] Hesselmann and Rosentritt, *Hansa Rostock*, p. 26.

## Unsocialist spectatorship: fans behaving badly

In April 1950, ZSG Horch Zwickau travelled to Dresden for a title-deciding match against SG Dresden Friedrichstadt. In a heated local derby, pitting a new workers' team (Horch) against the popular heir to the last champions of the Nazi era, the away team emerged with a 5–1 victory that owed a great deal, according to many witnesses, to aggressive tackling and friendly refereeing. At least 60,000 people watched the game, including Walter Ulbricht, who expressed post-game sympathies for the victorious, and red-shirted, 'worker sportsmen' from Zwickau.[30] The troubles that other incarnations of the Horch club gave the regime (SG Planitz in 1949, for example, or Motor Zwickau in 1951) remind us that, despite the party leader's wishes, a working-class label was no guarantee of political loyalty.

The result, combined with overcrowding on the terraces – 'like a surging cornfield', as Fritz Gödicke's wife recalled in 1982[31] – led to trouble. At the final whistle, thousands of Ulbricht's fellow onlookers broke through a police cordon onto the pitch. A Zwickau player was assaulted and it took mounted police to eventually restore order. Friedrichstadt's home ground was closed for six months. The team, whose future had been uncertain before the game, was disbanded. By the time that its remnants were handed over to the minnows of BSG Tabak Dresden, most of the players, including the later West German coach Helmut Schön, had left for West Berlin.[32]

There was nothing new about spectator unrest in Germany. Between 1924 and 1933, as football became an essential part of Weimar mass culture, fans in Mannheim alone caused no fewer than thirty disturbances. The press recounted similar incidents in cities such as Breslau, Dresden, Frankfurt, and Leipzig. Violent confrontations, usually on the occasion of local derbies, continued in many places under the Nazi dictatorship.[33] Reports from rural West Germany during the 1950s reveal that matches – like festivals, fairs, and weddings – were regular sites of aggression, as fans fought each other, staged pitch invasions, and attacked referees.[34] According to the socialist theory of spectatorship,

[30] Dieckmann, "Nur ein Leutzscher", p. 313.

[31] Archivgut des DFV, XV/63/4/1, letter from Gerda Gödicke to Klaus Huhn, 26 August 1982.

[32] Leske, *Enzyklopädie*, pp. 7–11; Hesse-Lichtenberger, *Tor!*, pp. 225–6.

[33] Oswald, *"Fußball-Volksgemeinschaft"*, pp. 261–82.

[34] Hubert Dwertmann and Bero Rigauer, 'Football hooliganism in Germany: a developmental sociological study', in Eric Dunning, Patrick Murphy, Ivan Waddington, and Antonios A. Astrinakis (eds.), *Fighting Fans: Football Hooliganism as a World Phenomenon* (Dublin: University College Dublin Press, 2002), p. 79.

things should have been otherwise in the GDR. Yet, from Schwerin in the north to Dresden in the south, spectator unrest was commonplace, showcasing unwelcome parallels with the tainted football past and the rival football present. In Halle, four grounds were closed following spectator brawls during the 1952/3 season. Seven years later in the same county, the police reported three pitch invasions, and two further minor incidents, in the first two months of the season.[35] Before the more ritualised fan violence of the 1970s and 1980s, and the extensive measures to counter its proliferation, stadia were less heavily policed. But crowds were larger and, arguably, more unpredictable. Three cases of spectators behaving badly, taken from *Oberliga* and county league matches between 1955 and 1963, provide a fascinating glimpse of everyday life in Ulbricht's GDR.

'Why are we protecting the referee? Hand him over to the crowd'. These were the words allegedly spoken by Wilhelm Hoffmeyer, an SC Turbine Erfurt defender, after his team's match with Empor Rostock on 23 October 1955. The referee in question, Karl Schönebeck, had enraged home players and fans alike with a performance that even *Die Neue Fußball-Woche* described as inadequate.[36] It culminated in the awarding of a late penalty to the visitors, who escaped with a 2–2 draw. Hoffmeyer and Turbine's star player, Helmut Nordhaus, hotly contested the decision. The latter kicked the ball off the penalty spot, spat in Schönebeck's direction, and called him a cheat. Spectators poured onto the pitch at the final whistle. They bundled past an inadequate security presence (122 stewards for a crowd of 16,000) and, armed with beer bottles, headed for Schönebeck. Nobody was seriously injured, as players and functionaries formed a cordon around the officials, though Schönebeck was scratched in the face by one fan as he neared the safety of the main stand. Riot police dispersed the crowd. Schönebeck left the ground safely.[37] The Turbine squad, *Oberliga* winners in the past two seasons, publicly apologised for behaviour 'unworthy of the reputation of our champion team' and condemned the 'small percentage of our fans'

[35] LHASA, MER, RdB Halle, Nr. 4053, Massnahmen zur Verbesserung der Arbeit auf dem Gebiete des Fussballsportes im Bezirk Halle, 26 May 1953, fo. 10; LHASA, MER, BDVP Halle 19, Nr. 133, Stellungnahme zu den Vorkommnissen anläßlich des Fußball-Oberligaspiels ASK-Vorwärts Berlin gegen SC Chemie Halle am 16.11.1960 im Kurt Wabbel-Stadion in Halle, 30 November 1960, fo. 175–85.

[36] 'Notbesetzung prüfte die Empor-Abwehr ernsthaft', *Die Neue Fußball-Woche*, 25 October 1955, 3.

[37] SAPMO-BArch, DY 12/307, Protokoll über die Rechtsausschuß-Tagung am 4.11.1955 in Berlin Deutscher Sporthalle, fo. 5–13.

who tried to attack the referee.[38] The DFV banned Hoffmeyer for three months and Nordhaus, a former national team captain, for five months. Turbine's ground was closed for three months.[39]

Five years later the army team Vorwärts Berlin, league champions in 1958, travelled to Halle knowing that victory against relegation-threatened SC Chemie could ensure a second title in three years. The match on 16 November 1960 followed a familiar pattern: a poor refereeing performance (again from the unfortunate Karl Schönebeck), epitomised by the awarding of a dubious penalty to the visitors (in this case to give Vorwärts a 2–0 lead), that sparked anger on the terraces. At the final whistle, a group of 150–200 youths gathered at the Western exit of the stadium. They abused the officials ('we'll snatch the ref and attack him!') and the Vorwärts players, who were described in politically loaded terms as 'pros . . . state amateurs'. Fans attacked an army vehicle parked near the exit. Plans to prevent the Vorwärts team bus from departing were foiled only when police moved it to another location. Fifteen people were arrested for public order offences.[40]

On 16 June 1963 Motor Wema Plauen and Motor Eisenach met in a county league play-off match to decide who would be promoted to the second division. Played at a neutral venue in Rudolstadt, the game was heading Eisenach's way with fifteen minutes remaining, as they held a 2–0 lead. The referee, Karl Trautvetter, then disallowed a Plauen goal. One enraged Plauen fan vaulted the security barrier onto the pitch and struck him on the head with an umbrella. The match was delayed for five minutes while Trautvetter received medical treatment and other fans were cleared from the pitch by stewards. On resumption Plauen reduced the arrears to 2–1, but could not find an equaliser. At the end of the match 400 Plauen fans invaded the pitch, threw beer bottles at the stewards, and tried to attack the referee, who received a cut to the shin. Order was restored only after police intervention.[41]

[38] SAPMO-BArch, DY 34/3800, Stellungnahme der Oberligamannschaft des SC Turbine Erfurt zu den Vorfällen im Spiel gegen SC Empor Rostock am 23.10.1955 in Erfurt, n.d.

[39] SAPMO-BArch, DY 12/307, Protokoll über die Rechtsausschuß-Tagung, fo. 12–13; Leske, *Enzyklopädie*, p. 339.

[40] LHASA, Mer, BDVP Halle 19, Nr. 133, Stellungnahme zu den Vorkommnissen, fo. 183–97.

[41] SAPMO-BArch, DY 12/5335, Gemeinsame Erklärung der Leitung der BPO, BGL, BSG und des Werkleiters des VEB Automobilwerk Eisenach zu den Vorkommnissen des Qualifikationsspieles zwischen Motor Wema Plauen und Motor Eisenach am 16.6.1963 in Rudolstadt, n.d., fo. 214–16; letter from BSG Einheit Rudolstadt to the DFV, 27 June 1963, fo. 366–7; Bericht des Schiedsrichters über die Vorkommnisse im Spiel BSG Motor Wema Plauen/Motor Eisenach, 17 June 1963, fo. 395–6.

The recriminations were as heated as the match-day unrest. Motor Eisenach officials condemned the 'fascist-like riots', pointing out that they had occurred on the eve of the tenth anniversary of the June 1953 Uprising, and accused their opponents of staging the umbrella attack in order to get the game called off.[42] Motor Plauen robustly attempted to keep alive their promotion hopes. Officials charged Eisenach with fielding an ineligible player. Somewhat brazenly, given the identity of the culprit, they argued that the referee was unfit to officiate after being struck on the head and had subsequently failed to keep time.[43] Plauen fans sent petitions to the DFV protesting against the 'shameful result' of the promotion decider. One threatened strike action. Others pointed out that the referee was from Immelborn, only twenty-two kilometres from Eisenach, and that one of the DFV's leading officials, Karl-Heinz Benedix, was from Eisenach.[44] When the dust settled in early July, the DFV rejected Plauen's protests and upheld the original result.[45]

There are several recurring themes in the three incidents: questionable officiating; frustrated players; pitch invasions; the consumption of alcohol; inadequate stewarding; violence, or threatened violence, towards the referee; and police intervention. What do they tell us about spectatorship and society during the Ulbricht era? It is instructive to begin with an analysis of who took part in fan disorder in Erfurt in 1955, Halle in 1960, and Rudolstadt in 1963. In the former case, we know little more than what the match report in *Die Neue Fußball-Woche* tells us: that the thousands who invaded the pitch 'to vent their wrath on the referee' were mostly 'children and young people'.[46]

Somewhat more detailed information can be gleaned from the petitions sent by Motor Plauen fans to the DFV in 1963, though there is no way of checking whether they participated in the pitch invasion that followed the game against Motor Eisenach. Some communications were anonymous, such as the handwritten letter from 'thousands of Plauen football supporters' that – echoing the Wismut *Kumpels* in Aue nine years earlier – threatened a strike.[47] Individuals generally gave little personal information. But, clearly, they were ordinary East German males, not anti-socialist provocateurs. Many worked at the factory that

[42] *Ibid.*, Gemeinsame Erklärung, fo. 214–16.
[43] *Ibid.*, letter from Motor Wema Plauen to the DFV, 1 July 1963, fo. 307–12.
[44] *Ibid.*, petitions from Plauen football fans, Klaus B., and Heinz Z. to the DFV, 18 June 1963, fo. 376, 372, 389–90.
[45] *Ibid.*, Protokoll über die Berufung der BSG Motor Eisenach gegen das Urteil des Spielausschusses vom 5.7.1963, fo. 219–22.
[46] 'Notbesetzung prüfte die Empor-Abwehr ernsthaft', 3.
[47] SAPMO-BArch, DY 12/5335, petition from Plauen fans, 18 June 1963, fo. 376.

sponsored the Plauen team. Those who pleaded Plauen's case included 31-year-old Heinz Z., who blamed the DFV, rather than the fans or the referee, for what happened; a factory doctor who asserted that the referee ignored his advice not to return to the pitch after being struck on the head; and a 'neutral' supporter (from Plauen!) who claimed to have kept accurate time at the match and that the second half lasted only forty minutes. There was even a letter from a fan who helped to apprehend the fellow Plauen supporter who struck the referee with an umbrella.[48]

The most penetrating profile of football troublemakers came from the Chemie Halle–Vorwärts Berlin match in 1960. Halle police emphasised the influence of the 'class enemy' in fomenting unrest at football grounds, just as they blamed Western pop culture for unsavoury manifestations of youth subculture based around leather jackets, motorbikes, sex, and rock'n'roll.[49] The evidence, though, painted a more complex picture. Six of those arrested at the stadium on 16 November faced criminal charges. All were from Halle, of working-class origins, and in regular employment. Five of them were FDGB members. Four were members of the FDJ. Only one of the six, the plumber Horst N., was not a member of any mass organisations. He had been a member of the Evangelical Church youth group, the *Junge Gemeinden* – a major target of the Ulbricht regime during the period of 'accelerated socialist construction' in 1952 and 1953[50] – and had twice tried to leave the GDR for the West. A twenty-six-volume cache of Western 'pulp' literature, the kind of cheap novels and comics whose corrupting influence was repeatedly flagged up in SED and FDJ reports during the 1950s, was confiscated from his home. Various political and educational red flags were raised against the other five. Eberhard R., an instigator of the thwarted attack on the Vorwärts team bus, had been warned about his 'uncouth' behaviour in his neighbourhood. His father, a former Nazi Party member, had died in 1953 and his mother lacked influence on him. The bricklayer Peter R., born out of wedlock and raised by his mother, had been dismissed from his volunteer work with the police when he started hanging around pubs with 'negative' youths. The welder Uwe A. had spent three months in prison for assault earlier in 1960. His father lived in West Germany.[51]

48 *Ibid.*, see various petitions/letters to the DFV, 18–20 June 1963, fo. 383–5, 389–90.

49 LHASA, Mer, BDVP Halle 19, Nr. 133, Stellungnahme zu den Vorkommnissen, fo. 173–4. On youth subcultures of the 1950s, see Fenemore, *Sex, Thugs and Rock'n'Roll*, especially chs. 6 and 9.

50 See e.g. McDougall, *Youth Politics*, pp. 42–7.

51 LHASA, Mer, BDVP Halle 19, Nr. 133, Stellungnahme zu den Vorkommnissen, fo. 188–92.

Yet, by the police's own admission, this was not an organised 'pack' (*Meute*), i.e. not the kind of macho gang that colonised public spaces such as street corners, parks, and cinemas during the 1950s.[52] No contacts with the West or even previous association with each other were proven among the six. Two were active contributors to socialist society. Apprentice welder Rainer K. was a member of four mass organisations and had a leadership role in the paramilitary sports organisation, the Society for Sport and Technology (*Gesellschaft für Sport und Technik*, GST). Klaus-Peter S., also an apprentice welder, was a member of three mass organisations and sang in the factory choir. His stepfather was an SED member and officially designated 'victim of fascism'.[53] Just as the Halle football hooligans arrested in 1988 were average young East Germans (as shown in Chapter 10), so the Halle six arrested in 1960 offered a cross-section of GDR youth. They were working-class boys born and raised in the Halle area, whose behaviour and experiences embodied major themes of growing up in 1950s East Germany. Some of them came from fatherless homes, a legacy of the destruction wrought by the Second World War: in 1955 there were 7.97 million men in the GDR, compared with 9.86 million women.[54] One had twice attempted *Republikflucht*: 36.1 per cent of all emigrants to West Germany between 1957 and 1960 were aged between fifteen and twenty-five.[55] All six were drawn to the cultural products of capitalism, including enemy influences such as Radio Luxemburg and 'Wild West' pulp fiction. Yet they participated, sometimes quite actively, in communist organisations. It was this kind of young male, we can surmise, that was likeliest to participate in spectator unrest. In a society characterised by grumbling conformity, football was exemplary, offering a relatively safe means of rebellion against the Ulbricht dictatorship.

Football supporters replicated the 'mixture of *Resistenz*, *Eigen-Sinn*, and non-conformity' that was typical of cultural life in the 1950s.[56] Their identities, at least when it came to football, were rooted in their own team, evincing little interest in the national project of building socialism.

52 LHASA, Mer, BDVP Halle 19, Nr. 342, Wortbericht für Monat November 1960, 9 December 1960, fo. 119–20. On *Meuten*, see Fenemore, *Sex, Thugs and Rock'n'Roll*, pp. 85–9.

53 LHASA, Mer, BDVP Halle 19, Nr. 133, Stellungnahme zu den Vorkommnissen, fo. 191–2. Those deemed to have been persecuted by the Nazis were members of the *Komitee der antifaschistischen Widerstandskämpfer in der DDR* (Committee of Anti-Fascist Resistance Fighters), founded in 1953.

54 Fulbrook, *The People's State*, p. 146.

55 Peter Skyba, *Vom Hoffnungsträger zur Sicherheitsrisiko: Jugend in der DDR und Jugendpolitik der SED 1949–1960* (Cologne: Böhlau Verlag, 2000), p. 415.

56 Richthofen, *Bringing Culture to the Masses*, p. 40.

From the communist perspective, this was unhealthy. Too often, as *Die Neue Fußball-Woche* noted of a 'chorus of whistles' at a Wismut Karl-Marx-Stadt game in 1956, fans overstepped the boundaries of 'a healthy local patriotism'.[57] Conspiracy theories amorphously directed against the authorities were common to the unrest in Erfurt, Halle, and Leipzig. Responding to a *Neues Deutschland* article on the Turbine–Empor game in October 1955, Erfurt-based readers asked why the Turbine team had been disadvantaged for years.[58] Indignant Motor Plauen fans accused the DFV of favouring their Eisenach rivals in 1963, highlighting the fact that the head of the organisation's legal commission hailed from Eisenach and had encouraged the referee to continue officiating after receiving treatment for his head injury.[59]

The fluidity of local patriotism was exemplified in the case of SC Chemie Halle. Having been created in the *Oberliga* reforms of 1954, Chemie was an initially unloved team, resented for usurping players from popular 1952 *Oberliga* champions BSG Turbine Halle.[60] By 1960, the same side united a crowd of 28,000 against the 'state amateurs' of Vorwärts Berlin. In the flux of the 1950s, local rallying points were far likelier to be new creations than 'tradition clubs'. Fans in Halle, as in Dresden (with Dynamo), became adept at cultivating *Eigen-Sinn* around clubs that were SED inventions, but that continued to provide outlets for local or regional pride. Like practitioners of *Heimat* in the Thuringian village of Holungen, where locals evaded *Kulturbund* efforts to co-opt a festival to mark the one-hundredth anniversary of priest and author Hermann Iseke in 1956, they appropriated socialist spectacle for their own ends.[61]

Spectator unrest revealed the grassroots disorganisation of SED rule, a phenomenon that was not confined to football stadia during the 1950s.[62] In Erfurt, Halle, and Plauen, security measures proved inadequate. There were not enough stewards or police to prevent trouble and it took time, up to an hour after the end of the match, to restore order. At the Chemie Halle–Vorwärts Berlin match in 1960, only forty policemen were on duty. The officer who took over the security operation as unrest escalated in the second half was on holiday and only at the match, with his son, by chance. Police units, focused on protecting the referee, were

[57] 'Ein ernstes Wort an einige Zuschauer', *Die Neue Fußball-Woche*, 4 September 1956, 3.
[58] SAPMO-BArch, DY 34/3800, 'War der Schiedsrichter wirklich schuld?' (*Neues Deutschland*, 10 November 1955).
[59] SAPMO-BArch, DY 12/5335, petition from Klaus B. to the DFV, 18 June 1963, p. 372.
[60] See Chapter 5. [61] Palmowski, *Inventing a Socialist Nation*, ch. 7.
[62] See e.g. McDougall, *Youth Politics*; Mark Allinson, *Politics and Popular Opinion in East Germany 1945–1968* (Manchester: Manchester University Press, 2000).

slow to move to the post-match centre of unrest. Confusion abounded, as individual officers spread misinformation – for example, that the tyres had been cut and the windows smashed on the Vorwärts team bus, or that one Vorwärts player had been hit by a fan. The many policemen at the game in mufti, rather than helping out their over-worked comrades when trouble began, 'turned their backs on the whole incident' and went home – a tendency to keep one's head down that was much in evidence among officials during the June 1953 Uprising.[63]

The latter point reminds us of the porous boundaries between state and society. Policemen in Halle represented a repressive organisation integral to the SED's attempts to create 'socialist governance' in the 1950s.[64] But they were also football fans and thus ordinary East Germans. The same was true of officials at Turbine Erfurt, who condemned the unrest at the game against Empor Rostock in 1955, but could not help mentioning, as the players did in their public statement, the bad refereeing performance that had triggered it and the belief among locals that their team was disadvantaged.[65] So sprawling and multi-layered was the GDR's organisational apparatus, in sport as elsewhere, that it makes more sense to talk about the 'societalisation' (*Vergesellschaftung*) of the communist system rather than a blanket imposition of power from on high.[66] Football was an arena in which the dictates of central authority regularly gave way to more complex realities on the ground. Local patriotism was not just a means for fans to assert their *Eigen-Sinn*. It subverted and fragmented the party state, pitting neighbouring BSG functionaries against each other (as at the Motor Plauen–Motor Eisenach game in 1963) or the periphery against the centre, as in the stand-off between Dynamo Schwerin and BFC after their match in 1968.

Disorder at football matches in the 1950s and 1960s reinforces the idea that stadia, like the picture houses that magnetised street gangs in the same period, were liminal spaces.[67] The authorities, in the shape of the host club and the police, had power, but it could slip quickly from their grasp. Fans had power, but it lacked direction and was short-lived. A linesman at the Turbine Erfurt–Empor Rostock match in 1955

[63] LHASA, Mer, BDVP Halle 19, Nr. 342, Information der Woche, 25 November 1960, fo. 115–16; McDougall, *Youth Politics*, pp. 56–8.

[64] Thomas Lindenberger, 'Creating socialist governance: the case of the Deutsche Volkspolizei', in Jarausch (ed.), *Dictatorship as Experience*, pp. 124–41.

[65] SAPMO-BArch, DY 12/307, Protokoll über die Rechtsausschuß-Tagung, fo. 8–10; SAPMO-BArch, DY 34/3800, Stellungnahme der Oberligamannschaft, n.d.

[66] On Ralph Jessen's 'societalisation' concept in a sporting context, see Wilton, 'The "societalisation" of the state', pp. 102–5.

[67] Fenemore, *Sex, Thugs and Rock'n'Roll*, p. 86.

observed that most spectators regarded the post-game tumult as 'just fun'. He argued that they were curious to see what would happen next, a conclusion shared by the Turbine Erfurt chairman.[68]

The adventure-seeking response, common among young protestors in June 1953,[69] suggests a spontaneous desire to let off steam, or to watch steam be let off, consistent with raucous sports spectacle. As in the Soviet Union, football matches in the GDR were never 'truly carnivalesque'. Only a minority of fans participated in disturbances. Order was never more than temporarily overthrown and unrest, at least in the Ulbricht era, rarely spread beyond the stadium. Equally, though, neither Soviet nor East German football functioned as a state-directed 'safety valve' along the lines of the Circus Maximus.[70] Matches, like local festivals, served, in Jan Palmowski's words, 'to euphemize [citizens'] distance from state and party', rather than to bring them more firmly under communist control.[71] Functionaries did not welcome pitch invasions, attacks on referees, or anti-army chants. In East Germany and elsewhere, stadia were sites of dispute and negotiation, where authority could never be taken for granted. The game offered a cultural space that existed between, and sometimes beyond, formal power structures.

## Armchair fans: the rise of mediated spectatorship

The nature of live spectatorship in the 1950s and 1960s changed relatively little. Crowds at matches were largely male and local, attired in the hats and overcoats typically worn for any outdoor public activity. It was not until the 1970s that a new fan culture emerged on the terraces. More significant change during the Ulbricht era came in the area of mediated spectatorship, particularly through the spread of television. Most East Germans, like their neighbours, followed West Germany's triumph over Hungary in the 1954 World Cup final on the radio. By 1964, a collection of children's essays on the topic 'how I spent last weekend' identified watching television as by far the most common activity. Listening to the radio and watching live sport were the preserve of a small minority.[72] Adults' leisure-time habits evolved in a similar way. As across much of Europe during the 1960s, entertainment came inside, as family life in East Germany coalesced around the hub of the television.

68 SAPMO-BArch, DY 12/307, Protokoll über die Rechtsausschuß-Tagung, fo. 7–8.
69 McDougall, *Youth Politics*, pp. 52–3.
70 Edelman, 'A Small Way of Saying "No"', 1457–8.
71 Palmowski, *Inventing a Socialist Nation*, p. 254.
72 Fulbrook, *The People's State*, p. 68.

Sports spectatorship shifted accordingly. Beginning in 1956, the East German state broadcaster (*Deutscher Fernsehfunk*, DFF) incorporated sports shows into its regular programming. In 1961, sport obtained an independent editorial unit within the DFF. Though technical limitations meant that, until 1965, weekend events were generally shown on delay on Mondays, sport's televisual appeal was undeniable.[73]

Television altered, and expanded, how football was consumed. In November 1963, East Germany drew 3–3 with Hungary in Budapest in a qualifying match for the 1964 European Championship. Letters of complaint about the Yugoslavian referee's performance reached the DFV from all corners of the GDR. They variously demanded a replay on neutral territory, the submission of a formal complaint to FIFA, and an end to the appointment of low-quality Soviet-bloc officials to the GDR's matches.[74] The complaints showed how the much-maligned national team could serve as a focal point for disgruntled fans, especially when ire was directed eastwards. In terms of spectatorship, what is important is how the complainants experienced the Hungary game, as 'attentive television viewers'.[75] The DFF transmitted it live on 3 November. Highlights were shown the following day. A vast audience of armchair fans thus saw Roland Ducke's wrongly disallowed goal and the consequent end of the GDR's qualification hopes.

The evolving nature of spectatorship allowed people to watch, and comment upon, games without leaving the comfort of their living rooms. When the DFF sports unit proposed extensive coverage of the 1966 World Cup finals in England, a tournament for which the GDR did not qualify and for which West Germany was one of the favourites, the justification was simply the 'enormous interest in football in our country'. Any other approach, it argued, would leave the DFF 'hopelessly set back'. Fans in the East would simply turn on the two West German stations providing blanket coverage of the tournament instead.[76] Football supporters caused the authorities enough headaches by attending games. Watching games in the privacy of one's home, as Robert Edelman observed of developments in the Soviet Union, created spaces for

73 Jorg Friedrich, Lothar Mikos, Hans-Jörg Stiehler, and Lutz Warnicke, 'Sports coverage on GDR television', *Historical Journal of Film, Radio and Television* vol. 24, no. 3 (2004), 420–1.

74 SAPMO-BArch, DY 12/5335, various petitions/letters sent to the DFV, 3–8 November 1963, fo. 70–4, 76, 79–80, 91, 94.

75 *Ibid.*, petition from J. Ulbricht (and four others) to the DFV, 8 November 1963, fo. 71–2.

76 SAPMO-BArch, DR 8/53, Fußballweltmeisterschaften 1966 in England (Sendevorhaben der Sportredaktion), 25 April 1966.

'free-flowing banter and unmonitored drinking' that placed them even further beyond the state's reach.[77] Armchair fandom left East German football more opinionated, more vulnerable to Western influence, and, arguably, more ungovernable than ever. It also embodied the shift towards domestic life characteristic of the 'new consumerism' of post-Stalin communist societies.[78] If the 1960s, as Paul Betts has argued, was 'the GDR's real age of social reconstruction,'[79] a burgeoning televisual culture was central to the process, prefiguring the retreat into the private sphere associated with the 1970s. Fluidly straddling public and private notions of spectatorship, football would be well placed to comment on the complexities of this retreat during the Honecker era.

[77] Edelman, *Spartak Moscow*, p. 282. [78] Pittaway, *Eastern Europe*, pp. 124–5.
[79] Betts, *Within Walls*, p. 12.

# 8 Fan culture in the Honecker era

## Another side of East German youth

During the 1987/8 *Oberliga* season, a crew from the state-run German Film Studios (DEFA, *Deutsche Film-Aktiengesellchaft*) followed one of Union Berlin's fan clubs, Berliner Sportverein (BSV) Prenzlauer Berg. Director Ernst Cantzler filmed interviews with fan-club members; recorded footage of gatherings at their local pub, the *Grüne Hölle* ('Green Hell'); and had the cameras rolling when Union fans travelled to watch their team in cities such as Leipzig. The resultant documentary, *Und freitags in die 'Grüne Hölle'*, offered a compelling glimpse of everyday life and popular culture in the dying days of East German communism.[1] The official image of GDR youth – the healthy, choreographed bodies on display at the Gymnastics and Sports Festivals, or the orderly marchers at FDJ rallies – could hardly have been more strongly contradicted. Cantzler's film depicted another world, where young people had long hair, drank and sang on train journeys to away matches, and confronted rival fans and the police. Unsurprisingly, given the chaotic match-day images that it captured and its frank depiction of articulate, independent-minded fan-club leaders, the film found little official support when it was released in 1989. After one screening at a festival in Neubrandenburg, *Und freitags in die 'Grüne Hölle'* was shelved. It did not gain wide circulation until 2006.[2]

Ernst Cantzler's documentary depicted a new type of fan culture. Its roots could be found in Europe-wide changes in fan behaviour during the 1970s. Young males in Britain, West Germany, and elsewhere – financially independent, scornful of their parents' generation, and with increased leisure time to occupy – gathered on the terraces. They organised more aggressively and more tribally than their predecessors.

[1] *Und freitags in die 'Grüne Hölle'* (dir. Ernst Cantzler, 1989). Theo Körner, who features in the film, describes it as a 'realistic' portrait of the Union fan scene. Interview with Theo Körner.

[2] See the booklet accompanying the DVD of *Und freitags in die 'Grüne Hölle'*, pp. 2–4.

They travelled in closed groups to away matches and wore some sort of identifying clothing. In England supporters formed gangs and firms that developed a mobile, violent, and widely imitated hooligan culture. In Italy *ultrà* (ultras) focused on creating a dramatic, intimidating atmosphere in the stadium. The 'carnival armies' of the Scots and the Danes posited a more celebratory image of travelling fans.[3] The English and Italian models were youthful, autonomous, and contemptuous of authority – a combination that caused sleepless nights among politicians in democracies and dictatorships alike.

The generational conflict that played out on French, West German, and American university campuses in 1968 did not bypass the GDR, despite SED claims that it was impossible under socialism. The tropes of youth culture that had older people shaking their heads in the West, such as the music of The Beatles and The Rolling Stones, were met with a similar lack of comprehension by their peers behind the Iron Curtain. The fact that 'beat music', not to mention long-haired males, motorbikes, and transistor radios, was the product of the capitalist class enemy only added to its subversive appeal.[4] Western-oriented youth subcultures that paid little or no heed to socialist ideology sprang up throughout the GDR.[5] The emergence of a fan culture that drew inspiration from England and Italy, and evinced a lively interest in West German football, was part of this trend. Further east in the early 1970s, similar role models inspired the advent of the raucous and independent-minded *fanaty* (fanatics) of Spartak Moscow.[6] Across Europe passive spectatorship was rejected in favour of attention-seeking and confrontational behaviour.

In the GDR as elsewhere, the new model was unashamedly masculine. But women were present too – and not just as reluctant companions of husbands and boyfriends. Kathrin Gaebel regularly went with friends to FC Magdeburg matches in her home-made blue and white scarf, and then headed to the disco, a social calendar followed by many of her male peers.[7] One Union Berlin supporter estimates that, for every 400 or 500 men who went to away games in the 1970s, 10 or 15 women came too. Christa Moog's 1985 short story 'Die Fans von Union' suggests a similar ratio among the Union *Schlachtenbummler* ('away fans') who watch their team play Lokomotive Leipzig.[8] This was an indisputably male world,

[3] Goldblatt, *The Ball Is Round*, pp. 546–9.

[4] On the impact of The Beatles in the GDR, see McDougall, *Youth Politics*, pp. 177–201.

[5] See e.g. Fenemore, *Sex, Thugs and Rock'n'Roll*.

[6] Edelman, *Serious Fun*, p. 192.

[7] Gröschner, *Sieben Tränen*, pp. 130–2.

[8] Luther and Willmann, *Eisern Union!*, p. 102; Moog, *Die Fans von Union*, p. 87.

where women, as Kathrin recalled, had to prove that they could drink and shout as well as the men.[9] But the presence of a minority of female spectators suggests that gender stereotypes surrounding football, often perpetuated (as we shall see in Chapter 12) by the communist authorities, were not watertight.

Football, like music, offered a means by which rebellious youths could thumb their noses at the communist state. Chemie Leipzig fans travelled to away matches in large, boisterous groups. There, as Jens Fuge recollected, they purchased black-market items such as *kicker* and photos of bands such as Kiss and AC/DC. They indulged in the popular pastime of 'plucking' (*Rupfen*) scarves from around the necks of rival supporters, an activity indicative of the importance of clothing – treasuring what you wore and taking what your enemy wore – to the new generation of fans.[10] Numerous interviewees recalled the ubiquity of such trophy hunts, emphasising their relatively non-violent nature ('more comical than brutal', in Frank L.'s words).[11]

These outings grew out of developments in the 1960s, when young East Germans, like their Western counterparts, became a leisure group in their own right, with more money and more time in which to spend it.[12] The five-day working week, introduced in 1967, allowed committed supporters to get to away games throughout the republic – and thereby experience a travel freedom that was rarely available beyond the GDR's borders. When Honecker came to power four years later, the government expanded the *Stasi* apparatus, but also promised the improved provision of consumer goods, conferring at least partial legitimacy on demands for more openness to products from the West.[13] The emergent fan culture of the 1970s was symptomatic of the accommodationist strand in SED thinking, which encouraged citizens to use the private sphere 'as theatres of pent-up individuality and subcultural pursuits'.[14] Similar pragmatism could be found across the Soviet bloc, as communist leaders tacitly made peace with Western consumer culture.

Studies of the GDR, including the present one, continue to draw a temporal distinction between the Ulbricht and Honecker eras. There were important shifts after 1971, in areas ranging from *Stasi* surveillance and relations with Bonn to consumerism and youth culture. Honecker's accession to power marked a retreat from the reform-minded idealism

[9] Gröschner, *Sieben Tränen*, p. 132.
[10] Jens Fuge, 'Von Fußball-Anhängern und Schlachtenbummlern', in Willmann (ed.), *Fußball-Land DDR*, pp. 93–100.
[11] Interview with Frank L.; interview with Jens Genschmar; interview with Sven S.
[12] See e.g. Richthofen, *Bringing Culture to the Masses*, pp. 101–5.
[13] Wolle, *Die heile Welt*, p. 45. [14] Betts, *Within Walls*, pp. 141–3.

that characterised Ulbricht's rule during the 1960s. In various fields – economics (the New Economic System, 1963), education (the Youth Communiqué of the same year), and the private sphere (the 1965 Family Law) – there were genuine, albeit unsuccessful, attempts to create a more motivated, educated, and resourceful socialist citizenry.[15] But, as recent works have emphasised, Ulbricht's ousting did not necessarily mark a significant rupture.[16] The reformist ethos of the early 1960s was in retreat long before 1971, partly because of Honecker's role in curbing liberal trends in economic, cultural, and youth policy after 1965.[17] Moreover, long-term socio-economic patterns – related, for example, to the solidification of the private sphere and the increased importance of leisure time and consumption – 'straddled the GDR's middle two decades'.[18]

Changes at home and abroad fed the development of a new model of spectatorship in the Honecker era. At the same time, watching football remained remarkably cheap. In 1988 an *Oberliga* ticket cost just 1.10 Marks – a sporting equivalent of the bread roll, which famously cost five pfennigs throughout the GDR's existence.[19] A typical match-day weekend for a young Union Berlin fan – Friday night at the 'cultural house' (*Kulturhaus*) disco in Köpenick, the overnight train to an away game in somewhere like Rostock, the match itself, and the return journey that took him back to the disco on Saturday night[20] – did not require deep pockets.

In examining fan culture in the Honecker era, this chapter highlights many of the signal features of GDR football: the *Eigen-Sinn* that coloured supporters' relations with the state and each other; the reach and ultimate limits of communist power, in a sport that consistently practised 'the art of the unforeseeable';[21] and the constrained sense of autonomy that made fan culture behind the Berlin Wall representative of wider trends and uniquely East German. It offers a vivid summation of football's importance in shaping everyday experiences, not only in the GDR – where fan disaffection played its part in 'chipping away at the state' during the 1980s[22] – but in every modern society where it has put down roots.

15 See e.g. McDougall, *Youth Politics*, pp. 153–63; Betts, *Within Walls*, pp. 100–8.
16 See e.g. Betts, *Within Walls*; and many of the essays in Fulbrook (ed.), *Power and Society*.
17 Fulbrook, *The People's State*, pp. 39–42.
18 Betts, *Within Walls*, p. 12.
19 SAPMO-BArch, DY 30/4969, letter from Klaus Eichler to Krenz, 13 June 1989, fo. 163–4; Josie McLellan '"Even under socialism, we don't want to do without love": East German erotica', *Bulletin of the German Historical Institute* Supplement 7 (2011), 49.
20 Interview with Theo Körner.
21 Galeano, *Soccer in Sun and Shadow*, p. 209.
22 Jeffrey Kopstein, 'Chipping away at the state: workers' resistance and the demise of East Germany', *World Politics* no. 48 (April 1996), 393–4.

## Around the wall: encounters with football in the West

In the 1970s, West Germany dominated European football. The national team won the European Championship in 1972 and the World Cup two years later. Clubs from the thriving *Bundesliga*, led by Bayern Munich, excelled in European competition. Given the less exciting fare on offer at home, and the ready availability of West German television, many East Germans turned westward for a football fix during the Honecker years. They did not necessarily forget about domestic football or value West German teams more highly than their own. Fan identities were more complex than such reductions allow.[23] But supporters, like other consumers, gravitated to the highest-quality product that they could find. When asked in a 1987 survey of young fans to name a favourite 'international' team, between 70 and 80 per cent of respondents chose clubs from West Germany.[24] Many interviewees followed, with varying degrees of enthusiasm, a second team in the *Bundesliga*, such as Eintracht Frankfurt, FC Cologne, or 1860 Munich.[25]

Television and radio provided the simplest, least risky way to follow West German football. Most East German households had television sets by the early 1970s and watching television became by far the GDR's most popular pastime. By 1987 85 per cent of citizens admitted that programmes from the capitalist West were a regular part of their viewing schedule.[26] In sport as elsewhere, communist efforts to combat this inner emigration – by reducing the educational content of programmes, introducing colour broadcasts, and opening a second sports channel[27] – had limited success. West German programmes such as *Sportschau* were widely available and popular. Klaus L. gathered with friends at a bar in Prenzlauer Berg every Saturday to listen to Hertha BSC games on a West Berlin radio station.[28] The *Bundesliga*, in the words of one West German journalist, 'belonged to everyday life in the GDR'. The exception was an area of poor reception in and around Dresden, jokingly labelled the 'valley of the clueless' (*Tal der Ahnungslosen*). The lack of Western television boosted Dynamo Dresden's status as the GDR's best-supported club.[29] Dynamo fans viewed their

23 Hesselmann and Ide, 'A tale of two Germanys', p. 43.
24 SAPMO-BArch, DC 4/721, Neuere Ergebnisse zum Verhältnis Jugendlicher zum Fußball (Fanverhalten) – Expertise des ZIJ zur Untersuchung "Sport '87", fo. 8.
25 Interviews with Tino C.; Tim E., 25 May 2011; Frank L.; Klaus L., 12 May 2011.
26 Betts, *Within Walls*, p. 144.
27 Friedrich *et al.*, 'Sports coverage on GDR television', 421.
28 Interview with Klaus L.
29 Leske, *Erich Mielke*, p. 92.

cluelessness with pride. Visiting supporters were told that ‘your team is so shit that you have to watch the *Bundesliga* too’.[30]

Some fans took greater risks, actively cultivating ties with West German supporters, players, and clubs. Football thereby served as a site of ‘cultural transfer’ in divided Germany, transgressing politically closed borders and giving GDR citizens access to, and contacts with, the outside world.[31] A strong affinity developed in the 1970s and 1980s between fans of Union Berlin and West Berlin’s leading team, Hertha BSC. In Cantzler’s documentary, the head of the Union fan club, Andreas Schwadten, is filmed in a jean jacket that displays the Hertha club badge. The walls of the *Grüne Hölle* pub where the club meets every Friday night are covered with Union and Hertha memorabilia. When Hertha came to the GDR to play Dynamo Dresden in 1978, 120 Union fans were in attendance, one-third of whom sported Hertha shirts, badges, and flags.[32]

By this time, the friendship between Union and Hertha fans was assiduously promoted on both sides. Hertha fans crossed into East Berlin to watch Union games at the ramshackle An der Alten Försterei stadium in Köpenick.[33] Union fans, denied the possibility of reciprocal travel to the West, took advantage of a revival in Hertha’s fortunes in the late 1970s to watch them play European games elsewhere in the Soviet bloc. Illegal Hertha fan clubs were monitored by the secret police.[34] In the mid 1980s a pub landlord in East Berlin was jailed for two years for secretly hosting a Christmas party for Hertha and Union fans.[35] The *Stasi* concluded on the basis of such evidence that ‘negative-decadent youths’ from in and around Berlin regarded Union as a ‘synonym’ for ‘“oppositional” attitudes’.[36]

The difficulties borne by exiled Hertha fans were exemplified by Helmut Klopfleisch. A leading figure in the ‘Hertha society’, disguised variously as a pools group or bingo club, that met on a monthly basis in changing locations in East Berlin,[37] Klopfleisch was a self-confessed West German football fanatic. With contacts at Hertha and Bayern

[30] Interview with Jens Genschmar.

[31] Merkel, ‘The GDR – a normal country’, pp. 197–200.

[32] BStU, MfS HA XX/AKG/6684, Gesellschaftswidriges Verhalten vorwiegend dem Anhang des 1. FC Union Berlin angehörender negativ-dekadenter Jugendlicher im Zusammenhang mit dem Fußballspiel der SG Dynamo Dresden gegen Hertha BSC Westberlin am 26.4.1978, n.d., fo. 73–4.

[33] Luther and Willmann, *Eisern Union!*, pp. 103–5.

[34] Wiese, ‘Wie der Fußball Löcher in die Mauer schoss’, pp. 257–68.

[35] Braun and Wiese, ‘DDR-Fußball’, 208.

[36] BStU, MfS HA XX/AKG/6684, Gesellschaftswidriges Verhalten, fo. 74.

[37] Wiese, ‘Wie der Fußball Löcher in die Mauer schoss’, pp. 246, 250–2; Kuper, *Football against the Enemy*, p. 20.

Munich, he became the subject of a bulging *Stasi* file on his 'anti-state' activities. These included sending a good luck telegram to the West German team before the 1986 World Cup finals in Mexico, attending private meetings with Hertha officials, and travelling outside the GDR to watch West German sides in action.[38]

When Hertha travelled to Czechoslovakia in 1979 for a UEFA Cup match against Dukla Prague, Klopfleisch was one of 300 East German Hertha fans in attendance. This was common practice in the 1970s and 1980s, as citizens used the limited freedom of movement at their disposal – which included after 1972 visa-free travel to most Soviet-bloc states[39] – to watch live West German football. Between 1979 and 1981, approximately 5,000 of them travelled to neighbouring socialist countries to watch thirteen games involving West German teams.[40] When West Germany played Poland in Warsaw in 1971, the *Stasi* estimated that 204 of the 1,303 East Germans in attendance openly cheered the class enemy. Banners posted around the ground included 'Leipzig greets Kaiser Franz and co.' and 'Guben greets the German eleven'.[41] If the fan friendship between Hertha and Union illustrated how surviving local allegiances could subvert communist intentions, the crowd response in Warsaw, and at matches elsewhere in the Soviet bloc, showed the durability of notions of shared German identity. Public opinion surveys throughout the Honecker era highlighted a strong awareness of, and sympathy with, the other Germany among citizens, even as they described the GDR as their country.[42] That *Abgrenzung* failed in football, as it did in other areas from music to environmental politics, is shown by the fact that the 200 GDR citizens who saw West Germany play Hungary in Budapest in 1987 behaved much as their fellow supporters had done in Warsaw sixteen years earlier. Fans had photographs taken with West German players outside the team hotel. Banners at the venue included 'Cottbus greets the 1988 European champions' (inaccurate, as it turned out), as well as the German flag bearing the DFB insignia. The people displaying open sympathies for the visiting team were aged between eighteen and forty-five.[43] Largely born and raised in the GDR, they

[38] Kuper, *Football against the Enemy*, pp. 18–26; Wiese, 'Wie der Fußball Löcher in die Mauer schoss', pp. 269–77.

[39] Major, *Behind the Berlin Wall*, p. 197.

[40] Braun and Wiese, 'DDR-Fußball', 206.

[41] Blees, *90 Minuten Klassenkampf*, pp. 38–9.

[42] Mary Fulbrook, *German National Identity after the Holocaust* (Cambridge: Polity Press, 1999), pp. 192–8.

[43] BStU, MfS ZOS/1342, Information über politisch-operative Sicherungsmaßnahmen und deren Ergebnisse im Zusammenhang mit dem Fußball-Länderspiel UVR-BRD am 18. November 1987 in Budapest, n.d., fo. 1–2.

rejected any identification with the socialist fatherland that precluded cheering for West Germany. For Sven S. and fans like him, it was possible to support 'two national teams'.[44]

Pilgrimages to socialist countries were fuelled by the difficulties of watching West German teams anywhere else. The SED strictly controlled all 'tourist delegations' that travelled to football matches outside the Soviet bloc. As the local party leadership stated before Dynamo Dresden's UEFA Cup match in Stuttgart in 1979, tickets were reserved for 'model' workers, comrades and 'bloc party friends', party and state functionaries, women, DTSB members, and those who had been on previous sports trips to West Germany.[45] As a young Carl Zeiss Jena fan, Christoph Dieckmann went directly to DFV headquarters in East Berlin in 1981 to plead for a ticket for his team's European Cup Winners' Cup final against Dynamo Tbilisi in the West German city of Düsseldorf. He was predictably unsuccessful.[46] It is small wonder that the 'dream job' for young fans such as Frank Willmann and his friend Ralf, growing up in Weimar in the Honecker era, was to be 'either a successful footballer or a trusted *Reisekader*', one of the select few who, like Ralf's uncle, could travel abroad.[47]

It was not much easier to watch West European teams at home. Ticket allocation was managed to keep out undesirable elements. Of the 19,000 tickets released for BFC's European Cup match against Austria Vienna in September 1985, 6,500 were sold to *Stasi* and Interior Ministry officials. A further 6,900 tickets were allocated to pre-selected outlets including customs and police officers, the DFV, BFC functionaries and members, and the SV Dynamo leadership. This left at most 5,600 tickets, less than one-third of the capacity at the Jahn Sportpark, for ordinary fans.[48] It was worse if BFC's opponents came from England or West Germany. The only options then were the black market or private connections. Klaus L. regularly got tickets for European matches through a neighbour whose son played for BFC.[49] When BFC hosted Hamburg in September 1982, one supporter later recounted, 'the big

44 Interview with Sven S.

45 HStA Dresden, 11857 SED-Bezirksleitung Dresden IV/D-2.16 Nr. 848, Vorschlag für die politische und organisatorische Vorbereitung der Touristendelegation zum UEFA-Pokalrückspiel Dynamo Dresden–VfB Stuttgart am 7.11.1979, 11 October 1979.

46 Dieckmann, '"Nur ein Leutzscher"', pp. 331–2.

47 Frank Willmann, 'Wir wollen hier nur entspannen', in Willmann (ed.), *Zonenfußball*, p. 44.

48 BStU, MfS HA XX/10313, Vorgesehener Kartenvertrieb für das Europapokalspiel des BFC Dynamo gegen Austria Wien am 18.9.1985, um 20.00 Uhr, im Friedrich-Ludwig-Jahn-Sportpark, n.d., fo. 44.

49 Interview with Klaus L.

wigs (*Bonzen*) dragged their stepmothers and daughters into the stadium and the fans had to stand outside'.[50] A joke that arose from this game has West German radio asking a BFC official before kick-off if the stadium will be full. He replies, *mit Sicherheit, mit Sicherheit*. This can be translated as 'certainly, certainly'. More literally, it means 'with security, with security', a pointed reference to the many spectators who worked for the GDR's police state.[51]

The frustration caused by such restrictions was apparent in a petition sent by eight BFC fans to the Dynamo leadership in 1980. Long-time season-ticket holders, they were repeatedly put off when trying to get tickets for the club's European Cup quarter final against Nottingham Forest and then told that the game was sold out. They asked why tickets for one of the biggest games in BFC's history were unavailable to the club's loyal supporters and distributed instead to 'supporters from [elsewhere in] the GDR, who otherwise never come to Berlin for BFC games'.[52] SV Dynamo's reply blamed high demand for the petitioners' lack of success, skating over an allocation policy that ensured that as many tickets as possible were kept in reliable hands.[53]

The danger of releasing so few big-match tickets to the public was illustrated ahead of the UEFA Cup semi-final between Dynamo Dresden and VfB Stuttgart in April 1989. Knowing the situation from previous matches, fans camped out at the box office two days before tickets became available. By 5 p.m. the next day there were 5,000 people waiting in line, many of whom were drinking heavily. The Dresden police chief consequently decided to open the sales counters early. The result was a stampede. Seventeen people were injured, a number of them seriously, just days before the deaths of ninety-six Liverpool fans at the Hillsborough Stadium in Sheffield brought into tragic perspective the difficulties of safely managing large crowds of football fans. Only police intervention restored order.[54]

Evidently, many of the fans denied tickets for big matches were not West German football fanatics like Helmut Klopfleisch. The 1987 survey of youth and football showed that 85 per cent of self-proclaimed fans had

50 Luther and Willmann, *BFC*, pp. 145, 155.

51 Interview with Klaus L.

52 SAPMO-BArch, DO 101/027/3–4, petition from Stefan K. to SV Dynamo, 14 April 1980.

53 *Ibid.*, letter from Mieder (BFC) to Stefan K., 2 May 1980.

54 BStU, MfS BV Dresden Stellvertr. Op. 70, Information zur Störung der öffentlichen Ordnung und Sicherheit im Zusammenhang mit dem Vorverkauf der Eintrittskarten zum UEFA-Pokal-Halbfinal-Rückspiel SG Dynamo Dresden–VfB Stuttgart am 7.4.1989, 8 April 1989, fo. 24–5; Genschmar, *Mit Dynamo durch Europa*, pp. 133–4.

a favourite 'international team' and that the *Bundesliga*, led by Bayern Munich (named by 42 per cent of fans), dominated this category. Bayern's role, though, was largely a surrogate one. The survey depicted lively support for a range of GDR clubs, based on factors that included playing style, team character, and 'local patriotism'.[55] When Dynamo Dresden hosted Bayern Munich in the European Cup in 1973, the city, in the words of one fan and club historian, stood 'like a wall' behind its team. Heiko H. might have preferred the West German national team to its East German counterpart, but he always supported his club, Lokomotive Leipzig, when it played West German opposition.[56] Domestic football was capable of forging home-grown identities, though it was played and watched in the West's shadow. Even the small and rebellious East German punk scene, while drawing inspiration from Western bands such as The Sex Pistols and The Clash, had indigenous characteristics that rooted it, however reluctantly, in GDR culture.[57] Just as citizens tended to prioritise local news and local newspapers,[58] so they often threw their weight behind the local football team. The game in East Germany was an amalgam of community and international concerns, neither of which corresponded readily to socialist notions of spectatorship.

## 'Dear comrades': football petitions

Football's importance was illustrated by the many petitions that it inspired. They constituted an essential part of the dialogue, which was uneasy and subject to mutual misunderstandings, between supporters and the authorities. Much has been written about the centrality of petitions, in the absence of conventional democratic markers, as a means of registering complaints about life under socialism – and the problems that historians face in analysing such stylised forms of discourse with the state.[59] Being based around conflict and conflict resolution, petitions showcased 'disturbances in everyday life'.[60] They were not written in ways that necessarily reflected popular attitudes to the GDR. Petitioners were adept at 'speaking socialist'.[61] Rhetorical tricks deployed by citizens

55 SAPMO-BArch, DC 4/721, Neuere Ergebnisse zum Verhältnis Jugendlicher zum Fußball, fo. 7–11.
56 Interview with Jens Genschmar; interview with Heiko H., 13 October 2011.
57 Dennis and Laporte, *State and Minorities*, pp. 158–62.
58 Palmowski, *Inventing a Socialist Nation*, p. 98.
59 For an overview of the GDR's petition culture, see Fulbrook, *The People's State*, ch. 13.
60 Ina Merkel and Felix Mühlberg, 'Eingaben und Öffentlichkeit', in Ina Merkel (ed.), *"Wir sind doch nicht die Mecker-Ecke der Nation": Briefe an das DDR-Fernsehen* (Cologne: Böhlau Verlag, 1998), p. 11.
61 Betts, *Within Walls*, p. 186.

who wrote to the television programme *PRISMA* about problems with housing, work, holidays, and consumer goods were replicated by petitioners on football: an introduction outlining the writer's commitment to socialism, followed by a specific and detailed complaint. The complaint was sometimes accompanied by a threat or choice quotation from a high-ranking individual (Honecker, for example) or public document (the constitution) highlighting discrepancies between what the party said and did.[62] It was possible, even desirable, for a petitioner to portray himself or herself as both faithful citizen and outspoken critic, an archetypal representative of what Alf Lüdtke has called the 'disaffected loyalty' (*mißmutige Loyalität*) of the GDR population towards the SED regime.[63]

It is not by chance that the hero's socialist mother in Wolfgang Becker's critical yet wistful film about the end of the GDR, *Goodbye Lenin* (2003), writes sharp letters to the authorities complaining on behalf of fellow citizens about ill-fitting women's clothing. Petitions were an integral part of the East German social fabric. They opened windows into citizens' private lives and highlighted 'patterns of individualisation' that often undermined the GDR's collectivist goals, in much the same way as letter-writing to the authorities in the Soviet Union during the 1930s shed light on the turbulent relationship between the personal and the public there.[64] Whatever constraints shaped the dialogue between the state and its citizens, both sides took the process seriously. Petitions illustrated what people expected from the regime, expectations that changed over time, and what they wanted for themselves. They showcased the limits of communist power, limits that were paradoxically exposed by the state's all-embracing ambitions. Petitions, finally, were critical to understanding how East Germans engaged with, and sometimes challenged, the SED dictatorship, defending autonomous or semi-autonomous interests in the face of state interference and indifference. They exemplified Lutz Niethammer's argument that some of the best insights into everyday life come when 'silent normality break[s] down'.[65]

62 Merkel and Mühlberg, 'Eingaben und Öffentlichkeit', pp. 24–7; Betts, *Within Walls*, pp. 186–8.

63 Alf Lüdtke, '"Helden der Arbeit" – Mühen beim Arbeiten: Zur mißmutigen Loyalität von Industriearbeitern in der DDR', in Hartmut Kaelble, Jürgen Kocka, and Hartmut Zwahr (eds.), *Sozialgeschichte der DDR* (Stuttgart: Klett-Cotta, 1994), pp. 188–213.

64 Fulbrook, *The People's State*, p. 271; Betts, *Within Walls*, p. 174. On Soviet petition culture, see Fitzpatrick, 'Supplicants and citizens', pp. 78–105; Sarah Davies, *Popular Opinion in Stalinist Russia: Terror, Propaganda and Dissent, 1934–1941* (Cambridge: Cambridge University Press, 1997), pp. 157–63.

65 Lutz Niethammer, 'Zeroing in on change: in search of popular experience in the industrial province in the German Democratic Republic', in Lüdtke (ed.), *The History of Everyday Life*, p. 279.

While not as common a cause of complaint as housing or foodstuffs, sport exercised the pens (or typewriters) of many GDR citizens. A grievance culture appears to have become more firmly entrenched among sports fans (and practitioners, as we shall see in Chapter 14) during the 1970s. SV Dynamo, for example, received fourteen petitions in 1968. That number rose steadily over the next decade, reaching 60 in 1974 and 118 in 1977.[66] The increase was probably related to the 'petition law' included in the 1974 constitution, which required all letters to be answered within four weeks.[67] It indicated a broader retreat from politics into the personal in this period, not only in East Germany but across the Soviet bloc, which led to increasingly vocal individual complaints about goods and services that the state failed to provide. Football was part of the development of this 'socialist private sphere'.[68]

The upsurge in petitions reflected television's growing role in broadcasting sport. The shows *Sport aktuell* (Saturday evenings) and *Sport speziell* (usually midweek) attracted higher viewing figures for football games than for anything outside special events such as the Olympics. Dynamo Dresden's European matches against Liverpool in 1972 and Bayern Munich a year later drew 25.6% and 58.4% of the total television audience respectively. BFC's home and away legs against Werder Bremen in the European Cup in 1988 attracted 31% and 24.7%.[69] These figures are worth emphasising. When a quarter or a half of television viewers are tuning in to football, its power as a collective cultural experience has few equals.

Football's lack of importance, one might say, made it important. The sense that this topic was not off limits in the way that, for example, criticising the Berlin Wall was, created a site of relatively open discussion. This was reflected in the range and vibrancy of fan correspondence with the authorities. Petitions addressed anger at the perceived favouritism of referees towards BFC (discussed in Chapter 10) and perennial bugbears, such as player transfers and the national team's performances. But they also dealt with other complaints that illuminate football's ubiquitous presence in everyday life, at least for men, the authors of the overwhelming majority of football-related petitions.

The starting point for many petitions, even when they went on to talk about something else, was the national team. In the eyes of many fans, international and domestic stagnation – the *Auswahl*'s shortcomings and

[66] SAPMO-BArch, DO 101/027/1–2, Analyse, 12 February 1969; Analyse der Eingaben 1976, 23 February 1977; Analyse der Eingaben im Jahr 1977, 7 June 1978.
[67] Grix, 'The decline of mass sport provision', 411.
[68] Betts, *Within Walls*, p. 9.
[69] Dennis, 'Behind the wall', 57–8.

BFC's domination – went hand in hand, cementing policies that avoided 'new, modern paths' for the game in the East.[70] Key elements of supporters' complaints offered insights into the political and economic malaise of the 1980s. An unwillingness to take risks, outmoded strategic thinking, an emphasis on stopping the opposition rather than creative play, the trumpeting of minor successes that papered over the cracks, and an over-reliance on older players:[71] systemic problems in football were relevant to key areas of East German life, as a conservative gerontocracy presided over an unreformed planned economy that was heading for the rocks.[72] Like the complaints after the GDR–Hungary match in 1963 or the elation that followed the triumph over West Germany eleven years later, the critiques of the 1980s showed that many citizens cared about the national team. But they also highlighted that patience was wearing thin, an attitude not confined to football by the middle of the decade.

Like the FA Cup in England, the FDGB Cup was open to everyone. Almost 6,000 teams entered the knock-out competition in 1967, by which time it was an established and popular part of the football calendar.[73] Complaints focused on the location and scheduling of matches. They often emphasised that the tournament bore the name of an organisation that claimed to represent the working class. A petition from one Magdeburg worker in 1972, for example, incredulously questioned the DFV's scheduling of the forthcoming round of cup matches for 1 p.m. on a Wednesday afternoon. How, he asked, was such a decision possible if the workers are meant to go to work? Have the floodlights been scrapped? The FDGB's response, a telling reminder of the supply problems that dogged the GDR's economy, blamed the 'current energy situation' for the decision to schedule matches at the inconvenient time.[74] The sense that the authorities were uninterested in meeting fans' wishes was reinforced by the decision to permanently play the cup final in Berlin from 1975 onwards. A petition

[70] SAPMO-BArch, DY 30/4982, petition from Manfred H. to the ZK sports department, 12 April 1985, fo. 247–8.

[71] *Ibid.*, petition from Ernst H. to Hellmann, 27 July 1984, fo. 180–1; SAPMO-BArch, DY 30/4986, petition from Ralf R. to Ewald, 29 August 1985, fo. 101–4; SAPMO-BArch, DY 30/4987, petition from Walter S. to Hellmann, 9 May 1983, fo. 159–61.

[72] On the economic problems of the 1980s, see e.g. Jeffrey Kopstein, *The Politics of Economic Decline in East Germany* (Chapel Hill, NC: University of North Carolina Press, 1997), especially chs. 3 and 6; Jonathan Zatlin, *The Currency of Socialism: Money and Political Culture in East Germany* (Cambridge: Cambridge University Press, 2007), chs. 3 and 4.

[73] SAPMO-BArch, DY 34/17719, Anlage I: Einschätzung der Pokalwettbewerbe, 1968.

[74] SAPMO-BArch, DY 34/12125, petition from A. W. to the FDGB leadership, 10 December 1972; reply to A. W. from Jochen Teubner, 15 December 1972.

from 1983 claimed that the 'overwhelming majority' of trade union members opposed this custom, particularly as the capital lacked a suitable stadium for the event. The authors vainly demanded a return to the earlier practice of choosing a venue based on the location of the two teams contesting the final.[75]

In 1972 the trade union newspaper *Tribüne* asked readers to write in with comments on the re-designed trophy for the FDGB Cup. Their responses were blunt and humorous. It was universally pointed out that the design had little to do with football. 'My first impression', wrote one bemused reader from Blankenhain, 'was that a small group-sex scene was being depicted'. This view was shared by Herbert S. from Colditz, whose breezy letter hinted at the famously relaxed East German attitude to nudism: 'It's a good thing that you wrote new football cup alongside it! Otherwise you'd think that three naked, intertwined volleyball players are making propaganda for group sex'.[76] The prevailing sentiment was summed up by a great grandmother from Birkenwerder. She opened her letter to *Tribüne* with the comment 'but, but colleagues, what is that supposed to be?' and closed by asking 'Why can't you simply show a player doing a nice backheel?'[77]

Some readers derided the college collective that came up with the design. Active players should be consulted, suggested Johannes F. from Niedersteinbach, 'not art students who only have beards, long manes, and naked women in mind'. Such unapologetic philistinism, reminiscent of the regime-endorsed stereotype of anti-socialist youth (the *Gammler*, or 'long-haired layabout') that emerged in the 1960s,[78] was interspersed with comments that gently reminded the party leadership of its shortcomings. 'Even today in a time of material savings', wrote a factory collective from Pirna, 'you don't play football naked. The players should at least be allowed a loincloth!'[79] Amid the humorous and disbelieving comments, respondents put forward detailed suggestions about what the new trophy should look like. The dialogue, albeit on a minor issue, offered an example of the interaction between citizens and the state that typified the GDR's 'participatory dictatorship', where legitimacy, or at

75 SAPMO-BArch, DY 30/4981, petition from K. W. and H. F. to the ZK sports department, 7 December 1983, fo. 335.

76 SAPMO-BArch, DY 34/17715, letter from Hubert M. to *Tribüne*, 3 April 1972; letter from Herbert S. to *Tribüne*, 31 March 1972. On the GDR as a 'naked republic', see McLellan, *Love in the Time of Communism*, ch. 6.

77 SAPMO-BArch, DY 34/17715, letter from Elsbeth O. to *Tribüne*, 29 March 1972.

78 See e.g. McDougall, *Youth Politics*, pp. 188–90.

79 SAPMO-BArch, DY 34/17715, letter from Johannes F. to *Tribüne*, 29 March 1972; letter from the Wilhelm Oswald collective to *Tribüne*, 14 April 1972.

least the illusion of it, was constantly sought.[80] In this case, public opinion counted for something. The draft design was shelved. A more apposite, if equally uninspired creation, showing a player with a ball hoisted on the shoulders of two team-mates, was made in its place.

As a new design for the FDGB Cup was debated in the spring of 1972, the quarter finals of that year's competition took place. Following Carl Zeiss Jena's 5–2 victory over Wismut Aue on 12 April, seventeen Aue fans and FDGB members wrote to the trade union leadership to protest against the result. Their petition contained the usual complaints about poor refereeing. The fact that the officials came from the same region, Thuringia, as the victorious home team reinforced the sense of injustice. The petitioners averred that there was 'no bribery' in the socialist sport, but posed the following question: 'would it have been a scandal for our football if another BSG team besides Sachsenring Zwickau had stayed in the running?'[81] The implication was clear. Carl Zeiss Jena was one of the heavily favoured FCs, created in the mid 1960s to raise standards. Wismut Aue, like Sachsenring Zwickau, was a factory team, lacking the financial or political clout to make, or be allowed to make, an impact in big games.

This kind of populist grievance, decrying the deliberate (or otherwise) disadvantaging of BSGs, was an interesting feature of petitions in the Honecker era. In 1983, Hans H., a party member of twenty years' standing, wrote to Rudi Hellmann about the declining fortunes of twice *Oberliga* champions Chemie Leipzig. References were made to the team's roots in the working-class Leutzsch district and to its home ground, named in honour of the murdered communist Georg Schwarz. The narrative placed Chemie 'in the foremost ranks of our socialist sports movement'. It urged the party to protect a proud representative of 'progressive development' and to draw on its energy to drag East German football out of the mire.[82]

H.'s letter returns us to the concept of invented socialist tradition, a technique of self-appropriation that was apparent among fans and players as far back as the 1950s.[83] In the absence of 'tradition clubs', all of which were dissolved after the Second World War, the factory teams – themselves artificial and initially unloved creations – became

[80] On the concept of 'participatory dictatorship', see Fulbrook, *The People's State*, pp. 10–17.

[81] SAPMO-BArch, DY 34/12125, petition from Klaus F. to the FDGB leadership, 14 April 1972.

[82] SAPMO-BArch, DY 30/4982, petition from Hans H. to Hellmann, 22 April 1983, fo. 141–5.

[83] See Chapters 5 and 7.

GDR football's closest approximation to the likes of Hertha BSC and Schalke 04. Using socialist rhetoric to attain individualised goals, their fans emphasised an underdog status that was artfully contrasted with the privileges accorded to teams such as BFC and Lokomotive Leipzig, party-mandated creations that lacked working-class roots. SED member Rainer K.'s petition to Honecker in August 1984 about the declining fortunes of BSG Sachsenring Zwickau aggressively pursued this strategy. Based on Zwickau's great service to GDR football over the years, he argued, the town's workers had a right to enjoy *Oberliga* football. This right was taken away when the team was relegated in 1983. K. charged the DFV with systematically disadvantaging Zwickau in favour of FC Karl-Marx-Stadt, the region's elite football centre.[84] Ironically, FCK often ran into a roadblock in the shape of another neighbouring BSG, as Heinz Werner discovered when he coached there between 1985 and 1988. Wismut Aue, 'led from Moscow', was beyond the SED's control, a reminder of both the hierarchy of power within the Soviet bloc and the ambiguities that could complicate a BSG's hard-luck story.[85]

K.'s petition began a testy correspondence with the DFV that lasted through the autumn. Meetings brought no quick resolution. The DFV saw K. as a 'fanatic' unconcerned about the fortunes of East German football. K., in a second petition to Honecker in October, accused a leading DFV official of brushing him off with comments such as 'we aren't at all interested in traditions such as . . . Zwickau football'. A truce was reached in late November, in part because officials needed to placate K., 'an influential personality in Zwickau football-supporting circles', in order to staunch anti-DFV sentiments in the town.[86]

Functionaries repeatedly found themselves drawn into this world of local grievances. Fans who knew how to press the right political buttons consequently exerted considerable influence. A petition to Egon Krenz 'in the name of more than 5,000 football fans of Fortschritt Bischofswerda' in 1986, for example, framed the DFV's disadvantaging of the newly promoted BSG in a provocative context: 'As workers we are of the opinion that our football is just as professional as football in the capitalist countries'.[87] The DFV's lack of interest in BSGs, its alleged

[84] SAPMO-BArch, DY 30/4983, petition from Rainer K. to Honecker, 1 August 1984, fo. 218–20.

[85] Interview with Heinz Werner.

[86] SAPMO-BArch, DY 30/4983, Eingabe zu Fragen der Entwicklung des Zwickauer Fußballs, 12 October 1984, fo. 215–16; petition from Rainer K. to Honecker, 19 October 1984, fo. 208–9; letter from Hellmann to Rühmke, 8 December 1984, fo. 207.

[87] SAPMO-BArch, DY 30/4988, anonymous petition to Krenz, 5 July 1986, fo. 175.

unwillingness to provide Bischofswerda with a large enough squad to survive in the *Oberliga*, was presented as an affront to socialist principles, a consequence of the elitism and closet professionalism of GDR football. Petitions tested negotiable boundaries. They gave people a sense of agency, however limited, in their dealings with the state, which tended towards conciliation rather than escalation in its responses to disgruntled citizens. The ZK sports department spent considerable time and energy trying to mollify public opinion in Bischofswerda.[88] Squad reinforcements did not save the BSG from relegation. But the team's fans had made their point. *Eigen-Sinn* was asserted, even if in a losing cause.

Supporters were not shy about airing grievances. Nor were they wary of reminding the SED regime of its self-proclaimed commitments to football, a holding to account that was evident in complaints about numerous areas of everyday life, from housing shortages to the availability of drinkable coffee or Mediterranean oranges.[89] In February 1989, 400 Dynamo Dresden supporters travelled to Romania to watch their team play Victoria Bucharest in a UEFA Cup match. They slept overnight at Bucharest train station and purchased match tickets on the black market.[90] Having allowed Dynamo fans into Victoria's ground to hang up banners, the Romanian police turned on the 'German tourists', frog-marching them outside and ripping up tickets. One group was threatened with truncheons and corralled into a side street by policemen with machine guns and un-muzzled dogs. Under a hail of rubber bullets, forty-five fans fled to the GDR embassy, where their flustered representative initially demanded political asylum. Others went to the West German embassy.[91] Three hundred fans were eventually allowed into the ground to watch the match from the beginning. A further fifty were let back in at half time. The rest did not see the match at all.[92]

In petitions written shortly after returning home, two Dynamo Dresden fans expressed outrage at what had happened. Jens V. from Berlin asked how 'peaceful football-loving young people from our state' could be subject to such violence 'in a socialist (!) foreign country'.

[88] *Ibid.*, memo from Hellmann to Krenz, 22 July 1986, fo. 164–5.

[89] Mark Allinson, '1977: The GDR's most normal year?', in Fulbrook (ed.), *Power and Society*, pp. 256–65.

[90] Pätzug, *Was wir niemals waren*, pp. 118–19; interview with Jens Genschmar, one of the Dresden fans who made the trip.

[91] SAPMO-BArch, DY 30/4985, petition from Andrea P. to the State Council, 8 March 1989, fo. 51–3; petition from Jens V. to the State Council, 3 March 1989, fo. 55–7; interview with Jens Genschmar.

[92] Pätzug, *Was wir niemals waren*, pp. 118–19.

He demanded financial recompense for the trip, which had cost 1,000 Marks and five days of holiday and ended with fans 'really in fear of their lives', as well as a written apology from the Romanian embassy and free tickets for the GDR's upcoming match against the Soviet Union. Andrea P. from Schmölln also addressed the cost of the trip ('I had to work and save for a long time'), the possibility of banning Victoria Bucharest from European games, and the need for discussions with the Romanian government about 'these excesses'.[93]

Like the Union Berlin fan club leaders in *Und freitags in die 'Grüne Hölle'*, these supporters articulated identities that simultaneously placed them within and beyond the parameters of state-approved behaviour. Clearly not hooligans, they emphasised that their behaviour abroad was peaceful and un-provocative (for example, not approaching Victoria's ground with the usual display of flags and scarves) and thus worthy of the East German state. Yet the Dresden fans, as the chilly tone of the *Stasi* report made clear, were no friends of the SED regime. They travelled to Romania independently, disregarding reports that the game was sold out, and purchased black-market tickets in Bucharest.[94] The trip reiterated the fact that the space occupied by football fans was liminal, neither regime-endorsing nor anti-communist, but containing a degree of uncertainty (or, in Victor Turner's words, 'anti-structure') that fed the construction of dynamic local identities.[95]

## 'Three cheers for our champions!'[96] Fan mail to Dynamo Dresden

If any team could have inspired a large-scale, privately-organised trip to Romania for a match against obscure opposition, it was Dynamo Dresden. Crowds at the Rudolf Harbig Stadium were larger than anywhere else, with an average home attendance of 22,754 even in the BFC-dominated 1980s.[97] Despite its sponsorship by the police, Dresden's reputation for good football, not to mention its status as the team likeliest to topple BFC, ensured that Dynamo fans were located throughout the republic. It is thus instructive to look at the fan mail received by Dynamo Dresden between 1969 and 1977, the period of its greatest success,

[93] SAPMO-BArch, DY 30/4985, petition from Andrea P., fo. 53; petition from Jens V., fo. 56–7.

[94] Pätzug, *Was wir niemals waren*, pp. 118–19.

[95] Palmowski, *Inventing a Socialist Nation*, p. 303.

[96] SAPMO-BArch, DO 101/079, letter from Rudolf H. to SG Dynamo Dresden, 5 June 1971.

[97] www.european-football-statistics.co.uk/attn/archive/avezddr80.htm.

beginning with promotion to the *Oberliga* and culminating in a second league and cup double. A less-reported aspect of fan culture emerges here, one that reminds us that debates about power and resistance, or *Eigen-Sinn* and conformity, do not tell the full story of GDR football. Woven deeply into the fabric of everyday life, the game – like music, television, gardening, fishing, or love – provided personal pleasures that transcended politics. Fan mail shows how, even in 'seemingly grand-scale, abstract, or impersonal systems of hegemony', such as communism, people 'act[ed] upon themselves and others' to build social relationships.[98] In this reading of everyday texts, football operates as 'an ideal vehicle' for analysing the role of social and cultural practices in shaping identity in modern societies.[99]

A range of individuals and organisations sent letters, cards, and telegrams to the Dynamo leadership. They were of all ages, from children as young as nine to pensioners. When Dynamo eliminated the Italian side Juventus from the UEFA Cup in 1973, it received congratulatory messages from, among others, a young Vietnamese worker living in Dresden, who – combining fan fervour with a nod to state-approved atheism – 'prayed to Buddha for the last time' to help the team before the second leg.[100] Of interest was the incursion of young female fans into a largely male world. A fourteen-year-old girl from Priestewitz, who went to Dynamo games with her father, wrote to the club in 1971 with ideas for cleaner terrace chants. An earlier letter asked whether it would be possible for a girl to become an *Oberliga* referee.[101] Ahead of the first all-German European Cup match in 1973, a pair of schoolgirls wrote a song that opened with the instructional couplet: 'Dynamo Dresden are the best/Beat "Bayern Munich" from the West'.[102]

The content of the messages was as diverse as the club's fan base. They included formal letters from other institutions; letters and postcards from factory collectives and individuals; artwork, mostly from children; and songs and poems from all manner of people. In general, these were happy communications. There were occasional gripes about the overly physical approach of some of Dynamo's opponents. One seventy-four-year-old fan, a retired policeman, made brief reference to the 'painful' departure

98 Steege *et al.*, 'The history of everyday life', 371.
99 Stieglitz, Martschukat, and Heinsohn, 'Sportreportage', 24.
100 SAPMO-BArch, DO 101/078, letter from Sam Ul K. to SG Dynamo Dresden, 3 October 1973. On the experience of Vietnamese 'guest workers', see Dennis and Laporte, *State and Minorities*, ch. 4.
101 SAPMO-BArch, DO 101/079, letters from Heike P. to SG Dynamo Dresden, 9 May 1971 and 23 November 1970.
102 *Ibid.*, song by Camelia L. and Martina W., n.d. This match is discussed in Chapter 5.

of the original Dynamo Dresden team to Berlin in the early 1950s.[103] But, even in these letters, the tone was celebratory. Football here served as an expression of both routine (the repetitive act of supporting Dynamo) and breaking out of routine (the less common act of articulating that support in writing). It created a sense of belonging through an imagined community.[104]

Children contributed regularly to the mailbag. Roberto L., a twelve-year-old who played for Motor Heidenau, wrote to the Dresden players in January 1971 to congratulate them on their good form during the first half of the season. He enclosed a skeletal drawing of a ball flying past the opposition goalkeeper and a 'little poem' of two stanzas that expressed his pride in the black and yellow club flag, which 'has never fallen' and 'which Kreische will carry around the world'. Nine-year-old Steffen J. from Freiberg displayed a sharper eye for detail in the drawing that he sent to the club after its *Oberliga* triumph in 1973. It depicted a joyous crowd scene at the Rudolf Harbig Stadium, with flag-waving fans dressed in black and yellow. On the pitch the referee blows his whistle, as the ball nestles in the away team's net. The scoreboard reads 2–1 to Dynamo.[105]

Among some adult fans, the urge to suggest new club songs was taken very seriously. The starting point was often the unsuitability of existing terrace chants – an approach calculated to appeal to club officials looking for ways to bypass Dynamo's more volatile supporters, who responded to the club's European exit at the hands of Leeds United in 1970 by throwing bottles onto the pitch and threatening the English players.[106] Konrad H. from Freiberg attended Dynamo's European Cup game against Ajax the following autumn. Though the atmosphere had been 'brilliant', he reported, the songs and chants had lacked tunefulness, 'to say nothing of their lyrical quality': 'damage to one's hearing was unavoidable'. H. wrote a new composition, entitled simply 'Dynamo'. Though any football song with a last verse urging an end to abuse of referees is probably doomed to failure, he immodestly suggested that it was 'rhythmically attractive, youthful, and catchy' and could become the club anthem. The club's apparently lukewarm response was made

[103] SAPMO-BArch, DO 101/078, letter from the TKO collective at the VEB SBS Dresden to SG Dynamo Dresden, 21 June 1973; SAPMO-BArch, DO 101/079, letter from Rudolf H. to SG Dynamo Dresden, 5 June 1971.

[104] Chris Stone, 'The role of football in everyday life', *Soccer & Society* vol. 8, no. 2/3 (April/July 2007), 175, 179.

[105] SAPMO-BArch, DO 101/079, letter from Roberto L. to SG Dynamo Dresden, January 1971; SAPMO-BArch, DO 101/078, letter from Steffen J. to SG Dynamo Dresden, n.d.

[106] SAPMO-BArch, DO 101/078, Kurzbericht über die Durchführung von internationalen Sportveranstaltungen in der DDR, n.d.

comprehensible by the poem 'Rudolf Harbig Stadium' that H. appended to the second of his two letters. Its memorably bad opening stanza referenced the distinctive floodlights at Dynamo's home ground: 'Not far away from Dresden zoo, you see giraffes/Gigantically large, craning their necks up into the air/They look with dignity at the throng and tumult/When a football feast is celebrated in the oval'.[107]

Konrad H. over-estimated his writing skills, but he was not alone in expressing support for Dynamo in an earnest and rather touching manner. From the marching song proposed by a pensioner to numerous compositions by schoolgirls and schoolboys, with titles such as 'Dynamo story' or 'our Dynamos', chants and poems articulated the bond that fans felt for their heroes in black and yellow.[108] Embracing both sexes and all ages, the mail collected by Dynamo Dresden testified to the club's popularity and to football's ubiquity in the GDR's sporting space. The letters, cards, poems, and songs conveyed the normal pleasures of watching football – in contrast, for example, to petitions, which focused attention on tensions and problems related to spectatorship. Few cultural activities had this kind of reach. Fan mail revealed football's central role as an 'extension of the everyday', a site for imagined communities that were fluid but enduring.[109] In this sense, a poem that lyricises the iconic floodlights spying on the action at the Rudolf Harbig Stadium is as relevant to the social history of East German football as a letter about biased referees.

## The state and football subculture: fan clubs

Dynamo Dresden's popularity placed the club at the forefront of an important element of fan culture: the fan club. Of the 353 officially registered clubs in 1988, Dynamo, the 'extreme case', had 74, the largest amount of any team.[110] Union Berlin had forty-eight, BFC only twelve.[111] In March of that year, the Dynamo Dresden representative

[107] SAPMO-BArch, DO 101/079, letters from Konrad H. to SG Dynamo Dresden, 26 February and 31 October 1972.

[108] SAPMO-BArch, DO 101/079, letter from Rudolf H. to SG Dynamo Dresden, 5 June 1971; letter from Bernd K. to SG Dynamo Dresden, 18 April 1974; letter from Gerd-Uwe H. to SG Dynamo Dresden, 30 September 1973.

[109] Stone, 'The role of football', 171, 180.

[110] BStU, MfS HA XX/221, Bericht zum Stand der Sicherheit und Ordnung bei Fußballspielen im Spieljahr 1987/88, 15 July 1988, fo. 263.

[111] *Ibid.*, Berichterstattung über die Ergebnisse der Erhöhung von Sicherheit und Ordnung bei Fußballspielen, 14 June 1988, fo. 251–7; Einschätzung zum jugendlichen Anhang des 1. FC Union Berlin und zur Erhöhung von Sicherheit und Ordnung bei Fußballspielen der 1. Halbserie 1988/89, 30 December 1988, fo. 303.

Christian Coun reported to the DFV that the club had undertaken fan-club work since 1982, liaised regularly with supporters' representatives, and supported numerous activities, from organised trips to away matches, football tournaments, and dance events.[112]

By the late 1980s, GDR clubs were making stronger efforts than ever to bring supporters into the fold. The primary motive was security. Fan clubs, at least in theory, provided a means of curbing hooliganism – community outreach projects that would tame wilder elements of a team's fan base through discounted travel to away games, autograph sessions with players, and a sense of participation, however nominal, in club affairs. The reality was more complicated. There was one telling statistic in Coun's report. For every registered (and therefore monitored) Dynamo Dresden fan club in 1988, there were four that were unregistered – and thus illegal.[113]

When fan clubs emerged in the GDR during the 1970s, they – like the amateur bands that sprang up in imitation of The Beatles in the mid 1960s[114] – were a grassroots phenomenon, without official input or support. Like jeans, music, and television, they were illustrative of the virtual border transgressions that characterised the GDR's engagement with Western popular culture. Taking inspiration from the West German fan scene, supporters congregated in loose, independent organisations. Chemie Leipzig's first fan club, the Green Angels, was founded in 1975. Looking wild like 'the uncle of the spirit of the Sudeten mountains (*Rübezahls Onkel*)' and constantly provoking the police, its members were heroes to young Chemie fans like Jens Fuge.[115] The writer and BFC fan Andreas Gläser recalled how he and a group of friends decided to call the fan club that they founded in the early 1980s Bobbys: a dual reference to Dynamo's role as East Germany's police team and to 'the cool motherland of football and punk rock', England.[116]

In December 1977, fans of Rot–Weiß Erfurt issued a home-made proclamation, inviting supporters to found a fan club in the city.[117] Investigations revealed that the two fans behind the announcement got the idea through 'long-standing' ties to West German fans, particularly those of Hertha BSC. Using a friend's typewriter, they wrote the

[112] Erfahrungsaustausch zu Problemen der Ordnung und Sicherheit bei Fußballveranstaltungen am 10.03.1988, 28 April 1988, fo. 218–19.
[113] *Ibid.*, fo. 218.
[114] McDougall, *Youth Politics*, pp. 179–81.
[115] Fuge, 'Von Fußball-Anhängern und Schlachtenbummlern', p. 97.
[116] Gläser, *Der BFC war schuld*, p. 43.
[117] ThHStAW, Bezirksparteiarchiv der SED Erfurt, Bezirksleitung der SED Erfurt IV D/2/16/603, Bekanntmachung 1/77, fo. 23.

proclamation on Christmas Eve, printing seventy copies that were to be circulated in Erfurt, Weimar, Leipzig, and Berlin.[118] The trio was hauled before a meeting with representatives of the football club, the city council, the police, and the DTSB on 30 December and reminded that the distribution of unauthorised written material was prohibited. The message was clear: 'there will be no fan club in Erfurt'.[119]

Power in East Germany though, as numerous recent studies have shown, was rarely just imposed by the few on the many.[120] The SED was repeatedly forced to bend policies to popular demands. The need for a more conciliatory approach to fan work than the one shown by the Erfurt authorities gradually became apparent. In 1970 the 'youth working group' (*Arbeitsgruppe Jugend*) at Union Berlin spoke sternly of disassociating the fan base from professional clubs in the West, stamping out excessive drinking and abusive chants, and following police orders. Ten years later, the same body was discussing boat trips, forums with club officials, and small dance events.[121] At the start of the 1980s, Chemie Leipzig fan clubs 'shot up out of the ground like mushrooms'. Jens Fuge counted eighty in the city alone, 'all of them organised independently and provisionally'.[122] Similar trends were noticeable at Dynamo Dresden, BFC, and Union.[123] Fan clubs were only one expression of a lively grassroots activism in this period, which was also apparent – though generally involving smaller numbers – in Church, environmental, and peace circles.[124] The apparent paradox between a re-born civic sphere and a smothering secret-police presence points to what we saw in Chapter 6: the deeper the state's tentacles went, the less certain its grip seemed to be.

As was the case with Beatles-inspired guitar groups in 1964 and 1965, straightforward repression did not work with fan clubs. They were fluid and small groups that met either privately or as rarely distinguishable parts of a larger match-day crowd, a crowd that at Union Berlin embraced a 'colourful' and 'strange' cross-section of the local population, including

118 *Ibid.*, Aktennotiz über die Aussprache betreffs Bildung eines Fan-Clubs in Erfurt, 30 December 1977, fo. 27–8.

119 *Ibid.*, fo. 28; untitled report [front page missing] on the same meeting, fo. 30–1.

120 See e.g. Betts, *Within Walls*; Palmowski, *Inventing a Socialist Nation*; Port, *Conflict and Stability*; Richthofen, *Bringing Culture to the Masses.*

121 Union Berlin Archive, untitled report (AG Jugend, 1970); Programm der Arbeitsgruppe Jugend des 1. FC Union Bln., 28 February 1980.

122 Fuge, 'Von Fußball-Anhängern und Schlachtenbummlern', pp. 97–8.

123 Union fan Sven S., like Fuge, talks of fan clubs that 'sprang up like mushrooms'. Interview with Sven S.

124 See e.g. Fulbrook, *Anatomy*, ch. 8.

hippies, punks, and heavy metal fans.[125] In both examples, the authorities ran into youth subcultures that were not easily defined or permeated. Subtle, multi-faceted tactics were required. In terms of fan clubs, two distinctive strands emerged by the mid 1980s, encouraging the climate of 'repressive tolerance' that typified SED youth policy under Honecker.[126] One was surveillance. Informants were deployed in as many unregistered fan clubs as possible, providing information about members' behaviour, habits, and attitudes. When he read his own *Stasi* file after reunification, Sven S., a member of the Union fan club FC Momme, discovered that four of his friends had worked for the secret police.[127]

The second, soft-power strategy centred on co-option. There was growing recognition in leadership circles that 'to dissolve fan clubs is an illusion. They will go into "illegality", which will only increase their attractiveness to young people and make the thing even more uncontrollable'.[128] An SED report from 1984 was typical of the uncertain approach – part olive branch, part gloved fist – that the authorities adopted. It began with an overview of the proliferation of fan clubs, estimating that there were at least fifty groups in each of the GDR's fifteen counties. The report then dwelt on a bureaucratic issue: the fact that no fan club had applied for state recognition according to the provisions of the 1975 law on 'the founding and activity of associations'. Throughout we are reminded that the party leadership correlated the existence of fan clubs and the threat of hooliganism. The report concluded with a series of questions. Is a 'certain legalisation' required? Are fan clubs to be considered associations as per the 1975 law? How can incentives such as cheap travel to away games be used to separate decent supporters from troublemakers?[129]

Subsequent reports on security at football grounds were rarely without a paragraph or two on fan clubs, a telling illustration of the way in which the communist regime, as with Church and environmental activism in the 1980s, had to adjust policies in the face of grassroots initiatives. Co-option took various forms, usually beginning (and sometimes ending) with the registration of fan clubs. In this process fans used the authorities – registering, for example, to get easier access to tickets – as much as *vice versa*. More engaged football clubs organised activities for registered supporters, including recreational tournaments and trips to

[125] Interview with Tim E.; Luther and Willmann, *Eisern Union!*, pp. 99–101.

[126] Ohse, *Jugend nach dem Mauerbau*, pp. 351–2. [127] Interview with Sven S.

[128] SAPMO-BArch, DY 30/IV 2/2.2039/251, Zur Lage auf den Fußballplätzen und den Schlußfolgerungen, n.d., fo. 31.

[129] *Ibid.*, Standpunkt zu einigen Fragen der weiteren Arbeit mit Fan-Clubs im Fußball, 8 May 1984, fo. 41–5.

away matches. The liaison officer at BFC held weekly fan meetings and 'did a great deal' for supporters.[130] At Rot–Weiß Erfurt in 1988, fan-club members were included in club affairs in typical GDR fashion. They were given pickaxes and sledgehammers to help with pre-season renovations to the Georgi Dimitrov Stadium.[131]

Some of the more creative ideas stemmed from the FDJ leadership. This should come as no surprise. The SED leadership in Potsdam had complained as far back as 1967 that FDJ officials were 'only concerned with the organisation of dance events'.[132] Sensing the possibility of connecting with young people through popular culture rather than politics, the youth organisation favoured a catholic approach to event programming in many areas. This was illustrated by the FDJ's support for the creation in Köpenick of a Union Berlin youth club with a purely 'sporting focus'.[133] The FDJ leadership argued in 1985 that 'the chief method [of influencing fans] must be to talk to them (at the moment we're only talking about them!)'.[134] The most influential proposal for drawing supporters to official fan clubs came from the FDJ's Youth Tourist travel bureau. In an effort to outflank unruly *Schlachtenbummler*, it created 'football expresses', organised train trips to away matches for registered fan club members. Eight expresses ran on four routes (Berlin–Dresden, Erfurt–Dresden, Erfurt–Berlin, and Leipzig–Magdeburg) during the 1984/5 season.[135] For Union Berlin's match against Lokomotive Leipzig in April 1988, 210 fans paid 32 Marks each for a package that included reserved seating on a special train, a pre-match cultural programme (including a visit to the city's sports museum), a ticket, and food in the canteen at the Karl Marx University.[136]

The attempt to canalise fan clubs, though, had little impact. Just as *Stasi* efforts to infiltrate other uncooperative subcultures, from Jehovah's Witnesses to punks, often fell flat, so the limits of dictatorship became apparent in the state's dealings with self-directed groups in football.[137]

[130] Luther and Willmann, *BFC*, p. 139.

[131] 'Auf der Halde tat sich etwas ...', *Die Neue Fußball-Woche*, 16 August 1988, 10.

[132] Richthofen, *Bringing Culture to the Masses*, pp. 137–8.

[133] Interview with Theo Körner.

[134] SAPMO-BArch, DY 30/IV 2/2.2039/251, Standpunkt des Zentralrats der FDJ zur Erhöhung von Ordnung und Sicherheit bei Oberligafußballspielen, n.d., fo. 33–5.

[135] *Ibid.*, Information zur Lage auf den Fußballplätzen der DDR und Vorschläge zur besseren Gewährleistung von Ordnung und Sicherheit im Zusammenhang mit Fußballspielen, n.d., fo. 27.

[136] SAPMO-BArch, DY 24/21223, Information zum Fußballexpreß von "Jugendtourist" anläßlich des Spiels 1. FC Lok Leipzig–1. FC Union Berlin am 23.4.1988, n.d.

[137] On Jehovah's Witnesses and punks, see Dennis and Laporte, *State and Minorities*, chs. 3 and 6.

Many supporters ignored the perks that accompanied official recognition. The *Stasi* noted in 1986 that BFC had six registered fan clubs and twenty-two that did not meet DFV guidelines. At Union, about thirty of seventy-eight fan clubs were unregistered at the end of 1988.[138] Neither *Stasi* surveillance nor FDJ initiatives achieved the desired breakthrough. At FC Momme, a closely knit Union fan club that met in Monbijou Park in the centre of Berlin, outsiders were viewed with suspicion. Anyone with a Saxon accent who showed up was regarded as a likely IM or policeman.[139]

All of this left the SED's initial assessment of the scene as valid in 1989 as it was in 1985: 'despite some efforts football clubs as well as state organs and societal organisations have little or no influence on the atmosphere in these [fan] clubs'.[140] The unchanging picture illustrated the governing dysfunctionality that was acute in, though by no means confined to, football. Central directives were applied inconsistently, if they were applied at all. For every football club that registered fan-club members, there was another where officials declared that 'we have no posts for fan work' and did nothing.[141]

Registration in any case offered no guarantee of influence. The official Dynamo Dresden fan club in Zittau, founded in 1984, contained thirty-three members aged between sixteen and thirty. None were SED members. Five had criminal records, four had received stadium bans, and one was applying to emigrate to West Germany.[142] Even in a supervised environment, supporters were capable of behaviour hardly befitting socialist youth. One Union fan who took part in the FDJ-sponsored trip to the game against Lokomotive Leipzig in April 1988 gave the *Heil Hitler* salute in front of a bust of the communist martyr Werner Seelenbinder. Two brothers in the group, which consisted of members of six registered Union fan clubs, then abused and spat at FDJ officials who took the prankster to task.[143] Fans took what they could get from these

138 BStU, MfS ZOS/3212, Bericht zum negativen Fußballanhang des BFC Dynamo in der Spielsaison 1985/86 und die Ergebnisse der Arbeit des Hauptsachgebietes negativer Fußballanhang, 11 July 1986, fo. 27–8; BStU, MfS HA XX/221, Einschätzung zum jugendlichen Anhang des 1. FC Union Berlin, fo. 303.

139 Interview with Sven S.

140 SAPMO-BArch, DY 30/4949, Information zur Lage auf Fußballplätzen und Vorschläge zur besseren Gewährleistung von Ordnung und Sicherheit im Zusammenhang mit Fußballspielen, n.d., fo. 2.

141 BStU, MfS HA XX/221, Bericht über den Stand der Realisierung der Aufgabenstellung der Information des ZK der SED "Zur Lage auf den Fußballplätzen und Vorschläge zur Gewährleistung von Ordnung und Sicherheit im Zusammenhang mit Fußballspielen, 30 December 1985, fo. 33.

142 HStA Dresden, 11857 SED-Bezirksleitung Dresden Nr. IV E – 2/16/719, letter from Parpaloni to Lothar Stammnitz, 27 July 1984.

143 SAPMO-BArch, DY 24/21223, Information zum Fußballexpreß.

package trips, most notably a safer means of travel to away games in a period of increased spectator violence. For the authorities, the special trains, expensive to run and offering little in the way of improved socialist consciousness, were of minimal political benefit.[144]

The independent-minded spirit of fan clubs, whether registered or not, was apparent in their names. Some were based on geographical location (the Momme in FC Momme, for example, was local slang for Monbijou Park) or the name of a favourite player. As with beat bands in the 1960s, English-language names were common. Among the twenty-eight BFC fan clubs listed by the *Stasi* in 1986, nine had English names, referencing the political (Black Panther, from Birkenwerder), the pop cultural (Beatles BFC Club, from Pankow), the inclusive (Accept, from Lichtenberg), the obscure (The Golden Monster), and the boastful (The Champs, from Bergfelde).[145]

Particularly interesting were references to German football or political traditions that had been eliminated after the Second World War. Two of the BFC fan clubs listed by the MfS in 1988 were Little Preussen and Madness Boys of Preussen. Both Anglo-Germanic names referred to the dismembered region of which Berlin was the capital (Prussia), a word redolent in SED discourse of Junker militarism and fascism. In the latter case, this was united with a double allusion to wild behaviour and an English ska band.[146] One of the six Union fan clubs on the Youth Tourist trip to Leipzig in April 1988 went by the quietly provocative name of VSG Victoria 84. Based in the Western district of Tempelhof, Viktoria Berlin was one of the city's oldest football clubs. 'VSG' stood for *Volkssportgemeinschaft* ('folk sports club'), a term with unmistakeable Nazi connotations.[147]

Through the names they adopted, fan clubs expressed identities that were as fluid and multi-layered as the fan scene itself. Alongside the national and the international, the homage to English bands and West German teams, there were names that emphasised domestic and regional concerns. Andreas Gläser recounts the rule of thumb for naming BFC fan clubs in the early 1980s: '*BFC Okay – Dynamo nee!*' and '*Berlin ja – Zone nein*!' His account draws a line between the city in

[144] Interview with Theo Körner; interview with Tino C.
[145] BStU, MfS ZOS/3212, Bericht zum negativen Fußballanhang des BFC Dynamo, fo. 27–8.
[146] *Ibid.*, Bericht zum negativen Fußballanhang des BFC Dynamo in der Spielsaison 1987/88 und zu den Ergebnissen der politisch-operativen Bearbeitung, 13 June 1988, fo. 242–3.
[147] Interview with Tino C. (founder member of Victoria 84).

Figure 12. A member of the Black Eagle fan club at a BFC home game in the Friedrich-Ludwig-Jahn-Sportpark, 1980. Note the customised scarf (with Anglophile name), jean jacket, and long hair – all standard features of the new fan culture of the 1970s and 1980s. Notorious for its unruly behaviour, Black Eagle was closely monitored by the *Stasi*. By 1986 it had disappeared from the terraces.

which he lived and the *Zone*, the commonly used Western media term for East Germany, the inhabitants of which (*Zonis*) 'often transferred their displeasure at the GDR to the members and fans of BFC'.[148] Berlin-based identities sometimes trumped bitter local rivalries – witness the short-lived attempt among Union and BFC fans in the mid 1980s to create a 'Berlin front' against hooligans from the rest of the GDR.[149] Outside the capital, local sentiments were equally pronounced. One feared Chemie Leipzig fan club was known as the Saxon People's Front – a regional badge of pride worn more modestly by Dynamo Dresden fan club Elbflorenz, named in honour of the city's reputation as the 'Florence on the Elbe'.[150] Football allowed the expression of horizontal as well as vertical *Eigen-Sinn*, encouraging identities that not only distanced fans from the state, but also differentiated them

[148] Gläser, *Der BFC war schuld*, pp. 43–5. [149] Interview with Frank L.

[150] Fuge, 'Von Fußball-Anhängern und Schlachtenbummlern', p. 98; Pätzug, *Was wir niemals waren*, p. 224.

from each other. In the collectivist framework of the GDR, where class, regional, and gender differences were elided, this was important in individualising and localising citizens.

State socialism, like capitalism prior to the 1990s, failed to sanitise football or tame its fan culture. For example, the FDJ proposed cleaning up the terraces in the mid 1980s with songs and chants that were distinct from 'the often unpleasant texts' in circulation at *Oberliga* matches.[151] Fans, of course, utterly ignored this appeal to their better nature and continued to follow the standard global practice of aiming abuse at their rivals. 'Dynamo, you are a shit club' was directed at both Dynamo Dresden and BFC. The latter inspired chants such as 'down with the armed eleven' and 'cops are work-shy',[152] broadsides at the guardians of order that were also audible ('get the cops') when Dynamo Moscow crossed town to play local rivals Spartak in the Soviet Union.[153] Chemie Leipzig fans asked 'Which whores, which dogs created 1. FC Lok?', in much the same way as supporters of the Hungarian team Honvéd taunted Budapest rivals MTK with the charmless couplet 'Shit on you/Your mother's a whore!'[154] When Union followers travel to Leipzig for a game against Lokomotive in the short story 'Die Fans von Union', the supporters trade insults – 'Saxon dagos', 'run Prussian, run, or we'll string you up' – based on regional identities that communism had tried to efface.[155] It was these identities that informed people's everyday lives, in ways that centralised state power did not. They created local spaces where the party, reluctantly or otherwise, was forced to make concessions to popular culture.[156]

On the contested terrain of East German football, fan clubs offered a striking illustration of the limits of dictatorship, the victory of autonomy over co-option. At the same time, these victories were always incomplete and had few direct political consequences. Umberto Eco, in a scathing article on Italy's national obsession, once posed the following question: 'Is it possible to have a revolution on a football Sunday?'[157] The answer was as obvious to Eco as it was to neo-Marxist sports scholars writing in the same period. Spectatorship ignored the possibility of political action

[151] SAPMO-BArch, DY 30/IV 2/2.2039/251, Standpunkt des Zentralrats der FDJ, fo. 33.

[152] *Ibid.*, Information zur Lage auf den Fußballplätzen der DDR, fo. 23; Koch, 'Rasen-Rivalen', p. 56.

[153] Edelman, *Spartak Moscow*, pp. 94–5.

[154] Koch, 'Rasen-Rivalen', p. 56; Karády and Hadas, 'Soccer and Antisemitism in Hungary', p. 232.

[155] Moog, *Die Fans von Union*, pp. 90–1.

[156] Palmowski, 'Regional identities', 524–5.

[157] Umberto Eco, 'The World Cup and its pomps', in *Travels in Hyperreality*, trans. William Weaver (New York: Harcourt, 1986), p. 172.

and thus reinforced the status quo, be it capitalist or communist.[158] Much depends, though, on how the word 'political' is defined. Fan clubs marked a retreat from politics in the sense that their primary concern was football (dressing for it, discussing it, travelling to it, and watching it). But in the SED worldview, such autonomous behaviour was far from a bread-and-circuses distraction. To watch football, in the words of Roland Barthes, 'is to call the whole world to witness: in a word, it is to communicate'.[159] The communists often disliked what they saw and heard from the *Schlachtenbummler* in their midst. *Und freitags in die 'Grüne Hölle'* presented Union Berlin fans as anarchic, joyous, dishevelled, and – despite the presence of security fences and police – free. Football supporters did not cause the gentle revolution of 1989. But the world that they inhabited, the fan clubs where *Eigen-Sinn* meant drinking beer with friends, fare-dodging, obscene chants, and keeping an eye out for *Bundesliga* results, formed part of the crumbling backdrop for the momentous events that autumn. This subculture, moreover, survived the *Wende*, providing supporters in the East with self-help strategies that were re-directed against the perils of free-market football.[160] Fan clubs constitute one of the lasting cultural legacies of GDR football.

158 On the neo-Marxist critique, see e.g. Allen Guttmann, *Sports Spectators* (New York: Columbia University Press, 1986), ch. 6.

159 Roland Barthes, *What is Sport?*, trans. Richard Howard (New Haven and London: Yale University Press, 2007), p. 61.

160 See Chapter 15.

# 9 The 'wild East': hooliganism in the GDR

## Fighting socialism: fan disorder behind the Iron Curtain

The *Oberliga* matches on 16 and 17 October 1987 ended with a familiar-looking table. After a 2–2 draw at Hallescher FC, BFC – league champions for nine years running – led the way, one point clear of Lokomotive Leipzig. Lok's 2–0 victory away to Union Berlin ensured that the capital's other team remained last, facing the latest in a long line of relegation struggles. In mid-table, BSG Stahl Brandenburg's 1–0 win at home to FC Magdeburg left the two teams level on points.

Off the field too, the weekend's action was typical of GDR football in the mid 1980s, a period during which, as one Union Berlin supporter recalled, hardly a game passed by without 'some sort of violence between [rival] fans'.[1] Two HFC fans were arrested during the draw with BFC, one for making 'fascist remarks', the other for climbing over the security fencing to invade the pitch. The game was briefly stopped after a firework thrown from the stands impeded the linesman's view of proceedings. After the home defeat to Lokomotive Leipzig, 300 Union fans went to Schönefeld train station in East Berlin to start a fight with 100 Lok supporters. A dozen policemen wielded truncheons to maintain order. Meanwhile, disappointed Magdeburg fans en route from the stadium to the station in Brandenburg caused 5,000 Marks worth of damage to five tram cars, by smashing windows, ripping up seats, and breaking lamps. Three people were arrested, one for making anti-GDR comments and two, under Section 215 of the state legal code, for 'hooliganism' (*Rowdytum*).[2]

By 1987 football hooliganism had well and truly broken through the Iron Curtain, to the puzzlement of communist authorities everywhere. The fact that the *Stasi* considered a weekend on which twenty-five people were arrested for slandering the state and various public order offences to

[1] Interview with Sven S.

[2] BStU, MfS HA XX/2700, Übersicht zu den Fußballoberligaspielen des 9. Spieltages am 17.10.1987, 18 October 1987, fo. 70–1.

Figure 13. Union Berlin fans invade the pitch in Karl-Marx-Stadt, May 1988. Crossing the line that separated fans and players, pitch invasions were commonly seen as acts of hooliganism. Often, though, they were joyous rather than menacing occasions. Harald Hauswald here captures the moment just after Union midfielder Mario Maek had scored the last-gasp goal against FCK that saved his team from relegation. Bedlam followed, as Union fans scaled the fences to mob their heroes.

be a normal, even quiet one tells us much about the East German, and indeed global, landscape at this time.[3] In Western Europe, England led the way, and – through the success of its teams in European competition – regularly exported a drink-fuelled, xenophobic brand of violence, a menacing phenomenon superbly captured in Bill Buford's *Among the Thugs*.[4] West Germany also grappled with an entrenched hooligan culture. In 1979 a Schalke 04 supporter slipped and fell to his death while fighting. Two years later, fans in Saarbrücken beat to death a passer-by after they had been thrown out of a bar. In 1982 the West German Ministry of the Interior, in a report entitled *Sport und Gewalt* ('Sport and violence'), introduced measures aimed at improving safety and fan behaviour in and around stadia.[5]

[3] *Ibid.* [4] Bill Buford, *Among the Thugs* (London: Arrow, 1992).

[5] Guttmann, *Sports Spectators*, p. 160; Dwertmann and Rigauer, 'Football hooliganism in Germany', p. 82.

Football, as we see throughout this study, served as a vehicle of Cold War cultural transfer, fostering interests and behaviour that transcended the Iron Curtain. Hooliganism was part of this crossover. Spectator violence was widespread in many communist states by the mid 1980s. In the Soviet Union, the *perestroika* era was punctuated by regular outbreaks of football-related disorder, most commonly involving the supporters of Spartak Moscow ('the team of intellectuals and hooligans'), but also reflective of growing nationalist tensions in areas such as the Ukraine (Dynamo Kiev) and Lithuania (Žalgiris Vilnius).[6] In Hungary, stadia became magnets for neo-fascism, as anti-Semitic chants ('Dirty Jews! Dirty Jews!/Gas chambers! Gas chambers!') were directed against supporters of MTK, a Budapest club with middle-class, Jewish origins.[7] In Czechoslovakia, the press documented an alarming increase in football hooliganism between 1980 and 1987, reporting the kind of incidents – fights between rival fans, vandalised trains, and pitch invasions – that were commonplace in East Germany. The authorities aired a documentary entitled *Proč?* ('Why?'), which followed a group of Sparta Prague fans to an away match. The intention had been to educate supporters about the right ways to behave, but it only inspired copycat violence, even among crowds of youths on their way out of cinemas where the film was shown.[8]

As a live spectator sport, from England to the Soviet Union, football was in precipitous decline during the 1980s. In West Germany aggregate crowds at professional matches shrank from 26 million in the late 1970s to about 18 million in 1990.[9] During a similar period in East Germany (1976–90), aggregate *Oberliga* attendance dropped from 2.5 million to 1.5 million.[10] On 19 May 1985, the *Sunday Times*, with characteristic contempt for the sport that later became the cash cow of its proprietor, Rupert Murdoch, described football as 'a slum game played in slum stadiums watched by slum people'. Ten days later, at the European Cup final at the Heysel Stadium in Brussels, crumbling facilities and inadequate policing allowed Liverpool fans to charge their Juventus counterparts, causing thirty-nine deaths in front of a horrified television audience of millions.[11] In the aftermath, the British Prime Minister

[6] See Edelman, *Serious Fun*, pp. 208–14; Edelman, *Spartak Moscow*, pp. 293–5.

[7] Karády and Hadas, 'Soccer and Antisemitism in Hungary', pp. 227–8, 232.

[8] Vic Duke and Pavel Slepička, 'Bohemian rhapsody: football supporters in the Czech Republic', in Dunning *et al.* (eds.), *Fighting Fans*, pp. 52–4.

[9] Goldblatt, *The Ball Is Round*, pp. 546–7.

[10] Horn and Weise, *Das große Lexikon*, p. 420.

[11] Goldblatt, *The Ball Is Round*, pp. 542–5.

Margaret Thatcher apparently asked football officials whether supporters were an essential component at matches.[12]

The Heysel disaster did not go unnoticed in East Germany. State television broke off live coverage after the scale of the tragedy had become clear and before the game, a meaningless 1–0 victory to Juventus, was played. Public opinion in Dresden the next day largely supported the decision, though some people switched to Czechoslovakian television to continue watching. Local DTSB functionaries and those attending a referees' course argued that such bloodshed was unthinkable in the GDR.[13] Others were not so sure. The *Stasi* issued a directive to all unit leaders on 30 May, warning of the possible impact of Heysel on GDR hooligans and the need to tighten security ahead of the cup final between BFC and Dynamo Dresden.[14] Shortly after that controversial game (to be discussed in Chapter 10), an irate Dresden fan wrote the following to the DFV: 'You should be happy by the way that despite all attempts to the contrary by [the referee] sports friend Roßner Dynamo Dresden won. Everyone can guess what would have happened otherwise. I don't want to meet the trouble in Brussels halfway, but such tendencies are also possible here'.[15] When it came to hooliganism, the moral high ground on which the communist authorities stood was uncertain. During crowd disturbances at a match between Dukla Banská Bystrica and Sparta Prague on 19 June 1985, Sparta fans were heard to chant 'Liverpool, Liverpool'. The Heysel final, as we saw, was shown right through to its conclusion live on Czechoslovakian television.[16]

In assessing the history of hooliganism in Honecker's East Germany, this chapter examines the extent of football-related disorder, the response of the authorities to spectator violence, and the social and political reasons behind an ugly development at odds with the peaceful and collective values of socialism. Hooliganism served as an extreme manifestation of sporting *Eigen-Sinn*, a violent rejection of the socialist state and its notions of healthy spectatorship. It illustrated the limits of the SED dictatorship, which devoted plentiful resources, from police units to academic studies, to misbehaving fans, but failed, just as West

12 Eric Dunning, Patrick Murphy, and Ivan Waddington, 'Towards a sociological understanding of football hooliganism as a world problem', in Dunning *et al.* (eds.), *Fighting Fans*, p. 225n.

13 HStA Dresden, 11857 SED-Bezirksleitung Dresden Nr. IV E – 2/16/719, Information über Meinungen zum Fußball-Europa-Cup-Finale am 29.05.1985 in Brüssel, 30 May 1985.

14 BStU, MfS HA XX/1000, directive from the general lieutenant to all unit leaders, 30 May 1985, fo. 318–9.

15 SAPMO-BArch, DY 30/4984, petition from Alfred M. to the DFV, 9 June 1985, fo. 113.

16 Duke and Slepička, 'Bohemian rhapsody', pp. 54–5.

European governments of the period failed, to reduce, let alone eradicate, football unrest. The truest picture of East German society during the Honecker era can be found in the liminal spaces – stadia, town centres, trains, and railway stations – in which hooliganism prospered. GDR hooliganism was part of a European, even global, discourse on 'the quest for pleasurable excitement' characteristic of industrial societies.[17] It was also an accurate gauge of the socio-economic and political decline that contributed to the SED's downfall in 1989.

## The state and 'real existing' hooliganism

Violent incidents at German football matches, as we saw in Chapter 7, long predated communist rule. Leading officials and coaches in the Weimar Republic frequently condemned the 'sick people', 'hollow heads', and 'beasts behind barriers' who flocked to the game after the First World War.[18] As in the 1920s, spectator unrest in the 1950s and 1960s was spontaneous and largely confined to the stadium. In the 1970s, as fan culture became more youthful, mobile, and organised, this changed. When BFC and Union Berlin met in 1977, the *Stasi* noted that much of the hooligan behaviour that led to the arrest of seventy-nine Union fans took place outside the stadium. Young supporters at train stations in the districts of Mitte and Friedrichshain chanted 'down with the pack of cops' and '1, 2, 3, truncheon police – smash them in the gob'. Flag poles were used to break windows and light fittings on trains and in stations. Two policemen were assaulted.[19] Leipzig police estimated that between 100 and 300 disorderly fans were attached to the city's two teams, Lok and Chemie, during the 1976/7 season. Much of the trouble, it was observed, occurred in train stations and the city centre.[20] As in England, GDR hooligans learned to disperse their activities, avoiding the concentrated police presence in the stadium.

The case of Union Berlin, popular local rivals to Mielke's BFC, highlights the scale and political resonance of football hooliganism in the 1970s. Matches at Union's ground in Köpenick were regularly interrupted by supporters throwing bottles, firecrackers, and toilet rolls onto

[17] Dunning, *Sport Matters*, p. 147.

[18] Oswald, *"Fußball-Volksgemeinschaft"*, p. 253. The quotes are from Peco Bauwens and Otto Nerz.

[19] BStU, MfS ZAIG/4117, Information über erneutes rowdyhaftes Verhalten von "Anhängern des 1. FC Union Berlin" im Zusammenhang mit dem Oberliga-Punktspiel BFC Dynamo gegen den 1. FC Union Berlin am 26.8.1977, 27 August 1977, fo. 1–4.

[20] Dennis, 'Soccer hooliganism', p. 58.

the pitch. After a stormy encounter with Wismut Aue in 1976, the club seriously contemplated moving all home games to the larger, more distant World Youth Stadium – a venue change that was usually enforced only when BFC were the visitors.[21] The club leadership wrote directly to unruly fans. Some letters asked them to attend personal hearings about recent misbehaviour, a reminder that the SED had not entirely abandoned the principles of the 'educational dictatorship' of the 1960s.[22] Others imposed one-year stadium bans.[23]

The sense among Union supporters that they were being unfairly targeted surfaced in October 1977, at a rock concert in Alexanderplatz in the centre of East Berlin to mark the GDR's twenty-eighth anniversary. During the concert, nine young men climbed up some scaffolding, which collapsed. All of them were injured, three seriously. Unaware of what had happened, spectators took umbrage when the police cut power to the stage and aggressively cleared a path to the injured youths. Many of those in attendance were Union Berlin fans, for whom this was one provocation too far. They charged the police and engaged in mass chants such as 'Down with the GDR!', 'Germany awake' (a phrase redolent of Nazism), and 'Honecker out – Biermann in!', the latter a reference to the poet and songwriter who had been expatriated the previous year. Sixty-six people were injured in the confrontation. In total 468 people were arrested on the day and, after further investigations, 95 of them received custodial sentences.[24]

Showcasing again the subversive intersection of music and football in socialist popular culture, the 1977 unrest revealed the explosive potential for youth disaffection in Honecker's East Germany. The *Stasi* reported a growth both in the number and in the seriousness of incidents of football hooliganism between 1978 and 1981, drawing attention to the prominent role of Union fans in the escalating disorder.[25] In 1984, the SED summarised the situation as follows:

> A minority of football supporters, among them many young people aged between 14 and 22, influence the general sporting atmosphere [at matches] and have a disturbing impact in public. According to estimates, we are talking about three to

[21] Union Berlin Archive, letter from Günter Mielis to Karl-Heinz Benedix (DFV), 11 January 1977.

[22] See Dorothee Wierling, 'Die Jugend als innere Feind: Konflikte in der Erziehungsdiktatur der sechziger Jahre', in *Sozialgeschichte der DDR*, pp. 404–25.

[23] See e.g. Union Berlin Archive, Aufforderung, 22 March 1979 (Mielis); letter from Hillert to Jörg S., 24 October 1974.

[24] See Allinson, '1977: the GDR's most normal year?', pp. 271–2; Frank Willmann, 'Wie alles anfing . . . und zu Ende ging', in Willmann (ed.), *Zonenfußball*, pp. 109–10.

[25] Dennis and LaPorte, *State and Minorities*, p. 137.

Figure 14. Damage caused by BFC hooligans at the ironically named *Stadion der Freundschaft* (Friendship Stadium) in Frankfurt/Oder, 1981. This was the kind of clean-up job that stadium staff frequently faced in the 1980s, as hooliganism became a major social and political problem in the GDR, as it did across Europe.

> five per cent [of all fans]. These young people manifest themselves more or less united in groups or blocs. This applies to the behaviour of this group of people in football stadia as well as upon arrival and departure.[26]

Between 1984 and 1988, there were on average slightly more than 1,000 arrests per season for football-related offences.[27] During the 1985/6 season, for example, 889 supporters were arrested at *Oberliga* matches, an average of 35 people per match day; 408 of them were fined and 31 faced criminal proceedings.[28] To put this in comparative perspective, in Division One of the English league, a much larger

[26] SAPMO-BArch, DY 30/IV 2/2.2039/251, Information zur Lage auf den Fußballplätzen der DDR, fo. 21.

[27] Dennis, 'Soccer hooliganism', p. 60.

[28] BStU, MfS ZOS/3212, Bericht über die Ergebnisse der politisch-operativen Sicherung von Fußballspielen und damit verbundene instructive Tätigkeit des ZOS, 11 June 1986, fo. 22–3.

and better-attended competition than its GDR equivalent, there were 2,008 arrests during the 1986/7 season.[29]

Interviewees who attended games in the 1980s offered mixed perspectives on the gravity of football-related violence. Serious trouble, it was not uncommonly suggested, was largely avoided.[30] Weapons, according to one Union fan, were 'scorned'. Supporters did not shy away from physical confrontations, but nor did they seek them out. A Dynamo Dresden supporter differentiated the largely spontaneous clashes between rival fans during the 1980s from the more serious violence that accompanied the *Wende*.[31] Interestingly, these reflections unwittingly echoed the SED's view that hooligan culture was more brutal in the capitalist West – witness, for example, the highly organised, weapon-wielding violence unleashed by Manchester United fans in Turin after a UEFA Cup game against Juventus in 1984.[32] Nothing quite so organised or dangerous, interviewees seemed to argue, was possible in the GDR. Yet a low level of violence became a permanent and unquestioned feature of the football scene during the 1980s, encouraging even those not inclined to fight to accept that 'you had to [do it] when the chips were down'.[33]

The 'battle excitement' that attracted English hooligans to 'aggro', reinforcing ideas of masculinity and territoriality, no doubt impacted in similar ways on young East Germans, who lived in a state where 'everything was provided for, but it was also boring'.[34] From the early 1980s onwards, the GDR's nascent network of skinheads, taking inspiration from peers in England and West Germany, began to infiltrate football crowds, bringing a radical edge to the hooligan scene. The numbers were small. Reports in 1988 noted a group of roughly 100 skinheads that regularly attended BFC's away games, reflecting the growing perception – fully realised after the *Wende* – that this was the 'club of the skinheads'.[35] There were about thirty 'Skins' among Union's followers, and limited skinhead activity in cities such as Leipzig, Dresden, Halle, Erfurt, and Frankfurt/Oder.[36] For a regime that cultivated a stylised abhorrence of 'Hitler fascism', the small numbers mattered less than

[29] 'Fact Sheet 1: Football and Football Hooliganism', Sir Norman Chester Centre for Football Research (January 2001), 3: www.furd.org/resources/fs1.pdf.
[30] See e.g. interview with Tino C.; interview with Heiko H.
[31] Interview with Sven S. [32] See Buford, *Among the Thugs*, Part I.
[33] Interview with Frank L.
[34] Dunning, *Sport Matters*, pp. 145–7; interview with Tino C.
[35] Luther and Willmann, *BFC*, p. 130.
[36] BStU, MfS HA XX 221, Bericht zum negativen Fußballanhang des BFC Dynamo, fo. 243; Bericht zum Stand der Sicherheit und Ordnung bei Fußballspielen im Spieljahr 1987/88, 15 July 1988, fo. 260–1.

the offensive political message. Attired in dark bomber jackets and laced boots, the young skinheads of Honecker's East Germany, who celebrated Hitler's birthday, chanted 'My father was an SS soldier', and called foreign workers 'wogs', were a slap in the face of state socialism.[37]

The authorities were at a loss to convincingly explain the hooligan upsurge. Communist societies had, by their own reckoning, overcome class conflict, leaving no objective reason for spectator violence.[38] Things should have been different there. The fact that they were not, as was clear by the mid 1980s, was usually blamed on the class enemy, culpable in transmitting values that glorified violence and fomented right-wing extremism.[39] More discerning voices recognised that this explanation was inadequate. The head of the Central Institute for Youth Research (ZIJ), Walter Friedrich, suggested in 1987 that the internal causes of the growing discontent with socialism among young East Germans needed to be carefully examined. Football fans who goaded the security forces with provocative chants, he argued, were not necessarily bent on causing political 'affront'.[40] Three years earlier an SED report admitted that the causes of hooliganism, beyond the usual suspects, included 'a certain boredom' among some youths 'who still have too few chances to "get some action" in their free time' and alarmingly high rates of alcohol consumption.[41]

Part of the problem in pursuing more empathetic approaches lay in defining football hooliganism. The party and the secret police deployed the phrase 'negative-decadent forces' to describe all manner of non-conformist youth, including skinheads, Goths, punks, and misbehaving supporters.[42] A distinction was theoretically made between the majority that got drunk and chanted abusive songs and the hardcore minority that harassed fellow citizens, vandalised public property, and espoused racist views. In reality, many of the 'hooligan' groups under *Stasi* observation were guiltier of creating a good match-day atmosphere – by dancing in the street, building snowmen, and getting opposition fans to sing with them – than of fomenting violence.[43] Distaste and a lack of insight, whether wilful or otherwise, combined with the political barriers to open

[37] On hostility to foreign workers (especially Mozambicans) in the 1980s, see Dennis and LaPorte, *State and Minorities*, pp. 112–17.
[38] Guttmann, *Sports Spectators*, p. 148.
[39] Dennis, 'Soccer hooliganism', pp. 65–6. [40] *Ibid.*, pp. 66–7.
[41] SAPMO-BArch, DY 30/IV 2/2.2039/251, Zur Lage auf den Fußballplätzen, fo. 31.
[42] Dennis, 'Soccer hooliganism', p. 56.
[43] BStU, MfS ZOS/3212, Bericht zum negativen Fußballanhang des BFC Dynamo, fo. 30–1.

debate, ensured that communist officials, rather like their counterparts in Thatcher's Britain, often tarred fans with the same brush.

If sympathy was in short supply, solutions were not. Just as West European governments and law-enforcement bodies busied themselves with combatting the hooligan menace, so a raft of guidelines on curbing anti-social behaviour was tabled in the GDR. In its mixture of force and persuasion, a joint statement issued in 1985 by the ZK departments for sport and security questions was typical. The report began by outlining the type of misdemeanours committed by the minority of unruly (and usually drunk) football fans: insults and provocative behaviour towards rival supporters, passers-by, policemen, and stewards; boorish behaviour on trains and at stations; and, in more serious cases, damage to public property and assault. It then provided a relatively nuanced, if cursory analysis of the causes of such behaviour, one notable for making no mention of the class enemy. Unsporting behaviour, the party argued here, was primarily the result of young males wanting 'to cause a stir' and prove their 'supposed strength' to themselves and others. Contributory factors included refereeing mistakes – a striking admission, made at the peak of the crisis about institutional bias towards BFC. The nine proposals for improving the situation contained an interesting mixture of the ideological, the educational, and the organisational. Copious space was devoted, as in Western Europe, to increasing the police presence in and around stadia, improving 'operative measures' against hooligan groups, and imposing tough sentences on ringleaders and repeat offenders. But there was also recognition of the need for 'differentiated' work among troublemakers, improved training of *Oberliga* referees, and better catering facilities at grounds.[44] The paternalistic mixture of 'care and coercion' on display typified the GDR's 'welfare dictatorship'.[45]

Of particular interest among the plethora of directives were those related to improving facilities at the GDR's 'clapped-out' stadia.[46] The European context was again important, not only the Heysel disaster in May 1985, but also the fire that broke out among the wooden seats at Bradford City's stadium earlier in the same month, resulting in the death of fifty-six supporters. The DFV reported in 1987 on special measures, including a ban on smoking and the creation of additional emergency exits, that had been introduced at grounds with wooden stands in Erfurt, Jena, and Leipzig. Recent improvements at BSG Stahl

44 SAPMO-BArch, DY 30/4949, Information zur Lage auf Fußballplätzen, fo. 1–7.

45 Konrad Jarausch, 'Care and coercion: the GDR as welfare dictatorship', in Jarausch (ed.), *Dictatorship as Experience*, pp. 59–60.

46 Interview with Tino C.

Brandenburg's ground included the construction of a covered stand that raised the seating capacity from 500 to 2,500, new car parks to house an additional 3,000 vehicles, and an increase in the number of snack facilities from one to eight.[47] At Dynamo Dresden, an agreement was reached with a girls' fan club to allow it to sell from vendor trays inside the Rudolf Harbig Stadium on match days, a measure that enhanced the snack options on offer and helped, in a small way, to feminise a largely male public space.[48]

Spectator-friendly improvements were designed to increase attendances and to encourage a more respectable audience (older men, families, and women) to turn up for matches, thereby reducing the threat of hooliganism. On paper, this looked like a socialist preview of the gentrification that occurred after ninety-six Liverpool fans were crushed to death on the terraces of Sheffield Wednesday's Hillsborough Stadium in April 1989, a disaster that led to the introduction of expensive all-seater stadia throughout Western Europe in the 1990s. In reality, the straitened economic cirumstances of the 1980s meant a persistent shortage of funds for stadium renovations. *Oberliga* grounds, not unlike recreational facilities (as we shall see in Chapter 14), often remained in a state of disrepair. The case of Stahl Brandenburg, where Hans-Joachim Lauck bankrolled a modernisation project that included floodlights, a hotel, and indoor pitches,[49] was the exception rather than the rule.

The impact of the state's multi-level campaign against hooliganism was remarkably limited. A *Stasi* report from July 1988 admitted a 'light increase' in the number of people arrested for football-related offences during the 1987/8 season, up from 960 in the previous season to 1,076.[50] The 1988 cup final in Berlin, in which BFC defeated Carl Zeiss Jena 2–0, was preceded by a march of up to 150 skinheads through the Pankow district to the World Youth Stadium. They bellowed fascist chants and clashed with other fans. At the match, 300 BFC fans tried to invade the pitch during the victory ceremony, causing extensive damage to 60 seats. Thirty-four people were arrested, three of whom were held in custody on charges of assault or brawling.[51]

47 SAPMO-BArch, DY 30/4966, Ergänzende Information zum Material "Maßnahmen des DFV der DDR zur Durchsetzung von Ordnung und Sicherheit bei Fußballveranstaltungen", 28 January 1987, fo. 15–20.

48 BStU, MfS HA XX/221, Erfahrungaustausch, fo. 219.

49 Interview with Heinz Werner.

50 BStU, MfS HA XX/221, Bericht zum Stand der Sicherheit und Ordnung, fo. 259.

51 Dennis, 'Soccer hooliganism', p. 62; BStU, MfS HA XX/221, Information über Vorkommnisse im Zusammenhang mit dem FDGB-Pokalendspiel im Fußball, 6 June 1988, fo. 238–9.

Reports emphasised coordinated anti-hooligan measures, but this was often wishful thinking. The behaviour of police units suggested a more complex reality on the ground, one that reminds us that authority was more directly shaped by ordinary citizens in the state's employ than by directives issued from East Berlin. Regional and operational differences often conditioned responses. Union Berlin supporters, for example, noted how local units in such places as Magdeburg and Rostock needed little excuse to wield their truncheons against the 'big eaters' from the capital.[52] In these situations, the Berlin transport police who accompanied Union supporters to away matches were allies rather than enemies: 'they often defended us against the other policemen'.[53] For one Lokomotive Leipzig follower, police and fans were simply two sides of the same coin ('it's hooligans on both sides'). Policemen were certainly capable of wading in with 'brute force', one Union Berlin supporter agreed. But units were often 'over-matched' and lacked clear-sighted strategies for dealing with large crowds. Their main concern was to hold on to their riot helmets, rather than to test them in clashes with supporters.[54]

In the case of hooliganism, the more things changed, the more they stayed the same. A *Stasi* report from early in the 1988/9 season showed a situation that was at best unaltered from earlier in the 1980s, and arguably slightly worse. At the seven *Oberliga* matches on 16 and 17 September 1988, 102 people were arrested. Magdeburg fans arriving at Schönefeld station for their team's match against BFC provoked brawls with Union supporters by chanting 'Berlin, Berlin, Jewish Berlin'. One of them subsequently assaulted two passers-by en route to the stadium, where thirteen rows of seating in the away end were later vandalised. FCK fans, whose team visited Stahl Brandenburg, were variously arrested for throwing beer bottles out of train windows, disturbing public order in a restaurant, and resisting police orders.[55] The persistence of this noisy, anti-social subculture suggested something rotten at the heart of the GDR. But it was also part of a wider pattern of violence, tribalism, and disillusionment among certain sections of (usually, though not always, working-class) European youth in the 1980s, one that encompassed the liberal democracies of the West and the creaking communist dictatorships of the East.

52 Interview with Theo Körner; interview with Sven S.
53 Luther and Willmann, *Eisern Union!*, p. 146.
54 Interview with Heiko H; interview with Sven S.
55 BStU, MfS HA XX/221, Übersicht zu den Fußballspielen des 5. Spieltages am 17.9.88, 18 September 1988, fo. 268.

## The hooligan in profile

Who committed acts of football-related violence? A dissertation by a Humboldt University student in 1988, based on *Stasi* reports compiled between 1983 and 1987, provided some interesting answers. All of those arrested in this period were men. Only 10.8% of them were over twenty-five years of age. Levels of political organisation, as with fan-club members, were low. Not a single one of those arrested was an SED member. Barely 30% were members of either the FDJ or the FDGB, the two broadest churches open to young East German men. Most offences were committed by away fans in the GDR's largest cities (Berlin, Leipzig, and Dresden), usually (in almost 88% of cases) under the influence of alcohol.[56]

The dissertation's findings inadvertently undercut communist attempts to pass off anti-social behaviour as the product of tendencies found only on the margins of socialist society.[57] It showed, for example, that most offenders were in regular employment. Indeed, 51.4% of them were skilled workers, earning wages that comfortably funded the regular purchase of tickets, alcohol, and transport to away matches. Financial independence was further encouraged by a lack of 'fixed ties' (i.e. wives and children) in 73% of cases and the fact that 75.7% of offenders still lived with their parents. In terms of leisure-time habits, offenders most frequently enjoyed three common pastimes: going to the pub, going to discos, and either playing or watching sport. Most of those arrested (58.15%) were not hardcore troublemakers, but first-time offenders.[58]

While they were by no means model citizens, hooligans represented a cross-section of ordinary young East German males. The conclusion tallied both with the results of a study of East Berlin hooligans during the 1980s and 1990s (among twenty-five interviewees there were 'no dramatic childhood traumas' or 'hardship cases') and with the characters in Christa Moog's short story 'Die Fans von Union', which brilliantly captured the loosely anti-authoritarian *Schlachtenbummler* culture of the late Honecker era, replete with beer drinking, abusive chants, casual violence, fare-dodging, and listening out for Hertha's results on the transistor radio.[59] It was also largely consistent with the findings of research into the hooligan demographic (young, male, working-class, employed) in capitalist countries such as Belgium, England, Italy,

[56] BStU, MfS JHS/22036, Untersuchungen zu Straftaten und Ordnungswidrigkeiten im Zusammenhang mit Fußballveranstaltungen, 6 May 1988, fo. 1–112.

[57] Dennis, 'Soccer hooliganism', p. 66.

[58] BStU, MfS JHS/22036, Untersuchungen zu Straftaten, fo. 1–112.

[59] Farin and Hauswald, *Die dritte Halbzeit*, p. 7; Moog, *Die Fans von Union*, pp. 82–99.

Scotland, and West Germany.[60] The GDR's research into the neo-fascism in its midst concluded that skinheads, like football hooligans, were 'our children': young men who were integrated into socialist society, popular at school and work, and from stable, predominantly working-class families.[61]

In July 1988, 250 HFC supporters travelled on an overnight train, organised by club officials, to watch their team play a pre-season game against Baník Ostrava in Czechoslovakia. A court case was later brought against seven of the group for various acts of hooligan behaviour. On the train, they let off fire extinguishers, smashed light fittings, threw objects out of the window, and (in one case) elbowed in the kidneys the wife of the HFC delegation leader. At a stopover station, they smashed at least ten windows and damaged a barrier on the concourse. After drinking at a pub upon arrival and clashing with Baník fans, the accused headed to the ground. During the game, they chanted abuse at their hosts ('Czech pigs', 'you asocial Czechs', 'Ostrava will be German') and attempted a pitch invasion, forcing intervention by the Czechoslovak police. The match was interrupted for five minutes, while the HFC captain and chairman implored the away fans to calm down. After the final whistle, the accused blockaded the exit from the stadium, refusing to follow police orders to move. The demonstration was broken up with the aid of police dogs, truncheons, and tear gas. After the HFC fans had been escorted back to the train, four of the seven threw objects, including beer bottles, bread, and a curtain rod, at the policemen waiting, no doubt anxiously, for the departure of their badly behaved guests. The journey home passed off in relative tranquillity.[62]

The seven defendants against whom the public prosecutor in Halle directed the lengthy charge sheet were all residents of the city, aged between nineteen and twenty-six years old. They knew each other from attending HFC matches, an activity often bound up with heavy drinking. All seven were described as single. Only one of them had children. Four of the group, including the two ringleaders, Michael R. and Dietmar S., had multiple previous convictions. The other three were first-time offenders. Replicating the findings of various studies of the occupational profile of English hooligans in the 1980s,[63] all seven were in regular

[60] Guttmann, *Sports Spectators*, pp. 168–9; Dunning, Murphy, and Waddington, 'Towards a sociological understanding of football hooliganism', pp. 17–22.

[61] Dennis and LaPorte, *State and Minorities*, pp. 182–4.

[62] SAPMO-BArch, DP 3/361, letter from the public prosecutor to the deputy SED leader in *Bezirk* Halle, 17 August 1988; Anklageschrift, 19 October 1988.

[63] Dunning, Murphy, and Waddington, 'Towards a sociological understanding of football hooliganism', p. 19.

employment, in various skilled and unskilled blue-collar jobs: pipe fitter, drill worker, maintenance mechanic, castings cleaner, boiler cleaner, and removal man. There were no complaints about their attitudes at work. The welder Steffen S., for example, was regarded as a good employee. He held the position of FDJ secretary in a youth brigade at his factory. Only one of the seven came from difficult family circumstances: Bernd S., who had served an eighteen-month prison sentence for attempted *Republikflucht* in 1985, had grown up in various children's homes.[64] The profile of the defendants in Halle in 1988 – single, under the age of twenty-six, in regular employment, politically uncommitted but not necessarily hostile, a mixture of first-time and repeat offenders – broadly corresponded to the findings in the above-cited Humboldt University dissertation from the same year. The HFC fans who so poorly represented the GDR in Czechoslovakia were representative of the average East German hooligan.

This was true not only in terms of who they were, but in terms of how they behaved. Excessive alcohol consumption was central to football-related violence in the GDR, just as 'intentionally self-destructive drinking' underpinned English hooligan behaviour.[65] The seven defendants drank steadily from the moment of their train's departure to Czechoslovakia in the evening of 2 July to their arrival at the stadium the following afternoon – a marathon session that left one of the accused, Helmut K., able to fall asleep during the match, despite the commotion around him.[66] The Humboldt study showed that offences were split relatively evenly among five time periods: en route (25.7%), immediately before the game (24.9%), during the game (18.3%), immediately after the game (13.5%), and upon departure (17.6%).[67] The behaviour of the HFC fans mirrored this distribution, from the various incidents on the train to Czechoslovkia (property damage, physical aggression), via the pre-match clashes with Baník fans, to the unrest at the stadium (xenophobic chanting, an attempted pitch invasion, and the post-match 'sit-in') and the bottle-throwing departure for home. Much of this was alcohol-fuelled loutishness. But it shaded at times into more serious offences, including a mélange of anti-police, nationalist, and racist chanting that referenced the West German national anthem (*Deutschland über alles*), Nazism (*Sieg heil* chants), and the heartland of hooliganism ('Germany, Germany,

64 SAPMO-BArch, DP 3/361, Anklageschrift.
65 Goldblatt, *The Ball Is Round*, p. 551. The astonishing rate of alcohol consumption among English hooligans is discussed in Buford, *Among the Thugs*, especially Part I.
66 SAPMO-BArch, DP 3/361, Anklageschrift.
67 BStU, MfS JHS/22036, Untersuchungen zu Straftaten, Table 31.

Engeland, Engeland [*sic.*] and hooligans').[68] The prison sentences that the prosecutor's office proposed for the seven HFC fans in the autumn of 1988 ranged in length from six months to two years. They indicated how seriously the authorities judged such anti-social (and anti-socialist) behaviour, particularly when it occurred on the territory of a fellow communist state.[69]

## Hooliganism and the state of socialism

What does football violence tell us about the state of the GDR during the 1980s? An interesting starting point for discussion is the public's response to hooliganism. After all, this was – in contrast to listening to Western music on a tape cassette or taking part in Church activities – a highly visible form of non-conformist behaviour. Unruly supporters took over public spaces, made lots of noise, dressed distinctively (with club scarves and scruffy, badge-covered jean jackets), and freely consumed alcohol. Their otherness in the drab landscape of Honecker's GDR, as just a glance at Ernst Cantzler's documentary on Union Berlin fans confirms, was striking.

Dan Wilton has argued that citizens displayed greater understanding towards 'rebellious subcultural groups' such as punks and misbehaving football fans during the 1980s than in the previous two decades, when there was widespread support for repressive measures against *Rowdytum* – a shift suggestive of a disillusionment with communist rule that permeated all areas of society.[70] The widely suspected manipulation of matches in BFC's favour certainly encouraged some petitioners to adopt more sympathetic attitudes. 'The responsibility for disturbances at the grounds doesn't lie as often with the spectators as is claimed', wrote Horst D. from Dresden in 1986, echoing the linkage between corrupt refereeing and a possible East German Heysel disaster made the previous summer by another Dresden-based complainant.[71] At the same time, the aggression (or threat of aggression), drunkenness, and offensive political utterances associated with hooliganism ensured that its practitioners were seldom embraced warmly. The empathy deficit was even more

[68] SAPMO-BArch, DP 3/361, Anklageschrift.

[69] *Ibid.*, letter from Klotz to Heyer, 25 October 1988. The file does not contain information about the sentences eventually given to the seven.

[70] Dan Wilton, 'Regime versus people? Public opinion and the development of sport and popular music in the GDR, 1961–1989', unpublished Ph.D. thesis, University College London (2005), pp. 220–1.

[71] SAPMO-BArch, DY 30/4981, petition from Horst D. to Hellmann, 25 March 1986, fo. 83; SAPMO-BArch, DY 30/4984, petition from Alfred M. to the DFV, fo. 113.

pronounced with punks, who were directed to labour camps and even gas chambers by hostile members of the public.[72]

Citizens of all ages complained to the authorities when they encountered anti-social behaviour from fans, usually on public transport. In October 1987, a group of sixth-form students from Werdau wrote to the DFV about the behaviour of Chemie Leipzig fans during a train journey from Quedlinburg to Leipzig. Emitting a 'bestial stink', drunken supporters threatened fellow passengers, displayed their genitalia, and groped the female students. A large number of them shouted out Nazi songs and words ('Gauleiter, SS-Sturmbannführer, etc.').[73] A similarly traumatic experience was reported by an older party member, whose journey from Berlin to Erfurt on 4 June 1988 was disrupted by several hundred Carl Zeiss Jena fans returning from that day's cup final against BFC. The supporters drunkenly blocked off entranceways, let off fireworks, left beer bottles everywhere, and (right in front of the petitioner's eyes) groundlessly attacked a seventeen-year-old student. When the comrade and his wife alighted at Erfurt, they could hear the West German national anthem being loudly sung. 'Whether this lot can master our national anthem', he concluded, 'is questionable'.[74]

The letters emphasised the state's inability to cope with hooliganism. Both the party member and the students acknowledged the regularity of such disturbances ('a general trend', 'every 14 days'). Both drew attention to inadequate security measures. The six transport police on the train to Leipzig in October 1987 were 'not in a position to protect citizens' against obnoxious Chemie fans. The two or three transport police accompanying Jena fans the following June were likewise 'not at all masters of the situation'.[75] Such incidents, as the SED member from Erfurt recognised, raised questions that went beyond the operational shortcomings of the police and football clubs: 'has our socialist education of young people in school and the socialist youth organisation failed?'[76]

The party and secret police devoted considerable resources to combating hooliganism in the 1980s: the directives on order and security, stadium renovations, work with fan clubs, increased police visibility and numbers, and *Stasi* surveillance. By the end of the decade, one in every

[72] Dennis and LaPorte, *State and Minorities*, p. 165.

[73] BStU, MfS HA XX/2700, petition from the collective at the Jürgen Lange School to the DFV, 23 October 1987, fo. 68–9.

[74] BStU, MfS HA XX/221, petition from [name blacked out] to the State Council, 5 June 1988, fo. 236–7.

[75] BStU, MfS HA XX/2700, petition from the collective at the Jürgen Lange School, fo. 69; BStU, MfS HA XX/221, petition from [name blacked out], fo. 237.

[76] BStU, MfS HA XX/221, petition from [name blacked out], fo. 237.

ten skinheads in East Berlin was an IM.[77] But the problem did not go away. If anything, it got worse. How was this possible? The *Stasi* often found ways to successfully infiltrate the grassroots political networks that emerged in the 1980s. IMs, for example, helped to drive a wedge in the environmental movement, whose message largely failed to reach ordinary citizens.[78] The anti-hero Klaus Uhltzscht's remark in Thomas Brussig's novel *Helden wie wir* that seasoned protestors in Berlin in the autumn of 1989 constituted a group 'small enough to fit into a short U-Bahn train' was cruel but not wholly inaccurate.[79] A *Stasi* report from 1986 estimated that the 18 peace and environmental groups in Berlin numbered a total of 350 members, roughly 37 times smaller than Union Berlin's average home crowd in the *Oberliga* that year.[80] The fan scene – with its fluency, size, and ingrained suspicion of outsiders and authority – was a tougher nut to crack.

When it came to football, the vast, multi-layered nature of the state apparatus, the swollen bureaucracy that grew in place of Marx's predicted 'withering away' of the state, paradoxically limited its authority. The cooperation of large numbers of organisations and individuals was required in order for there to be a chance of being able to prevent unrest. While power was concentrated in the hands of a small number of decision-makers in the Politburo and *Stasi* headquarters, the way in which it was received by supporters was largely determined by the likes of local policemen, train personnel, club officials, and fan-club leaders. Match stewards (*Ordner*) played a particularly important role. Directives in the 1980s emphasised the need for stewards to be carefully selected, provided with proper training (so that they would stay in position throughout the game), and made a visible and effective part of match-day operations.[81] They were assigned a demanding range of tasks. It included, according to 1984 DFV regulations, checking tickets, removing drunken fans from the stands, securing the press

[77] Farin and Hauswald, *Die dritte Halbzeit*, pp. 9–10.

[78] See e.g. Leon Quinn, 'The politics of pollution: government, environmentalism and mass opinion in East Germany, 1972–1990', unpublished Ph.D. thesis, University of Bristol (2002), ch. 3B.

[79] Thomas Brussig, *Helden wie wir* (Berlin: Verlag Volk und Welt, 1996), pp. 281–2. Thanks to Leon Quinn for drawing my attention to this quote.

[80] Wolle, *Die heile Welt*, p. 266; www.european-football-statistics.co.uk/attn/archive/avezddr80.htm.

[81] See e.g. SAPMO-BArch, DY 30/IV 2/2.2039/251, Maßnahmen zur Erhöhung von Ordnung und Sicherheit bei Fußballgroßveranstaltungen, 23 March 1984, fo. 14; SAPMO-Barch, DY 24/21223, Information zum Stand der Gewährleistung der öffentlichen Ordnung und Sicherheit im Zusammenhang mit Fußballspielen, 8 October 1987.

area and the away fans' section, and ensuring a trouble-free exit for all supporters at the end of a game.[82]

But these were volunteer positions, often filled, as one 1986 *Stasi* report noted, by young people looking for 'a cheap and comfortable way to go to football games'.[83] One BFC steward's motivation was simple and typical: to watch European matches for which he would otherwise have been unable to get tickets.[84] There were high fluctuation rates. Training programmes were either basic or not held at all.[85] The state's first line of defence in the fight against hooliganism was unreliable, in some cases including the 'negative-decadent' youths that careful stewarding was meant to weed out. Four of the volunteers ostensibly supervising the Union contingent at an away match against FCK in 1988, for example, incited their peers to go on the 'rampage' and were subsequently sacked.[86] Older colleagues were not always more dependable. A DTSB report from the same year bemoaned the disruptive and drunken behaviour of stewards, many of whom were pensioners.[87]

Football matches and music concerts allowed certain young people to use official positions to act out violent tendencies. Event security at FDJ evenings in Karl-Marx-Stadt, for example, sometimes consisted of aggressive and drunk heavy metal fans and known football hooligans.[88] Stewarding thus helps to explain why it was difficult to quash hooligan activity. Like the leaders of registered fan clubs, stewards both participated in the structures of power and behaved or talked in ways that subverted communist rule.[89]

The SED regime never seriously or publicly contemplated policies that required self-critical analysis of the causes of football hooliganism. Whether out of conviction or convenience, the class enemy remained its preferred scapegoat for 'explaining the inexplicable'.[90] In a centralised, authoritarian, and militarised society, the match-day emphasis was on security – a heavy uniformed presence, a network of informers, and segregation and fencing inside the stadium – rather than empathy. As in the West, the law-and-order approach tended to fan the flames rather

[82] BStU, MfS JHS MF WS 750/85, Anforderungen an den Bereich Organisation des BFC Dynamo zur Gewährleistung der politisch-fachlichen Aufgaben bei der Absicherung internationaler Wettkämpfe, 12 August 1985.

[83] BStU, MfS ZOS/3212, Bericht zum negativen Fußballanhang des BFC Dynamo, fo. 37

[84] Interview with BFC fans.

[85] BStU, MfS ZOS/3212, Beratung mit MA der BV Berlin, 21 December 1986, fo. 63.

[86] BStU, MfS HA XX/221, Einschätzung zum jugendlichen Anhang des 1. FC Union Berlin, 30 December 1988, fo. 302.

[87] Dennis and LaPorte, *State and Minorities*, p. 143.

[88] Wilton, 'Regime versus people?', p. 200n.

[89] Fulbrook, *The People's State*, p. 236.

[90] Dennis, 'Soccer hooliganism', p. 65.

than extinguish them, by dispersing violence beyond the stadium, increasing the sense of solidarity among hooligans, and attracting a larger number of extremists to the game.[91] Even attempts to reach out to unruly elements, such as the work with fan clubs, were undertaken with control rather than partnership in mind. Communist hypocrisy, clearly displayed in the failure to take responsibility for the role of BFC's dominance in undermining the *Oberliga*, drove a wedge between the party and football supporters that undermined attempts to rally support for anti-hooligan measures. Public disquiet with the loutish and drunken behaviour of a minority of fans mattered less than public disquiet with the football and political cultures that hobbled the GDR in its final decade.

Following a game with Dynamo Dresden on 28 October 1989, 800 BFC supporters marched through Prenzlauer Berg to the centre of East Berlin, heading first to Alexanderplatz and then down Unter den Linden to Friedrichstraße. The 'demonstration-like appearances', as the *Stasi* termed the unrest, were unusual for the absence of known skinhead groups and the lack of violence. Passers-by were ignored rather than abused. 'Not a single fascist slogan' was heard. In the uncertain weeks that followed Honecker's resignation on 18 October, the peaceful nature of anti-SED demonstrations across the country appears to have affected football supporters. The BFC fans, though, were not coming from quite the same place as the Monday-night demonstrators in Leipzig. The chants heard en route to the city centre included the standard 'BFC'; expressions of civic pride ('Berlin, Berlin'); songs directed at rival Dynamo Dresden fans ('the Saxons sleep under bridges or on benches, they have no homes'); and openly anti-regime remarks that would have been unthinkable a month earlier ('*Stasi* out', 'bigwigs out'). There were also nationalist and racist sentiments such as 'Germany awake' and, when a group of Polish citizens was encountered near Friedrichstraße, 'foreigners out'[92]

The eclectic character of these chants, seamlessly embracing local patriotism, anti-communism, and xenophobic nationalism, speaks to an ambiguity and elusiveness at the core of football hooliganism in the GDR's final years. Reflecting the looseness of the groups that they formed and dissolved, the motives of hooligans are hard to pin down. The line between letting off steam, the drinking and aggressive behaviour

[91] Dunning, *Sport Matters*, p. 152.

[92] BStU, BV Berlin/AKG 22, Information zu demonstrationsartigen Erscheinungen im Stadtzentrum nach dem Fußballspiel des BFC Dynamo gegen den SC Dynamo Dresden am 28. Okt. 1989, 28 October 1989, fo. 49; Bericht zum Vorkommnis nach dem Fußballspiel BFC Dynamo gegen SG Dynamo Dresden, 28 October 1989, fo. 50–3.

common to masculine youth culture in many parts of the world, and more serious offences was not always easy to discern. Hooliganism embraced a variety of actions and attitudes, from drunken vandalism to violent clashes with the police or rival fans. Only a small minority of troublemakers were skinheads. Instances of neo-Nazi provocation, moreover, did not necessarily reflect genuine political convictions. At least part of the 'drift to the right' among some young East Germans during the 1980s was rooted in a desire to position oneself wherever the state was not.[93] What one Union fan called GDR youth culture's 'lax' attitude to extremism was part of a 'better brown than red' attitude rooted in disillusionment with communism.[94] This is not to trivialise the ugly displays of racism that marred football in this period. The seriousness of the problem was fully revealed amid the political and economic upheaval that accompanied the *Wende*. But there was more to GDR hooliganism than neo-Nazism.

How much more, and what it signified, is difficult to say. Hooligans did not bring down the GDR, nor did they attempt to. Yet, chaotic and disorganised as it generally was, football-related unrest was one of the most constant threats to public order in the 1980s, involving greater numbers of people than the widely studied peace and environmental movements. Troublemaking supporters fitted into a wider context of youthful disaffection with the communist regime that spawned a number of Western-influenced subcultures, including punks, skinheads, heavy metal fans, and Goths. These groups all offered sites for *Resistenz* to authority, a means of engaging in widespread, but relatively low-risk, opposition to the political manipulation of apolitical pastimes and of maintaining identities (individual, local, national, or international) that were anathema to those in power. Hooliganism illustrated another facet of the communists' failure to understand or control football. It exposed too the quietly rotting edifice of East German socialism. The Potemkin village of mass choreographed FDJ parades was undercut by images of aggressive, disrespectful, scruffy, and alienated young men surrounded by police and high-security fencing in crumbling stadia. Hooligans, even if they did not realise it, reflected, and contributed to, the disintegration of the East German state in the autumn of 1989.

These images were at once GDR-specific and part of a European, even global story. What occurred on match days in and around grounds in East Berlin and Leipzig was replicated in London and Cardiff – and in places further east. The 1985 Bulgarian cup final between Levski Sofia

[93] Farin and Hauswald, *Die dritte Halbzeit*, p. 9.
[94] Interview with Sven S.; Fulbrook, *German National Identity*, pp. 165–6.

and CSKA Sofia was marred by fan and player violence so severe that both clubs were effectively dissolved.[95] When Spartak Moscow travelled to play Dynamo Kiev in September 1987, several hundred visiting fans were attacked in the railway station as they waited for their train home. A pitched battle ensued, resulting in numerous injuries and serious property damage. This was one of many incidents that involved Spartak's *fanaty* during the 1980s, as football violence reached the heart of the Soviet empire.[96]

East German hooligans were aware of this international context. Though their concerns were rooted in local antipathies and shaped by the GDR's singular political circumstances, they drew inspiration, not to mention names and dress codes, from fan scenes elsewhere, especially in West Germany and England. The small Lok Leipzig fan club *Härte 10* ('Force 10'), for example, was known for its neo-fascist tendencies and glorification of West German paramilitarism.[97] Such groups were part of a transnational community, whose members were seen by hostile governments and police forces across the continent (and regardless of ideological stamp) as animals to be corralled, segregated, and caged up. The fact that the GDR did not experience an equivalent to the Hillsborough disaster, or the horrific crush that killed as many as 340 Spartak fans on the icy steps of the Luzhniki Stadium in Moscow during a UEFA Cup match seven years earlier,[98] perhaps had more to do with the *Oberliga*'s smaller attendances than immunity to the cycle of repression, alienation, and violence that characterised European football, whether communist or capitalist, during the 1980s.

[95] Wilson, *Behind the Curtain*, pp. 185–90. [96] Edelman, *Spartak Moscow*, pp. 293–5.
[97] Dennis and LaPorte, *State and Minorities*, p. 172.
[98] Edelman, *Spartak Moscow*, pp. 294–5.

# 10 'Crooked champions': the BFC problem

## 'Together it works': a football conspiracy theory

Late in the afternoon of 13 May 1988, and shortly before his team's game against BFC, a young FC Karl-Marx-Stadt fan was observed distributing a small batch of handbills outside the Friedrich-Ludwig-Jahn-Sportpark in Berlin's Prenzlauer Berg district. Slightly built and wearing a faded jean jacket, the man was flanked by eight or nine fellow FCK supporters. They ensured that the offending material was not given to anyone in a suit and tie, the usual attire of plain-clothes *Stasi* officers.[1]

The handbill contained an anti-BFC ditty entitled 'Together it works' (*Gemeinsam klapps!*). It ran as follows:

> Beim BFC geht's gut voran
> mit Prokop, Stumpf und Habermann.
> Auch Roßner, Scheurell sorgen prompt,
> daß der BFC nach vorne kommt.
> Und fragt man sich, wie heißt der Mann,
> der so gezielt setzt Schirie an?
> Heinz Einbeck ist's, kommt von der Spree,
> ist Mitglied auch beim BFC.
> Er reguliert mit viel Geschick
> für seinen Club das Fußballglück.
> Und bei der Schieberei vier Wenzel
> sind Peschel, Ziller, Supp und Stenzel.
> So schafft man mit vereinter Kraft
> für den BFC die Meisterschaft.
> Doch ist der Schirie mal neutral,
> bleibt auch der BFC nur zweite Wahl.
> Im Meistercup gibt's schwere Stunden:
> BFC gewogen und zu leicht befunden!!![2]

[1] BStU, MfS HA XX/221, Zur Verteilung von Handzetteln provokativen Inhalts anläßlich des Fußballoberligaspiels BFC Dynamo–FC Karl-Marx-Stadt, 14 May 1988, fo. 221.

[2] *Ibid.*, *Gemeinsam klapps!*, fo. 222. A translation of the handbill is given here:

> At BFC things are grand
> With Prokop, Stumpf and Habermann.

Referencing its collusion with referees, cosy relationship with the DFV, and inability to translate domestic success to the European stage, the scurrilous attack took aim at the most controversial topic in GDR football during the 1980s: the BFC problem.

After a fractious encounter between BFC and Dynamo Dresden in December 1978, the *Stasi* boss and BFC patron Erich Mielke allegedly walked into the Dresden dressing room and told the players 'You must understand, the capital city needs a champion'.[3] Dynamo Dresden had won a third consecutive *Oberliga* title earlier that year. But its dominance now ended. For the next ten years, BFC were champions, an unprecedented run of success that, as one petitioner sardonically noted in 1986, turned GDR football into a 'farce': 'This has never happened in Albania or Malta, to say nothing of England, the Soviet Union, Czechoslovakia, Hungary, or Italy'.[4] To most football followers, the reasons for this string of triumphs were obvious. *Stasi* patronage ensured that BFC, a team with a modest fan base – average home gates of just over 11,000 even in the golden years of the 1980s[5] – had access to the best facilities, the best young talent, and the best players from rival clubs. Above all, it was widely assumed that BFC received preferential treatment from referees. Last-minute penalties, controversial red cards, disallowed goals, and dubious offside decisions ensured that the *Stasi* team remained ahead of the pack.

Roßner and Scheuerell too of course ensure
That BFC comes to the fore.
And you ask, who's the guy
Who picks refs so specifically?
It's Heinz Einbeck from the Spree,
A member too of BFC.
He controls with great finesse
His club's football happiness.
And four knaves in the wangling
Are Peschel, Zill, Supp and Stenzel.
This is how with united force
BFC gets the championship.
But when the ref's merely neutral
Then BFC is just second level.
In the European Cup there's difficult times:
BFC weighed and deemed too light!

(The Spree is the river that runs through Berlin; Einbeck was head of the DFV's referee commission, though only until March 1986; the nine other individuals mentioned were *Oberliga* officials.)

3 Pleil, *Mielke, Macht und Meisterschaft*, p. 11.

4 SAPMO-BArch, DY 30/4986, petition from Gerd R. to Hellmann, 24 March 1986, fo. 35.

5 www.european-football-statistics.co.uk/attn/archive/avezddr80.htm.

Figure 15. Erich Mielke congratulates *Oberliga* champions BFC, June 1987. This was BFC's ninth consecutive league title. In front of the cameras, the players look far less happy about their run of success than the *Stasi* boss and club patron. Public hostility towards BFC was almost universal in the mid 1980s.

Like the notorious fans of English club Millwall, who chanted 'no-one likes us, we don't care' at their many detractors, BFC supporters took a perverse delight in unpopularity. The 1980s, one fan recalled, 'were my greatest years, as we always had glorious success in provoking other fans'. At this time, another supporter noted, 'we were really hated by everyone: fans, residents of towns hosting away matches, cops, transport police, *Stasi*'.[6] This hatred was reflected in the epithets and chants directed BFC's way, such as 'every second person a spy' and 'the eleven pigs'.[7] In its 1987 survey of young football fans, the ZIJ concluded that hostility to BFC was the 'prevailing mood' (*Grundstimmung*). Their main beefs (in 53 per cent of cases) were listed under the headings 'unwarranted preferential treatment' and, more bluntly, 'deceit/rigging'.[8] In the

[6] Interview with Rainer, 29 May 2011; Luther and Willmann, *BFC*, p. 141.

[7] BStU, MfS HA XX/221, untitled ZOS report, 11 December 1988, fo. 295; Kuper, *Football against the Enemy*, p. 17.

[8] SAPMO-BArch, DC 4/721, Neuere Ergebnisse zum Verhältnis Jugendlicher zum Fußball, fo. 11–13.

perennially fractured world of football, BFC created unity in antipathy. Across the GDR, supporters gathered in stadia, or around television and radio sets, cheered the club's every defeat.

This chapter examines BFC's controversial role in GDR football. The theory that there was a state-sanctioned order to favour the club is shown to be less persuasive than the idea that match officials took preventative action. Working in a society in which foreign travel was conditional upon reliable behaviour, they appear to have engaged in an East German version of what Ian Kershaw termed 'working towards the *Führer*', 'not waiting for instructions before using [their] own initiative' to further the regime's (perceived) goals.[9] Attention focuses primarily on citizens' indignant responses to the manipulations that were seen as integral to BFC's success. Petitions on this subject were extraordinarily blunt – and had potentially dangerous political ramifications. They reveal the state's willingness to meet fans halfway, as BFC's corrupt ascendancy threatened to discredit the game and the regime that sanctioned it. No other collective cause in the 1980s – certainly not in the Church, peace, or environmental movements – was as public, popular, united, or effective as the anti-BFC campaign. It is no coincidence that the club's precipitous decline at the end of the decade paralleled that of the East German state.

## BFC in the lean years

BFC's unpopularity did not spring up overnight. In the *Oberliga* reforms of 1954, controversy clouded the founding of SC Dynamo Berlin. Dynamo Dresden, the 1953 league champions, were forced to move mid-season to the capital to bolster football's fortunes there, creating a lasting enmity between the two clubs. The surviving shell of a team in Dresden went into a party-imposed decline from which it took more than fifteen years to recover.[10] The newly created Dynamo team, known after the further reforms of 1965/6 as Berliner FC Dynamo, spent much of the following two decades in the successive shadows of Vorwärts Berlin, Carl Zeiss Jena, and a resurgent Dynamo Dresden, winning just one trophy, the 1959 FDGB Cup. Lack of success kept disapproval in check. But as a representative of both the secret police and the capital, BFC were viewed with more suspicion than affection. The sense that BFC benefited from soft refereeing decisions was not a post-1978 invention, as illustrated by

[9] Ian Kershaw, 'Hitler and the Nazi dictatorship', in Mary Fulbrook (ed.), *Twentieth-Century Germany: Politics, Culture and Society 1918–1990* (London: Hodder Arnold, 2001), pp. 117–18. The term was coined by Nazi functionary Werner Willikens in 1934.

[10] Leske, *Erich Mielke*, pp. 138–40.

the controversial game against Dynamo Schwerin in 1968 (recounted in the introduction to Part II). In an extensive and typically paranoid study of media coverage of BFC games in 1969 and 1970, the *Stasi* linked the club's negative image to newspaper criticism of pro-BFC officials – a reminder that, even within party organisations and publications, as one Lok Leipzig fan put it, football never inspired 'a strict homogeneity'.[11] Two petitions to the DFV from Union Berlin supporters, following Union's controversial loss to their local rivals in February 1977, radiated an outrage about refereeing injustices similar to that found in petitions a decade later. 'Unclean' officiating, one argued, endangered fairplay, 'not only on the pitch, but in the stands too'. The other emphasised his right as a 'paying customer' to see 'fair matches'.[12]

BFC always had an 'image problem'.[13] Until the late 1970s, though, there was no correlation between its apparent status as the regime's favoured team and its results. Why things then improved so markedly is not an easy question to answer. If the *Stasi* were so powerful, why did Mielke wait so long to flex his muscles? If match officials always practised 'pre-emptive obedience' (*vorauseilender Gehorsam*) towards BFC, why did it bear fruit only after 1978?[14] The archives, as BFC fans keenly point out, have never yielded a document that mandated *Stasi* bribery of match officials.[15] A confluence of factors seems to have brought BFC to prominence: Mielke's annoyance at Dynamo Dresden's success and popularity in the 1970s; the cyclical decline of some of its rivals (such as FC Magdeburg); the MfS's growing stranglehold on elite sport, including referees; and the BFC first team benefiting from what journalist Horst Friedemann called its 'exquisite youth work', which produced players of the calibre of Lutz Eigendorf, Andreas Thom, and Thomas Doll.[16]

Complaints about favouritism towards BFC inevitably increased as the team became more successful. A turning point was the match at which Mielke allegedly made his remark about bringing the championship to Berlin, BFC's 3–1 victory over Dynamo Dresden on 2 December 1978. The Dresden party leader, Hans Modrow, blamed the unrest at the Rudolf Harbig Stadium, which led to thirty-five arrests and snowballs being thrown at the departing BFC team bus, on inept officiating.[17]

11 *Ibid.*, pp. 491–6; interview with Heiko H.
12 Union Berlin Archive, petition from Wolfgang Q. to the DFV, 23 February 1977; petition from Klaus H. to the DFV, 1 March 1977.
13 Leske, *Erich Mielke*, p. 486.
14 This term was used in interview by two Union fans: Tim E. and Sven S.
15 Interview with Olaf S. 16 Luther and Willmann, *BFC Dynamo*, p. 75.
17 SAPMO-BArch, DY 30/IV 2/2.036/25, letter from Hans Modrow to Paul Verner, 5 December 1978, fo. 56–7.

The match triggered such heated discussion in the city's factories and institutions, one SED report claimed, that work output in the early part of the following week was adversely affected. There was open talk of the result being 'manipulated' ('only Dynamo Dresden didn't keep to the arrangement by taking the lead'). The inexperienced linesman who contentiously allowed BFC's equaliser to stand came in for strong criticism: 'Supp certainly got a new Lada for this decision'.[18]

Local patriotism was arguably more pronounced in Dresden than anywhere else. Residents warned that 'if there's to be manipulation, then not with the Dresden public' and suggested that this was not the first time that the city had received the short end of the stick: 'we're ripped off everywhere, even on the pitch'. Such comments, as the party leadership in Dresden noted, were conditioned by 'a widely held anti-Berlin attitude'. Locals asserted that 'the SED wants a Berlin football champion, that's why referees have been bribed'.[19] A spiky, defensive regional pride that posited Berlin-directed conspiracies was a recurrent feature of complaints about BFC. In an era characterised by GDR historians' increased focus on the progressive aspects of Prussian historical figures such as Frederick the Great, it is interesting to note how a football team from Prussia's major city (and a police team, no less) was the target of so much vitriol. BFC supporters gleefully fanned the flames, emptying out crates of bananas and oranges – perishable symbols of the capital's favoured status – on match-day visits to Dresden's stadium.[20] Union supporters engaged in similarly provocative activities, taking old Cuban oranges to matches against the likes of FC Karl-Marx-Stadt.[21] Enmity between East Berlin and 'the Zone' (i.e. the rest of the GDR) – fed by discrepancies in the supply of not only fruit, but also coffee, toys, and Christmas decorations[22] – was emblematic of the difficulties that the SED faced in creating a sense of socialist nationhood that buried these rivalries once and for all.

The fallout from the Dynamo Dresden–BFC clash raised wider political fears. Modrow noted that the bad officiating led to discussions extending 'into the ranks of the party' that were 'foreign' to the socialist sports movement. He warned against unnecessarily providing 'explosive material' for 'negative manifestations' among the sizeable part of the population that watched football.[23] As one party member in Dresden remarked, 'political decisions in football are currently generating just as

[18] HStA Dresden, 11857 SED-Bezirksleitung Dresden IV/D-2.16 Nr. 848, Negative Erscheinungen im Zusammenhang mit dem Oberligaspiel Dynamo Dresden gegen Dynamo Berlin am 02.12.1978, n.d.

[19] *Ibid.* [20] Interview with BFC fans. [21] Interview with Sven S.

[22] Allinson, '1977: the GDR's most normal year?', p. 259.

[23] SAPMO-BArch, DY 30/IV 2/2.036/25, letter from Modrow to Verner, fo. 57.

bad an atmosphere among the population as the poor supply situation'.[24] Umberto Eco may have been right about the incompatibility of football and revolution, but – given the game's popularity – the SED regime did not want to take chances. In the following decade, it spent considerable time and effort attempting, largely unsuccessfully, to assuage public hostility to BFC.

## 'The damned right to watch honest sport':[25] petitions on BFC

The championship quickly became an annual procession. BFC won its fourth successive *Oberliga* title in 1983 by twelve points, without losing a single game. Even among the team's fans, such predictability wore thin. Attendances plummeted, from an average of 15,577 in the 1980/1 season to an average of 8,792 in 1987/8.[26] Jokes about bent officials ('hustle and bustle, panic, corruption – Adolf Prokop has it already done!') fell flat. Unlucky cup final defeats bolstered morale more than 'the expected league title'.[27] Meanwhile, anger among supporters of other teams grew steadily. By the mid 1980s, the BFC problem dominated the public discourse on football.

Petitions on the subject took one of two forms. A minority were mailed anonymously, allowing the writer, or writers, a degree of cover to make more threatening remarks than might otherwise have been possible. In 1982, for example, the DFV received a 'declaration on the carrying through of clean *Oberliga* games' from a self-proclaimed 'circle of terrorists'. Outlining fan anger at 'obvious manipulations' in BFC's favour, the circle advocated direct action: 'The customs of our country do not allow open discussion of this outrage. The only way to force a change is via pressure on referees'. It then listed various measures, all rather mild for a terrorist group, to be taken against officials who continued to collude with BFC: smashed windows on their flats and vehicles, spray-can-painted cars and punctured tyres, weed-killer-strewn gardens, and 'ravaged' bungalows.[28]

Anonymous or semi-anonymous complaints were often reasonable in tone. A petition sent to the DFV in 1984 by the violent-sounding

[24] HStA Dresden, 11857 SED-Bezirksleitung Dresden IV/D-2.16 Nr. 848, Negative Erscheinungen.

[25] SAPMO-Barch, DY 30/4982, petition from Hans-Jürgen H. to Hellmann, 12 May 1986, fo. 337.

[26] www.european-football-statistics.co.uk/attn/archive/avezddr80.htm.

[27] Gläser, *Der BFC war schuld*, pp. 43–4.

[28] SAPMO-BArch, DY 30/4959, Deklaration zur Durchsetzung "sauberer Spielabläufe" in der Oberliga, n.d., fo. 45–6.

Dynamo Dresden fan club *Blutiger Knochen* ('bloody bones') opened with strongly worded criticism of the referee's performance in BFC's recent 4–2 victory over Dynamo. It then emphasised how such 'wangling' encouraged 'crazy spectator disturbances', expressed grudging respect for BFC's run of success, and conceded how difficult it was for referees to make split-second decisions: 'that's why we don't just talk, but also send talented friends to [officiating] courses'.[29] The constructive approach, the modest goal of which was to air pertinent issues in *Junge Welt*, featured in the terrorist declaration two years earlier. This group too ultimately sought a partner in dialogue and a public space in which their views could be heard: 'Allow publication of an item in the *Sport-Echo* [newspaper] stating that referees have been instructed to take better general care of fairness in the stadia'.[30] The SED, as we shall see, eventually met these popular demands.

Even when complainants did not give their names and were clearly very angry, they deployed rhetorical devices that both appropriated and targeted SED discourse. An anonymous petition to the ZK in 1985, for example, framed its biting critique of institutional bias towards BFC ('from Rostock to Aue every child knows about it and it's on everyone's lips') within the following argument: 'Nobody in our country really understands why a team is favoured so strongly by the top brass when three of its players have recently committed treason [*republikflüchtig wurden*]: Eigendorf, Schlegel, Götz'. Criticism and conformity, as in many petitions on the BFC problem, were not opposite, but mutually reinforcing categories. They suggested how citizens' outward loyalty to the regime, a key factor in most accounts of the stability of the GDR, could itself be 'potentially destabilizing'.[31] The petitioner established his credentials as a loyal citizen, praising BFC's play and condemning traitors to the GDR, in order to legitimate his attack on the corruption that was ruining football: 'You can't treat millions of honest football fans as idiots for years to come!'[32]

Most petitioners identified themselves openly to the authorities. Their letters arrived from all parts of the republic, from cities with *Oberliga* clubs such as Dresden (the biggest source of complaints), Berlin, and Erfurt to small communities where top-flight football was only available on television. Petitioners were invariably men – of all ages, from youth

29 BStU, MfS HA XX/2669, petition from the *Blutiger Knochen* fan club to the DFV, fo. 42.

30 SAPMO-BArch, DY 30/4959, cover note from 'the circle' to the DFV, n.d., fo. 44.

31 Port, *Conflict and Stability*, p. 5.

32 SAPMO-BArch, DY 30/4980, anonymous petition to the ZK, 27 October 1985, fo. 2–3. The *Republikflucht* of BFC players is discussed in Chapter 6.

brigade members to pensioners, and all social classes: industrial workers, but also writers, teachers, and doctors. Many were unaffiliated football fans, but others were active sports functionaries and some were even party members.

What lay behind this groundswell of public opinion? Some answers are suggested by five petitions written during the 1985/6 season, when disillusionment about BFC was at its peak. Between one and six pages in length, these petitions, sent to party headquarters between October 1985 and May 1986, provided a representative cross-section of the anti-BFC demographic. They came from just outside Berlin (Potsdam and Babelsberg), from Leipzig, from Erfurt, and from the small community of Breitungen-Werra (near Suhl). Two of the five petitioners were SED members. Two BFC matches prompted their letters of complaint: the 3–2 win away over Rot–Weiß Erfurt on 26 October and the 1–1 draw at Lokomotive Leipzig on 22 March. The latter match, in which BFC escaped with a point thanks to a dubious penalty awarded long after referee Bernd Stumpf should have blown the final whistle, has a strong place in the collective memory of East German fans. BFC eventually beat Lok to that season's *Oberliga* title, their eighth in succession, by two points.[33]

The petitioners were generally at pains to emphasise their objectivity. Party member Jens G. from Potsdam opened his letter in March 1986 with the caveat 'please note that I am no fanatical or loyal fan of one of our *Oberliga* teams', before adding in parentheses the possibly telling aside 'years ago I especially liked BFC Dynamo'.[34] In the early lines of his letter in November 1985, fellow comrade Wolfgang S. from Breitungen-Werra made a similar plea, the accuracy of which was unwittingly enforced by his bizarrely optimistic assessment of the *Auswahl*: 'I am no football fan, though I follow with interest *Oberliga* matches and the upwards trend in our national team'.[35] Just two of the quintet supported a particular team: Hans-Jürgen H. from Erfurt (Rot–Weiß Erfurt) and Heiko H. from Leipzig (Lokomotive Leipzig).[36] Detachment from the label 'fan', which had pejorative connotations in the GDR as across much of the rest of Europe during the 1980s, suggested an internalisation, whether genuine or pragmatic, of the sober values of the socialist sports movement.

33 On the Lok–BFC game, see Leske, *Erich Mielke*, pp. 518–29.

34 SAPMO-BArch, DY 30/4982, petition from Jens G. to Krenz, 22 March 1986, fo. 40.

35 SAPMO-BArch, DY 30/4987, petition from Wolfgang S. to Hellmann, 1 November 1985, fo. 68.

36 SAPMO-BArch, DY 30/4982, petition from Hans-Jürgen H. to Hellmann, 12 May 1986, fo. 339; private archive of Heiko H., petition from Heiko H. to the DFV, 24 March 1986.

There was an interesting mixture of caution and bluntness in the language chosen to criticise BFC's pre-eminence. Both party members used reported speech, creating a sympathetic space, but a space nonetheless, between themselves and the football-loving public. Jens G., following the model of SED public opinion reports, gave a long list of 'questions or points of view' provoked by favouritism towards BFC, including 'in the *Oberliga* you play for second to fourteenth place, BFC has to be GDR champions', 'why do so few Berliners support BFC?', and 'are referees being manipulated and who is responsible for it?'[37] Michael R. from Babelsberg, in his petition from October 1985, created a similar distancing effect, citing a discussion that he had had two years earlier with a DFV functionary to support the commonly heard argument that referees favoured BFC in order to be nominated for international matches.[38] Hans-Jürgen H. pulled fewer punches, describing the referee's decisions in the Erfurt–BFC game as 'a scandal!!!'[39] Heiko H. was even franker, though only in his second petition to the DFV, after a first, more modestly phrased letter had, unlawfully, gone seven weeks unanswered: 'for me it's all reduced to the question of whether you are hopelessly unqualified to do your job responsibly, or whether you are rather misusing your position for deliberate cheating'.[40]

The latter two petitioners were most alive to the detrimental impact of BFC's dominance on the reputation of East German football and the East German state. Hans-Jürgen H's letter included a detailed account of dubious decisions made throughout the 1985/6 season, unknowingly echoing a secret investigation that the DFV commissioned on the same topic a year earlier.[41] The 'special role' that unseen forces had granted BFC during the past ten years, he emphasised, 'hampered the natural development' of the game. It left clubs unprepared for European competition, ridiculed the cliché that 'a referee can't score a goal', and created problems so extensive that 'it's hardly credible that there are still functionaries with nothing to say about them'.[42] As Heiko H. noted, it

[37] SAPMO-BArch, DY 30/4982, petition from Jens G. to Krenz, 22 March 1986, fo. 41.

[38] SAPMO-BArch, DY 30/4986, petition from Michael R. to the ZK, 27 October 1985, fo. 50–1.

[39] SAPMO-Barch, DY 30/4982, petition from Hans-Jürgen H. to Hellmann, fo. 340.

[40] Private archive of Heiko H., petition from Heiko H. to the DFV, 5 May 1986. According to the 1974 constitution, petitions were to be answered within four weeks.

[41] SAPMO-Barch, DY 30/IV 2/2.039/247, Zusammenstellung von Informationen zur Problematik der Schiedsrichterleistungen und -verhaltensweisen in Zusammenhang mit den Spielen des BFC Dynamo, der SG Dynamo Dresden und dem 1. FC Lok Leipzig in der Saison 1984/85, n.d., fo. 88–92.

[42] SAPMO-BArch, DY 30/4982, petition from Hans-Jürgen H. to Hellmann, fo. 337–8.

reinforced the attractiveness of West German football to players and spectators alike: 'I too see how football can look at Bayern Munich'.[43]

A conspicuous feature of the petitions was the media's role in disseminating and talking around the BFC problem. Jens G., for example, framed his petition as an immediate response to the injustices that he witnessed in the highlights of the BFC–Lok Leipzig match on the *Sport aktuell* show. Michael R. wrote to the ZK five months earlier after watching the Rot–Weiß Erfurt–BFC match on television.[44] Mediated spectatorship meant, first and most obviously, a wider audience for suspicious refereeing performances, turning what in the 1950s might have been a series of local incidents into a nationwide debate. Manipulation in the television age was harder to deny, which made the awkward attempts to turn a blind eye to it all the more damaging. In his diary of the injustices of the 1985/6 season, Hans-Jürgen H. made frequent and pointed references to the reluctance of state television to criticise poor refereeing decisions that favoured BFC or, in highlights programmes, to show them at all.[45] It was the mass visibility of the consistent and blatant manipulations that finally forced both the media and the authorities to speak out against incompetent refereeing, though not against its root causes, in the mid 1980s. Likewise the 'sheer visibility', as well as taste and smell, of pollution prevented the SED leadership from keeping green issues out of the public eye, as escalating environmental decline undermined the 'socialist transcript' of the beautiful *Heimat*.[46]

The petitioners acknowledged that perceived injustices on the football field could have a destabilising political impact. Jens G., like many concerned party leaders, noted that negative discussions about refereeing performances spilled into the workplace the following Monday, with 'criticisms in this connection [...] often not confined to BFC'. Hans-Jürgen H. asserted that the current situation damaged not only BFC's reputation, but also that of its patron, the police: 'If you get points weekend after weekend through one-sided refereeing decisions and these [police] units are also responsible for order and security at the venue, a very complicated case arises'.[47] Moreover, as Wolfgang S. anxiously remarked, it left comrades in an uncomfortable position: 'For me as a party member, it's about making honest arguments to sports fans and

43 Private archive of Heiko H., petition from Heiko H. to the DFV, 5 May 1986.

44 SAPMO-BArch, DY 30/4982, petition from Jens G. to Krenz, fo. 40; SAPMO-BArch, DY 30/4986, petition from Michael R. to the ZK, fo. 50.

45 SAPMO-BArch, DY 30/4982, petition from Hans-Jürgen H. to Hellmann, fo. 339.

46 Fulbrook, *Anatomy*, pp. 225–34; Palmowski, *Inventing a Socialist Nation*, pp. 187–8.

47 SAPMO-BArch, DY 30/4982, petition from Jens G. to Krenz, fo. 40–1; petition from Hans-Jürgen H. to Hellmann, fo. 338.

citizens and being able to ascertain that we're only talking here about gaffes (*Ausrutscher*) that can happen but that aren't typical'.[48]

By 1986, however, few fans believed that officiating errors in BFC games were innocent. The knock-on effects of the growing cynicism were significant: angry discussions in the workplace that shaded from football into economic or political issues; encouragement for those who believed that 'you can only influence our game by throwing bottles and fireworks and by wanton destruction';[49] a point of attraction for anti-communist forces (by the mid 1980s, the West German media commented regularly on the corrosive impact of BFC's dominance);[50] lack of confidence in the security forces; and a fractured, suspicious relationship between the party leadership and the populace. Such developments return us to the 'chipping away' at the East German state that occurred during the final decade of its existence.[51] This generally unconscious subversion of the structures of power, as expressed through grumbling and complaints about various aspects of everyday life, was expressed nowhere more powerfully than in the anti-BFC crusade. Football fans' actions help to explain how the edifice of communist power crumbled so rapidly and completely in 1989 and 1990.

## State responses to the BFC controversy

The five petitions were just the tip of the iceberg. Hundreds more were dispatched to the authorities on the same theme, particularly in 1985 and 1986. Nor was the upsurge in anti-BFC sentiment confined to the page. BFC players were booed when they played in the national team's colours at grounds across the republic. At Leipzig's Zentralstadion, a frequent venue for international fixtures, only Andreas Thom escaped this 'merciless' treatment.[52] Terrace chants and slogans became increasingly numerous and virulent ('death to BFC', 'DDT for BFC', 'Zyklon B for BFC').[53] In a hostile climate, BFC supporters responded by becoming more organised and more aggressive, revelling in, and thereby feeding, the hatred that their team inspired. People voted with their feet. The predictability of the league championship was a vital factor in the declining attendances of the 1980s. Average crowds at FC Magdeburg, for example, dropped by more than half, from 13,654 in the 1980/1 season

48 SAPMO-BArch, DY 30/4987, petition from Wolfgang S. to Hellmann, fo. 68.

49 Private archive of Heiko H., petition from Heiko H. to the DFV, 24 March 1986.

50 See e.g. the West German articles on GDR football collected by the *Stasi* in 1985–6 in BStU, MfS HA XX/221, fo. 24, 46–54, 59–61.

51 Kopstein, 'Chipping away at the state', 393–4.

52 Gläser, *Der BFC war schuld*, p. 44.

53 Moog, *Die Fans von Union*, p. 90.

to 6,615 in 1988/9. Other clubs, including (as previously noted) BFC, experienced similar losses.[54]

The authorities were not insensitive to the problems caused by BFC's success. Conciliatory replies to petitions on this vexed subject illustrated a responsiveness to public opinion that might at first seem out of place in an authoritarian state, but was in fact common. Answering petitions effectively and quickly was seen as a key part of the state's contribution to the 'co-formation of the citizen's developmental possibilities', as well as a socialist version of 'customer care'.[55] Jens G. was 'very surprised' to find his petition to Egon Krenz in protest against the referee's performance in the Lok Leipzig–BFC match in March 1986 answered with a personal meeting with Rudi Hellmann in Potsdam two weeks later, at which the head of the ZK sports department discussed in detail the fallout from this game, including the decision to bar the referee, Bernd Stumpf, from top-level fixtures for a year.[56] Other responses from Hellmann to the angry, accusatory missives that landed on his desk after the same game were equally placatory. The outspoken Hans-Jürgen H. was informed that his 'basic position is completely justified, though you'll certainly understand that we can't agree in every detail with your statements'. Horst D. from Dresden was politely assured that steps were being taken to improve refereeing standards and to guarantee 'modern, spectator-friendly, and fair' football.[57] This was a damage limitation exercise, in which referees such as Stumpf were sacrificed to the altar of public opinion. But the authorities' replies were not just window dressing. The call and response of the petition process may in some ways have shored up the regime, reproducing socialist discourses in relatively safe civil spaces.[58] But the fact that the SED, as in the case of anti-BFC complaints, had to venture onto less comfortable terrain suggests a different way of looking at petitions. By championing a grievance culture based on individual complaints, the East German state sometimes had to negotiate on its citizens', rather than on its own, terms, thereby undermining the collective ethos that supposedly underpinned socialist ideals.

The 1985 cup final provided a particularly interesting case study of the complex, media-influenced interplay between concession and denial in

[54] www.european-football-statistics.co.uk/attn/archive/avezddr80.htm.

[55] Betts, *Within Walls*, p. 182; Fulbrook, *The People's State*, p. 281.

[56] SAPMO-BArch, DY 30/4982, letter from Hellmann to Krenz, 4 April 1986, fo. 37.

[57] *Ibid.*, letter from Hellmann to Hans-Jürgen H., 26 May 1986, fo. 335; SAPMO-BArch, DY 30/4981, letter from Hellmann to Horst D., 1 April 1986, fo. 84.

[58] Judd Stitziel, 'Shopping, sewing, networking, complaining: consumer culture and the relationship between state and society in the GDR', in Pence and Betts (eds.), *Socialist Modern*, pp. 272–3.

the party's response to the BFC problem. The match took place at the end of a season in which, as the DFV concluded in a frank report, systematic favouritism towards the champions could no longer be denied. In the *Oberliga* in 1984/5, the report noted, BFC earned only one-third of the yellow cards incurred by Dynamo Dresden. The DFV identified nine league and cup matches that were probable sites of crooked officiating and spoke of 'targeted pressure' on referees and the press from BFC officials, including the case of one leading referee allegedly given a holiday home at the club's expense.[59]

Dynamo Dresden defeated BFC 3–2 in the cup final. However, by most accounts, Dynamo won despite the best efforts of the experienced referee, Manfred Roßner, to shape a different outcome. The DFV and *Die Neue Fußball-Woche* received roughly 700 letters of complaint about the referee's performance on 8 June.[60] Petitions were sent in considerable numbers to the ZK sports department and state television. Their content was as unanimous as their authorship was diverse. Erik Neutsch, author of the prize-winning novel *Traces of Stones* (1964),[61] exulted in Dynamo Dresden's triumph against the odds. When BFC scored in the eighty-eighth minute to reduce the arrears to 3–2, he noted, Roßner restarted the game with three red-shirted players still in the Dresden half! Alfred M. from Dresden, a party member of forty years' standing, highlighted the scarcely credible incompetence of the officials: 'I can tolerate a poor performance but the mistakes should be evenly distributed. Roßner's one-sidedness in the cup final could have hardly been bettered'. M., like Neutsch, drew attention to the spineless television coverage of the game: 'are our sports reporters incapable of recognising [bad refereeing], or are they not allowed to speak about it?' As a mechanic from Bischofswerda put it, the manipulations were so obvious that 'even the party leadership must have seen it'.[62]

Top sports functionaries did indeed view the cup final, and the uproar that followed it, with consternation. The report on the 1984/5 season had already spoken of the 'great damage' that officiating bias did to the reputations of BFC and the embattled DFV, and outlined a number of

[59] SAPMO-BArch, DY 30/IV 2/2.039/247, Zusammenstellung von Informationen, fo. 88–92. It is unclear whether this report was written before or after the cup final.

[60] SAPMO-BArch, DY 30/4986, Aktennotiz zur Aussprache mit Sportfreund Roßner am 11. Juli 1985, n.d., fo. 115.

[61] On Neutsch's novel and the idealised socialist *Heimat*, see Palmowski, *Inventing a Socialist Nation*, pp. 65–6.

[62] SAPMO-BArch, DY 30/4985, petition from Erik Neutsch to *Die Neue Fußball-Woche*, 12 June 1985, fo. 10; SAPMO-BArch, DY 30/4984, petition from Alfred M. to the DFV, fo. 111–14; SAPMO-BArch, DY 30/4987, anonymous petition to the ZK, 18 June 1985, fo. 137.

measures to clean up the game.[63] Now the SED demanded further action. On 21 June an eight-man DFV panel gathered in Leipzig to undertake a video review of the performance of the officials – Roßner and the two linesmen, Klaus Scheurell and Widukind Herrmann – in the fateful game a fortnight earlier. The results confirmed what most fans had claimed for years. Of the ten most egregious mistakes, nine went against Dynamo Dresden. These included a wrongly disallowed goal by Ralf Minge and repeated failures to give BFC players yellow cards for crude fouls, including one by the captain Frank Rohde on Minge so obvious that all of the players stopped playing to wait for a whistle that never came. The DFV's analysis concluded that seventeen of the referee's sixty decisions (about 30%) were wrong, a very high ratio for an experienced official – the average figure was around 10%. Fourteen of these seventeen errors benefited BFC, including all of the decisions that carried possibly game-changing consequences, such as Minge's disallowed goal.[64] Nothing emerged to indicate that the *Stasi* had bought Roßner's compliance. It seems likelier, rather, that the referee followed the pattern of 'pre-emptive obedience' that had long shaped the relationship between officials and the Dynamo organisation. This pattern was replicated elsewhere in the Soviet bloc. Asparuh Yasenov, who refereed the riotous 1985 Bulgarian cup final between Sofia's army and police clubs, later remarked that 'Nobody tried to put pressure on me before the match, but it was always difficult to referee matches between CSKA and Levski. We all knew who was behind the clubs and that we had to be faultless. Sometimes the psychological pressure leads to mistakes'.[65]

On the basis of the video evidence, the DFV barred Roßner from refereeing international and *Oberliga* games, demoting him to second division matches for one year. Scheurell was de-selected for duties in the first round of the following season's European Cup matches. The cup final had been Herrmann's last game before retirement.[66] It was thereby established that officials who performed badly in games involving BFC could face consequences. After BFC's controversial victory over Rot-Weiß Erfurt in October 1985, the referee Reinhard Purz was suspended until the end of the year and the linesman Günter Supp for three games.[67]

[63] SAPMO-BArch, DY 30/IV 2/2.039/247, Zusammenstellung von Informationen, fo. 92.

[64] SAPMO-BArch, DY 30/4963, Protokoll der Videoauswertung des Endspiels im FDGB-Pokal vom 8. Juni 1985 zwischen dem BFC Dynamo und der SG Dynamo Dresden zur Beurteilung der Schiedsrichterleistung, 3 July 1985, fo. 195–6.

[65] Wilson, *Behind the Curtain*, p. 188.

[66] SAPMO-BArch, DY 30/4963, Protokoll der Videoauswertung, fo. 196–7.

[67] SAPMO-BArch, DY 30/4983, letter from Hellmann to Dr Alfred I., 22 November 1985, fo. 3–4.

The referee Bernd Stumpf was banned from international and *Oberliga* matches for a year as a result of his performance in BFC's contentious 1–1 draw at Lokomotive Leipzig five months later, at which point the DFV's refereeing commission was also overhauled, with the unpopular Berliner Heinz Einbeck being replaced as its head by the ex-referee Rudi Glöckner.[68]

Roßner and Stumpf, like the supporters who criticised them, sent petitions to the authorities. Roßner's letter to Krenz in July 1985 conceded that he performed poorly in the cup final, but that this was unintentional and unrepresentative of his impressive record. The DFV's punishment, he argued, was 'very harsh' and had been publicised in such a way that 'everything comes back to me personally'. Stumpf's petition to Honecker in March 1986 adopted a similar tone, emphasising his previous good service to GDR football and criticising the recent trend to scapegoat officials for decisions made in BFC games (and BFC games only).[69]

Roßner offered interesting perspectives on behind-the-scenes discussions of the BFC problem that were largely absent from party or DFV reports. He claimed that the DFV deputy general secretary Volker Nickchen had approached him before the cup final and confidentially requested 'no BFC-friendly decisions'. Afterwards the incensed DFV vice president Franz Rydz took Roßner to task for his performance, allegedly emphasising that 'you can't always go by the book, but have to officiate in a way that placates the Dresden public'. Such responses suggested the DFV's sensitivity to public opinion: the flood of anti-BFC petitions was making its mark. They also remind us of the football association's ambiguous position, caught between loyalty to the regime, on the one hand, and representing the wishes of fans and players on the other. As if to emphasise the fractured nature of communist authority in football, Roßner also cited rumours circulating in his home town of Gera that Mielke ordered his demotion because BFC had lost the cup final.[70] Referees, in this reading, were caught between a rock and a hard place, between the DFV's party-backed attempts to mollify anti-BFC sentiments and the MfS's desire to advance the interests of the club that it sponsored.

68 SAPMO-BArch, DY 30/IV 2/2.039/251, Stellungnahme des DFV der DDR, n.d., fo. 157–9; Baingo and Horn, *Die Geschichte der DDR-Oberliga*, p. 246.

69 SAPMO-BArch, DY 30/4986, petition from Manfred Roßner to Krenz, 23 July 1985, fo. 120–2; SAPMO-BArch, DY 30/IV 2/2.039/251, petition from Bernd Stumpf to Honecker, 31 March 1986, fo. 113–5.

70 SAPMO-BArch, DY 30/4986, petition from Roßner to Krenz, fo. 121.

Neither Roßner nor Stumpf was granted clemency. The DFV confirmed their one-year suspensions. Suggestions that the organisation acted under outside pressure, as Stumpf in particular claimed, were strenuously denied.[71] These measures indisputably marked a victory for public opinion, a reminder that football fans were a powerful constituency even in authoritarian states such as the GDR. The party and the DFV were forced by the scale of popular outcry in 1985 and 1986 to disassociate themselves from, and discipline, referees perceived to favour BFC. An interesting comparision can be made here with the fallout from the 1985 Bulgarian cup final between fierce rivals Levski Sofia and CSKA Sofia, a match that featured fan unrest, a mass on-field brawl, and assaults on the referee. The Bulgarian football association, condemning the match as a 'breach of socialistic morals', subsequently dissolved both clubs. Coaching staff and management were sacked. Players were handed long suspensions or, in four cases, banned for life.[72]

The DFV's response to a controversial, if less unruly, cup final was more circumspect. Whereas Bulgarian football was turned upside down in June 1985, GDR football, at first viewing, stayed much the same. The triumph of public opinion was incomplete or, one might argue, delayed. The tougher line against referees did not prevent BFC from winning the league title in either the 1986/7 or the 1987/8 season. It was simple to scapegoat figures such as Roßner and Stumpf, leaving them to shoulder the burden of public anger, which in both cases apparently stretched to death threats.[73] It was more difficult, though, to tackle the underlying causes of BFC's unpopularity, just as the regime struggled (as we saw in Chapter 9) to address the root causes of hooliganism. This would have required an open reckoning with the secret police, whose network of informers included leading referees (such as Prokop, Stumpf, and Supp),[74] coaches, and players that nobody in football was prepared to countenance – nobody except the fans. Their role in BFC's eventual decline, while difficult to quantify, cannot be underestimated.

In the meantime, BFC's bullying presence was inescapable. The DFV report on the 1984/5 season spoke of journalists being threatened by anonymous secret-police representatives.[75] Following his team's victory

71 SAPMO-BArch, DY 30/IV 2/2.039/251, petition from Stumpf to Honecker, fo. 113–15; letter from Krenz to Stumpf, 2 April 1986, fo. 119–20.

72 See Wilson, *Behind the Iron Curtain*, pp. 185–90.

73 SAPMO-BArch, DY 30/IV 2/2.039/251, petition from Stumpf to Honecker, fo. 114; SAPMO-BArch, DY 30/4986, Aktennotiz über die Aussprache mit Genossen Manfred Roßner am 19.8.1985, 20 August 1985, fo. 113.

74 Leske, *Erich Mielke*, pp. 531–2.

75 SAPMO-BArch, DY 30/IV 2/2.039/247, Zusammenstellung von Informationen, fo. 91.

at Rot–Weiß Erfurt in October 1985, the BFC chairman Manfred Kirste sent angry letters to various media outlets about reporters who fomented anti-BFC sentiments. He accused television commentators, widely excoriated for their silence in the face of pro-BFC manipulations, of failing to correct the 'varied eyesight' of the 26,000 Erfurt supporters at the game. A young *Junge Welt* journalist was charged with tricking Frank Rohde into conceding in a post-match interview that the home team should have been awarded a penalty for his last-minute barge on Martin Busse. The conspiracy theories that circulated about BFC's shady influence were turned on their head, with the *Stasi* club now the injured party: 'In previous weeks we were rightly criticised for the poor fitness level in our team. Now, when performances have improved, when the team is playing well and fighting ... allegedly "dubious decisions" by the refereeing collective are being sought out and pushed to the fore!'[76] The club's defensiveness echoed the defensiveness of its fan base, a small minority in the schools, pubs, and discos of East Berlin, who felt themselves to be more sinned against than sinners.

*Stasi* power did not silence dissenting voices. Resentment at BFC's supremacy among not only fans, but also the media, the DFV, and some party leaders was palpable. The journalists attacked by Kirste stood their ground. The *Junge Welt* reporter whose interview with Rohde after the Erfurt game had angered the BFC chairman justified the decision to publish the BFC captain's candid assessment of the penalty incident ('It was certainly not entirely clean on my part. You could give a penalty for that') on the grounds that millions of viewers had seen and were discussing it.[77] At a meeting with the DFV leadership on 30 October 1985, journalists expressed indignation at Kirste's attempted coercion of the press. Ulrich Meier, the head of sport at East German television, remarked on his 'scandalous attempts' to handpick reporters for BFC games, leading to the impression that the club had 'its reporters' just as it had 'its referees'. Again such arguments were supported with reference to public opinion, in this case the anti-BFC petitions put forward 'in mass numbers' in recent years. The DFV, it should be noted, concluded that media coverage of the Erfurt–BFC game, in particular of the errant refereeing decisions that helped to ensure victory for the away side, had been accurate.[78] In the realm of football, the East German dictatorship

[76] SAPMO-BArch, DY 30/IV 2/2.039/251, letter from Manfred Kirste to Ulrich Meier, 29 October 1985, fo. 100–2; letter from Manfred Kirste to Volker Kluge, 29 October 1985, fo. 104–5.

[77] *Ibid.*, Erklärung, 31 October 1985, fo. 107–8.

[78] SAPMO-BArch, DY 30/4964, Information über eine Beratung mit den Sportredaktionen der zentralen Medien am 30.10.1985, fo. 244–6.

was a head with many voices. Though the GDR was no friend of media plurality, it is striking how often – for example, in match reports on the 1984/5 season[79] – local and regional SED newspapers took issue with pro-BFC refereeing performances.

Ultimately, there were only limited outlets for discontent among football followers, just as there was only so much a disaffected citizen could do about housing shortages, lack of replacement parts for cars and televisions, or shortfalls in the provision of fruit or coffee. As one Lok Leipzig fan noted, individual protestors could achieve surprising things in the GDR. The problems arose when it came to collective action.[80] Petitions provided a vent for anti-BFC sentiment, but long-term solutions – to problems in and beyond football – did not appear to be imminent. The result was far-reaching disillusionment, not only with BFC and the football authorities, but also with the system that condoned a one-horse title race. Alfred M.'s petition to the DFV after the 1985 cup final came to a telling conclusion: 'The comment of my daughter (18 years old, Dynamo Dresden fan) shows just how much political porcelain is being destroyed by the above-named machinations: "I would never have believed that such things are possible in our state"'.[81]

## BFC and (the decline of) the GDR

BFC's run of success ended in the 1988/9 season, when Dynamo Dresden won the league title for the first time in ten years, eight points clear of their old rivals. What might have been a blip in other circumstances quickly became a terminal decline amid the political changes that began in the autumn of 1989. When the *Wende* came, BFC – shorn of the support of the disbanded *Stasi* – fell from its exalted position as rapidly and completely as the socialist state that it controversially represented. Indeed, BFC's decline serves as a persuasive metaphor for the collapse of the GDR: a seemingly impregnable institution, outwardly successful despite widespread domestic grumbling, but always struggling for international credibility, suddenly reduced to impotence. BFC at least survived unification, albeit in a much reduced capacity. But Mielke's all-powerful club, with the pick of the GDR's young players and referees, was – just like the SED dictatorship – history.

What conclusions can be drawn from analysis of the BFC problem? In the first place, it offers a concretisation of the argument that football's relative unimportance was what made it important in the GDR. In an

[79] See Leske, *Erich Mielke*, pp. 506–7. [80] Interview with Heiko H.
[81] SAPMO-BArch, DY 30/4984, petition from Alfred M. to the DFV, fo. 114.

authoritarian society, where human rights were highly restricted, everyday concerns assumed an ersatz political importance that they lacked in democracies. Like popular music or the Church, football offered a mass civil space that was difficult to police and impossible to dissolve – and from which it was possible to fire shots across the bows of an unpopular regime. It would have been rash to send a petition to the authorities complaining about the ubiquity of the *Stasi*. But it was quite possible to send a petition, or partake in a chant, that offered a veiled critique of the *Stasi* via direct and often virulent criticism of its football team. Whether fans viewed their complaints about BFC as some form of surrogate protest against the state is questionable. Even Union Berlin fans concede that it is a stretch to call BFC's chief local critic 'a resistance club' ('politics was not the main interest'). For some, Union's dissident reputation was a 'post-*Wende* legend'.[82] But there can be little doubt that football provided legitimate cover for comments and activities that undermined the reputation of one of the pillars of East German socialism. Both petitioners and petitioned were aware, moreover, that such dissent was not a curative venting. Trouble in football could have political ramifications. At least until 1989, no other public campaign – laudable as the work of Church, peace, and environmental activists was – matched the popularity and influence of the anti-BFC drive. Protests about an unpopular football club did not bring down the Berlin Wall. But disillusionment at corruption and stagnation within the game was not easily separated from growing cynicism about life under socialism.

If football was a 'small way of saying "no"', it was expressed by fans throughout the GDR in opposition to BFC's dubious winning ways. In the process, they posited identities that clashed with communist values, articulating local or regional sentiments, anti-Berlin attitudes, and criticism of powerful state institutions. An *Eigen-Sinn* of a particularly interesting kind was noticeable among the small but committed core of BFC supporters. As one fan later recalled, 'it was simply great to be hated by everyone'. Republic-wide antipathy created a siege mentality that manifested itself in numerous ways: the development of a radical and violent hooligan following; contempt for the so-called *Zonis* and their 'shit Eastern life' without Levi's, bananas, and Western television (all readily available in the capital); mockery of Union Berlin's lack of success and *faux* working-class identity; distaste for the labelling of BFC as the '*Stasi* club'; and bridling against the familiar charge that BFC were 'crooked champions' (*Schiebemeister*).[83] In stark contrast to the team that

[82] Luther and Willmann, *Eisern Union!*, p. 102; interview with Tim E.
[83] Luther and Willmann, *BFC*, pp. 149–56.

they supported, BFC fans cultivated an underdog image – and took just as much pride in the peculiarities of their 'club egoism' as supporters of more popular teams such as Union and Dynamo Dresden. If Union's home ground was a gathering place for people 'who did not entirely approve of the state',[84] it was also a venue for making a statement about local identity, one that revelled in the raucous atmosphere frequently absent from BFC games.

The BFC controversy reiterates the dysfunctional character of the SED dictatorship, showcasing the limited ability of the authorities to shape football in the way that they shaped Olympic sports. Though publicly unspoken, tensions existed between the *Stasi* and the SED about perceptions of officiating bias towards BFC by the mid 1980s. While BFC chairman Manfred Kirste complained of 'a wedge being constructed between the population and a team of the armed organs', the DFV came under intense pressure 'from "outside"' (in this case the ZK sports department) to take action against referees who favoured BFC.[85] As noted earlier, the result was a triumph for public opinion, as leading officials such as Roßner and Stumpf were banned. The SED could not bring fan culture to heel – and ended up making concessions to it instead. The damage, though, was done. Terrace chants, banners, jean jacket badges, and even tattoos took aim at BFC, the hated frontrunners of GDR football, indicating a sporting culture that, like socialism in theory (if not in practice), prized a level playing field. Anti-BFC protests could not be silenced any more easily than terrace culture – noisy, rude, aggressive, and boozy – could be bent to the SED's will. The game and its supporters confounded attempts to place them safely within the framework of GDR sport.

In the final reckoning, the BFC problem epitomised the liminal space occupied by football under the East German dictatorship. There was much contested terrain between the small constituency that welcomed and even connived at the success of the BFC juggernaut between 1978 and 1988 and the larger group, or rather groups, that chafed against it. The game could be both regime-endorsing and rebellious. BFC fans reminisced in the post-*Wende* era about great European nights, pitch invasions to celebrate title triumphs, and chance encounters with Mielke ('Erich had a bit of a short fuse. He was a true BFC fan') – yet also made the questionable claim that their club was 'a gathering point for subversive characters' in the Prenzlauer Berg area.[86] Supporters of other teams

[84] Luther and Willmann, *Eisern Union!*, p. 102.

[85] SAPMO-BArch, DY 30/IV 2/2.039/251, letter from Kirste to Meier, 29 October 1985, fo. 101; petition from Stumpf to Honecker, fo. 113.

[86] Luther and Willmann, *BFC*, p. 132, 142–4, 154.

often framed their complaints about BFC within an acceptable discourse that called for the re-establishment of socialist values – yet represented a popular cause that had indisputably anti-socialist implications. The much-maligned DFV, arguably, had a liminal position of its own, one in which it served both as a mouthpiece for popular discontent against BFC's dominance and as an accomplice in this dominance. Unruly and unpredictable, even when the destination of the league title was all too predictable, football was emblematic of the mixture of conformity and quiet rebellion that characterised society in the GDR's final decade.

*Part III*

# The people's game

## 'King football': the game as *Massensport*

In the GDR, wrote Christoph Dieckmann in 1999, there were 'three kinds of football'. On Saturday afternoons at 4 p.m., he and countless others tuned in to live second-half radio updates from all seven *Oberliga* matches, hosted by anchorman Herbert Küttner. On Saturday nights there was 'Western television ... at Uncle Rittmüller's on his country-style sofa' and the illicit charms of the Munich derby between Bayern and 1860. The third kind, less publicised and less glamorous, took place on Sundays: 'the relegation battle in the Magdeburg *Bezirksklasse*, division C, between Traktor Dingelstedt with "Boxer" Könnecke in goal and Stahl Elbingerode'.[1] A photograph by Bernd Cramer (Figure 16), taken in Leipzig in 1987, shows two men's teams, one representing a local collective farm and the other a visiting delegation from a Soviet agricultural machine factory. They are posing for the camera on a rough pitch on what looks like an overcast day. The players' tight-fitting, sweat-stained shirts betray incontrovertible physical evidence that these are not performance athletes. This is recreational football – the people's game as *Massensport* ('mass sport').[2]

Football's uniqueness in the GDR, as in many countries, stemmed from its popularity as both a spectator and a participatory sport. In 1990, on the eve of its dissolution, the DFV numbered 5,534 clubs, 30,200 teams, and 424,587 members.[3] Roughly one in every forty GDR citizens was

[1] Dieckmann, '"Nur ein Leutzscher"', p. 311. The *Bezirksklasse* was the fourth tier of GDR football.

[2] SED functionaries used the term *Massensport* primarily during the 1950s. West German scholars referred to the practice as *Breitensport* ('popular sport'), a term not used in the GDR. From 1967 onwards, mass sport was known there as 'free time and recreational sport' (*Freizeit- und Erholungssport*). See Jochen Hinsching, 'Der Bereich "Freizeit- und Erholungssport" im "ausdifferenzierten" Sport der DDR', in Hinsching (ed.), *Alltagssport in der DDR*, p. 16.

[3] Archivgut des DFV (no *Signatur*), Konzeption des DFV der DDR zur Vorbereitung der Beratung der beiden Präsidien DFV–DFB am 19.05.1990 in Berlin (West), 7 May 1990; DDR-Bezirksverbände, n.d.

Figure 16. Recreational football in Leipzig, 1987. Local collective farmers take on a visiting team from a Soviet agricultural machinery factory.

a footballer. The estimate excludes the many others who played outside official structures, such as the steel workers in Thale, who organised fixtures beyond the DFV's purview, and the fans of Union Berlin, who founded an unsanctioned league in 1981, playing wherever pitches were available.[4]

No other sport rivalled football's appeal, at least among men.[5] In large sports organisations, such as the railway industry club Lokomotive and the army club Vorwärts (according to statistics from 1960 and 1972 respectively), the game was the leading sport in terms of registered players, sections (i.e. clubs), coaches, and referees.[6] Football's favoured status spanned the GDR's history. In 1955 it accounted for 316,262 of the almost 1.14 million members of the DS, the forerunner to the DTSB. Gymnastics, the second-largest sport, had 147,477 members.[7] Figures compiled thirty-two years

[4] Uwe Karte, 'An der Basis', in Willmann (ed.), *Fußball-Land DDR*, p. 171. The Union *Fan-Liga* ('fan league') is discussed in Chapter 11.

[5] Women's football is discussed in Chapter 12.

[6] SAPMO-BArch, DY 12/2416, Mitgliederstatistik des Deutschen Turn- und Sportbunds: SV Lokomotive, 30 September 1960; SAPMO-BArch, DY 12/2440, Organisationsstatistik des Deutschen Turn- und Sportbunds: Armeesportvereinigung "Vorwärts", 31 December 1972.

[7] SAPMO-BArch, DR 5/866, Statistischer Bericht 1955, n.d.

later for a survey on young people's sporting habits showed that football was the game that young men played most often, as well as the game that young men wanted to play the most, regardless of material or other circumstances.[8]

Football's deep roots in East German society can be traced to the factors that made it the world's foremost sporting activity in the twentieth century. Being 'a simple and elegant game, unhampered by complex rules',[9] football was easy to organise and relatively cheap to play. Basic facilities were widely available. The 1987 survey found that football pitches, including those without permanently installed goals, were more readily reachable within twenty minutes than any other type of sports facility in the republic.[10] Smaller communities often lacked indoor swimming pools or tennis courts. Most of them had numerous football grounds of one description or another.

Football's predominance was not always to the SED's liking. Commenting in 1963 on trade union neglect of mass sport, the party leadership in Guben noted that 'often the entire sporting activity [within a factory] consists only of football'.[11] A textile factory that employed 1,750 women in the Berlin district of Lichtenberg was criticised in 1956 for ploughing the majority of its sports budget into football, more specifically the factory-sponsored men's team, which played in the second district division and had only three factory workers among its members.[12] Football's supremacy in mass sport occasioned just as ambiguous a response from party officials as its pre-eminence in performance sport. On the one hand, it was a trump card. A winning side showcased local patriotism, bringing reflected glory to the individuals and institutions that supported it. Getting a successful men's team is the obsession of the mayor of the fictional town of Sonnethal in Joachim Hasler's football musical *Nicht schummeln, Liebling!* (1973). But the focus on football retarded the development of other sports, undercutting the SED's programme to create a healthy, motivated, and collective-minded workforce through regular exercise.

8 SAPMO-BArch, DC 4/716, Körperkultur und Sport – fester Bestandteil der sozialistischen Lebensweise der Jugend der DDR (Untersuchung "Jugend und Massensport 1987"), December 1987.

9 Eric Hobsbawm, *Age of Extremes: The Short Twentieth Century, 1914–1991* (London: Penguin, 1994), p. 198.

10 SAPMO-BArch, DC 4/716, Körperkultur und Sport (Tables 55 and 56).

11 BLHA, Rep 930 Nr. 911, Einschätzung der Erfüllung des Beschlusses der Bezirksleitung vom 15.2.1962 "Die Aufgaben bei der Entwicklung von Körperkultur und Sport bis 1965 im Bezirk Cottbus", sowie des gegenwärtigen Standes der Wahlen im DTSB, 22 March 1963.

12 SAPMO-BArch, DY 34/3879, Den Massensport weiterentwickeln!, 21 August 1956.

A small but growing body of scholarship exists on mass sport in the GDR.[13] Studies of football as a recreational activity, though, are conspicuous by their absence. The dearth in part reflects the distribution of available archival sources on football, which in turn reflects the SED's primary focus – whatever its public statements to the contrary – on performance rather than mass sport. In 1959 the SED leader Walter Ulbricht pushed his stolid frame around a volleyball court in East Berlin at an event organised to launch a campaign to encourage 'everyone everywhere' to 'play sport once a week' (*Jedermann an jedem Ort, einmal in der Woche Sport*). Eight years later, he increased the dosage, recommending that citizens should play 'several times' per week.[14] Leading sports functionaries, however, had other, Olympic-based priorities. Their colleagues on the ground often lacked the time or resources to realise Ulbricht's injunction.

Older accounts tended to accept the party line, commonly cited by governments today, about the 'virtuous cycle' of sport. This portrayed elite and mass sport as mutually supportive components in a system that was both successful and popular.[15] In reality, in East Germany as elsewhere, elite sport was estranged from everyday sport, existing in a privileged world of training centres and specialist clubs that was inaccessible to the average citizen.[16] In 1989 there were 25 elite sports schools in the GDR, with an average of 10.2 pupils per class and a total student population of just 10,053.[17] A two-tier system existed in sport, as it did in shopping, where those with access to sufficient Western currency could (after 1974) purchase items from the high-end Intershops, while everyone else made do with the basic fare on sale at state-run stores.[18] Top-class facilities were available, but only to the favoured few.

Lip service was paid to mass sport, but it was not the primary means by which the GDR established its international reputation as a *Sportland*. This unwritten rule applied to football as it did to other sports. The central authorities prioritised the national team and leading *Oberliga* clubs. Individual SVs and BSGs gave precedence to their top teams. The results, as one 1953 report noted, could be seen at Turbine Halle, where 68,000 M

[13] See e.g. Braun, 'The people's sport?'; Grix, 'The decline of mass sport provision'; Hinsching (ed.), *Alltagssport in der DDR*; Johnson, *Training Socialist Citizens*.

[14] Kluge, *Das Sportbuch DDR*, pp. 178–9; Hinsching, 'Der Bereich "Freizeit- und Erholungssport"', pp. 16–18.

[15] See e.g. Doug Gilbert, *The Miracle Machine* (New York: Coward, McCann & Geoghegan, 1980), p. 9. On the 'virtuous cycle' model, see Dennis and Grix, *Sport under Communism*, pp. 173–6.

[16] Grix, 'The decline of mass sport provision', 406–9.

[17] Fulbrook, *The People's State*, pp. 79–80.

[18] Wolle, *Die heile Welt*, pp. 74–8.

was spent on the first team (*Oberliga* champions in 1951/2) and only 771 M on the 'lower-level teams' under the BSG's tutelage.[19]

Inattention to mass football was an inevitable consequence of the centralised and hierarchical system of East German sport. It is of course not a phenomenon that was confined to the GDR. Simon Kuper observed in 2006 how little media or scholarly attention is paid to the mass of 'goofs' who play the game for fun: 'Given how rich we goofs are as human material, it's strange that over the last decade we have been eclipsed in popular culture by supporters'. Mainstream coverage of football throughout Europe means the Champions' League, rows between rival coaches, transfer rumours, and player bust-ups – all catering to the fan, 'an epic figure whose happiness supposedly depends on his team's results'. 'For us goofs', Kuper reminds us, '[football] is a game you play'.[20]

Part III turns attention away from *Oberliga* stars and fervent supporters to examine the experiences of ordinary citizens who played football under communist rule. It constructs a worm's-eye view of the people's game, focusing on four themes: men's football at the grassroots (Chapter 11); women's football (Chapter 12); football encounters between lower-level teams from East and West Germany (Chapter 13); and the material difficulties, in terms of facilities and equipment, that complicated the SED's vision of football for the masses (Chapter 14).

In the process, the book's three key arguments will be reinforced. Recreational football first emphasises new ways in which citizens – from the steelworkers at SV Stahl to the women's team at Turbine Potsdam – approached the sport on their own terms, using it as a vehicle for an *Eigen-Sinn* that did not necessarily accord with, or was largely detached from, the SED's goals. Second, mass football reveals further aspects of the limited power and disjointed character of the communist dictatorship. In a regime with an organisational apparatus so vast and multi-levelled that the line between state and society was often unclear, communist power was 'societalised' (i.e. delegated to citizens as active carriers of the system) as much as society was 'communised'.[21] This was particularly apparent in mass sport, with its strong reliance on volunteer activism. Innovation and improvisation, rather than enforced central planning, were the norm here.[22] Recreational football, third and lastly, can be seen as a hugely

[19] 'Leistungssteigerung – das "A und O"'.
[20] Simon Kuper's afterword in Hans van der Meer, *European Fields: The Landscape of Lower League Football* (Göttingen: SteidlMACK, 2006).
[21] Wilton, 'The "societalisation" of the state', pp. 102–5.
[22] Hinsching, 'Der Bereich "Freizeit- und Erholungssport"', p. 27.

popular liminal activity, at once dependent on the centralised state and curiously detached from it. Playing the game meant probing and negotiating uncertain boundaries between *Eigen-Sinn* and authority. The results illustrated football's often unintended ability to act as a thorn in the side of dictatorial governments.

# 11 Football and everyday life

## The view from the pitch

Eisenhüttenstadt was the GDR's first socialist town. Like Nowa Huta in Poland, Sztálinváros in Hungary, and Dimitrovgrad in Bulgaria, it symbolised the high hopes and hardships that accompanied the communist transformation of Eastern Europe in the early 1950s.[1] Located close to the redrawn German–Polish border, Eisenhüttenstadt – known between 1953 and 1961 as Stalinstadt – was home to a vast steelworks integral to the GDR's heavy industry. It was an exemplar of the new socialist community, a place with affordable housing, no church towers, good schools and hospitals, and a wide range of cultural amenities. Despite its reputation for difficult work and living conditions, many residents looked back with pride on the collective spirit that drove Eisenhüttenstadt's construction during the first decade of SED rule.[2]

The cultural amenities included football, as popular in *Bezirk* Frankfurt/Oder as it was elsewhere in the GDR. The steelworks held an annual recreational football championship. The 1955 final pitted a team from the Mechanik II department against a team representing the works transport section. The match report, written by a representative of the factory sports club, BSG Stalinstadt, began with a detailed description and tactical analysis of the game, which 'the blokes from Mechanik II' won 7–2 in front of 500 supporters. Attention was drawn to the victor's 'desire to win' and the shortcomings of their opponents ('you had to ask yourself, what is up with the works transport team today?'). Not everything ran smoothly off the pitch. A 'shadow' was cast over the post-match ceremony, after a colleague left the winners' trophy in his flat. The report concluded by remarking on the value of such matches in identifying players for the BSG's first and second teams, provided that talented individuals were

[1] Pittaway, *Eastern Europe*, pp. 110–11.
[2] Fulbrook, *The People's State*, pp. 58–61.

not held back by 'so-called clubmanship (*Vereinsmeierei*)', i.e. loyalty to their department team.[3]

With its microhistorical observations, the match report offers rich insights into football's importance in the 'history of everyday life' (*Alltagsgeschichte*) in the GDR. As it was in other countries around the world, the game was a site for ordinary social relations, building friendships, and sharing experiences. Footballers who played together in Wittenberg in the 1950s remembered card games on the train to away matches and regular post-match gatherings at the Black Bear pub, where they grouped around the in-house pianist to sing, regardless of the result.[4] When Rotation Prenzlauer Berg hosted a stronger team from Warsaw in the 1980s, the players tried to level the playing field by getting drunk with the visitors the night before the game. The result was a narrow defeat rather than a blowout.[5]

The 'humanizing impulse'[6] of *Alltagsgeschichte* gives voice and agency to ordinary people. The approach has been fruitfully applied to studies of German society under Nazism, shedding new light on popular resistance to, and complicity in, the crimes of the Third Reich.[7] It has been adopted as a framework for examining GDR society – as, for example, in Jan Palmowski's study of how state-promoted concepts of *Heimat* and national identity were 'appropriated, subverted, and even resisted' by the inhabitants of Mecklenburg and Thuringia.[8]

Through three case studies – examining, respectively, the football tournament run by SV Stahl in the 1950s; the history of an ordinary BSG, Rotation Prenzlauer Berg; and the 'fan league' (*Fan-Liga*) created by Union Berlin supporters in the 1980s – this chapter reconstructs football 'on the spot':[9] what it meant to its participants and what it tells us about class and power relations in the GDR. Clubs ultimately relied on the state for material and political support, yet fostered a culture of self-initiative that fed local pride and created separation, or distance, between citizen and regime. The case studies illustrate the growing independence that football won for its participants. The collective mobilisation of the 1950s, epitomised by the SV Stahl tournament, gradually gave way to the more autonomous solutions of the 1980s, as reflected in the Union fan league. Together with similar evolutions

[3] SAPMO-BArch, DY 46/2411, Mechanik II Titelträger 1955 "Meister des Eisenhüttenkombinates J. W. Stalin", 17 August 1955.

[4] Johnson, *Training Socialist Citizens*, pp. 101, 103–4.

[5] Interview with Klaus L.

[6] Steege *et al.*, 'The history of everyday life', 368.

[7] Alf Lüdtke, 'Introduction: what is the history of everyday life and who are its practitioners?', in Lüdtke (ed.), *The History of Everyday Life*, pp. 2–3.

[8] Palmowski, *Inventing a Socialist Nation*, p. 10.

[9] Lüdtke, 'Introduction', p. 20.

among fans and elite players, this shift was one of the strongest indicators of the individualisation of social and cultural habits, and the turning away from public life, that was the defining characteristic of society during the Honecker era.[10]

## Serious fun: the steelworkers' championship

In the 1950s, one historian has argued, 'the regular East German citizen, not destined for athletic greatness, remained at the center of East German efforts to promote athleticism'.[11] In this decade, and into the early 1960s, there was no shortage of ideas about how to mobilise people, and especially young people, to play football. In the optimistic wake of the SED's 1963 youth communiqué, with its reform-minded injunction to give 'trust and responsibility' to the young,[12] the DFV proposed to expand and diversify football's appeal through five-a-side competitions, football tennis, and street football.[13] Efforts were made to raise the game's profile in schools and in smaller communities, for example, by holding the finals of the FDGB Youth Cup, played over the Whitsun weekend, in provincial towns such as Belzig (1960) and Quedlinburg (1963).[14] In a letter to *Die Neue Fußball-Woche* in 1956, a frustrated footballer from Brüssow in *Bezirk* Potsdam complained that 'we in the rural population are the poor relations in sport, as in many other areas'.[15] His remark reflected a general dearth of available leisure activities ('nothing is happening in the village', young people frequently complained in the early 1960s),[16] as well as the fact that both football and communism were urban phenomena. 'You play like farmers' was not meant as a compliment.[17]

As was the case with the policing of hooliganism, mass football was only as strong as the people (administrators, coaches, and referees) who ran it. Many schemes fell by the wayside for lack of resources, especially in rural areas, or were implemented in an uneven fashion. The more enduring

10 On this shift, see e.g. Betts, *Within Walls*, pp. 12–13; Richthofen, *Bringing Culture to the Masses*, pp. 196–203.

11 Johnson, *Training Socialist Citizens*, p. 203.

12 See e.g. McDougall, *Youth Politics*, pp. 153–63.

13 ThHStAW, Bezirkstag und Rat des Bezirkes Erfurt KK 24, Kinder-, Jugend- und Volkssportprogramm des Deutschen Fußballverbandes für das Sportjahr 1964, fo. 10–16.

14 SAPMO-BArch, DY 34/22575, Um den Wanderpokal des FDGB im Fussball der Jugend, 1960; memo from Stephan to Büro Naß, 14 June 1963.

15 'Hilfe, Hilfe, Hilfe!', reader's letter to *Die Neue Fußball-Woche*, 11 September 1956, 13.

16 McDougall, *Youth Politics*, p. 113.

17 'Ihr spielt ja wie die Bauern', reader's letter to *Die Neue Fußball-Woche*, 9 November 1964, 11.

structures took root when local activism and state sponsorship were combined effectively. Such was the case with the mass football tournament organised by the Stahl (steelworkers') sports association during the 1950s. This was a nationwide competition, first played in 1954. It began with inter-factory matches, progressed through district (*Kreis*) and county (*Bezirk*) rounds, and culminated in a final that determined SV Stahl's best recreational football team.

The steelworkers' football tournament, as one 1957 directive stated, was meant to be a fun and friendly means of keeping fit and thereby serving 'the construction of socialism'. Instead, as the same directive complained, matches were so fiercely contested that many players sustained injuries serious enough to keep them off work for long stretches of time.[18] An evaluation of the tournament a year earlier drew attention to its numerous unpalatable features, including the use of ineligible players, the protest letters submitted by defeated teams, overly aggressive play, and abuse of referees.[19]

In the 1956 tournament, almost every game appeared to be mired in controversy. Three of the four semi-finalists, Stahl Gröditz, Stahl Merseburg, and Stahl Torgelow, were accused of cheating. The Torgelow and Merseburg teams were charged by their opponents with fielding non-recreational players. Gröditz, it was alleged, broke a tournament rule stipulating that factories with workforces larger than 2,000 should be represented by a team taken from a single factory department. The Gröditz team apparently included players from four different departments.[20] The only untainted semi-finalist, Stahl Thale, got a bye into the last four after both potential quarter-final opponents, Stahl Eisleben and Stahl Hettstedt, were expelled from the competition. Their match was abandoned just before half-time following a mass brawl.[21]

The flood of complaints and flagrant attempts at rule-bending that typified the steelworkers' tournament in the mid 1950s suggests a natural antagonism between football and the state that was less evident in more middle-class forms of *Resistenz*, from the allotment to the Church. Of course, badly behaved footballers were hardly confined to socialism;

[18] SAPMO-BArch, DY 46/2411, letter from Sommer to all BGLs, 5 July 1957.

[19] *Ibid.*, Auswertung Stahlwerkturnier im Fußball um den Wanderpokal der SV Stahl 1956, n.d.

[20] *Ibid.*, Protesteinlegung zum Spiel Betriebsfußballmannschaft VEB Gus-Stahl Torgelow gegen VEB Walzwerk Burg am 14.10.1956 in Torgelow, 15 October 1956; telegram from Maxhütte to SV Stahl ZL, October 1956; Pokalspiel der Betriebsfußballmannschaft Karl-Marx-Stadt-Reichenhain gegen Gröditz am 14.10.1956, 15 October 1956.

[21] *Ibid.*, Fernschreiben von der BSG Stahl Hettstedt, Walzwerk, 11 October 1956; letters from SV Stahl ZL to Stahl Hettstedt and Stahl Eisleben, 13 October 1956.

in the same period in rural West Germany, matches were regularly called off after fights between players and attacks on referees.[22] But local as well as global conclusions can be drawn here. The tournament inverted the 'virtuous cycle' sports model promoted as the defining feature of GDR physical culture. Instead of mass sport feeding into elite sport, and the latter then encouraging greater mass participation, recreational teams sneaked first-teamers into their starting XIs and, as the report on the 1955 championship at the Eisenhüttenstadt steelworks complained, sometimes refused to make their own players available for higher-level competition. As in fan culture, football in the factories went along almost impervious to directives from above – a self-sustaining sphere of working-class life.

Second, the intensity of competition reminds us that local patriotism was not the sole provenance of elite teams and their supporters. In mass football, *Eigen-Sinn* was as much about distance from one's peers as it was about distance from the state. Eisleben and Hettstedt, for example, the two teams disqualified from the 1956 tournament following their violent quarter-final encounter, came from towns less than ten miles apart. Even when rivalries were not local, the sense of local identity seemed to trump any sense of cross-class or cross-industry solidarity, among fans and amateur players at least. Stahl Burg's complaints about Stahl Torgelow in 1956 were not confined to the latter's alleged fielding of 'active' (i.e. elite) players. Burg players were also unhappy that the referee came from Spechtberg, a district in Torgelow.[23] Steelworkers, it is safe to assume, did not get together after games to 'exchange production experiences' as often as the Stahl leadership would have liked.[24]

In recreational football, as in other cultural forums such as rural choirs,[25] ostensibly socialist structures were rarely repositories for socialist *Lebensweisen* ('modes of life') during the 1950s.[26] Indeed, football was perhaps the key site of proletarian detachment from the SED's project. Recreational players appropriated state resources for their own purposes, but by and large attempted to keep the state at arm's length, repeating the 'patchwork' of cooperation and 'self-willed distance' that characterised German workers' behaviour under Nazism.[27] Participants in the steelworkers' tournament

[22] Dwertmann and Rigauer, 'Football hooliganism in Germany', p. 79.

[23] SAPMO-BArch, DY 46/2411, Stellungnahme zum Fussballspiel um den SV-Pokal zwischen Stahlwerk Burg und GUS Torgelow am 14.10., 14 October 1956 (BSG Stahl Torgelow).

[24] *Ibid.*, letter from Sommer to all BGLs.

[25] Richthofen, *Bringing Culture to the Masses*, pp. 32–7.

[26] Lüdtke, 'Introduction', p. 11.

[27] Alf Lüdtke, 'What happened to the "fiery red glow?" Workers' experiences and German fascism', in Lüdtke (ed.), *The History of Everyday Life*, p. 227.

frequently ignored the precepts of 'our democratic sports movement', as the SV Stahl leadership noted in a letter to BSG Stahl Calbe in 1955, in which the latter was reprimanded for its behaviour during and after a loss to Stahl Badeleben (refusal to shake hands with the victors, as well as complaints about the referee and ineligible opposition players).[28] The litany of grievances surrounding the relatively small issue of recreational football competitions reinforces the view of the GDR as a 'grumble *Gesellschaft*',[29] foreshadowing the entrenched culture of complaint that emerged during the 1970s and 1980s.

The evidence suggests that, in sport as in other politically less sensitive areas, the SED 'tended to tolerate widespread grumbling', partly because of its therapeutic value (as a vent), partly because it allowed the regime to gain insights into public opinion, and partly because many lower-level officials understood, and were affected by, the problems that ordinary citizens identified.[30] As in fan culture, though, complaints in recreational sport did not always function as a safety valve. When representatives of the team at a rolling mill in Karl-Marx-Stadt suggested that Stahl Gröditz's alleged breaking of tournament rules in 1956 shook the 'democratic feeling (*Empfinden*) of our people',[31] it indicated how football's practitioners, like the regime whose rhetoric they sometimes adopted, had an intuitive awareness of the game's potential political impact.

## Rotation policy: life in the football sections

In May 1986 angry officials from the football section at BSG Fortschritt Heubach, a small community in *Bezirk* Suhl, wrote to Rudi Hellmann to complain about punishments meted out to the club following a district league game against Gleichamberg in March. Following an 'alleged disciplinary offence', left unspecified in the petition, the referee abandoned the match. The DFV consequently banned several Heubach players and closed the team's home ground for three games. Heubach representatives argued that the stiff penalties purposely disadvantaged their team, allowing local rivals Heßberg to gain promotion instead. The persecution complex was strengthened when Heubach received a two-point penalty for failing to provide a referee for another match later in the season.[32]

28 SAPMO-BArch, DY 46/2411, letter from SV Stahl to BSG Stahl d. Eisenwerke West (Calbe), 15 November 1955.

29 Port, *Conflict and Stability*, p. 115.

30 *Ibid.*, pp. 102–3.

31 SAPMO-BArch, DY 46/2411, Zweierlei Disziplin, 24 October 1956.

32 SAPMO-BArch, DY 30/4979, petition from the football section at BSG Fortschritt Heubach to Hellmann, 22 May 1986, fo. 138–41.

In building their case, Heubach officials highlighted the voluntary hours put in by club members over the years to renovate the sports hall, fix the water supply, and clear snow from the pitches, at once affirming the self-help discourse integral to communist propaganda and chiding the central powers for their neglect of the grassroots. Relegation, they argued, would mean the end of the football section and possibly of the entire BSG. Many Heubach players talked openly of resignation from the DTSB. More alarmingly from the SED's perspective, the petitioners were 'unable to stop' parents and others associated with the BSG from refusing to vote in recent national assembly (*Volkskammer*) and county council elections as a protest against the injustices of the past few months.[33]

The football authorities in *Bezirk* Suhl seem to have lobbied successfully to have the two-point penalty pushed back to the start of the following season. The Heubach team thus avoided relegation and the dissolution of its football section. The petition was not closed until November 1986. Numerous individuals and organisations were dragged into it, including the DFV's deputy leader, the DFV justice commission, the Suhl county FA, and the SED county leadership in Suhl.[34] As was typical of East German football, the authorities were forced to spend far more time and energy than they would have liked in untangling the minutiae of local interests that motivated citizens to defend their sporting *Eigen-Sinn*.

The Heubach case offered a compelling example of the intensity with which local football interests could be pursued. As with most petitions, though, it documented dissent rather than consent, the ruptures in everyday activities rather than their more enduring features. What was the day-to-day existence of BSG football sections like? Some answers to this question can be found in the biography of Klaus L., a player and football section leader at BSG Rotation Prenzlauer Berg. Founded in 1950, under the sponsorship of the printing press for the SED newspaper, *Neues Deutschland*, Rotation was one of the main recreational sports clubs in the East Berlin district of Prenzlauer Berg.[35] Its football section numbered roughly 300 members and was renowned for its strong youth teams (among the players to come through the ranks was BFC captain Frank Terletzki). The men's team generally played in the *Kreisklasse* (district class), the fifth tier of GDR football.[36]

Born in the late 1940s, Klaus L. grew up in Prenzlauer Berg and first played football at Rotation. On his older brother's advice, he moved to Vorwärts Berlin, one of the GDR's premier clubs, and, aged fourteen,

[33] *Ibid.*
[34] *Ibid.*, various correspondence on the Fortschritt Heubach petition, fo. 128–37.
[35] www.rotationpb-fussball.de/unser-verein/. [36] Interview with Klaus L.

was part of a team that won the Berlin schoolboys' championship in 1960. He was then delegated to a lower-level Berlin club, Motor Treptow, where he played for three years, before returning to his local team. Aside from a spell at county league side Vorwärts Spremberg during military service, Klaus L. remained at Rotation Prenzlauer Berg, as player, coach, section leader, and deputy chairman, until 1988.[37]

The history of Rotation Prenzlauer Berg suggests both how mass football could be politicised and how it cultivated *Resistenz* to politics. In the early 1960s, Klaus L. was delegated from Vorwärts Berlin to Motor Treptow ostensibly on performance grounds, but in reality because he had been reluctant to do the requisite *Aufbaustunden* ('construction hours') required of young Vorwärts players at a local sports facility.[38] This kind of compulsory voluntarism was expected of young players elsewhere too, as the recollections of footballers in Wittenberg attest.[39] Failure to fulfil one's civic duty in such matters – as in Nazi Germany and the Soviet Union – left a political black mark that was hard to escape. Klaus L.'s football options were narrowed after his 'first political defeat', in much the same way as young people's educational options shrank if they decided not to join the FDJ, a mass organisation also built around a coercive voluntarist culture.[40]

Klaus L. became deputy chairman of Rotation Prenzlauer Berg in 1976 and football section leader in 1982. In 1988 he resigned from this position, citing (as was common in the GDR) personal reasons, usually, or ideally, related to work or health. Klaus L.'s decision, though, was really made for what he later termed 'political reasons'. Recent research has shown that the 1980s saw increased signs of disillusionment with SED policies among grassroots 'regime carriers' within the DTSB and other organisations.[41] In Klaus L.'s case, resignation was not the product of a single issue or moment, but rather of a long-term weariness with the political strings attached to his work at Rotation. Like many lower-level cultural and sports functionaries, he was an intermediary between society (in this case, the BSG members) and the state (most immediately here, the sponsoring factory). It could be a thankless task. Rotation's sponsoring factory, the printing press for *Neues Deutschland*, expected political as well as sporting returns on its investment. Rotation's footballers generally had no interest in politics and regarded Klaus L., who had to write reports on trips abroad, march under a red flag on 1 May, or man a stand at a press

[37] *Ibid.* [38] *Ibid.* [39] Johnson, *Training Socialist Citizens*, p. 128.

[40] On student FDJ membership, see McDougall, *Youth Politics*, pp. 117, 169–70, 205.

[41] Wilton, 'Regime versus people?', ch. 6; Richthofen, *Bringing Culture to the Masses*, pp. 192–6.

festival, with some suspicion, 'especially after they had drunk a couple of beers'. Although, on a day-to-day basis, the football section was largely left to its own devices, the general climate of political pressure (and the distance it created from peers who called him 'red sock') took its toll. After his resignation, Klaus L. left Rotation Prenzlauer Berg for good.[42]

In football, competition for resources was fierce, as was the satisfaction that functionaries displayed in defending the interests and achievements of teams under their supervision. This sense of competition, and the rivalries that it engendered, was felt in even the smallest neighbourhoods. Rotation Prenzlauer Berg shared training facilities with SG Nordring, one of the GDR's rare private clubs. Their men's teams generally played at the same level. Nordring's stronger financial backing allowed it from time to time to poach players from Rotation. Though relations between club officials and players improved over the years, an old Nordring saying remained in circulation: 'only a good and dead Rotation member is a good Rotation member' (*Nur ein guter toter Rotationer, ist ein guter Rotationer*).[43]

There were inter- as well as intra-club rivalries. At Rotation Prenzlauer Berg, as at many BSGs, the main dividing line was between football and other sports. The men's football team, languishing in the fourth or fifth tier of national competition, received a small collective bonus (300 M) whenever it avoided relegation. The Rotation men's volleyball team, who played in the GDR's elite league, received the same amount for their endeavours. Monthly meetings of the BSG leadership, at which all section leaders reported on recent performances, could be tense. Football struggled to match sports such as volleyball and boxing, with its successes in multiple weight divisions at the *Spartakiad*, the contests across various disciplines, named after the Roman gladiator Spartacus, that promoted competitive sport among young East Germans.[44] As in elite sport, football's popularity in ordinary BSGs made it something of an outlier.

In a country that extolled the virtues of organised sport, football's prosperity as a recreational activity depended less on what the centre dictated than on what local officials did to support it. Klaus L.'s biography illustrated this point, though it also showed how sport, and sports functionaries, could not avoid politics entirely. There were figures like him at every BSG. Lothar Köhler joined Rotation Leipzig 1950 in 1959. He played for various successful junior teams and was a ballboy when England played the GDR in Leipzig in 1963. He contributed at least twenty hours per year of volunteer work to the rebuilding of the club's stadium. After injury forced him to retire in 1970, he became a referee, officiating in more than

[42] Interview with Klaus L. [43] *Ibid.* [44] Interview with Klaus L.

1,000 games in and around Leipzig.[45] At Empor Beelitz, some of the youth-team coaches were 'weird creatures' – an alcoholic and heavy smoker, who was succeeded by a man with a beer gut who was rumoured to work for the *Stasi*.[46] GDR football possessed a wide variety of regime carriers. Some were more politically reliable than others. The limits of the SED dictatorship were inherent in the expansiveness of the state apparatus, which blurred the lines between rulers and ruled and allowed local actors to claim agency in their everyday sports or cultural work.

## Keep off the grass: the Union Berlin *Fan-Liga*

Contrary to stereotypes of the armchair supporter, there was substantial crossover between those who watched and those who played football in the GDR. A 1987 survey found that fan-club members were just as likely as not to play the game in their spare time.[47] Most of the time, recreational players were incorporated into official structures. Perhaps the most interesting exception to this rule was the 'fan league' (*Fan-Liga*) started by supporters of Union Berlin in 1981. Being independent both of the DTSB and of the Union administration, the league was a unique example of self-organisation. The players set the playing schedule, found venues for matches, appointed referees, and created a set of league rules. Six teams took part in the inaugural championship. Numbers grew rapidly through the 1980s, with thirty-four participating teams in the 1988/9 season. The fan league survived the *Wende* and the financial upheavals at Union Berlin in the early 1990s. It remains a thriving entity, home to forty-seven teams across three divisions.[48]

Like the fan clubs that emerged at Union and other clubs in the 1970s, the fan league was an expression of football autonomy. Both fostered flexible structures where supporters were in charge and the state's influence was minimal. There were no fixed venues for *Fan-Liga* matches. Tino C.'s team, VSG Victoria, played without permission on an asphalt pitch in the Wuhlheide, a large park in the Köpenick district where Union were based. Frank L.'s side, one of the league's founder members, FC United Karlshorst, played in the same park, as the pitches were always free for impromptu six-a-side games. He served variously as the team's manager, goalkeeper, and striker, and even designed

[45] Beyer, *Rotation Leipzig*, pp. 62–3. [46] Interview with Tim E.

[47] SAPMO-BArch, DC 4/721, Neuere Ergebnisse zum Verhältnis Jugendlicher zum Fußball, fo. 5.

[48] Luther and Willmann, *Eisern Union!*, p. 351; www.unionliga.de/index.php/geschichte/geschichte-der-unionliga.

match programmes.[49] Interviewees emphasised similar motivations for their participation in the league. It was a space where you could play 'without referees, without coercion' (Frank L.), where something fun and 'anarchic' could escape the attentions of the FDJ and organised youth life (Tino C.), and where 'we could decide things for ourselves outside GDR sports management' (Theo Körner).[50]

How did the authorities respond to the emergence of a self-governed football competition among Union fans? It happened in a period when autonomous or semi-autonomous Church, peace, and environmental bodies were quietly beginning to shake up the moribund political landscape.[51] This predominantly middle-class political activism quickly drew the attention of the state's vast surveillance apparatus. Moves towards football independence received greater latitude. In the words of one Union fan, 'there was no support [for the fan league], but there were also no obstacles'.[52] The Union chairman regarded it as an acceptable face of fan culture, preferable to the hooligan elements that gave Union a bad press. There were state attempts at co-option, primarily through the FDJ, which created a Union youth club to exert a stronger influence on the club's fan base. But this had little impact on the *Fan-Liga*, other than to perhaps make it easier to find pitches on which to play.[53] Pragmatism was displayed on both sides. The authorities tolerated the fan league, according to one organiser, because 'it was no danger' and because 'you could not have banned it' anyway.[54] Stopping people playing football for fun was no easier than stopping people listening to Western pop music in the comfort of their homes. The players in turn made 'certain compromises', safe in the knowledge that FDJ sponsorship of the Union youth club had no influence on the day-to-day running of the league.[55] Reflecting the nebulous lines between state and society, official and unofficial leisure actitivities were not mutually exclusive. Tino C., Frank L., and Theo Körner were all FDJ members (and in the latter's case an FDJ activist). 'The FDJ didn't bother me', Tino C. recalled, 'if the offering was OK, I went to FDJ parties [or] concerts'.[56]

Throughout the 1980s, the Union fan league prospered. On Theo Körner's initiative, a cup competition was added to the league schedule during the 1983/4 season. A year later, there were sufficient teams for

[49] Interview with Tino C.; interview with Frank L.
[50] Interview with Tino C.; interview with Frank L.; interview with Theo Körner.
[51] See e.g. Fulbrook, *Anatomy*, pp. 201–15.
[52] Interview with Tino C. [53] Interview with Theo Körner.
[54] Interview with Tino C. [55] Interview with Theo Körner.
[56] Interview with Tino C.

two divisions to be created.[57] As with fan clubs, fan league teams adopted names that were distinctly unsocialist, referencing their autonomous roots (many clubs had the appellation FSV, meaning *Fansportverein*, or 'fan sports club'), local identity (VSG Weinbergstraße, for example, after a street in Köpenick), older German club traditions (Alemannia Karlshorst), or Anglophilic tendencies found in football as in music (FC United Karlshorst).[58]

The ways in which the *Fan-Liga* became embedded in the everyday life of Union recreational players can be seen in a four-page, handwritten programme that accompanied VSG Union's match against VSG Wuhlheide on 3 October 1981, part of the third round of fixtures in the 'first East German championship for pure-bred amateurs'. Entitled *UZ: Die Union-Zeitung für alle* ('The Union newspaper for everyone'), the programme began with a detailed preview of 'the duel between the basement dwellers'. There followed a humorous profile of the visiting team, in which the players were described as 'famous, well-known, and notorious' (*berühmt, bekannt und berüchtigt*). VSG Wuhlheide's striker was compared to West German star Rainer Bonhof; Theo Körner, the team's 'great thinker', was said 'to have an artist's name, like every good Brazilian'. The last two pages gave updated statistics from the *Fan-Liga* (standings, results, and top scorers) and an eclectic selection of results from around the football world, taking in places where Union fans could be found, including England, Luxemburg, Portugal, Spain, and West Germany.[59] As with the fan mail sent to Dynamo Dresden in the 1970s, *UZ* offered unmediated insights into the ways in which ordinary East Germans made football a game of their own, creating structures and communities that were integral to their everyday lives.

The emergence of the Union *Fan-Liga* in the 1980s pointed to the greater individualisation of social and cultural practices that characterised the Honecker era, impacting on areas as diverse as interior design and residential disputes.[60] The shift from the more collective ethos of the 1950s was noticeable. Recreational football then, as with the steelworkers' tournament, was pursued through official channels, even when players and teams behaved in ways that deviated from socialist values. In the steel factories, as was the case for the villagers of Holungen when dealing with projects such as the National Reconstruction Effort and 'Join in! – our

[57] Interview with Theo Körner; www.unionliga.de/index.php/geschichte/geschichte-der-unionliga.

[58] www.unionliga.de/index.php/geschichte/geschichte-der-unionliga.

[59] *UZ: Die Union-Zeitung für alle*, 3 October 1981. Thanks are due to Gerard Karpa for providing this document.

[60] See e.g. Betts, *Within Walls*, pp. 141–3, 169–70.

towns and communities more beautiful' (*Mach mit! – schöner unsere Städte und Gemeinden*),[61] state initiatives were adapated to local needs. The Union fan league showcased a new kind of *Eigen-Sinn*, one in which the authorities were bypassed rather than met halfway. It might not have had the political significance of the new organisations and *samizdat* publications that marked the largely middle-class protest sphere in the 1980s, but, in its small way, the *Fan-Liga* expressed a more plebeian disengagement from socialism that left the SED regime bereft of popular support in the autumn of 1989.

## A matter of life and death? Conclusions on *Alltagsfußball*

Football, in the famous words of Liverpool manager Bill Shankly, was 'not a matter of life and death ... it was much, much more important than that'. A 1987 ZIJ survey sought to reject such hyperbole. Passion for the game, it stated, was merely 'the most beautiful triviality in the world'.[62] Yet the triviality was bound up with life and death, in the GDR as elsewhere. DTSB statistics showed that twenty-one of the ninety sports-related fatalities between 1982 and 1985 involved footballers. This made it the GDR's most 'dangerous' sport, ahead of bowling (fifteen deaths) and mountain climbing (twelve). The most common cause of death was a heart attack (in ten cases), followed by traffic accidents en route to and from matches (five), and brain injuries (four, including a nine-year-old boy struck by a falling goalpost).[63] Behind the statistics, the short reports on individual lives cut short offer poignant reminders of football's centrality to the fabric of everyday life (and death): Siegfried T., a fifty-two-year-old former *Oberliga* player, who died of a heart attack in 1981 during a veterans' tournament in Stendal, where he worked as a coach at the local training centre; a thirty-two-year-old player from Empor Quedlinburg, who died in the same year of a broken neck, after he fell from an unsecured crossbar while doing push-ups, leaving behind a wife and two children; and the four players from Aufbau Marienwerder, who were killed in a car accident in Bernau as they returned home from a game in 1983.[64]

61 Palmowski, *Inventing a Socialist Nation*, pp. 235–9.

62 SAPMO-BArch, DC 4/721, Neuere Ergebnisse zum Verhältnis Jugendlicher zum Fußball, fo. 7.

63 SAPMO-BArch, DY 30/4973, Information über Todesfälle und schwere Verletzungen im Bereich des vom DTSB organisierten Sportbetriebes, 12 December 1985, fo. 74–86.

64 SAPMO-BArch, DY 30/4972, Information, 11 February 1981, fo. 2; Information, 13 February 1981, fo. 5; Information, 18 October 1983, fo. 116.

For *Alltagsgeschichte* to be more than a mundane backdrop to 'more important aspects of life',[65] or romanticised detail on the nameless masses, it needs be firmly harnessed to the larger historical picture.[66] What, then, can *Alltagsfußball* tell us about the GDR? State support for recreational football was inconsistent. In some areas, it was strong; in others, it was skeletal. The variances showcased a leadership incoherence (and indifference) that was the antithesis of the tightly run Olympic programme that brought GDR sport to international prominence. For all of the talk about making football 'the people's sport in reality', as the Erfurt authorities pledged in 1961,[67] political and economic realities framed less resplendent horizons. The prioritisation of elite football left responsibility for its mass counterpart largely in the hands of local activists, a voluntarist sporting culture that the regime promoted both in the belt-tightening 1950s, when citizens fashioned their own goalposts and volleyball nets, and during the more affluent 1970s, when Herculean volunteer efforts ensured the construction of new facilities in many small communities.[68]

The gulf between elite and mass sport, it has been argued, widened considerably over this period, particularly after the 1969 high-performance directive (*Leistungssportbeschluß*) prioritised a select number of Olympic sports and marginalised others such as basketball and ice hockey.[69] In football, this could be seen in the evolution of the FDGB Cup. During the 1950s and 1960s, the GDR's premier cup competition strove to maintain a populist touch. It was open to all teams, including factory sides that did not otherwise play in DFV-sanctioned competitions. A total of 5,915 teams entered the 1967/8 tournament, including 558 'people's sports teams' from factories and residential areas.[70] By the mid 1970s, trade union leaders appear to have resigned themselves to the separation between elite and popular teams in their flagship tournament, a distinction that was being made more sharply across the board, as the SED – with the introduction of an integrated talent-spotting system (1973) and State Plan 14.25 (1974), the key document in the GDR's clandestine doping programme – devoted increased time and resources to Olympic glory at the expense of mass sport.[71] The FDGB's head of sport spoke in 1974

[65] Stone, 'The role of football', 175. [66] Lüdtke, 'Introduction', pp. 20, 29.

[67] ThHStAW, Bezirkstag und Rat des Bezirkes Erfurt KK 24, Perspektiveplan für 1961–1965, n.d., fo. 53.

[68] On the 1950s, see Johnson, *Training Socialist Citizens*, pp. 125–33; on the 1970s, see Wilton, 'Regime versus people?', pp. 137–9; 'Erxlebener Chronik', *Die Neue Fußball-Woche*, 19 November 1974, 2.

[69] Johnson, *Training Socialist Citizens*, pp. 203–9.

[70] SAPMO-BArch, DY 34/17719, Einschätzung der Pokalwettbewerbe, 1968.

[71] Dennis and Grix, *Sport under Communism*, pp. 66–9, 97–8; Grix, 'The decline of mass sport provision', 409–10.

about the division of trade union-sponsored cup competitions, in football and other sports, into two categories, one with 'mass sport character' and the other for 'competitive DTSB teams'.[72] The optimism of the 1960s, as in many areas of East German life, gave way to 'a cooling off of ideals and reform zealotry',[73] and a more pragmatic understanding of how to run the FDGB Cup profitably and to the benefit of elite clubs.

Mass football appeared only intermittently on the communist leadership's radar. That did not necessarily matter. The game hardly needed the SED's blessing to earn, or rather retain, its status. Across different institutions and social classes, and almost regardless of the level of state support, football was never seriously challenged as the most popular form of competitive and recreational exercise among East German males. A 1987 ZIJ survey of youth sports facilities in two factories (in Jena and Schwerin), two small towns (Rudolstadt and Bernburg), and the Martin Luther University in Halle confirmed this point. Of the twenty-eight sports on offer in Rudolstadt's twenty sports clubs, where facilities often failed to meet minimum sanitary standards, football took pride of place alongside volleyball, swimming, and table tennis – with cup competitions run by the FDJ and FDGB, as well as tournaments for factory youth brigades.[74]

Football at the grassroots existed outside the spotlight that fell on *Oberliga* stars or hooligans. For many recreational players, the game was a relatively uncomplicated means of asserting both vertical and horizontal forms of *Eigen-Sinn*, of getting away from politics, and from work or family troubles, to play sport and to socialise in an informal setting. This at first sight seems to accord with Günter Gaus's description of the GDR as a 'niche society', in which 'outward conformity' was coupled with an 'inner emigration' that was enacted at holiday homes and allotments.[75] The concept, though, tends to pit state and society against each other, as grudging partners in an uneasy social contract, rather than addressing the huge overlap between the two that was apparent in mass sport, where lower-level functionaries (representing both state and society) ran kids' programmes, coached adults' teams, and – when they were not lobbying for better facilities – sometimes built them with their bare hands. Even the

[72] SAPMO-BArch, DY 34/17719, Interview mit Kollegen Hans Degebrodt, Leiter der Arbeitsgruppe Sport beim Bundesvorstand des FDGB, 2 April 1974.

[73] Betts, *Within Walls*, p. 12.

[74] SAPMO-BArch, DC 4/723, Zum Einfluß territorialer Bedingungen auf die sportliche Tätigkeit: Teilbericht zur Untersuchung "Jugend und Massensport 1987", July 1988.

[75] Günter Gaus, *Wo Deutschland liegt: Eine Ortsbestimmung*. (Hamburg: Hoffmann & Campe, 1983), pp. 156–233.

Figure 17. A district league match in Bad Berka, 1977. This is a photograph from Werner Mahler's 1977–8 project on everyday life in the Thuringian village. The SG Berka goalkeeper appears to be playing without gloves and in an outfield shirt.

autonomous Union Berlin fan league found a *modus vivendi* with the regime, in order to avoid unnecessary 'stress' and the pitchside presence of the 'green cars' of the *Stasi*.[76] The 'exit to niches' argument underplays the level of citizens' active participation in the regime's sporting structures.[77] In football this meant dispatching petitions about the unjust deduction of points (for example, BSG Fortschritt Heubach) or lodging appeals with competition organisers about the opposition fielding ineligible players (as at the steelworkers' tournament). It meant participation in the myriad of mass sport competitions such as the FDGB Cup or the district and county *Spartakiade* that the DFV organised on a regular basis, a process that required an army of volunteers, including coaches, referees, groundsmen, and administrators. It meant playing on the weekend or after work in factory leagues and student leagues, in indoor and *Kleinfeld* ('small field') tournaments. Neither a niche activity nor subject to oppressive state control, mass football existed in a liminal space that allowed its participants both to retreat from, and to make use of, the communist state.

[76] Interview with Theo Körner. [77] Wilton, 'Regime versus people?', pp. 120–2.

# 12 Women's football

## Women on the ball

In 1973 DEFA released the musical comedy *Nicht schummeln, Liebling!* ('Don't cheat, darling!'). Directed by Joachim Hasler and starring two of the GDR's biggest stars, Frank Schöbel and Chris Doerk, the film was set in the fictional town of Sonnethal, where the mayor's chief concern was to develop a men's football team good enough to gain promotion to the county league. In order to remind him of other priorities, in particular the construction of a youth clubhouse, the new female director of the town's vocational college founds a women's team that threatens to put its male counterpart in the shade. The plot is slight and the songs less memorable than those that distinguished Hasler's previous collaboration with Schöbel and Doerk, *Heißer Sommer* ('Hot Summer') in 1968. In the end, the clubhouse is successfully built via the joint efforts of the men's and women's teams (the collective message distinguishing socialist musicals from their capitalist counterparts). The film's two prospective couples – the mayor and the college director and the captains of the two teams – are happily paired up. Though flimsy, the film's treatment of women's football was not without significance. At a time when football was attracting growing interest among female athletes, *Nicht schummeln, Liebling!* suggested that *Frauenfußball* was still primarily a humorous diversion. As the players from Sonnethal's men's team watch the first women's match in the town from the terraces, one remarks that 'this just isn't football'. Bernd, the team captain, agrees: 'A circus is what it is!'[1]

Fifteen years later, another DEFA production showed the strides that the women's game had made. *Frauen am Ball* ('Women on the Ball') was a short documentary on the GDR's most successful women's team, BSG Turbine Potsdam. It opens with the players being put through gruelling training exercises to the off-camera exhortations of the coach, Bernd Schröder. There are interviews with the players, in which their sporting

[1] *Nicht schummeln, Liebling!* (dir. Joachim Hasler, 1973).

vocation is taken seriously. The film shows extensive highlights of an important game against Wismut Karl-Marx-Stadt. The camera at one point even follows the players into the showers. In these and other ways, Ted Tetzke's documentary treated Turbine much as it might have treated a leading men's team. Notable differences remained. Interviewees suggest that their husbands or boyfriends took some convincing to take their choice of sport seriously. The narrator offers several reminders that the women's game is still closer to being a hobby than a performance sport, despite Turbine's achievements. The film's closing images include the Turbine players leaving the sun-baked pitch after a training session. One of them is pulling along her young son in a buggy – a snapshot of the domestic pressures that made it hard for women to commit time to a sport that, as we shall see in this chapter, almost entirely lacked state support.[2]

*Nicht schummeln, Liebling!* and *Frauen am Ball* offer visual presentations of women's football that, despite their differences, highlight its status on the fringes of the GDR's most popular sport. Institutional indifference is reflected in the lack of archival sources. Historians are reliant on newspaper reports, interviews, private collections, and a smattering of documents in the DFV archive. Indifference of a different kind is illustrated by the limited treatment of the women's game in post-*Wende* histories of GDR football, where it is generally either mentioned in passing or not mentioned at all.[3] Scholarship on *Frauensport* has tended to focus on elite sport, where stars such as the ice-skater Katarina Witt became internationally recognised faces of the SED regime, and the deleterious impact of the state doping programme on women's bodies.[4] A few scholars have countered the prevailing trend, providing groundbreaking insights into the difficulties and pleasures of breaking into a male-dominated field. These works, importantly, have placed the women's game in a comparative context, particularly in relation to developments in West Germany.[5]

This chapter offers a detailed analysis of women's experiences playing the game in East Germany. It discusses the evolution of competitive structures for *Frauenfußball*, state and media attitudes to women's involvement in the game, and the grassroots initiatives (most notably at Turbine Potsdam) that allowed women to overcome the political and

[2] *Frauen am Ball* (dir. Ted Tetzke, 1988).

[3] For a summary of the historiography, see Carina Linne, *Freigespielt: Frauenfußball im geteilten Deutschland* (Berlin: be.bra verlag, 2011), pp. 9–13.

[4] See e.g. Gertrud Pfister, *Frauensport in der DDR* (Cologne: Strauss, 2002).

[5] See e.g. Linne, *Freigespielt*; Gertrud Pfister, 'The challenges of women's football in East and West Germany: a comparative study', *Soccer & Society* vol. 4, no. 2/3 (April/June 2003), 128–48.

socio-economic barriers that often made becoming a footballer difficult. Comparisons are drawn with the development of women's football elsewhere in Europe, highlighting another facet of the tension between isolation and internationalism in GDR football, and with the mobility blockages that women encountered in other areas of East German society. In women's football, while state apathy had its drawbacks, it also created a space that was, to a greater extent than any aspect of the men's game, free of official constraints.

## The development of the women's game

Most accounts state that the first women's football team in East Germany was founded at BSG Empor Dresden in 1968, on the initiative of a Bulgarian student enrolled at the city's Technical University.[6] Recent research, though, shows that women played football in the city as early as 1960 – and probably before that too, as a spontaneous activity that neither the press nor the DFV took seriously.[7] Statistics from the 1950s suggest that women footballers were not entirely absent from organised sports structures. At SV Wismut in 1957, for example, the 74 football sections numbered 11 women among their 6,917 members.[8] At SV Lokomotive, membership figures for the same year show 35 women footballers among 10,731 adults in the various football sections.[9] Though no information is given about how they played (whether in mixed or all-women's teams; on full-size pitches or only in six-a-side games), women were a very small but undeniable element in football culture at least a decade before Empor Dresden took to the field.

As in most of the world's football-playing countries, including West Germany, where women's football was banned on spurious health grounds from 1955 to 1970, and England, where the women's game had been ostracised since 1921,[10] football was an indisputably male domain in the early GDR. Women's involvement, or at least public perception of it, was mediated through men. A two-page spread in *Die Neue Fußball-Woche* in

[6] See e.g. Pfister, 'The challenges of women's football', 138.

[7] Linne, *Freigespielt*, p. 39.

[8] SAPMO-BArch, DY 12/2415, Mitgliederstatistik des Deutschen Turn- und Sportbunds, 25 October 1957 (SV Wismut), fo. 208.

[9] SAPMO-BArch, DY 12/2416, Mitgliederstatistik des Deutschen Turn- und Sportbunds: SV Lokomotive, 25 October 1957, fo. 178.

[10] Pfister, 'The challenges of women's football', 129, 132–4; Jean Williams, 'The fastest growing sport? Women's football in England', in Fan Hong and J. A. Mangan (eds.), *Soccer, Women, Sexual Liberation: Kicking Off a New Era* (London: Frank Cass, 2003), pp. 112–27.

November 1949 asked the question 'what does the footballer's wife do on Sunday afternoons?' The answers focused on support: watching husbands in action or, when they were playing out of town, keeping the house clean and mending shorts. When a little girl was seen kicking a ball on the pitch at half time of a game in Altenburg, the reporter jokingly remarked that 'she wants to be the footballer's wife of tomorrow!'[11] Fifteen years later, women's roles do not appear to have changed greatly. In an article to mark International Women's Day in 1964, the same newspaper asked 'where would our football be without our women', before praising their activities as secretaries and treasurers at clubs up and down the country.[12]

Even at later dates, media coverage of women's football was sparse and subject to gender stereotypes. One survey of *Deutsches Sport-Echo*, the GDR's leading sports newspaper, shows that just ninety-one articles on the subject were published between 1967 and 1990.[13] In East just as in West Germany, the press often portrayed women footballers either as sex objects or as unwomanly.[14] Unreconstructed popular attitudes can be seen in the provincial coach ('I'm absolutely not a misogynist') in Thomas Brussig's *Leben bis Männer*, who explains at considerable length why women's only role in football should be to look pretty on the sidelines, thereby inspiring the men on the pitch to play better.[15]

That women remained largely in the shadows can be seen in football-related petitions. Their rare appearances were usually in the guise of concerned 'soccer moms', rather than as players or fans in their own right. In 1973 BFC officials received two 'aggressive' letters from the mother of veteran defender Jochen Carow, asking why he did not play more regularly in the first team. She complained about a lack of support for Carow's vocational training and accused the club of abandoning a player who for years 'risked his neck' for the BFC cause.[16] In 1985 Doris B. lobbied Rudi Hellmann to cut through the bureaucracy that was holding up the move of her talented eleven-year-old son Torsten from the training centre at BSG Einheit Güstrow to the better-funded youth programme at Dynamo Güstrow – a move that Doris had initiated on her son's request, to the chagrin of Einheit officials, who were typically loath to lose one of their own to a local rival and so had him banned

[11] 'Was macht die Fußballbraut Sonntagnachmittag?', *Die Neue Fußball-Woche*, 11 November 1949, 8–9.

[12] 'Viele unserer Frauen im Dienste des Fußballs', *Die Neue Fußball-Woche*, 10 March 1964, 2.

[13] Linne, *Freigespielt*, p. 252. The survey excludes 1986.

[14] *Ibid.*, pp. 249–73.

[15] Brussig, *Leben bis Männer*, pp. 5, 60–7.

[16] SAPMO-BArch, DO 101/027/1–2, Dienstanweisung 1/73, 8 January 1974.

from competition for his new team. Torsten's abilities ensured that, though his mother went about the move in the wrong way, the SED met her wishes.[17]

Women's football was not taken seriously for reasons both universal and GDR-specific. The derisive sexism with which male-dominated media and crowds viewed the women's game under socialism, with jokes about 'beauty competitions' and post-match shirt-swapping, was replicated in capitalist countries, as witnessed by West German press coverage of the inaugural (unofficial) women's World Cup in Italy in 1970 and the DFB's attempt to ban advertising on women's shirts in 1976 because of its distracting tendency to highlight a certain feature of the female anatomy.[18] When Dynamo Dresden travelled to Scotland to play Rangers in the Fairs' Cup in 1967, the match programme's description of the Dynamo team doctor, 'the charming' Gisela Passehr, expressed patronising wonderment at her combination of brains and beauty.[19] Her best remembered contribution to the game was the stir caused by the lucky green and white dress that she wore, green and white being the colours of Rangers' bitter rivals, Celtic.[20] It did not work, as Dynamo lost 3–2 on aggregate. In East Germany, as in Scotland, women's presence in men's football as doctors, physiotherapists, board members, or match officials was negligible.

The struggle to gain respect was common to women footballers in many European, and indeed non-European, countries, regardless of the political climate.[21] But it is striking that the women's game in East Germany, where gender equality was enshrined in the 1949 constitution and regarded as a guiding principle of socialist rule, eventually came to lag behind its West German counterpart, despite the latter's arguably less impressive record in employment and higher education.[22] A national women's league was set up in West Germany in 1974. The national team began playing regular fixtures in 1982 and developed into one of the world's strongest sides.[23] The DFV sanctioned the creation of a national women's tournament only in 1979 and refused to permit it official status. A GDR women's XI contested one international match, against Czechoslovakia in May 1990, six months after the SED dictatorship had collapsed. In 1981,

[17] SAPMO-BArch, DY 30/4980, petition from Doris B. to Hellmann, 28 October 1985, fo. 188–9; letter from Hellmann to Doris B., 18 November 1985, fo. 185.

[18] Pfister, 'The challenges of women's football', 139–40, 134.

[19] SAPMO-BArch, DO 101/078, programme from Rangers vs. Dynamo Dresden, 4 Oct 1967.

[20] Interview with Gisela Passehr, in Genschmar, *Mit Dynamo*, p. 23.

[21] See e.g. the various essays in *Soccer, Women, Sexual Liberation*.

[22] On the mixed results of the SED's efforts towards gender equality, see Fulbrook, *The People's State*, ch. 7.

[23] Linne, *Freigespielt*, pp. 178–94.

the GDR had 6,000 registered women players in 360 teams. The FRG had 383,171 players in 2,701 teams.[24]

Part of the explanation for this contrast lay in official attitudes. The DFB, previously an organisation hardly known for its progressive credentials, began in the 1980s to create professional structures in *Damenfußball* (as it was called in West Germany). There was no equivalent shift in East Germany. When women's football received increased, if still guarded, state support in the 1970s, it was on the understanding that it remained a recreational, rather than a performance, sport.[25] Women athletes featured prominently in the GDR's 'sports miracle', consistently outperforming their male counterparts. At the 1980 Moscow Olympics, women constituted 36.4% of the GDR team and won 49% of its medals.[26] But these women were sprinters, javelin throwers, and swimmers, not footballers. *Frauenfußball* was seen as no more than a leisure pursuit.

This reduced status had advantages and disadvantages. On the one hand, it meant that financial resources for those who took the game seriously were usually scarce. While some sponsoring factories, most notably in the case of Turbine Potsdam, gave embryonic women's teams significant support, players elsewhere were less fortunate. *Frauenfußball* was in large part self-financed. Players at Empor Saßnitz on the Baltic coast bought their own boots and paid for all travels costs to away matches. At Rotation Schlema, the women's team had only three footballs between them.[27] Material constraints made it hard to organise training sessions and matches and, in the long run, to keep women interested in the game.

Family commitments further complicated matters. When women got married and had children, their football careers often ended.[28] Most of the players at Turbine Potsdam were young and single. The team's average age in 1971 was just over sixteen.[29] 'In my opinion', said a Turbine player in 1982, 'you either play football or are married'.[30] In the socialist family envisioned in the GDR, women continued to be assigned the nurturing role. To them fell the bulk of the responsibility for childcare and household tasks.[31] In the coverage of women's football in *Die Neue Fußball-Woche*, the maternal aspect was often foregrounded. A 1986 article on Turbine Potsdam opened with the following remark: 'the little ones are often at

[24] *Ibid.*, p. 276. [25] *Ibid.*, pp. 53–4.
[26] Dennis and Grix, *Sport under Communism*, pp. 49–50.
[27] Linne, *Freigespielt*, pp. 78, 95–6.
[28] Pfister, 'The challenges of women's football', 139.
[29] Linne, *Freigespielt*, p. 87. [30] *Ibid.*, p. 262.
[31] See e.g. Donna Harsch, 'Squaring the circle: the dilemmas and evolution of women's policy', in Major and Osmond (eds.), *The Workers' and Peasants' State*, pp. 164–6.

the ground to watch Mummy and to joyously greet her at the final whistle'. The photograph accompanying a shorter report on an indoor tournament in Dresden in the same issue focused on a player carrying her son off the pitch.[32] Football, like the daytrips organised by local women's groups in Thuringia,[33] was a break from workplace and domestic routines, but no more than that. Competitive play was difficult to sustain in this environment.

At the same time, state disinterest in women's football made it an arguably more attractive pastime. If there was none of the wealth or prestige that came the way of Katarina Witt, there was none of the pressure or surveillance. Like the recreational players in men's factory teams, women footballers prized the social aspect of their sport as much as the competitive: the camaraderie that developed on trips to away matches, the post-match celebrations, and the gatherings at weddings or birthday parties. As Sabine Seidel, one of Turbine Potsdam's leading players, said in a 2009 interview, 'I had fun at matches'. Like Doreen Meier from Post Rostock, she fondly recollected playing at sports festivals and village fairs throughout the republic, in what served effectively as 'publicity matches' for the women's game.[34]

## Determining the best? *Frauenfußball* between entertainment and competition

The development of the women's game echoed the combination of grassroots agency and state indifference found in other areas of mass sport. When Waltraud Horn wrote to the DFV in 1967 to ask for support in promoting women's football in Leipzig, she received little encouragement. President Wolfgang Riedel suggested that, instead of playing, Horn should try to make a name for herself as a referee.[35] The women's team at Turbine Potsdam was originally devised as a prank by two male sports friends. Nobody expected much reponse to the call for players that was posted at the club's sponsoring factory, VEB Energiekombinat Potsdam, in 1971. Only after thirty-six women had quickly expressed interest did sports functionaries begin to think seriously about women's football.[36]

As at Turbine Potsdam, the women's teams that emerged in the 1970s usually began as grassroots initiatives within existing BSG football sections. They were found throughout the GDR. The hub, as in men's football, was

[32] 'Zum Frauentag ein Jubiläum', *Die Neue Fußball-Woche*, 9 March 1986, 9.
[33] Palmowski, *Inventing a Socialist Nation*, pp. 102–3.
[34] Linne, *Freigespielt*, p. 75; Pfister, 'The challenges of women's football', 139.
[35] Linne, *Freigespielt*, p. 41. [36] *Ibid.*, p. 85.

Figure 18. An international women's tournament in Frankfurt/Oder, 1975. During a decade in which *Frauenfußball* developed steadily, the sparsely populated terraces here suggest that its public appeal remained limited. Though there were teams in the towns of Eisenhüttenstadt, Frankfurt/Oder, and Schwedt, *Bezirk* Frankfurt/Oder was not at the forefront of the women's game.

Saxony. There were five women's teams in the city of Dresden alone after 1969 and countless others in towns across the *Bezirk* of the same name. There were at least eight women's teams in Berlin, led by BSG EAB Lichtenberg 47, whose line-up included the former European discus champion and world record-holder Christine Spielberg.[37] The popularity of women's football in rural areas was notable. The village of Spornitz in Mecklenburg (population 1,200) had its own team, Traktor, and drew a large crowd for a match against BSG Hydraulik Parchim at the district *Spartakiad* in 1972.[38] While it might be a stretch to call the growth in the

[37] *Ibid.*, pp. 74–8. [38] Pfister, 'The challenges of women's football', 138–9.

1970s football 'fever', particularly in comparison with developments in West Germany, the women's game did spread at a steady rate.

Expansion was largely achieved by bypassing the organisation that ran football. The DFV's attitude to *Frauenfußball* in the 1970s was characterised by a mixture of indifference and hostility. Matches were confined to local and regional levels. Teams were generally left to their own devices. A 1974 proposal to raise the profile of the women's game – and, crucially, to bring it more firmly into the realm of organised sport – identified only six counties (Berlin, Cottbus, Erfurt, Halle, Karl-Marx-Stadt, and Neubrandenburg) in which the DFV organised regular competition for women.[39] Elsewhere it was apparently not on the organisation's radar, even as a recreational sport. In football, as in other areas of cultural activity, 'locality became an important forum ... for the representation ... of women in socialism'.[40] The game's survival and growth depended on the commitment of the players and of BSG coaches, such as Bernd Schröder at Turbine Potsdam, who invested time and money in an activity that was of little interest to those who ran sport.

The 1974 proposal was shelved. It was not until 1978 that the DFV, acting largely on pressure from below, authorised the creation of a nationwide competition 'for the best women's teams in each county'.[41] This was the so-called *Bestenermittlung* ('determination of the best'), which was first contested in 1979. The awkward formulation served as a reminder of the second-class status of women's football. Since it represented a mass rather than an elite sport, the new competition could not be called a 'championship' and its winners could not be called 'GDR champions', at least not officially. Instead, the inaugural winners, Motor Mitte Karl-Marx-Stadt, and their successors could only call themselves 'the GDR's best', a less prestigious title. The state's reluctance to promote women's football found unlikely supporters. After Motor's win in 1979, the Olympic swimming champion Kornelia Matthies told *Die Neue Fußball-Woche* that football was a man's sport 'not suited for women'.[42]

The impact of the *Bestenermittlung* on the women's game is hard to measure. It has been argued that it coincided with a period in which, after the expansion of the 1970s, 'women's enthusiasm for football gradually faded again'.[43] A survey of young people's sporting activities in 1987 showed that only 2% of young female workers and 3%–4% of female

[39] Archivgut des DFV, III/4, Empfehlung der Volkssportkommission an das Präsidium des DFV der DDR zur Entwicklung und Förderung des Frauenfußballs in der DDR, 6 September 1974.

[40] Palmowski, *Inventing a Socialist Nation*, p. 102.

[41] Linne, *Freigespielt*, p. 58.

[42] *Ibid.*, pp. 139–40.

[43] Pfister, 'The challenges of women's football', 139.

apprentices were interested in playing football.[44] By the end of the decade, there were fewer women footballers (5,500) and fewer women's teams (201) than there had been at the start of it.[45]

In keeping with the publicity-match traditions of the 1970s, the new women's tournament was largely contested in smaller communities. Between 1979 and 1984, the finals were held in Templin, Bad Blankenburg, Potsdam, Lauchhammer, Schwedt, and Grimma. Not until 1986 were they hosted by a large city, Dresden.[46] Attendance figures fluctuated. Whereas 3,677 spectators witnessed Turbine clinch their first title in Potsdam in 1981, two years later, only 679 people showed up for the finals in the new town of Schwedt in *Bezirk* Frankfurt/Oder. Crowds were generally small during the mid 1980s, before picking up again from 1988 onwards.[47] The tournament became an established part of mass sport. Women's teams from Czechoslovakia, Hungary, and Poland came to East Germany for indoor tournaments. Leading teams such as Turbine Potsdam and Aufbau Dresden-Ost went the other way, though – as in the men's game – the desire for international experience was stymied by the Cold War considerations that made matches against West German teams all but impossible.[48] Media coverage of the women's game – while still largely framed within traditional gender conventions (questions to players often focused, for example, on their marital status)[49] – improved. East German television covered the finals of the national championship. *Die Neue Fußball-Woche* published the results of women's matches from 1987 onwards.[50]

Nonetheless, frustration was palpable among those who wanted the women's game to be taken more seriously as an elite sport, as was now under way in the neighbouring Federal Republic, where – true to the 1979 DFB slogan 'give girls a chance!'[51] – increasingly professional structures for club and national competition contributed to a huge growth in *Damenfußball* in the 1980s. The 'socialist glass ceiling' that made it difficult for women to attain leading positions in East German economic and political life applied too in football.[52] The DFV working group on women's football, created in 1984 under pressure from female players seeking a stronger

[44] SAPMO-BArch, DC 4/727, Zur Entwicklung sportbezogener Wertorientierungen und Interessen sowie sportlichen Tätigkeit in der *Freizeit* bei Lehrlingen, Arbeitern und Studenten zwischen 1969 und 1987 – Trendanalyse, December 1988.

[45] Linne, *Freigespielt*, p. 277.

[46] Archivgut des DFV, III/4, Bestenermittlungen im Frauenfußball der DDR, n.d.

[47] *Ibid.*, Prüfungsprotokoll, 24 January 1982; Prüfungsprotokoll, 5 December 1983; Linne, *Freigespielt*, p. 135.

[48] Linne, *Freigespielt*, pp. 172–5, 240–1. [49] *Ibid.*, pp. 264–7.

[50] *Ibid.*, p. 176. [51] *Ibid.*, p. 191.

[52] See Dagmar Langenhan and Sabine Roß, 'The socialist glass ceiling: limits to female careers', in Jarausch (ed.), *Dictatorship as Experience*, pp. 186–9.

institutional voice, complained in 1987 that the *Bestenermittlung* did not provide sufficient motivation to take up football. Scheduling was irregular and the matches that took place, at only thirty minutes per half, did not meet international standards. For the 1987/8 season, two national divisions were created and matches extended to forty minutes each way.[53] Even at this stage, though, the head of the working group, Horst Müller, reaffirmed that 'women's football belongs to recreational sport and we must direct our activity towards this'.[54]

The major shift towards recognising women's football as a performance sport coincided with the collapse of the SED dictatorship. Though not as public as the anti-BFC campaign, it constituted another example of grassroots pressure forcing change in football. The belated promotion of *Frauenfußball* would not have happened without persistent lobbying from below. In October 1989, the DFV commission on recreational sport unambiguously recommended that the *Bestenermittlung* should be replaced by a GDR championship; that a women's football commission be created within the DFV; and that, in terms of hierarchy, the women's game should be placed above the third tier of the men's game, the *Bezirksliga*.[55] The women's commission was founded in April 1990 by the reformed leadership of the DFV, providing the impetus for the creation of an elite league structure along the lines of the men's game: a ten-team first division (*Damenoberliga* – the use here of the word *Damen*, rather than *Frauen*, illustrated West German influence), with two ten-team second divisions. Long anticipated, the official GDR women's championship, won in 1990/1 by the University of Jena, existed for just one season before it, like all other GDR football structures, was incorporated into a reunified football nation. Only the top two *Damenoberliga* teams received places in the new women's *Bundesliga*.[56]

The restructuring of women's football, like almost every other urgently needed reform within 'real existing socialism', was a case of too little, too late. This was particularly true when it came to the issue of a national team. DFV proposals from as late as October 1988 made no mention of it.[57] Concrete plans to build a squad to compete in international fixtures did not take shape until the following October, when twenty-six women participated in a training course at the national sports school in Leipzig. Dramatic political change then opened up the women's game,

[53] Pfister, 'The challenges of women's football', 140.

[54] 'Niveau, Organisation mit beachtlichen Fortschritten – FuWo-Gespräch mit Horst Müller', *Die Neue Fußball-Woche*, 23 February 1988, 11.

[55] Archivgut des DFV, III/4, Konzeption zur Weiterentwicklung des Frauenfußballes in der DDR, 25 October 1989.

[56] Linne, *Freigespielt*, pp. 210–27. [57] *Ibid.*, p. 195.

just as it did the men's. In April 1990, one month after the GDR's first free elections, the national team crossed the open border between East and West to play its first practice match against a West Berlin XI in Zehlendorf. The first official fixture, against Czechoslovakia, was set for May. In defiance of the momentum, in sport and elsewhere, towards reunification, the DFV envisaged two further internationals in October and November of that year.[58]

One of the training-course nominees, Doreen Meier, recalled in 2010 her feelings of entering 'a completely new world', replete with pristine pitches, shooting machines, outstanding medical facilities, and an endless supply of Adidas balls. She slept in a room where BFC star Thomas Doll usually stayed. If the upgraded facilities at the sports school came as a shock to players accustomed to the cruder environment of recreational sport, their eleventh-hour elevation also caught officials off guard. Meier remembered how, at the squad's final gathering in May 1990, DTSB officials sought to clothe the women in skimpy handball shirts. The players stood their ground and ran out to play against Czechoslovakia in Potsdam in kit borrowed from one of the junior men's teams. The GDR's one and only international match ended in a 3–0 defeat in front of 800 spectators. The result was predictable: the debutants' opponents were playing their 184th international fixture.[59] The contest was a fitting epitaph for the SED regime's half-hearted treatment of *Frauenfußball*. Afterwards, the DFV general secretary told reporters that the game would not be 'a flash in the pan' (*Eintagsfliege*). But the DFV's belated embrace of the women's game, possibly as a compensation for its rapid loss of control over all aspects of men's football at this time, could not save GDR football as a separate entity.[60] The creation of a national team, like the creation of a national league, came far too late to take advantage – as the West Germans had done – of the international growth of women's football in the 1980s.

## The tail wagging the dog: local agency and *Frauenfußball*

If the central authorities failed to take *Frauenfußball* seriously, the same could not always be said of local functionaries. The most successful attempt to bridge, or at least narrow, the gap between the game's status as a recreational activity and its elite aspirations occurred at Turbine Potsdam. As noted earlier, the women's team there was conceived in

58 *Ibid.*, pp. 199–204.
59 Doreen Meier, 'Meine Gegnerin war eine wahre Kampfmaschine', *11 Freundinnen* (April 2010), 24–5.
60 Linne, *Freigespielt*, pp. 207–8.

1971 as a joke. But the lively response to the advertisement for players encouraged the BSG leadership to appoint an experienced coach in former *Oberliga* player Bernd Schröder.[61] It was largely thanks to Schröder's efforts that Turbine Potsdam dominated women's football, winning the *Bestenermittlung* six times between 1979 and 1991. He succeeded in doing what the DFV and DTSB showed little interest in doing: putting the women's game on an equal footing with its male counterpart. As the 1988 film *Frauen am Ball* showed, the women's section at Turbine had access to the same facilities and comforts as the men's teams.[62] Schröder was a fierce advocate of equality. He argued in the factory newspaper in 1972 that the DFV's categorisation of women's football as a recreational activity was a mistake and compared the situation in the GDR unfavourably with that in Czechoslovakia, where a women's league had existed since 1970.[63] Schröder instituted regular training sessions (at least three times a week), jettisoned those who lacked talent or application, and arranged exhibition matches throughout the GDR. His charges were found one week in Berlin and the next in Schwerin in the north or Halberstadt in the south-west.[64] Schröder also knew how to spot talent. In 1980 he recruited a fifteen-year-old midfielder, Sybille Brüdgam, after watching her train with male footballers from nearby BSG Elektronik Teltow. A gifted handball player, Brüdgam had played football since the age of seven, though she was barred from competitive games after turning eleven. At Turbine she became the mainstay of the GDR's most successful team and, in May 1990, captain of the national team in its sole appearance.[65]

Aside from the role of dedicated individuals, women's football required a wider platform of support to flourish. At Turbine Schröder was supported in his endeavours, as the former player Elke Martens recalled in a 2010 interview, by 'engaged people' within the BSG, who pulled strings in the Energiekombinat leadership to ensure that players finished work at 2 p.m. and started training one hour later. A similar network existed at BSG Nährungsgütermaschinenbau Neubrandenburg, where Werner Lenz was the central figure in successfully integrating a women's team into the preexisting football section. In the absence of willing or available husbands, Lenz's wife regularly looked after the players' children during training sessions.[66] Women's football, like fan clubs and the Union Berlin fan league, was developed from the bottom up, in defiance of state priorities and in accordance with the dictates of individual and local *Eigen-Sinn*.

[61] Horn and Weise, *Das große Lexikon*, pp. 308–9.
[62] *Frauen am Ball.* [63] Linne, *Freigespielt*, p. 88. [64] *Ibid.*, p. 87.
[65] Horn and Weise, *Das große Lexikon*, p. 63. [66] Linne, *Freigespielt*, pp. 83, 88.

The best women's teams developed at factory sports clubs that did not have strong men's sections. There was no time or money for women's football at *Oberliga* and *Liga* clubs. The GDR's second most successful team, Rotation Schlema – national champions in 1987 and 1988 and provider of four of the starting XI for the match against Czechoslovakia in 1990 – hailed from a small town near Aue where there was little competition for resources from ambitious or resentful male teams. The Schlema players became role models for women's sport in the area, receiving a letter of congratulations from the SED district leadership in Aue after their title defence.[67] In the late 1980s, a successful women's team was parachuted into BSG Rotation Prenzlauer Berg, a club that had good resources, but little in the way of successful men's teams.[68] Like *Resistenz* in the niche activities that state political activity ignored, women's football prospered in gaps that the men's game left behind.

## True amateurs? Women's football and society

As Carina Linne concludes, the GDR's 'true amateur sport' was women's football.[69] Designated as a recreational activity, and given only piecemeal state support, it existed in a world far removed from the privileged one inhabited by top male players, for whom foreign travel, nice cars, spacious flats, and generous wages were the norm. The tenacity with which a minority of women pursued their interest in football, despite official discouragement and generally scarce resources, illustrated the agency that GDR citizens brought to bear on their lives. *Frauenfußball* did not, or was not permitted to, serve national sporting interests. It could not draw on a wellspring of local patriotism or regional pride to maintain it in lean times, as many struggling *Oberliga* and *Liga* clubs did. The survival and growth of women's football in an unsympathetic environment testified to the individual pleasure that women took from the sport, both for competitive and for social reasons.

Women's football developed in no small part thanks to a handful of dedicated individuals such as Bernd Schröder, Werner Lenz, and Rotation Schlema coach Dietmar Männel,[70] who consistently procured funds for their women's teams from sponsoring factories. As in other areas of mass sport, these lower-level activists, officially representatives of the state, served

[67] *Ibid.*, pp. 165–7; Horn and Weise, *Das große Lexikon*, p. 300.

[68] Interview with Klaus L.

[69] Carina Linne, 'Freigespielt – Frauenfußball zwischen der Ostsee und dem Erzgebirge zwischen 1960 und 1990', unpublished paper from the Schwabenakademie conference on 'The History of Women's Football in Germany', 5 February 2011, 15.

[70] For Männel's biography, see Horn and Weise, *Das große Lexikon*, pp. 308–9.

local interests in the face of SED hostility or indifference. They took advantage of the sometimes disjointed and always male-oriented governance of the game to establish a foothold for women's teams in ways and areas that did not threaten, or concern, the DFV: through publicity matches in rural areas, or by establishing sections at BSGs such as Turbine Potsdam and Rotation Schlema where the men's teams were relatively weak. They exerted pressure on leading officials to give stronger institutional support to women's football, pressure that resulted in the creation of a *de facto* national championship in 1979 and grudging acceptance in the DFV and the media that the women's game was here to stay. In this grassroots prodding of passive sports organisations, the GDR's experiences very much corresponded to the international pattern on both sides of the Iron Curtain – witness, for example, the central role of women 'pioneers' in getting the 'wait-and-see' football association to finally take the women's game seriously in Sweden.[71]

From its position at the margins of mass sport, East German women's football above all highlighted the multi-layered nature of the communist state apparatus and the, in this case largely self-imposed, limits of the centre's hold over the periphery. *Frauenfußball* was not seen as important enough for leading sports functionaries to worry about. This could be liberating. Young women's stays at residential hostels gave them a taste of 'freedom from domestic responsibility, the opportunity to mix with other girls of their own age and do what they liked with their spare time'.[72] Football provided a similar space for shared experiences: sleeping in barns after exhibition games at village festivals (BSG ZfK Rossendorf), or drinking a crate of beer on bus trips to matches in Neubrandenburg or Rostock (Empor Saßnitz).[73]

There was a price to pay for this freedom. Playing for the national team may have meant, in Sabine Seidel's words, 'a lot of stress', particularly given the extra domestic burdens that women footballers faced, but it was stress that she and countless others would have welcomed.[74] Leading footballers bumped against a glass ceiling not dissimilar to that which met ambitious women looking to become factory directors, university rectors, heads of schools, doctors, or national political figures.[75] No matter how successful they were, women footballers were excluded from the upper echelons of sport, being denied the material support and

[71] Jonny Hjelm and Eva Oloffson, 'A breakthrough: women's football in Sweden', in Hong and Mangan (eds.), *Soccer, Women, Sexual Liberation*, pp. 190–212.

[72] McLellan, *Love in the Time of Communism*, p. 39.

[73] Linne, *Freigespielt*, pp. 75, 78. [74] *Ibid.*, p. 75.

[75] Fulbrook, *The People's State*, pp. 162–3; Langenhan and Roß, 'The socialist glass ceiling', pp. 183–4.

access to international competition that was granted only to select Olympic disciplines and to men's football. The horizons of the largely autonomous women's game were limited by the communist regime that paid it so little attention. Only as that regime crumbled were the first steps taken towards establishing *Frauenfußball* as an elite sport in East Germany.

# 13 East plays West: amateur matches across the Iron Curtain

## Border games

On 16 November 1976, while he was on tour in West Germany, the SED leadership revoked the citizenship of the GDR's most rebellious cultural figure, the poet and songwriter Wolf Biermann. The move provoked public criticism from leading writers and artists, some of whom soon joined him in the West. Four days earlier, *Stasi* officers in Potsdam reported the elimination of a much smaller dissident threat. Twelve young East Germans from Hennigsdorf, just north of Berlin, intended to play a football match against students from West Berlin's Free University at a local sports ground on 14 November. The Hennigsdorf youths were all employed in local factories. They were described as drop-outs from the socialist system, characterised by their 'decadent appearance', 'asocial lifestyle', and criminal behaviour. The idea for the game had originated in a previous visit by two FU students to Hennigsdorf, during which a bond was forged over 'shared interests' that apparently included Maoism. The MfS quickly forestalled the unholy gathering. Three of the organisers were brought in for police questioning on 12 November. The authorities ensured that the planned venue was in use on 14 November, in case the Hennigsdorf youngsters and their friends from West Berlin wanted to try their luck. The match, it must be assumed, did not take place.[1]

Even with the powers at its disposal, the *Stasi* was not always so successful. Unannounced and illegal football contests between recreational teams from East and West Germany were part of the sporting terrain during the 1970s and 1980s, a period in which the secret police also devoted considerable resources to monitoring officially sanctioned matches between amateur teams affiliated with the DFB and their GDR counterparts. At earlier points, most notably the 1950s, sporting traffic between East and West was more loosely regulated. This meant football matches between

[1] BStU, MfS HA XX/2698, Information über ein geplantes Fußballspiel zwischen Jugendlichen aus Hennigsdorf und Westberliner Studenten am 14.11.1976, 12 November 1976, fo. 3–4.

leading clubs such as Wismut Karl-Marx-Stadt and Kaiserslautern, who played in front of 110,000 people in Leipzig in 1956, but also contests much further down the pyramid.

This chapter examines what happened when East met West in amateur football, focusing on how the game maintained notions of shared national interests and subverted the sense of separate socialist identity that the SED sought to cultivate among its citizens.[2] It charts change over time, from the numerous, lightly policed 'national' encounters of the 1950s to the strictly rationed and strictly observed 'international' matches of the Honecker era – arguing that, here as in other areas of football, the more the authorities sought control, the more it eluded them. Football matches between East and West, whether legal or illegal, opened cracks in the socialist façade. They revealed the desire to travel, and to remain connected to the world outside the Soviet bloc, that was an intrinsic part of GDR citizens' aspirations (if not always experiences), particularly in the 1970s and 1980s.[3] Cold War cultural exchange was not only about the avant-garde musical compositions of the Darmstadt school or the arthouse cinema of the likes of Krzystof Kieślowski.[4] It found far greater popular resonance in football's ability to go around the Wall, keeping alive interests shared by ordinary Germans, and indeed ordinary Europeans, on both sides of the Iron Curtain.

## Poor control? East–West matches in the 1950s

From the early stages of Germany's post-war division, football was regarded as a potentially effective propaganda weapon. Three months before the creation of the GDR, communist officials in the Thuringian town of Sonneberg, on the western border of the Soviet Zone, organised an impromptu football match between a local team and one from the neighbouring town of Neustadt bei Coburg, situated in the American Zone. As a publicity stunt, the border between East and West marked the halfway line of the pitch on which the contest was played. Citizens of the two towns, closely linked for centuries by cultural, economic, and family ties, watched from their own side, ensuring that, unlike the players, they did not require inter-zonal passes for the day's entertainment. Sonneberg won 2–0. Local Soviet military authorities opened the border to the West for

[2] The term 'amateur' is generally understood in this book to mean football beneath the top three tiers of the DFV pyramid (*Oberliga*, *Liga*, and county leagues). In this chapter, there is a slightly more flexible interpretation of the term, as county league sides regularly competed against West German amateur teams.

[3] Major, *Behind the Berlin Wall*, pp. 194–5.

[4] Körner, 'Culture', pp. 158–9.

the rest of the day to mark the occasion. In a surviving photograph, the two teams walk towards each other carrying banners. The Sonneberg one reads 'we want the unification of Germany'; the Neustadt response is 'and so do we'.[5] This previewed the competing claims to represent the nation that characterised inter-German sporting relations until the GDR first fielded a separate team at the Olympic Games in 1968.

During the 1950s, the SED's public commitment to reunification was reflected, less disingenuously, in popular opinion. GDR citizens widely assumed that political division was temporary and that there was still one German nation, even if there were two German states.[6] Youth opposition to remilitarisation was strongly shaped by distaste at the idea of taking up arms against friends and relatives in the West.[7] The SED closed the inter-zonal borders with West Germany in 1952, creating a heavily policed 'restricted area' (*Sperrzone*) that ran along the 1,380-kilometre border separating the capitalist West from the socialist East. But sporting outreach on the basis of 'socialist patriotism' remained high on the party's agenda. The three vast German Gymnastics and Sports Festivals held in Leipzig in the 1950s – the GDR moniker was not added until 1963 – made strenuous attempts to attract visitors from West Germany and to emphasise a sporting history that could be shared by progressive forces on both sides of the political divide.[8]

Football matches continued on a regular basis. In 1954 teams from the county of Erfurt played seventy-one matches against West German opposition. Twenty-one of the fixtures took place in West Germany, the remaining fifty in the GDR. The propaganda results, like those of the matches, were mixed. Footballers at Traktor Wechmar refused to accept food and gift packages from their West German hosts, suggesting instead that they be given to the unemployed there. The football section at Einheit Arnstadt was less scrupulous, fraternising with their West German counterparts in the unsupervised environment of a pub on a Friday night.[9]

A lively if controlled exchange between East and West German teams survived until the late 1950s, when the gathering Berlin crisis forced both sides to step back. Correspondence between the DFB and its East German counterpart was regular and, with some exceptions, amicable. In the era of the Hallstein Doctrine, as Schiller and Young argue, both

[5] Edith Sheffer, 'On edge: building the border in East and West Germany', *Central European History* vol. 40, no. 2 (2007), 310–11.
[6] Fulbrook, *German National Identity*, pp. 192–3.
[7] McDougall, *Youth Politics*, p. 29.
[8] Johnson, *Training Socialist Citizens*, pp. 36–7.
[9] ThHStAW, Bezirkstag und Rat des Bezirkes Erfurt KK 24, Bericht über die gesamtdeutsche Arbeit der Sektionen Fußball, Handball und Boxen im Jahre 1954, n.d., fo. 77–84.

sides simultaneously played up and kept in check Cold War politics.[10] During the 1954 *Deutschlandtreffen*, a festival organised by the SED to promote its all-German credentials, the authorities delighted in highlighting the 800 recreational footballers who defied a DFB ban to play in matches across the GDR.[11] The politicisation of such encounters was sometimes too crude for the SED's liking. A 1951 report criticised the 'sledgehammer politics' adopted by functionaries from lower-level teams when they hosted visitors from across the border. 'Hour-long speeches', it argued, were unlikely to convince West German footballers about the justness of the socialist cause.[12]

Encounters with West German teams triggered a variety of responses among participating East Germans, not all of which could be either condoned or controlled by the authorities. The arrival of a visiting team from West Germany offered a propaganda showcase not only for the regime, but also for a particular sports club or town, in the same way as the arrival of FRG citizens in Leipzig for the Gymnastics and Sports Festivals was an occasion for civic pride as well as to display the achievements (and, indeed, the shortcomings) of socialism.[13] It provided opportunities for cross-border dialogue, both within and beyond the confines of party-approved discourse. SC Rieste's trip to Klingenthal in June 1957 centred around three matches between the visitors' teams and those of BSG Wismut Klingenthal. But it also included a visit to a museum, a dance evening at a local restaurant, a concert, a hike into the Vogtland countryside, and the requisite 'all-German talks'.[14] To miss out on such an event was a bitter blow. In September 1957 officials at BSG Wismut Rödeltal Cunersdorf wrote to the SV Wismut leadership to complain about the last-minute cancellation of their team's trip to Bavaria for a friendly against SV Sonthofen. The cancellation was part of an SED-ordered boycott of matches against West German teams for the duration of the World Youth Festival in Moscow, to which the West German government had refused to send a delegation. The high politics behind the decision were evidently not explained, or not explained clearly enough, in Cunersdorf. Officials recounted the justified anger of their colleagues in Sonthofen, who waited in vain for their visitors' arrival. The head of the BSG football section

10 Schiller and Young, *The 1972 Munich Olympics*, p. 159.

11 SAPMO-BArch, DY 34/3672, Bericht zur Gesamteinschätzung des 2. Deutschlandtreffens in der Abteilung Körperkultur und Sport, 19 June 1954.

12 SAPMO-BArch, DY 12/2459, Bericht über die Arbeit nach Westdeutschland, n.d., fo. 148–50.

13 Johnson, *Training Socialist Citizens*, pp. 152–9.

14 SAPMO-BArch, DY 12/2659, Veranstaltungsplan für den Besuch des SC Rieste v. 1920, n.d., fo. 222.

resigned. The players demanded an explanation. The section's entire work allegedly suffered as a result of the aborted trip west.[15]

Reports compiled by SV Wismut in 1957 suggest that some football encounters with West German opponents went more smoothly than others. A four-team tournament hosted by Wismut Stollberg in April, for example, was described as a political and sporting success. Three thousand spectators attended the matches. The competition was won by the single visiting West German team, SV Gosterhof from Nuremberg, whose young, largely apolitical squad was apparently impressed by what they saw in the GDR and criticised the attacks on civilians by American soldiers and 'almost daily bank robberies' that characterised life in their home town. The propensity of certain lower-level functionaries to write what was expected of them has to be taken into consideration here, just as officially sanctioned citizens' essays on the Gymnastics and Sports Festival, in which Leipzig's 'unique' amenities appear to trump the availability in West Germany of Volkswagen cars, need to be treated with caution.[16] But there was generally a less formulaic approach to writing about East–West contests in the 1950s than was the case three decades later, an untutored enthusiasm that comes across in the BSG leadership's effusive summary of the Stollberg tournament.[17] This lends the rose-tinted accounts of the early years a degree of authenticity that is lacking in Honecker-era reports of the same ilk, as well as perhaps highlighting the more optimistic attitudes to reunification then prevalent among officials. They were not always willing or able to report such happy tidings, however. Functionaries at BSG Wismut Berga/Elster reported a 'regrettable incident' that marred the visit of the West German team EV Wunsiedel in June 1957. Three of the visiting players were assaulted by two drunken brothers, the oldest of whom worked for the border police in Plauen and apparently accompanied his blows with the comment 'you're not getting across the border, I'm throwing you back over there'.[18] GDR border police took full control of the inter-German border from the Soviets two years earlier and everywhere tightened security, erecting barbed wire and observation towers. The brothers' behaviour, consciously or otherwise, reflected an

[15] *Ibid.*, letter from BSG Wismut Rödeltal to the SV Wismut leadership, 17 September 1957, fo. 59; letter from the SV Wismut leadership to TSG Solnhofen [*sic.*]/Bavaria, 31 July 1957, fo. 113.

[16] Johnson, *Training Socialist Citizens*, pp. 153–5.

[17] SAPMO-BArch, DY 12/2659, Bericht über das von der BSG Wismut Stollberg Ostern 1957 durchgeführte nationale Fußballturnier, 23 April 1957, fo. 282–3. On the greater frankness of reports from the 1950s, see e.g. Johnson, *Training Socialist Citizens*, pp. 25–6.

[18] SAPMO-BArch, DY 12/2659, letter from the football section at BSG Wismut Berga/ Elster to the district DTSB leadership, 15 June 1957, fo. 199–200.

internalisation of party rhetoric about the importance of the GDR's guardians of the 'border between two worlds'.[19]

If Wunsiedel's trip to East Germany was blighted by socialist zeal, other exchanges were complicated by different interpretations of the past. In April 1957 FC Lauda brought two teams to Aue to play friendly matches against teams from the local Wismut club. Late one evening Wismut functionaries heard some of the West German players strike up in song with *O du schöner Westerwald*, a folk standard that was a popular Wehrmacht marching song during the Second World War. To make matters worse, some of the Aue players present joined in – a reminder of the shared experiences of National Socialism that post-war division had not erased. Needless to say, the song, cheerfully belted out when German soldiers entered conquered territories in 1939 and 1940, was unacceptable in the anti-fascist GDR. Officials from Lauda rather disingenuously pleaded ignorance. One apologised; another said that his players had come 'to play football games, not to practice politics', showcasing the kind of 'sport only' attitudes that the SED tried unsuccessfully to root out among GDR athletes. Wismut officials then lectured their guests on the 'path that young people had once taken with this song on their lips'. Despite the incident, and some talk among Lauda officials about a boycott, the scheduled matches went ahead without incident.[20] On both sides of the German border, as communist officials came to reluctantly recognise, grassroots mistrust of 'politicised sport' proved extremely difficult to overcome.[21]

From the late 1950s onwards, the number of sporting exchanges between East and West fell off noticeably. The criminalisation of unauthorised travel to the FRG and West Berlin, a consequence of the 1957 Pass Law, meant that East German athletes with close relatives on the other side of the border were barred from competition there.[22] The construction of the Berlin Wall in August 1961 announced a decade in which football, like many other social and cultural activities, was forced to turn inwards, as officials jettisoned shared traditions in favour of GDR-specific features of mass mobilisation.[23] Keeping open lines of communication with the West was difficult. A football functionary from Dessau complained in 1964 that he had put off invitations from 'West German sport friends'

[19] Major, *Behind the Berlin Wall*, pp. 108–9.
[20] SAPMO-BArch, DY 12/2659, Bericht über einige Diskussionen, die während des Aufenthaltes der westdeutschen Freunde aus Lauda geführt wurden, 25 April 1957, fo. 278.
[21] Kristin Rybicki, 'Sportler an einen Tisch! – Berlin und die "Westarbeit" des Deutschen Sportauschusses in den frühen 1950er Jahren', in Braun and Teichler (eds.), *Sportstadt Berlin*, p. 95.
[22] *Ibid.* [23] Johnson, *Training Socialist Citizens*, pp. 162–3.

at a club in Düsseldorf for five years, as he had been unable to gain authorisation to travel to the Federal Republic.[24]

## East–West encounters in the *Abgrenzung* era

The signing of the Basic Treaty in 1972 put political relations between East and West Germany on a more normal footing. Connections between the two sides – whether in the form of 'permanent representatives' (*de facto* ambassadors), telephone lines, or the traffic of persons and goods through fixed crossing-points[25] – were tentatively re-established. In May 1974 the DTSB and the DSB agreed to play a maximum of eighty annual contests across various sports, including football.[26] The relatively frequent, loosely policed 'national' meetings of the 1950s were now replaced by a much smaller, scrupulously monitored quota of 'international' matches between East and West. In 1984, for example, the SED authorised just six games between BSG football sections and West German amateur teams.[27]

GDR teams looking to play West German opposition had to go through a long and bureaucratic application process. Their squads were vetted for suspicious elements. Those with known contacts in the West were, with rare exceptions, excluded. Strict regulations governed the etiquette surrounding trips to West Germany. Interviews with television and radio were rationed and confined in subject matter to football. Gifts could be accepted only if they were of 'souvenir character'. The delegation leader was to be informed immediately if suspicious persons were seen lurking around the team hotel. The GDR flag was to be raised alongside the FRG's flag in the stadium, as would happen at any international football match.[28] The SED leadership, working closely with the *Stasi*, created a paranoid and joyless atmosphere, in which fraternal contact was kept to a minimum. Given the obstacles, and the pressure to secure victories for East German socialism, most clubs saw games with West German opponents as a privilege too burdensome to take up. The football section leader at BSG Rotation Prenzlauer Berg recalled that his club was 'much, much too small' to consider applying. Rotation's trips abroad were directed to the

[24] LHASA, MER, Bezirkstag/Rat des Bezirkes Halle, Nr. 9418, letter from the county council department for physical culture and sport to Comrade Klapproth, 29 October 1964, fo. 11.

[25] Major, *Behind the Berlin Wall*, p. 198.

[26] Braun and Wiese, 'DDR-Fußball', 203.

[27] SAPMO-BArch, DY 12/3102, Plan der Sportveranstaltungen für das Jahr 1984, BSG-Ebene, n.d., fo. 149–50.

[28] See e.g. SAPMO-Barch, DY 12/3104, Reisebericht: Durchführung eines internationalen Fußballspieles in der BRD am 14.10.84 – SC Willingen–BSG Lok Stendal, 16 October 1984, fo. 5–7.

safer political ground of Poland.[29] If *Oberliga* stars, with their privileged *Reisekader* status, were football's labour aristocracy, recreational players generally had the narrower travel horizons typical of ordinary East Germans.

How successful was the policy of relentless control? BSG Traktor Ziltendorf, a fourth-division (*Bezirksklasse*) team from Frankfurt/Oder, visited West Germany for a match against SV Neukirchen in May 1986. The lengthy report on the team's trip epitomised in language and content the guarded ideal to which the SED regime aspired. The prescribed schedule was followed unswervingly. Sequestered at a hotel twelve kilometres outside Neukirchen, the Ziltendorf team partook in a guided tour of the town, a forty-five-minute shop at a local department store, and a joint dinner between the two clubs. In front of 100 spectators, it won the match 2–0. The hosts adhered to the terms of the 1974 DTSB–DSB agreement, using the correct language to describe the GDR, removing advertising from around the pitch, and ensuring that media questions were kept to pre-approved topics. In this bloodless report, lacking the enthusiasm that characterised its counterparts from the 1950s, there were few cracks in the façade. Personal discussions with Neukirchen officials touched on interesting issues, most notably the recent Chernobyl disaster – but only so that GDR representatives, deaf to the scale of the catastrophe and the mobilising impact that it had on East Germans, could criticise the West's 'mass media campaign' against the Soviet Union. About the only point of tension during the entire trip, if the report is to be believed, was the delegation's rejection of a set of gift glasses, because the exchange had not been agreed in advance.[30]

Ziltendorf's trip to West Germany embodied the *Abgrenzung* ideal of the Honecker government. East–West cultural and sporting contacts were increased, but only under strict supervision – and with the goal of accentuating the GDR's identity as 'a socialist state within the German nation'. When the chairman of the Lichterfelder Sportunion club in West Berlin requested permission to scout games involving TSG Gröditz, ahead of the two teams' meeting in 1980, DTSB functionaries informed him that it was not standard practice for lower-level fixtures. Organisational questions about the match could be expedited in writing. 'The goal', as the *Stasi* office in Dresden emphasised, 'is to avoid any contact between [the chairman] and members of TSG Gröditz'.[31]

29 Interview with Klaus L.

30 BStU, MfS HA XX/2698, Bericht über die Reise der BSG Traktor Ziltendorf in der Zeit vom 16.5. bis 18.5.86 zum internationalen Freundschaftsspiel gegen die SV Neukirchen in Neukirchen/BRD, 28 May 1986, fo. 93–104.

31 *Ibid.*, Information zum internationalen Fußballwettkampf TSG Gröditz gegen Lichterfelde Sportunion (Westberlin) im Mai 1980 in Gröditz, 21 February 1980, fo. 11.

On the West German side, the strict policing of matches between amateur teams, a manifestation of what Braun and Wiese have called *Abgrenzungshysterie* ('demarcation hysteria'),[32] caused frustration and disappointment. Players from amateur side FC Schüttorf 09 criticised the killjoy functionary who presided over TSG Wismar's trip to West Germany in 1985 and put a damp cloth on every social activity, planned or otherwise. After officials prevented BSG Hettstedt players from exchanging shirts with their West German opponents, TuS Dornberg, following a game in 1982, Dornberg players asked whether such matches 'still had any purpose'.[33]

## Outside the lines: illegal football matches

The thoughts of the Hettstedt players, or other GDR citizens involved in games against Western opposition, went largely unrecorded in party and secret-police reports. Perhaps, as for elite players, the benefits of being allowed travel to the West at all outweighed the regulations that strictly attended the trips. A minority of recreational footballers, though, rejected the stifling environment of official East–West encounters. Like fans who travelled to socialist states to watch *Bundesliga* sides in action, they established ties to teams in the Federal Republic, and other West European countries, outside official channels. This subversive activity, as we saw in the case of the young Hennigsdorf footballers, regularly drew the attention of the secret police.

The DTSB's reluctance to authorise anything beyond a very small number of annual matches against non-socialist opposition was the root cause of many illegal encounters. In 1986, the *Stasi* authorities in *Bezirk* Dresden informed the SED leadership about a planned veterans' contest between BSG Chemie Radebeul and the Dutch team SV Koedijk. The DFV had repeatedly refused to sanction the match. But one of the Dutch players, who had previously lived in the Radebeul area, established 'private connections' (always a mark of suspicion in the outwardly collectivist GDR) with Chemie functionaries, with a view to organising it anyway.[34] What raised alarm bells was not any specific threat – there were no 'politically negative' discussions when players from the clubs met in 1985 – but the fact that sport might take place outside the SED's

[32] Braun and Wiese, 'DDR-Fußball', 208. [33] *Ibid.*, 204.

[34] BStU, MfS HA XX/2698, Information über eine beim Reisebüro der DDR nichtgebuchte Gruppeneinreise aus den Niederlanden zu einem Besuch von Angehörigen der BSG Chemie Radebeul, 3 June 1985, fo. 76–8; Information über ein geplantes Fußballspiel der BSG Chemie Radebeul gegen eine Mannschaft der Niederlande am 17.5.1986, 23 April 1986, fo. 91–2.

remit and, indeed, against its wishes. A blind eye could be turned to independent activities, such as the Union Berlin fan league, that were confined within domestic parameters. But matches against Western opposition, however informal, were always political as well as sporting affairs.

Such matches suggest, among other things, a desire for normal contact with the outside world – and a desire to be part of a normal society, where one could travel wherever, and dress however, one liked.[35] They created small tears in the Iron Curtain. In 1985, the Dresden *Stasi* office reported on another unauthorised game, between a team representing a Swiss company and a team composed of employees and customers from a local pub. As in the case of SV Koedijk and Chemie Radebeul, Western economic interests in the GDR – which were extensive by the early 1980s, due to the regime's increased reliance on Western banks to prop up the ailing economy – created personal contacts that were maintained via football. The only people in attendance at BSG Pentacon Dresden's ground on 10 August were family members of the home team's players. There was nothing in the match or the post-match revelries, which lasted until 3 a.m., that constituted a political threat, apart from the fact that they had been organised in the first place.[36] By making everything, or almost everything, beyond its control political, including nondescript football matches that were essentially social gatherings, the communist regime set impossible standards of surveillance and conformity. By making every point of contact with the West potentially subversive, it fed, rather than sated, curiosity about the people and lifestyles on the other side of the Wall.[37] At some level, citizens intuited this paradox, recognising that an unauthorised football game against the class enemy, like an impromptu concert or untoward Church meeting, could slip under the radar – at least for long enough for it to take place and with disciplinary consequences light enough to warrant the risk. The pub landlord who organised the match against the Swiss firm could expect a serious talking to from the authorities, as could the BSGs that allowed their players to participate in the match. But the *Stasi* lacked the time and resources to press for stiffer penalties.[38]

[35] On normality in the GDR context, see e.g. Merkel, 'The GDR – a normal country', pp. 194–203.

[36] BStU, MfS HA XX/2698, Information über die Durchführung einer unangemeldeten Sportveranstaltung mit Beteiligung einer Mannschaft aus der Schweiz auf dem Sportplatz der BSG Penatacon Dresden, 25 September 1985, fo. 85–7.

[37] Fulbrook, *German National Identity*, p. 198.

[38] BStU, MfS HA XX/2698, Information über die Durchführung einer unangemeldeten Sportveranstaltung, 25 September 1985, fo. 85–7. On the *Stasi*'s stretched resources in the 1980s, see Dennis and LaPorte, *State and Minorities*, p. 201.

The clash between the competing claims of state control and societal autonomy was exemplified by an unauthorised match in the town of Altenburg in *Bezirk* Leipzig in 1981. On 21 March customs officials stopped a West German BMW en route to the international trade fair in Leipzig and discovered a pair of Adidas football shirts bearing the name BSG Wismut Altenburg. Investigations revealed that the driver managed a football team, Gulf Atletico 71 from Frankfurt. The shirts, a full set of which existed, were a gift for Wismut Altenburg, whom Atletico 71 – unbeknown to the local authorities – were due to play in a 'training match' the following day. Perhaps as a consequence of the border search, the two sides moved the match forward to late in the afternoon of 21 March. To avoid 'political complications', and taking into account the short notice and lack of public interest (ten spectators were in attendance), local *Stasi* officers allowed it to go ahead. The visitors won 5–0.[39]

Subsequent investigations shed fascinating light on the methods and motivations of individuals who organised unlawful football matches with West German teams. The ringleaders at the GDR end, two functionaries at BSG Wismut Altenburg, were, like match-day stewards or leaders of officially recognised fan clubs, the kind of grassroots figures on whom the SED's authority depended. M. and S. were known as 'fanatical football supporters and especially as supporters of West German football'. S., an SED member, first met the Atletico 71 manager when he travelled to Prague to watch West Germany play Czechoslovakia in 1979. The idea for a game between retired players from Altenburg and the team from Frankfurt apparently developed from there, in almost complete secrecy.[40] At a meeting on 27 March, the pair readily conceded that they were aware of the gravity of their offence and that, if the DTSB leadership or BSG chairman got wind of it, 'things would go badly for us'.[41] They went to considerable lengths to conceal the true nature of the game, informing the local authorities merely that they planned to play a 'friendly match' on 21 March against unspecified opposition, telling the Altenburg groundsman a similarly vague story, and even informing some of their Wismut team-mates that their opponents hailed from the East German town of

[39] BStU, MfS HA XX/2698, Bericht über die Ergebnisse der Überprüfungen zur Austragung eines nichtgenehmigten Fußballspieles zwischen einer Mannschaft der BSG Wismut Altenburg und der BRD-Mannschaft Gulf Atletico 71 Frankfurt (a. Main), 30 March 1981, fo. 26–30.

[40] BStU, MfS ZAIG/3118, Information über die Austragung eines nichtgenehmigten Fußballspieles zwischen einer Mannschaft der BSG Wismut Altenburg und der BRD-Mannschaft "Gulf Atletico 71 – Frankfurt", 22 April 1981, fo. 1–2.

[41] SAPMO-BArch, DY 12/3352, Protokoll der außerordentlichen Vorstandsitzung der BSG Wismut Altenburg, Betriebssportgemeinschaft des Jugendbergbaubetriebes "Ernst Thälmann", 27 March 1981, fo. 35–9.

Hettstedt.[42] Given that the visitors wore Adidas shirts emblazoned with the words 'Gulf Atletico 71', and that the Altenburg team were dressed in the Adidas shirts brought across the border, it seems improbable that the Hettstedt story was believed. In the meeting on 27 March, the BSG leadership found unconvincing the player K.'s claim that he found out only at half time that Altenburg's opponents were from West Germany.[43] The entire team, it emerged, was complicit in spreading the fiction that this was a friendly match against a team from Hettstedt.[44]

The consequences were serious. Both M. and S. were expelled from BSG Wismut Altenburg and the DTSB for their 'reprehensible behaviour'. The Adidas shirts were confiscated. The local branch of the *Stasi* opened files on them, an act that meant the permeation of their friendship circles with informants and a possible lifetime under surveillance.[45] BSG officials set about destroying the 'negative concentration' in their football section, but with limited success. Not all players, it seemed, were convinced of the seriousness of the incident. Clarifying discussions with the team were still ongoing at the end of April, almost six weeks after Gulf Atletico's visit.[46]

The almost insouciant attitude of the Altenburg players, not to mention the seemingly breezy indifference to risk of M. and S., suggests that they were willing to test the resolve of the authorities – or at the very least thought that they could be got around. In a state as heavily policed as the GDR, this might seem surprising. But it matched the behaviour of footballers in Dresden, Hennigsdorf, and Radebeul, all of whom were willing to organise informal games with West European opponents, in the hope or belief that the SED had bigger fish to fry. As in the case of the FDJ functionary in Annaberg who sanctioned the founding of a Depeche Mode fan club in 1989, illegal matches were less an illustration of open resistance to the SED leadership than they were local instances of turning a blind eye to contraventions of the 'ideological purity and socialist morality' that the regime envisaged for its citizens.[47] This was a 'negotiated society',

[42] BStU, MfS ZAIG/3118, Information über die Austragung eines nichtgenehmigten Fußballspieles, fo. 2–3.

[43] SAPMO-BArch, DY 12/3352, Protokoll der außerordentlichen Vorstandsitzung, fo. 35–9.

[44] BStU, MfS HA XX/2698, Bericht über die Ergebnisse der Überprüfungen zur Austragung eines nichtgenehmigten Fußballspieles, fo. 35.

[45] *Ibid.*, fo. 39; SAPMO-BArch, DY 12/3352, Information über das besondere Vorkommnis in Altenburg am 21./22. März 1981, 28 March 1981, fo. 31–4; Protokoll der außerordentlichen Vorstandsitzung, fo. 35–9.

[46] BStU, MfS HA XX/2698, Bericht über die Ergebnisse der Überprüfungen zur Austragung eines nichtgenehmigten Fußballspieles, fo. 38; SAPMO-BArch, DY 12/3352, Information über das besondere Vorkommnis, fo. 31–4; Abschlußinformation über das besondere Vorkommnis in Altenburg am 21./22. März 1981, 30 April 1981, fo. 40–1.

[47] Wilton, 'The "societalisation" of the state, pp. 126–7.

in which the boundaries between state and society, and between state influence and established social patterns, were highly fluid.[48]

The Altenburg match also indicated a surviving sense of German national identity among GDR citizens (and, it should be added, among their West German counterparts). At the boozy post-match celebrations between Altenburg and Gulf Atletico players, both sides apparently spoke of sport's 'un-political' role in fostering cross-border ties – the kind of thinking that the SED regime had condemned since the early 1950s. The *Stasi* conceded that, just as the match had not been authorised by the East German authorities, so also it had not received any support from 'enemy offices' in West Germany.[49] This was an all-German encounter organised outside official channels.

The crossover between watching and playing the game is interesting to note in this context. The secret police reported that S. first met the Gulf Atletico manager at a West Germany game in Prague in 1979. Like Helmut Klopfleisch and thousands of other East Germans (as discussed in Chapter 8), he followed West German teams wherever possible behind the Iron Curtain, watching seven games in Poland, the GDR, Czechoslovakia, and Bulgaria between 1971 and 1980. Only a discussion with local *Stasi* officers prevented him from travelling to Czechoslovakia again on 10 March 1981 for Bayern Munich's European Cup quarter-final clash with Baník Ostrava, a match watched by 1,000 Bayern fans from the GDR and only 70 from West Germany.[50]

Both as a spectator sport and as a participatory sport, football acted as an unofficial bridge between East and West – and as a reminder that on both sides, but especially in the GDR, the concept of a single German nation, of shared interests and bonds that transcended the country's political division, had not been entirely abandoned.[51] *Eigen-Sinn* as enacted through the illegal matches played, or nearly played, during the Honecker era undermined *Abgrenzung* almost without trying. It showed another facet of football's role in chipping away at the state, of a piece with the withdrawal of popular support for socialism that was evident throughout the game in the 1980s, from the growing individualism of *Auswahl* players to the subcultural *Resistenz* in fan clubs and hooligan circles and the public resentment of BFC and its protectors.

48 Merkel, 'The GDR – a normal country', pp. 200–3.

49 BStU, MfS HA XX/2698, Bericht über die Ergebnisse der Überprüfungen zur Austragung eines nichtgenehmigten Fußballspieles, fo. 31, 39.

50 *Ibid.*, fo. 34; Braun and Wiese, 'DDR-Fußball', 206.

51 Fulbrook, *German National Identity*, pp. 192–8.

# 14 Football for all? The provision of facilities

## Material matters

In April 1989, the leader of the football section at BSG Traktor Hochstedt, a sports club in a village halfway between Erfurt and Weimar, sent a petition to the county council. He first recounted Traktor Hochstedt's contributions to socialism: the volunteer help that ensured the construction of a sports ground within three years of the club's founding in 1978; the expansion of the football section during the 1980s (70 members in 1989, in a village of 390 inhabitants); and the BSG's outstanding work in developing young footballers. The petitioner then came to the point. The BSG's good work, he argued, had been achieved under 'very bad conditions', despite, rather than because of, the communist state. Officials had campaigned unsuccessfully for more than a decade for a clubhouse with changing-room facilities. The only building currently available to Hochstedt players was a community hall 500 metres from the pitch. It had no sanitary facilities other than an outside toilet and was also used by the BSG's table tennis and chess sections, as well as by various mass organisations and the fire brigade. When the hall was double-booked on the day of a game against Molsdorf, Traktor Hochstedt's players retreated to the section leader's garage to get changed. 'In my opinion', he asserted, 'that is not right after 40 years of the GDR'.[1]

Complaints about inadequate sporting infrastructures were increasingly common during the last decade of the Honecker era, part of an upsurge in petitions to the authorities that reached the astonishing annual figure of more than one million in the late 1980s.[2] Amid political stagnation and economic decline, and in a period when the GDR's international standing was heavily reliant on the success of its Olympic teams, the lack of running water or indoor toilets at a small football ground in rural Thuringia was not

[1] ThHStAW, Bezirkstag und Rat des Bezirkes Erfurt Altregistratur Nr. 46939/1, petition from the football section at BSG Traktor Hochstedt to Erfurt county council, 21 April 1989, fo. 322–4.

[2] Betts, *Within Walls*, p. 189.

a priority for communist leaders. But such problems mattered a great deal to the many GDR citizens who organised and played recreational sport. They are also of considerable value to historians, as a window onto the ever-growing contradictions between rhetoric and reality under consumer socialism and the festering socio-economic grievances that left the SED dictatorship with so few supporters in 1989. Recent work on mass sport provision in the GDR's twilight years emphasises the dismal reality of neglect and deterioration behind the SED's claim to offer sport for all.[3]

This chapter discusses the challenges that citizens encountered in building and maintaining structures for recreational football. Evidence from the Ulbricht era shows that complaints about poor facilities were not inventions of the 1970s and 1980s. The problems, though, were magnified in these decades. While funds were lavished on performance sport, the inadequate provision of facilities for ordinary East Germans exposed the hollow promises of the Honecker era, revealing a regime that struggled to appease the demands of a disillusioned yet active citizenry. The gulf, or perceived gulf, between facilities for elite and recreational athletes replicated two-tier systems in other areas of society such as shopping and travel. Top-of-the range Adidas boots, just like Intershops and *Reisekader* status, were privileges of the few, not the many. Football's material shortcomings showed with particular clarity the dangers of politicising everything. East Germany in the 1980s arguably possessed better sports facilities than England, where the Thatcher government's Regulation 909 (1981) gave schools the right to sell off playing fields for commercial purposes.[4] But far more was expected of the SED than of the Conservative Party. The communists' theoretical commitment to, and subsequent neglect of, mass sport created a culture of expectancy, often framed in socialist rhetoric, that was bound to end in frustration and disappointment. This fed the popular discontent with the GDR, rumbling away in many areas of football culture, that came so dramatically to the surface in 1989.

## Recreational football in the Ulbricht years

Walter Ulbricht liked to portray himself as a 'friend of German athletes'. Publications emphasised his sporting roots in Leipzig, where he had joined a workers' gymnastics club at the age of fourteen.[5] Under his leadership, mass sport, in theory at least, was a major part of the SED's

[3] See Braun, 'The people's sport?'; Grix 'The decline of mass sport provision'.

[4] 'A playground for policy makers', *Times Educational Supplement*, 11 June 1999: www.tes.co.uk/teaching-resource/A-playground-for-policy-makers-310455/.

[5] Johnson, *Training Socialist Citizens*, p. 46.

social programme. One typical report from 1956 criticised factories where sport was regarded as a 'necessary evil' and granted only limited resources. Physical activity, it argued, was not an optional extra, but an integral means of improving workers' lives and reinforcing patriotic education.[6] The early Soviet model of *fizkultura* as civic duty was an important influence.[7] No less significant was the selective reading of German sports history – focusing on the early *Turnen* movement and the traditions of *Arbeitersport* ('workers' sports') – that underpinned the GDR's attempts to mobilise socialist patriotism through mass sport.[8]

It has been argued that SED commitment to mass sport was stronger in the 1950s than at later dates, when Olympic glory, and concomitant generous funding of performance sport, was prioritised.[9] Yet many of the problems faced by functionaries in the Honecker years – decrepit or misappropriated facilities, equipment shortages, and neglect of mass sport in favour of the elite – bedevilled their predecessors too. In the 1950s, as in the 1980s, a self-help culture ensured that things got done when the state lacked the resources or the political will to take the initiative. Amateur footballers, gymnasts, hockey players, hurdlers, and skiers all recalled in later interviews the time that they voluntarily gave to the rebuilding of war-ravaged sports grounds and clubhouses in the GDR's early years.[10] Footballers at Rotation Leipzig devoted more than 200,000 volunteer hours to the construction of their sports ground, the Sportpark Nordost, between 1958 and 1966.[11] This ethos survived into the supposedly more affluent era of consumer socialism. The sports hall opened in 1974 in the small community of Friedrichsgrün near Zwickau, for example, barely cost the authorities anything, since the vast majority of the 46,000 hours of labour on the project had been put in by a band of 800 volunteers.[12]

Voluntarism served the needs of the state, saving money and offering uplifting propaganda examples, and of its citizens, providing much-needed facilities and a bond forged through shared goals.[13] In the 1950s, initiatives to build facilities at one's own club existed alongside voluntary work as an expected 'social contribution'. Footballers in Wittenberg, for example, logged volunteer hours at the end of the workday or at the conclusion of a job training programme, in order to help with the construction of a new athletics stadium. The rapid construction of the Zentralstadion in Leipzig

6 SAPMO-BArch, DY 34/3879, Den Massensport weiterentwickeln!, 21 August 1956.
7 O'Mahony, *Sport in the USSR*, pp. 15–16.
8 Johnson, *Training Socialist Citizens*, pp. 35–47. 9 *Ibid.*, p. 203.
10 *Ibid.*, pp. 126–7. 11 Beyer, *Rotation Leipzig*, pp. 20–1.
12 Wilton, 'Regime versus people?', p. 137.
13 Johnson, *Training Socialist Citizens*, pp. 113–24.

in 1956 was likewise the product of an ambiguous voluntarism whereby pledges of manpower and labour hours were often state-initiated, if not state-enforced.[14]

Whether voluntary or compulsory (or, as was often the case, something in between), the rebuilding of mass sport facilities in the 1950s dovetailed with the self-identity of the reconstruction generation, those who had lived through Nazism and the Second World War and subsequently found pragmatic common ground with the communist leadership in raising the GDR from the rubble. The 'reconstruction myth' was based on hard work and, in the broadest sense, political orthodoxy.[15] Sport was an ideal arena in which to transfer the value system learned under Nazism, with its emphasis on self-sacrificing 'duty consciousness' (*Pflichtsbewußtsein*) and 'willingness to achieve' (*Leistungsbereitschaft*), to more productive socialist projects.[16] Grassroots sports initiatives were also a source of local pride. Club histories often emphasise the modest, community-based origins of post-war facilities and activities. The first useable grass pitch at Eintracht Mahlsdorf's ground on the outskirts of Berlin, for example, was laid with the help of a local farmer and his two horses.[17]

Citizens who played sport during the cash-strapped 1950s were encouraged to fund and build their own facilities, as well as to fashion rudimentary sports equipment. The SED's hands-off approach was shaped by political and financial priorities, both of which lay elsewhere, and a desire to mobilise popular participation in the building of socialism. Such cost-cutting exercises were by no means confined to impecunious communist regimes – witness the British government's promotion of 'low-cost facilities backed up by inspiring leadership' during the economic crisis of the 1970s.[18] Football, like volleyball and table tennis, was attractive in this regard, since it was relatively cheap. But GDR footballers, like other sports enthusiasts, expected something in return for their hard work. Letters to the SED in 1959 and 1960 complained about the neglect of rural sports clubs, the limited availability of facilities such as swimming pools (open to elite athletes before the public), and the lack of state funding for BSGs.[19] With rationing ended and the GDR supposedly set fair on the path to socialism, there was a growing tendency to call the state to account. As in the Stalinist Soviet Union, the media played an important role in

[14] *Ibid.*, pp. 127–8. [15] Wierling, 'The Hitler Youth generation', pp. 312–17.
[16] McDougall, 'A duty to forget?', 39–40.
[17] www.bsv-eintracht-mahlsdorf.de/Verein/verein3.htm.
[18] Hargreaves, *Sport, Power and Culture*, p. 189.
[19] SAPMO-BArch, DY 30/IV 2/18/1, Analyse der Post aus der Bevölkerung seit Anfang August 1959, 6 January 1960, fo. 10–10A.

amplifying citizens' complaints about available amenities.[20] A 1964 article in *Die Neue Fußball-Woche* exposed the 'most primitive conditions' at Einheit Strausberg's ground, where doors and windows were broken and there were neither lighting nor indoor washing facilities.[21]

If the 1960s marked the highpoint of reform projects in economic, family, and youth policy, change was less apparent in recreational sport. In February 1963 officials from the football section at BSG Lokomotive Weißenfels wrote to Halle county council to protest about ongoing problems with their ground. Four years earlier it had been dug up during the season for the installation of a sewerage system. Making it playable again required 1,800 hours of labour on the part of BSG members. In 1960 the club was promised a new sports ground, but 'it remained only a promise'. At the urging of football section leaders, the move to a new facility was finally granted in 1962. But the old pitch on which the club played in the meantime was dug up again, without consulting the BSG leadership, in order to drain off excess water. League fixtures were disrupted. The players once more stepped in, clearing building materials and mounds of earth from the playing surface, so that matches could resume.[22]

The communication from Lok Weißenfels contained many of the features that characterised petitions about mass sport during the Honecker era. The authors emphasised the self-help ethos that the SED lauded, not only the volunteer sacrifices that made the ground playable, but also the grassroots pressure that forced through the start of construction on a new facility in 1962. Unresponsive or politically unreliable officials populated the narrative. The first district councillor with whom the club dealt absconded to West Germany. His successor was not much better, showing 'no interest' in Lok's problems and allowing the factory that owned the land where the original facility was located to ignore agreements to respect playing schedules during construction. Local rivalry played a role as well. Lok Weißenfels's anger was fed by the fact that a newly founded neighbouring BSG, Traktor Bürgwerben, received 10,000 M in 1960 for the construction of a sports ground 'that is still not finished today' – a largesse, it was implied, that the more established club would have put to better use.[23]

[20] See e.g. Fitzpatrick, 'Supplicants and citizens', pp. 93–4.

[21] 'Primitivste Voraussetzungen fehlen!', *Die Neue Fußball-Woche*, 15 December 1964, 13.

[22] LHASA, MER, RdB Halle, Nr. 9418, petition from the football section at BSG Lokomotive Weißenfels to Halle county council's office for youth and sport, 13 February 1963, fo. 74–5. There is no reply to the petition in the file.

[23] *Ibid.*, fo. 74.

Supplying recreational facilities was problematic before Honecker came to power in 1971. It is thus difficult to confirm the argument that there was a decline in the provision of such services 'from the late 70s onwards'.[24] There were more complaints by then. But this most likely reflected growing intolerance of sub-standard facilities, rather than a clearly quantifiable decline. What might have been acceptable during the reconstruction era of the 1950s was no longer good enough in the supposedly more prosperous and stable period of real existing socialism. Perceptions of the state's shortcomings shifted, rather than the shortcomings themselves worsening. Petitioners adopted a 'rhetoric of decline' that reflected a growing scepticism about the SED's ability to create a more egalitarian society.[25] Their correspondence with the state became more confrontational, more sarcastic, and more assertive, foreshadowing the revival of civil society and popular disrespect for authority that characterised the protests of 1989.[26]

In November 1970, as Honecker manoeuvred behind the scenes to replace the ageing Ulbricht, the football section leader at BSG Motor Babelsberg wrote to the DTSB with the kind of problem that featured permanently on the GDR's recreational landscape. He had been informed that the floodlights at the BSG's ground would no longer be available, an apparent consequence of the 'tense energy situation', which forced the SED into a number of cutbacks in the late 1960s and early 1970s.[27] Since most of Motor Babelsberg's teams trained after work or school, and the club's sports hall was used by other sections, the floodlight ban would bring its youth programme to a halt. In order to prevent such a scenario, and at the same time respect the party's energy-saving drive, the section leader proposed a training schedule in which three of the five night-time sessions used the lights only at half power.[28] The art of compromise, of making reasonable demands that served community interests but did not upset the socialist applecart, was essential to the lower-level functionaries who effectively served as mediators between citizens and the state.[29] Whatever the shifts in the political and economic climate, this balancing act defined the work of BSG representatives

[24] Grix, 'The decline of mass sport provision', 409.
[25] Zatlin, *The Currency of Socialism*, pp. 286–8.
[26] Betts, *Within Walls*, pp. 188–9.
[27] On the energy consequences of the bitterly cold winter of 1969/70, see Wolle, *Die heile Welt*, pp. 33–5.
[28] BLHA, Rep. 545 Nr. 320, petition from the football section at BSG Motor Babelsberg to the DTSB leadership in *Bezirk* Potsdam, 6 November 1970.
[29] On the role of these intermediary figures in cultural life, see Richthofen, *Bringing Culture to the Masses*, ch. 1.

throughout the GDR's existence. It seemed particularly attuned to the leadership style of Honecker, 'the man of small compromises'.[30]

## Football facilities in the Honecker era

The transition years between Ulbricht and Honecker were marked by the SED's increased commitment to elite and mass sport. The 1969 Politburo resolution created a hierarchical system of resource distribution in which Olympic sports received the majority of state funding, while the likes of tennis, basketball, and ice hockey fell by the wayside. The new policy bore fruit at the 1972 Munich Olympics, where the GDR finished third in the medal table behind the Soviet Union and the United States and just ahead of West Germany. With the introduction over the next two years of comprehensive talent-spotting and doping programmes, the bedrock of the 'sports miracle' was in place.

At the same time, the SED expanded its commitment to recreational sport. Reduced time in the workplace, down to 43¾ hours per week by 1967, with weekends free, created a society, and a regime, that could focus more intently on leisure pursuits.[31] In the same year, the party announced an ambitious programme aimed at getting citizens to exercise several times a week. Starting in the early 1970s, the DTSB created 'joint sports programmes' with the FDGB and the FDJ. They organised mass sports festivals, as well as events such as the 'table tennis tournament for thousands' and the jogging campaign *Eile mit Meile* ('make haste with miles').[32] The latter mimicked mass jogging movements in the United States and West Germany, suggesting once more how sport's internationalism allowed it to cross political borders with relative ease and frequency.[33]

It was clear which was the more important of the two branches of socialist sport. Olympic athletes were the GDR's most successful export. They gave the regime international prestige that it enjoyed in few other areas. In comparison, how local bowling clubs were organised or how veterans' football teams were run was a minor concern, to be left, as before, to volunteers. This was nothing new, but expectations had changed. The apparent 'opening up' to a wider range of popular interests in sport and popular music in this period created greater hope among citizens that 'more personalised and localised concerns ... should

[30] Wolle, *Die heile Welt*, p. 44.
[31] Richthofen, *Bringing Culture to the Masses*, pp. 101–2.
[32] Wilton, 'The "societalisation" of the state', pp. 110–12, 114–15.
[33] Braun, 'The people's sport?', 418.

and could be resolved'.[34] The regime became a hostage to ambitions that, in the field of mass sport, it often lacked the time and money to fulfil. Disappointment at broken promises almost inevitably followed. The number of sports-related petitions, as we saw in Chapter 8, appeared to increase in the 1970s, in SV Dynamo's case from 14 in 1968 to 118 in 1977.[35] A more entrenched grievance culture reflected growing impatience with the SED regime among citizens no longer sustained by the more optimistic, or at least less expectant, spirit of the reconstruction generation.

Football facilities, it is important to emphasise, were not always crumbling or oversubscribed. When the journalist Doug Gilbert visited a factory sports club near Leipzig in the mid 1970s, he noted the 'beautiful layout' of football pitches, in constant use by the club's largest section, which had ten teams (including a woman's XI) in operation.[36] Perhaps more typical was the situation at Empor Beelitz, where the pitch used for matches was 'good', the changing rooms with 'age-old brickwork' were basic, and one of the training pitches possessed a rudimentary set of floodlights ('like street lamps') that were 'poor-quality' but at least allowed the excitement of evening games.[37] Particularly in rural areas, where indoor pools, fitness rooms, and tennis courts were in short supply, the local football ground, whatever its shortcomings, was a well-trodden gathering point for recreational sport.[38] Football's cheapness, as well as the large number of volunteers available to coach or referee, ensured that it did not suffer the deprivations of less popular or more expensive pastimes.

By the early 1980s, the provision of specialist footwear was problematic in numerous sports. Hiking and ski boots, for example, as well as trainers for handball or basketball, were scarce. Even in a low-maintenance sport such as running, the demand for footwear could not be met – despite, or perhaps because of, the worldwide boom in jogging under way at this time and the SED's *Eile mit Meile* campaign, which attracted 2.3 million participants in 1980.[39] 'I hadn't gathered', one petitioner from

34 Wilton, 'Regime versus people?', p. 119.

35 SAPMO-BArch, DO 101/027/1–2, Analyse, 12 February 1969; Analyse der Eingaben im Jahr 1977, 7 June 1978.

36 Gilbert, *The Miracle Machine*, pp. 92–3.

37 Interview with Tim E. From the author's experience, facilities for recreational football in England in the 1980s were no better – and sometimes considerably worse – than this.

38 SAPMO-BArch, DC 4/716, Körperkultur und Sport, December 1987 (Tables 55 and 56); SAPMO-BArch, DC 4/729, Zum Einfluß ausgewählter sozialer und materiell-technischer Bedingungen auf die sportliche Tätigkeit Jugendlicher: Teilbericht Untersuchung "Jugend und Massensport 1987", March 1989 (Table 6).

39 Grix, 'The decline of mass sport provision', 410–15.

Brandenburg wrote in 1983, 'that the *Eile mit Meile* movement was in fact a jog through the city's shops!'[40]

Systemic equipment shortages were less acute for footballers. Nonetheless, demand tended to outstrip supply. Shortfalls in domestic production were often made up via expensive imports from West Germany, such as the Adidas 'Argentina' boot in 1973.[41] A similar solution was required in 1988, when there was a gap of 115,000 between what the state could offer and what customers wanted.[42] The technology to produce plastic-covered (and thus weather-resistant) balls, like the technology to produce a home-grown boot to rival Adidas, was not yet in place in East German factories, one 1984 report noted. 'Specialist' balls made by Adidas and Puma were thus to be imported from the West.[43] Even if footballers were better off than skiers, tennis players, or runners, the best-quality boots and balls, manufactured by West German companies, were readily available only to elite footballers. Like ordinary citizens seeking cars, the waiting times for which in 1988 were as long as seventeen years,[44] recreational players became familiar with deferred consumer satisfaction. Alternatively, they contented themselves with inferior domestic products or relied on relatives in the West. A West German aunt sent Tim E. the Uhlsport goalkeepers' gloves that finally allowed him to replace his uncomfortable, GDR-produced ones.[45]

The major area of concern for footballers was facilities rather than footwear. Complaints here echoed those that addressed fraying infrastructures in other sports, most notably swimming. By the mid 1980s, the situation at outdoor and especially indoor pools was catastrophic.[46] Heating and sanitary problems were common. Buildings were in advanced states of disrepair.[47] At functioning venues priority access was often accorded to performance athletes. When recreational Friday-night swims at Dynamo's swimming pool at the Sportforum facility in East Berlin were discontinued in 1979, the city's SED leader, Konrad Naumann, received an indignant

40 Braun, 'The people's sport?', 418.

41 SAPMO-BArch, DY 30/IV B 2/18/2, Information über den Stand der Versorgung der Bevölkerung mit Sportartikeln, 26 July 1973.

42 SAPMO-BArch, DY 30/IV 2/2.039/248, letter from Krenz to Günter Mittag, 17 May 1988, fo. 95–6; Bedarf des organisierten Sports an Sportschuhen 1988 sowie Preise und Stand des Vertragsabschlusses per 30.4.1988, n.d., fo. 97–8.

43 SAPMO-BArch, DY 30/4981, Information über Ergebnisse der Parteikontrolle zum Stand und zu den weiteren Schritten der Ablösung von NSW-Importen für Sportgeräte und Sportmaterialien, 2 April 1984, fo. 203–8.

44 Wolle, *Die heile Welt*, p. 218.

45 Interview with Tim E.

46 Braun, 'The people's sport?', 418.

47 SAPMO-BArch, DY 30/4981, Information zum Nutzungsstand der Berliner Schwimmhallen, 6 July 1987, fo. 30–3.

petition signed in the name of 'many friends of swimming'. There were not enough pools in Berlin, it argued, for Dynamo to shut out the public in this arbitrary manner.[48]

Football facilities were not in such dire straits as swimming pools. But infrastructural problems in the two areas were part of the same discussion, one in which citizens questioned the gap between communist rhetoric and reality, and highlighted the gulf that separated performance athletes – a sporting equivalent of the party 'bigwigs' (*Bonzen*) – from their recreational counterparts. In a telling example of the two-tier nature of GDR sport, Rotation Leipzig's ground, the Sportpark Nordost, which had been built by members over an eight-year period, was handed over to the DTSB in 1976, in a deal done behind their backs. In the three years before it was reopened as an elite sports centre, and the football section was forced to leave, the facility witnessed a civil war of sorts between the BSG leadership and Rotation's footballers, who were barred from the on-site pub and had their bikes vandalised.[49] Sponsoring factories, as at Lokomotive Weißenfels in the early 1960s, did not always behave much better, pursuing construction projects with little regard for the inconvenience that it might cause their football teams. In 1986 the football section leader at BSG Einheit Steremat in Berlin wrote to Rudi Hellmann to protest against VEB Steremat's decision to plough up the section's grass pitch in Treptow before a suitable replacement facility could be found, leaving its 9 teams and 140 members reliant on neighbouring clubs for a place to train and play.[50] The problems facing participants in mass sport were not new. It was their immutability, as much as their worsening, that drove football section leaders to their desks or typewriters.

## 'Left alone with our difficulties': three petitions on facilities

Three petitions sent to officials between 1978 and 1989 help to illuminate this examination of football facilities in the Honecker era. The first was written by the football section leadership at Dynamo Forst to Erich Mielke in August 1978; the second is a pair of letters dispatched by the football section leadership at BSG Tiefbau Berlin to Rudi Hellmann in November 1981 and October 1982; and the third is the aforementioned

[48] SAPMO-BArch, DO 101/027/3–4, petition from Werner M. to Konrad Naumann, 14 May 1979.

[49] Beyer, *Rotation Leipzig*, pp. 20–6.

[50] SAPMO-BArch, DY 30/4979, petition from the football section at BSG Einheit Steremat Berlin to Hellmann, 3 June 1986, fo. 6–7.

petition from the football section leadership at BSG Traktor Hochstedt to Erfurt county council in April 1989.

The three petitions raised similar issues. As we have seen, failure to build the long-promised clubhouse and changing rooms at Traktor Hochstedt obliged players to share a community hall 500 metres from the football ground with everyone from the fire brigade to the chess club – and on one occasion to change for a match in the coach's garage for want of any other available space.[51] Petitioners from Dynamo Forst complained that there was only one pitch for seven football teams at the club's ground. Changing facilities were limited, the heating system unreliable, and the access road in poor condition. The section lacked money for footballs, kit, and transport to away games.[52] The chief concern at BSG Tiefbau was the lack of electricity at the club's home ground in Gosen, a small community on the eastern outskirts of Berlin. As a result, players (including, it was emphasised, children) changed in a 'primitive' hut, washed with cold water, and held team talks by candlelight.[53]

The communications displayed a firm sense of entitlement to greater support from a regime that repeatedly expressed the importance of sport. The act of writing was presented as a final plea for help that had been too long coming. In the most extreme case, the 1981 petition from BSG Tiefbau Berlin claimed that the club had been trying to get an electricity supply for its ground since 1958.[54] Blame for delays and broken promises was widely dispersed: the leadership of SG Dynamo Forst and its parent organisation Dynamo Cottbus attracted criticism in the example of the Forst football section, whereas the state electricity suppliers, the sponsoring factory, and the local party leadership were blamed in Tiefbau Berlin's case.[55]

The duality of citizens' relationship to the state, professing loyalty and distance in almost the same breath, was reflected in the stylistic approach of the petitioners. Local pride was framed within a narrative of the football section's contribution to socialism. Functionaries at Traktor Hochstedt highlighted the success of its teams under trying conditions and requested help 'in the interests of [GDR] football in general and especially for football in Hochstedt'. Using a common rhetorical device, football

[51] ThHStAW, Bezirkstag und Rat des Bezirkes Erfurt Altregistratur Nr. 46939/1, petition from Traktor Hochstedt to Erfurt county council, fo. 322–4.

[52] SAPMO-BArch, DO 101/027/1–2, petition from the football section at SG Dynamo Forst to Erich Mielke, 7 August 1978.

[53] SAPMO-BArch, DY 30/4979, petition from the football section at BSG Tiefbau Berlin to Hellmann, 17 November 1981, fo. 46–9.

[54] *Ibid.*, fo. 47.

[55] *Ibid.*, 46–8; SAPMO-BArch, DO 101/027/1–2, petition from Dynamo Forst to Mielke.

leaders at Dynamo Forst – after emphasising their own contribution to SV Dynamo's development – implied that the SED regime was failing to uphold socialist ideals. Facilities there, they claimed, were 'no advertisement' for a Dynamo sports club, adding the politically loaded reminder that the team's home venue was formerly a 'workers' sports ground'.[56]

A sense of optimism giving way to disillusionment – a feature of the 'breakdown of communication' between grassroots cultural activists and the state in the late 1970s and 1980s[57] – was marked at BSG Tiefbau Berlin. In their first petition in November 1981, officials noted that, despite terrible conditions at the club's ground, 'enthusiasm for sport had previously won out. But today's young people have no more patience for that'.[58] A second petition in October 1982, prompted by the fact that nothing had changed in the intervening period, expressed a brusquer sense of anger and disappointment:

> We cannot and will not just accept that we are being left alone with our difficulties, in a stadium in which our sports club with its 160 members is threatened with dissolution for the reasons mentioned in our correspondence of 17 November 1981. Is nobody then interested in our continued existence? Can you in that case so hugely disappoint the sportspersons and functionaries who for years and decades have voluntarily given themselves to the development of sport?

The petitioners then drew attention to the 'crass contradiction' between what was offered to ordinary East Germans and what was offered to the elite: 'We might rightly rejoice in the great successes of our leading sportspersons. But doesn't mass sport, the work done in factory sports clubs and sections, play a decisive role in these successes that are the envy of so many countries throughout the world?'[59]

There was nothing GDR-specific about this gulf, or perceived gulf, which cuts across modern political systems. In fascist Italy, a dearth of local facilities and coaches seriously compromised the mass sporting ideal of 'many participants and few spectators', especially in the 1930s. By this time, the regime's lavish funding of 'high sports', an important source of prestige at home and abroad, contrasted starkly with its modest support for the recreational activities sponsored by the mass leisure organisation, the OND (*Opera Nazionale Dopolavoro*). James Riordan's

[56] ThHStAW, Bezirkstag und Rat des Bezirkes Erfurt Altregistratur Nr. 46939/1, petition from Traktor Hochstedt to Erfurt county council, fo. 323; SAPMO-BArch, DO 101/027/1–2, petition from Dynamo Forst to Mielke.

[57] Richthofen, *Bringing Culture to the Masses*, pp. 190–6.

[58] SAPMO-BArch, DY 30/4979, petition from Tiefbau Berlin to Hellmann, 17 November 1981, fo. 48.

[59] *Ibid.*, petition from the football section at BSG Tiefbau Berlin to Hellmann, 2 October 1982, fo. 44.

pioneering 1977 study of sport in the Soviet Union noted a similar trend, 'towards an administrative separation and funding of sport with the serious sportsman who shows talent being channelled at an early age into a privileged environment of qualified trainers, good facilities and intensive training, and the casual sportsman independently following his inclination in a more or less unsupervised way'.[60] In Britain during the same decade, Sports Council (i.e. government) funding was disproportionately directed towards elite sport. Recreational programmes, especially in poorer areas, were often under-resourced.[61]

Nor was the gulf confined to football. The feelings of Tiefbau officials were shared by disgruntled GDR citizens in other sports, such as the aspiring marathon runner from Rathenow who found that training shoes were available only to elite athletes and the recreational swimmers in Dresden who were barred from a local pool because they apparently made it too dirty for the high-performance swimmers there.[62] A parallel can, finally, be drawn between growing resentment of SED elitism in the provision and maintenance of facilities and the populist strand that underpinned supporters' anger about the declining fortunes of BSG football teams such as Chemie Leipzig and Sachsenring Zwickau during the same period. Both suggest that citizens sometimes internalised, or at least knew how to use, the egalitarian ideals of socialism better than did the socialist regime itself. The end result, though, was disengagement, a turning inwards to resolve problems that the SED could not or would not resolve, thereby satisfying or at least keeping alive local sporting needs.[63] Failing facilities pointed to the larger failings of the socialist project. It is difficult not to see something of significance in the incredulous comments about primitive sporting conditions from the petitioners at Tiefbau Berlin ('and this in the year 1981!') and Traktor Hochstedt ('that is not right after 40 years of the GDR').[64]

The responses of the authorities to the petitions confirmed that scepticism about party promises was not misplaced. They also shed light on the often dysfunctional character of communist rule. Bureaucratic inertia

[60] Victoria de Grazia, *The Culture of Consent: Mass Organization of Leisure in Fascist Italy* (Cambridge: Cambridge University Press, 1981), pp. 170–9; James Riordan, *Sport in Soviet Society: Development of Sport and Physical Education in Russia and the USSR* (Cambridge: Cambridge University Press, 1977), p. 231.

[61] Hargreaves, *Sport, Power and Culture*, pp. 195–7.

[62] Grix, 'The decline of mass sport provision', 412–13; Wilton, 'Regime versus people?', p. 174.

[63] Wilton, 'The "societalisation" of the state', p. 122.

[64] SAPMO-BArch, DY 30/4979, petition from Tiefbau Berlin to Hellmann, 17 November 1981, fo. 47; ThHStAW, Bezirkstag und Rat des Bezirkes Erfurt Altregistratur Nr. 46939/1, petition from Traktor Hochstedt to Erfurt county council, fo. 323.

was a common feature of the petition process, as the state recognised in handbooks written in the 1970s that criticised 'heartless' bureaucrats for poorly serving the needs of citizens.[65] It was particularly hard for Tiefbau Berlin to overcome, as the club's second petition from October 1982 related. Despite protracted discussions involving the county DTSB and SED leaderships, officials at the club's sponsoring factory, and the putative energy suppliers, negotiations to ensure an electricity supply to the ground in Gosen had still not been concluded eleven months after the BSG's initial petition.[66] It was a similar story of delays and buck-passing at Traktor Hochstedt. The Erfurt county council emphasised in June 1989 the need for the 'strongest principles of thrift' in any clubhouse construction proposals, essentially re-directing the BSG's request for help to the village and district authorities that had provided so little support during the previous decade[67] – a hugely frustrating process that was commonly replicated in citizens' attempts to seek redress of the most contentious of all petition issues, the housing situation.[68]

The responses highlighted the financial constraints that governed mass sport during the last decade of the Honecker era. The best that officials in Erfurt could offer Traktor Hochstedt was possible inclusion in the county's 1990 financial plan. But any clubhouse project, it was emphasised, would have to be subsidised with manual labour on the part of BSG members.[69] Not much had changed since the early 1950s in this regard, when functionaries in Leipzig, Plauen, and elsewhere promoted mass voluntary work actions on sports stadia to save money.[70] Low-cost sport in East Germany was predicated on this ingrained volunteer ethos. As Doug Gilbert noted in the mid 1970s, 'GDR mass sports clubs have a very good record of taking care of themselves'.[71] This kept Tiefbau Berlin's football section going, despite the intermittent electricity supply. It allowed Traktor Hochstedt's youth team to stand undefeated at the top

[65] Betts, *Within Walls*, p. 179.

[66] SAPMO-BArch, DY 30/4979, petition from Tiefbau Berlin to Hellmann, 2 October 1982, fo. 44–5; Aktennotiz über eine Aussprache zur Klärung einer Eingabe der Sektion Fußball der BSG Tiefbau vom 2.10.1982, fo. 51.

[67] ThHStAW, Bezirkstag und Rat des Bezirkes Erfurt Altregistratur Nr. 46939/1, letter from Erfurt county council's office for youth and sport to the football section at BSG Traktor Hochstedt, 7 June 1989, fo. 325–6.

[68] See e.g. Allinson, '1977: The GDR's most normal year?, pp. 261–5; Port, *Conflict and Stability*, pp. 262–9.

[69] ThHStAW, Bezirkstag und Rat des Bezirkes Erfurt Altregistratur Nr. 46939/1, letter from Erfurt county council to Traktor Hochstedt, fo. 326.

[70] Johnson, *Training Socialist Citizens*, pp. 109–10.

[71] Gilbert, *The Miracle Machine*, p. 94.

of the district league table in the 1988/9 season. It prevented the heating system at Dynamo Forst's ground from freezing during the winter of 1977/8.[72]

In all three cases, functionaries responsible for mass sport were largely left to their own devices until such time as they felt compelled to call on the state for help. Even at Dynamo Forst, part of a sports organisation that was run on tighter lines than ordinary BSGs, micro-management was not the order of the day – as suggested by the lack of urgency in permanently filling the position of club groundsman and the unwillingness to support an upgrade to the access road that was being churned up by farm vehicles ('we can have no influence on changing this state of affairs').[73] The SED's hands-off approach to mass sport was particularly feasible in football, a cheap sport that could count on a large volunteer body of referees, coaches, and administrators.

This approach worked as long as basic levels of state support for recreational sport, or at least perceptions of such support, were maintained. During the 1980s, though, the unspoken social contract between citizens and regime broke down, less because facilities were worse than in the 1950s (they were generally better) than because football section leaders – and their peers in swimming, running, and tennis sections – were less willing to accept sub-par conditions, especially given the resources that were being pumped into the GDR's Olympic programme. The state's commitment to mass sport now came back to haunt it, creating, or at least fuelling, a sense of resentment among the people whom it short-changed. In their second petition to Rudi Hellmann in late 1982, football leaders at Tiefbau Berlin remarked bitterly that 'we seem to lack all credibility in the eyes of our sportsmen, as we cannot give them concrete information about when or even whether we are going to get a supply of electricity'. If all areas of society, they concluded, were run in 'such a complicated and irresponsible' manner, 'where would we be then!'[74] The petitioners were closer to the truth than they knew. The SED's grip on the tiller was less secure and all-encompassing than it seemed. The regime's inability to either effect or control change, in mass sport as in other areas from housing to travel, was dramatically exposed in the autumn of 1989.

[72] ThHStAW, Bezirkstag und Rat des Bezirkes Erfurt Altregistratur Nr. 46939/1, petition from Traktor Hochstedt to Erfurt county council, fo. 322; SAPMO-BArch, DO 101/027/1–2, petition from Dynamo Forst to Mielke.

[73] SAPMO-BArch, DO 101/027/1–2, Stellungnahme zur Eingabe der Sektion Fußball, 29 August 1978.

[74] SAPMO-BArch, DY 30/4979, petition from Tiefbau Berlin to Hellmann, 2 October 1982, fo. 45.

## The people's state and the people's game

In December 1989 *Neues Forum* ('New Forum'), one of the political organisations that emerged as the SED dictatorship began to collapse, noted that 'sport in the GDR – an enormous feather in the cap of both the Party and the government – is not rooted in the people'.[75] For a regime that portrayed mass sport as a key component in forging a healthy society, this was a damning indictment. In reality, as we have seen throughout Part III, the central organs of state power had limited influence on, and interest in, everyday sporting activities. In the case of football – whether it was the development of the women's game or the upkeep of decrepit facilities – the legwork was invariably undertaken by lower-level functionaries. These people were part of the state structure, yet not necessarily, or not only, regime loyalists. An unintended consequence of the SED's desire for a comprehensively ruled society was to open up the bloated state apparatus to elements whose support for socialism was conditional. The condition, in the case of mass sport, was that the voluntarist culture that kept football and other sections thriving would be supplemented when necessary with state funding for essential items such as buildings and equipment. By the 1980s, the SED could not keep up its end of the bargain, as the GDR's planned economy – hobbled by a plummeting currency, ubiquitous shortages, corruption, bottlenecks, and low worker morale – went into steep decline.[76] There was not enough money to maintain existing sports structures, let alone build new ones.[77] This had been true of the 1950s too. The big shift in the intervening thirty years was a growing impatience with restrictions and deficiencies that, if SED propaganda were to be believed, should have long since been eradicated.

The GDR's history was not static. Nor were the responses of its citizens to problems that they negotiated in their everyday lives. The sporting self-help strategies developed during the first decade of socialist reconstruction survived into the final decade of the GDR's existence, but in a manner that reflected growing popular detachment from socialist goals and an increased personalisation of interests that was also noticeable among *Oberliga* stars, fan-club members, and Union *Fan-Liga* players. Numerous BSGs turned away from traditional, communist-approved offerings in the 1980s and embraced instead politically suspect 'trend sports' such as karate, aerobics, skateboarding, and windsurfing[78] – a change also

[75] Braun, 'The people's sport?', 414. [76] See e.g. Zatlin, *The Currency of Socialism*, ch. 4.
[77] Grix, 'The decline of mass sport provision', 414.
[78] Braun, 'The people's sport?', 420–3; Wilton, 'The "societalisation" of the state', pp. 122–5.

apparent in the Soviet Union, where the authorities criticised bodybuilding for promoting 'a dandified culture of the body' and yoga and karate for encouraging 'individualism and mysticism'.[79]

Football remained immovably popular. Rather than giving up in despair, section leaders in Hochstedt, Gosen, and elsewhere made the best of the situation, meeting local needs and working around the climate of political stagnation and economic disrepair. In much the same way in fascist Italy, the OND, especially in smaller towns, 'simply adapted [its] activities to the lack of sports facilities'.[80] The SED regime relied on grassroots activism to reach the parts that it could not, or did not want to, reach. When activists became disillusioned in the 1980s – unhappier about filling shortfalls in the command economy through self-help campaigns – they fed a process of disintegration that suddenly and unexpectedly came to light during the *Wende*.[81]

Football, like the Church and popular music, occupied a liminal space between the public and the private, where ways of being were not determined solely, or even primarily, by the dictates of the state. Whereas fans and elite players were often subject to extensive state surveillance, lower-level footballers, with rare exceptions, led a less encumbered existence. For them football was a social bond, a fun form of exercise and competition, and a source of local pride. Even when facilities were far from ideal, the game survived. BSG Berliner Werkzeugmaschinenfabrik (machine-tools factory) Marzahn, today FC Nordost Berlin, kept a football section going, despite losing its home ground to the construction of new concrete-block (*Plattenbau*) flats in Marzahn during the early 1980s. Rotation Leipzig's football section, as we have seen, endured an acrimonious eviction from its home ground in 1979. Despite the departure of the equivalent of two teams' worth of players, it remained a strong presence on the local football scene.[82] In defending and following individual and local interests through a combination of engagement with and detachment from communist power, footballers safeguarded a sporting *Eigen-Sinn* that, in many cases, outlasted the country in which they lived and played.

79 Riordan, *Sport in Soviet Society*, p. 201.
80 De Grazia, *The Culture of Consent*, p. 178.
81 Wilton, 'The "societalisation" of the state', p. 128.
82 www.fc-nordost-berlin-web.de (Chronik); Beyer, *Rotation Leipzig*, pp. 26–8, 121–44.

# 15 Conclusion

## Drowning, not waving

In Rome on 8 July 1990, West Germany defeated Argentina 1–0 to win the World Cup for the third time. The winning goal, a contentious penalty converted by Andreas Brehme with five minutes left to play, was a fitting end to a tournament marked by cynical, defensive football. That mattered little in Germany. The victory captured the optimistic *Zeitgeist*. With reunification three months away, and supported by the majority of GDR citizens, Brehme's goal triggered celebrations in the East as well as the West. In Wolfgang Becker's 2003 film *Goodbye Lenin*, where the plot revolves around a son's attempt to prevent his convalescing socialist mother from discovering that the GDR had collapsed while she was in a coma, *Ossis* and *Wessis* watch the game side by side. After the final whistle, there are fireworks. Cars bedecked in the national flag honk joyously through the streets of Berlin.

In the still real existing GDR, West Germany's triumph engendered more complex responses. Police in *Bezirk* Frankfurt/Oder reported disturbances of public order in many towns on the night of 8 July. Celebrations, as in Becker's film, were mostly good-natured. But there were exceptions. In the town of Frankfurt/Oder, a crowd of 500 or 600 people marched through the city centre. They threw stones at the police and chanted 'Germany for the Germans', 'foreigners out', and 'communist pigs out'. At the border crossing with Poland, a smaller group chanted 'Poles go home' and 'this is Germany'. Twenty-seven people were arrested. In Schwedt, post-match celebrants headed towards the homes of Polish and Vietnamese workers. They chanted 'foreigners out' and 'Germany for the Germans'. Windows were smashed and vehicles damaged.[1]

[1] BLHA, Rep. 601 Nr. 26443, letter from Schettler (head of the DVP in Frankfurt/Oder) to Kunze, 12 July 1990.

Football violence in East Germany was nothing new. But the collapse of the SED dictatorship gave freer rein to the anti-foreigner, anti-communist, and anti-police sentiments that characterised the 'hard core' (*harter Kern*) of the fan scene. It created, in the words of one Dynamo Dresden fan, a 'lawless space' in which hooliganism thrived.[2] In consequence, as one former DFV functionary remarked, things got 'a bit nasty'.[3] In March 1991 Dynamo's European Cup quarter-final match at home to Red Star Belgrade was abandoned after seventy-eight minutes due to crowd unrest. The club was banned from European competition for two years. 'This way,' said coach Reinhard Häfner after the game, 'football is systematically killed'.[4] Death was not just a figurative term. Ahead of an *Oberliga* match between Sachsen (formerly Chemie) Leipzig and FC Berlin (formerly BFC) in Leipzig on 3 November 1990, an eighteen-year-old BFC fan, Mike Polley, was shot dead by police during clashes with visiting hooligans. Five others suffered serious injuries.[5] A planned 'festival of German football', featuring a match between East and West Germany in Leipzig on 21 November, was called off by the Saxon government out of fear of further unrest.[6]

In 1989 and 1990, a dam broke over GDR football. In its wake, violent troublemakers were often the last men standing. Simon Kuper attended a BFC game shortly after reunification. He remarked that so many of the crowd of 1,000 were hooligans that 'it was possible to speak of a lunatic majority'.[7] The recollections of one Rot–Weiß Erfurt fan powerfully encapsulate the despairing, almost nihilistic mood of the time: '1991 was anarchy in Germany. We didn't give a shit about politics. At first we still chased after police and rival fans. Later it was mostly about clearing out shops to get cheap electronics and brand-name gear'.[8]

Attendance figures reflected the new realities. The ugly atmosphere at many grounds, rising ticket prices, mass unemployment, and an understandable focus on things more important than the game all contributed to a precipitous decline. Average attendance in the 1990/1 season was 4,807, by far the lowest figure in *Oberliga* history.[9] As GDR football said farewell, it appeared to be drowning rather than waving.

[2] Interview with Jens Genschmar. [3] Interview with Holger Fuchs.
[4] Genschmar, *Mit Dynamo*, p. 179.
[5] Luther and Willmann, *BFC*, pp. 210–17; Fuge, *Leutzscher Legende*, pp. 152–4.
[6] Michael Barsuhn, 'Die Wende und Vereinigung im Fußball 1989/90', in Braun and Teichler (eds.), *Sportstadt Berlin*, pp. 407–11.
[7] Kuper, *Football against the Enemy*, p. 18. [8] Willmann, 'Wie alles anfing', p. 112.
[9] Horn and Weise, *Das große Lexikon*, p. 420.

### Transfers of power

The tenth round of matches in the penultimate *Oberliga* season took place on the night of Wednesday 8 November 1989. BFC's 0–0 draw at home to newly promoted BSG Stahl Eisenhüttenstadt was the latest indicator that its aura of invincibility had long disappeared. Dynamo Dresden strengthened its title defence with a 3–1 win over FC Magdeburg. Emerging frontrunner FC Karl-Marx-Stadt recorded a 1–0 win over the top flight's longest residents, struggling BSG Wismut Aue. The best game of the night was Hansa Rostock's 3–3 draw at home to Lok Leipzig.[10]

These unremarkable contests took place against a backdrop of revolutionary change. The following day, flustered communist officials in East Berlin – faced with mass protests, an uncertain party leadership, and the momentum of events elsewhere in the Soviet bloc – announced that the government was opening the Berlin Wall. By nightfall thousands of GDR citizens were gleefully and disbelievingly making their way into West Berlin. Interim leader Egon Krenz scrambled for position, using an unconvincing metaphor to remind Moscow of its security responsibilities: 'You know, in a game of football, when a free kick is awarded, a wall is formed in front of the goal. Free kicks are the results of fouls by the other team. Let us make sure together of fair play'.[11] But Moscow was no longer listening. The collapse of SED rule was under way.

East German football was never the same again. Almost overnight the *Oberliga* became a chore to be tolerated rather than the focal point of players' attention. Heads were turned by the changes at home and by the chance to play in the *Bundesliga*. In its first match after the fall of the Wall, a vital World Cup qualifier in Vienna against Austria on 15 November, the GDR meekly lost 3–0. As coach Eduard Geyer noted, 'the players were completely distracted, making telephone calls like crazy and in fact only worried about [finding] other clubs'.[12] The insular system in which players and coaches had lived for forty years had disappeared. East German football, like East German industry, was ill-equipped for a swift transition to the free-market economy.

Nowhere was this more evident than in the transfer market. In December 1989, Andreas Thom became the first *Oberliga* player to officially move from East to West, joining Bayer Leverkusen from BFC for 2.8 million Marks.[13] Leverkusen's general manager Rainer Calmund,

[10] www.rsssf.com/tablesd/ddr90.html. [11] Major, *Behind the Wall*, p. 254.
[12] Horn and Weise, *Das große Lexikon*, p. 125.
[13] Archivgut des DFV, I/2, Transfervereinbarung (Andreas Thom), 12 December 1989.

a prime mover in mining the East for talent during the *Wende*, allegedly arranged to repay part of the fee in kind, by delivering 300 motorbikes to BFC headquarters in Hohenschönhausen.[14] Whether or not inexperienced BFC negotiators allowed the club's star player to be bartered for cash plus Japanese motorbikes, most of the transfer fee disappeared into a black hole[15] This pattern repeated itself to ruinous cost at many East German clubs over the next few years, as agents, officials, and undeclared parties all took their slice of the pie.

Thom's transfer was part of an exodus of GDR athletes to the West that included almost the entire national cycling team, sixty amateur boxers, and the men's national handball squad.[16] At the end of the 1989/90 season, three more BFC players left for the *Bundesliga*, including the highly rated Thomas Doll. Dynamo Dresden's championship-winning squad was decimated by the departures of striker Ulf Kirsten (who joined Thom at Leverkusen), Matthias Sammer, who was sold to VfB Stuttgart, and three other first-team regulars who went to Fortuna Cologne.[17] *Bundesliga* clubs scoured highly regarded academies at clubs such as BFC, Dynamo Dresden, and Lok Leipzig for talented young players.[18] The end result was the selling off – or, as Günter Schneider put it, the 'sell-out' – of GDR football.[19]

Given the *Bundesliga*'s appeal and the political and economic situation at home, heavy losses were probably unavoidable. But the DFB did little to help matters. It provided minimal start-up help to clubs in the difficult transition from communism to capitalism. 'The arrogant DFB grandpas', Frank Willmann argued, let animosity towards the DFV get in the way of their self-proclaimed solidarity with football in the East.[20] Even Hanns Leske, a critical observer of GDR football, suggested that an 'annexation mentality' characterised the West German takeover.[21] Functionaries in the East, brought up in a closed system of political patronage and industrial protection, knew nothing of commercial sponsorship or transfer systems. This left the field open to the incompetent and the unscrupulous.

A sense of the changes in GDR football can be gained by examining club names. In the 1940s and 1950s, they were usually altered on

14 Alex Raack, 'Was hat euch bloss so ruiniert? 20 Jahre nach dem Fall der Mauer, das Schicksal des Ostfussballs', 3 *Ecken Ein Elfer* 6 (May 2009), 16.
15 Luther and Willmann, *BFC*, p. 201.
16 Braun, 'Sport frei!', pp. 354–6.
17 Baingo and Horn, *Die Geschichte der DDR-Oberliga*, p. 259.
18 Leske, 'Der Fußball-Osten'.
19 Archivgut des DFV I/2, 'Dokumentation über 45 Jahre Fußball'.
20 Willmann, 'Wie alles anfing', p. 102.
21 Raack, 'Was hat euch bloss so ruiniert?', 19, 21.

political orders. During the *Wende*, agency was reversed, as clubs began a process of identity reclamation from the dying communist state. In 1990, eight of the fourteen *Oberliga* teams changed names. FC Karl-Marx-Stadt became Chemnitzer FC, after the city was renamed in June.[22] Shorn of its notorious sponsor, BFC adopted the name FC Berlin in February – a vain attempt to distance the club from the *Stasi* that was unpopular among many fans and abandoned in 1999.[23] A similar process was under way in the second division. In *Staffel B* (Division B) of the *Liga* in 1990, all eighteen competitors changed names, sometimes more than once.[24]

Despite the chaotic circumstances, the 1989/90 season was played to an exciting conclusion. Late goals in its final game against Lok Leipzig gave Dynamo Dresden the win that narrowly secured an eighth championship, ahead of FC Magdeburg and FC Karl-Marx-Stadt. The team claimed the double for the third time by defeating minnows PSV Schwerin 2–1 in the cup final. The match, played at Berlin's Jahn Sportpark, was watched by just 5,750 people.[25] Domestic football was becoming irrelevant, as the shadow of the *Bundesliga* loomed ever larger.

The DFV declared defiantly in May 1990 that negotiations with West German officials 'are not about how GDR football integrates itself into the DFB, but about newly organising football in the whole of Germany'.[26] Like the GDR itself, the East German FA was swimming against the tide in advocating a partnership of equals. With the SED's collapse, any notion of a level playing field had been pulled from under the feet of organised sport. Faced with the withdrawal of state funding, the DFV reformed in an attempt to survive. Full-time staff numbers were reduced from sixty-seven to ten. In elections on 31 March 1990, delegates overwhelmingly chose outsider Hans-Georg Moldenhauer as the new president, ahead of the experienced Günter Schneider.[27]

Power in East German football, though, bypassed the DFV in the historical moment and headed straight for the DFB, just as political power would bypass the Party of Democratic Socialism (PDS) – as the SED renamed itself in December 1989 – and be delivered up to the West German Christian Democratic Union (CDU), leaving the PDS and other East German parties watching from the sidelines. By 1990, the East German FA was in too weak a position to dictate terms.

[22] www.rsssf.com/tablesd/ddr90.html. [23] Luther and Willmann, *BFC*, pp. 202, 240–4.
[24] www.rsssf.com/tablesd/ddr90.html.
[25] Baingo and Horn, *Die Geschichte der DDR-Oberliga*, pp. 255–8, 260.
[26] Archivgut des DFV (no *Signatur*), Konzeption des DFV, 7 May 1990.
[27] Barsuhn, 'Die Wende und Vereinigung', pp. 391–8.

Recommendations from a first meeting with the DFB in January, such as a list of un-transferable GDR players and full recognition of GDR coaching qualifications, were not adopted. Requests ahead of the subsequent meeting in May, including the provision of a joint fund to develop the game in the East, cut equally little ice.[28]

In a move emblematic of the fate of the GDR, the DFV, faced with its own powerlessness, dissolved itself at a meeting in Leipzig on 20 November 1990. The following day, it joined the DFB as a regional organisation, the North-East German FA (*Nord-Ostdeutscher Fußball-Verband*, NOFV). All GDR teams were withdrawn from international competition, thereby solving the problem briefly raised by the two German sides being drawn in the same group for qualifying matches for the 1992 European Championship. The GDR's 293rd and final fixture, a 2–0 win against Belgium in Brussels, had taken place in September. Matthias Sammer scored both goals. Three months later, in his new home town of Stuttgart, Sammer became the first East German to play for unified Germany. In the same game against Switzerland, erstwhile BFC hero Andreas Thom came off the bench to become the first East German to score a goal in German national colours.[29]

Unification was sealed with a photograph of Moldenhauer and DFB president Hermann Neuberger shaking hands across a car emblazoned with the logos of the two former rival organisations. Against the DFV's wishes, GDR football had been integrated into the DFB, almost entirely on the latter's terms. The process made it hard to support the claim that West German sports officials 'did not want to act the big shot' in 1990.[30] The DFB's attitude, though, was not simply a matter of kicking *Ostfußball* when it was down. West Germany was a larger and wealthier area, with more successful football traditions, than the GDR. From the outset, the balance of power in post-*Wende* football, as in politics and the economy, made inevitable (if not necessarily admirable) a mindset that quickly discarded East German organisations, practices, and personnel.

## Liminal moments: the final *Oberliga* season

During the heady days of the *Wende* – as political and economic structures collapsed and were born, as doors opened and closed for GDR citizens – anything seemed possible. The final *Oberliga* season in 1990/1

[28] Archivgut des DFV, I/2, Verhandlungen DFV der DDR/DFB am 10./11.1.1990, 12 January 1990; Archivgut des DFV (no *Signatur*), Konzeption des DFV, 7 May 1990.

[29] Horn and Weise, *Das große Lexikon*, pp. 65, 293–4, 341.

[30] Braun, '"Very nice, the enemies are gone!"', 178.

reflected the excitement and uncertainties of this 'liminal period'.[31] It began in the GDR and ended in reunited Germany. For the fourteen teams involved, it was an existential struggle. According to the 'two plus six' formula agreed between the DFB and the DFV, only the champions and runners-up would qualify for the *Bundesliga* the following season. The next six teams would join the *2. Bundesliga*. Everyone else would face the financial anxieties of amateur football. There was consequently a desperate quality, or lack of quality, to the football that year. The goal quota per game (2.52) was the third lowest in *Oberliga* history. As fans fought on the thinly populated terraces, the players fought on the pitch. There were 29 red cards and 544 yellow cards during the season. In more ways than one, the last days of GDR football 'border[ed] on anarchy'.[32]

Reminders of the changed landscape were everywhere. Teams wore shirts bearing sponsors' names. With restrictions on signing foreigners lifted, clubs quickly followed in the footsteps of *Liga* side Union Berlin, who – with the debut of Polish striker Jacek Menzel in March 1990 – became the first East German team to field a non-German player.[33] Hungarian national team goalkeeper Péter Disztl joined Rot–Weiß Erfurt. American defender Paul Caligiuri moved to Hansa Rostock.[34]

Western know-how was seen to offer the best means of joining the West German elite. This did not always work out, as the short and ill-fated tenure of Jimmy Hartwig as Sachsen Leipzig coach illustrated. Hartwig's inexperience of GDR football worked against him. He received a touchline ban for calling the referee 'a little swine' after Sachsen played Carl Zeiss Jena in October 1990, the only match in *Oberliga* history to be abandoned due to crowd trouble. He had little patience for, or understanding of, the backstairs intrigues swirling around the club. Despite sacking Hartwig less than halfway through the season, Sachsen ended it outside the top eight – and thus entered the ranks of amateur football.[35]

Hartwig was the second West German to coach an *Oberliga* side. The first enjoyed far greater success. In June 1990 Hansa Rostock appointed Uwe Reinders as first-team coach. A member of West Germany's 1982 World Cup squad, Reinders had most recently worked at Eintracht Braunschweig. His arrival in Rostock was primarily the work

31 Palmowski, *Inventing a Socialist Nation*, p. 295.
32 Baingo and Horn, *Die Geschichte der DDR-Oberliga*, pp. 261–4.
33 Luther and Willmann, *Eisern Union!*, p. 168.
34 Baingo and Horn, *Die Geschichte der DDR-Oberliga*, p. 262; Tim Jürgens and Alex Raack, 'Triumph des Vorkuhilas', *11 Freunde* 114 (May 2011), 64.
35 Baingo and Horn, *Die Geschichte der DDR-Oberliga*, pp. 262–3; Fuge, *Leutzscher Legende*, pp. 150–5.

of Hansa chairman Robert Pischke, an SED functionary who understood better than some of his peers the opportunities opened up for smaller clubs by the collapse of communist rule. While West German scouts cherry-picked the best players from BFC and Dynamo Dresden, Hansa's squad remained intact – and was then strengthened by the arrival of Caligiuri from SV Meppen. Reinders knew as little about East German football as Hartwig. Ignorance, though, was bliss in Rostock's undemanding environment. Hansa began the season on a twelve-match unbeaten run and never looked back, clinching the club's first *Oberliga* title with three games to spare. Reinders' team then completed the double, defeating Eisenhüttenstadt 1–0 to claim the last ever East German cup final in June 1991.[36] The unprecedented success secured a place in the *Bundesliga*, and the European Cup, for the following season.

On the day of Hansa's final league game against Lok Leipzig, a motorcade containing eight cars and one motorbike made its way through the streets of Rostock to the stadium. A time-honoured tradition of triumphant teams, such parades usually denote a public celebration, with fans lining the streets to honour their heroes. In Hansa's case, the only witness was an irate policeman. Neither Reinders nor the media knew what the players had organised. Most tellingly, no fans knew (or cared) either. The greatest season in Hansa's history was played in front of an indifferent public. Average home attendance was 10,031 – above the *Oberliga* average, but hardly commensurate with the team's sudden success and half the size that it had been just two seasons earlier.[37] Hooliganism was less of a problem than rising ticket prices. Before the *Wende* supporters could watch Hansa play for 60 *Ost-Pfennig*. In the new era of free-market football, and against a backdrop of widespread unemployment, the entry price had risen steeply to 6 DM.[38] Success, like failure, met with popular apathy.

Nowhere was the apathy more pronounced than at FC Berlin, as BFC had been renamed in 1990. The team finished the final *Oberliga* season in eleventh place, failing to qualify for the *2. Bundesliga*. Average home attendance that year was just 781.[39] In Andreas Gläser's words, FC Berlin was of chief interest to those 'who sought out a club on the basis of its riot potential'. Gläser watched Hertha Berlin in the *Bundesliga*

[36] On Hansa's 1990/1 season, see Hesselmann and Rosentritt, *Hansa Rostock*, pp. 96–106; Jürgens and Raack, 'Triumph des Vorkuhilas', 60–5.
[37] www.european-football-statistics.co.uk/attn/archive/avezddr80.htm.
[38] Jürgens and Raack, 'Triumph des Vorkuhilas', 65.
[39] Luther and Willmann, *BFC*, p. 218.

instead. The entertainment was better at the cavernous Olympic Stadium, even if the atmosphere was not.[40] FC Berlin began the 1991/2 season in the third tier of German football. The season opener against Post Neubrandenburg drew a crowd of seventy-six hardy souls. Though the team won the division, media headlines focused all too predictably on hooliganism. After unrest involving FC Berlin supporters outside an asylum seekers' shelter in Greifswald, SV Hafen Rostock postponed its match with the league leaders.[41] Notoriety accorded the club a pariah status that would have been unthinkable in the Honecker era, when BFC was hated but never ignored. FC Berlin's fate combined key elements in the closing chapters of the story of GDR football: managerial inexperience and financial negligence; a player exodus to the West; a surge in spectator violence and related collapse in attendance figures; and the harsh reality of life at a humbler station in the football pyramid. By the mid 1990s, even the last string to the club's bow – its reputation for developing young talent – had been stretched to breaking point. Money for such long-term investment was no longer available.[42] It is hard to imagine a more potent symbol of the decline of the game in the East after 1989.

## Football's grassroots revolution?

Literature on the *Wende* years has focused on hooligan unrest, the DFB takeover, and the struggles of *Oberliga* clubs. Less attention has been paid to the grassroots. With funding and infrastructure no longer guaranteed by the state, clubs were weakened across the board. In a time of flux, sport lost some of its meaning. People had new freedoms (to travel or to purchase goods), but also new worries, most notably the spectre of unemployment. 'Who in 1990', asked Holger Fuchs, 'wanted to be a member of a football club?'[43] The case of BSG Rotation Leipzig was typical. During the 1989/90 season, at least six first-team players moved to West Germany for family or economic reasons. Departures throughout the club meant that Rotation withdrew four teams from competition.[44] In this period, as the fictional coach of BSG Tatkraft Börde recalls in *Leben bis Männer*, 'I could be happy if I got eleven men on the pitch on a Sunday afternoon'.[45]

Financial difficulties overshadowed the transition from socialism to democracy. Factories closed down. Universities were restructured,

[40] Gläser, *Der BFC war schuld*, pp. 103–4. [41] Luther and Willmann, *BFC*, pp. 221–2.
[42] *Ibid.*, 224. [43] Interview with Holger Fuchs.
[44] Beyer, *Rotation Leipzig*, pp. 145–6. [45] Brussig, *Leben bis Männer*, p. 48.

leaving much of the intelligentsia out of work. East German divorce rates doubled between 1991 and 1996.[46] Football felt these stresses. The 1990/1 *Junge Welt* Cup, a nationwide competition for youth teams, was hampered by the withdrawal of teams such as PSV 90 Pasewalk who could not afford the travel, kit, and other expenses. Preparations for the 1990 football *Spartakiad* were curtailed for similar reasons, with teams in smaller communities able to train only once a week.[47]

Savage cuts to recreational budgets came as a shock to the coaches who, as we saw in Part III, did more than the party leadership to maintain the SED's mass sport programme. Cuts meant lost jobs, in football as elsewhere. Rot–Weiß Erfurt, for example, had eleven youth teams in the summer of 1990, but only three coaches on the payroll; the other nine had been let go for financial reasons.[48] In the 1970s and 1980s, petitions were directed by frustrated DTSB members against inadequacies in the communist state's provision of facilities and equipment. In 1990 the same device was deployed by the same people in protest against the cost-cutting measures of the post-communist government. The rapid dismantling of the DTSB – stripped of all state financial support in May and dissolved in December – left many full-time functionaries facing unemployment. There was uncertainty and anger about what would happen in the new era of what the DSB called 'autonomous sport'.[49] A fifty-three-year-old sports teacher from Forst, active in local sport for twenty-three years (including stints as chairman and deputy chairman of the district football committee), protested against the 'complete lack of democracy and collective decision-making' that suddenly ended his career. H. appended to his letter a clipping from the local newspaper, asking 'what's going to happen to our football?'[50]

As was the case under the SED regime, local agency was defended against government intrusions and government neglect when the CDU-led coalition came to power in March 1990. But the rules had changed. Petitions, an integral part of the dialogue between citizen and state in the GDR, were obsolete. In response to a letter from HFC coaches, the

46 Betts, *Within Walls*, p. 236.

47 Archivgut des DFV, X/10, letter of withdrawal from PSV Pasewalk 90, August; Auswertung der 22. DFV-Spartakiade für Knaben-Bezirksauswahlmannschaften (1.8.1977) vom 12.–19.05.1990 in Parchim, June 1990.

48 ThHStAW, Bezirkstag und Rat des Bezirkes Erfurt Altregistratur Nr. 46939/3, Vorlage für die Entwicklung der Nachwuchsabteilung, n.d., fo. 214.

49 Braun, 'Sport frei!', pp. 365–7.

50 SAPMO-BArch, DY 12/4080, petition from Gerhard H. to Martin Killian, 20 April 1990, fo. 33–4.

Figure 19. A boy kicks a football against a typically ramshackle and graffiti-covered building in the East Berlin district of Prenzlauer Berg, 1990. Amid the political and economic turmoil of the *Wende*, football remained an important part of East German popular culture.

Ministry of Youth and Sport advised that, 'based on our new democratic relations', the club's dismissal of staff was an in-house matter. It was not the Ministry's place to intervene in the working methods of individual associations or clubs.[51] This was the polar opposite of long-standing SED policy, which had been in place until just a few months earlier. It is small wonder that many DTSB activists felt cut adrift in the new world that they confronted. The long-term impact was significant. In 2004, participation rates in sport in the West fluctuated between 32% and 40%. In the East, they were much lower: 14.5% in Thuringia, for example, and just 10.5% in Brandenburg.[52]

Amid the changes, there was continuity, born of the fact that people continue to play football whatever the radical or violent upheavals going on around them. This was true of players in Nazi death camps such as Auschwitz during the Second World War. It was true of Iraq

[51] *Ibid.*, letter from Killian to Gerhard H., 3 May 1990, fo. 31; letter from Dr Iske (Ministry for Youth and Sport) to Axel R., 2 July 1990, fo. 127.
[52] Braun, 'Sport frei!', p. 374.

during the brutal regime of Saddam Hussein.[53] In the peaceful and rapid transition from communism to capitalism in East Germany, football was sufficiently robust to survive, and in many cases prosper, as a popular activity. Its impervious nature shines through, for example, in correspondence about the *Junge Welt* Cup in 1990/1. The Union Mühlhausen player Matthias M. was sent off in a game against HFC on 22 September 1990 for 'showing the finger' to his father, who was watching on the sidelines and criticised his son after a misplaced pass. A feisty match in rainy conditions between SV Wartburgstadt Eisenach and FC Suhl on the same day ended with four yellow cards and one red, awarded to an Eisenach player for a late and dangerous knee-high tackle on an opponent.[54] The incidents were striking for their normality. They could have happened in any season, regardless of what was occurring in the world or who was trying to take advantage of football for their own prestige or power. Amid the momentous changes of the *Wende*, the game struggled at times, adapted where necessary, but endured in ways that other mainstays of East German life, from the *Stasi* to the DTSB, were unable to do.

## 'Rotes Banner, I miss you!' The afterlife of GDR football

In 2009 the fanzine *3 Ecken Ein Elfer* ran a special issue on East German football twenty years after the fall of communism. It read more like a wake than a celebration. Experts gave gloomy summaries of the post-*Wende* period. They varied only in their degree of pessimism about the future. Hanns Leske predicted that the game in the East would be a 'wasteland' for at least the next decade, with just 'two or three rays of light'. The direst forecast, from Frank Willmann, declared *Ostfußball* 'dead', unless some 'idiot' pumped money into an ailing Eastern club – something that, ironically, was under way in 2009, as the energy-drink company Red Bull bankrolled the controversial creation of Rasen-Bull Leipzig.[55] What happened to football was a microcosm of the unification experience in the East. Initial euphoria gave way to disappointment,

[53] On football at Auschwitz, see e.g. Tadeusz Borowski, *This Way for the Gas, Ladies and Gentlemen*, trans. Barbara Vedder (London: Penguin, 1976), pp. 83–4. Football under the Hussein dictatorship is discussed in Simon Freeman, *Baghdad FC: Iraq's Football Story* (London: John Murray, 2005).

[54] Archivgut des DFV, X/10, Feldverweis gegen den Spieler Muth, M. im Pokalspiel der Junioren, SV Union Mühlhausen–HFC Chemie am 22.09.1990, 5 October 1990; Bericht zum Feldverweis beim Spiel JW-Pokal SV Wartburgstadt Eisenach Jun.–1. FC Suhl Jun. 0 : 3, am 22.09.1990, 23 September 1990.

[55] Raack, 'Was hat euch bloss so ruiniert?', 21.

Figure 20. A light that never goes out: BFC fans parade the GDR flag at a match in Zwickau, 2000. A year earlier, supporters had embraced the socialist past, voting – after nine years as FC Berlin – to return the club to its GDR-era name.

displacement, and – among some people at least – an embrace of the GDR past in all of its absurdities. Willmann's affectionate, tongue-in-cheek lament 'Rotes Banner, I miss you!'[56] for the passing of the Mecklenburg village team BSG Rotes Banner ('Red Banner') Trinswillershagen speaks volumes to this process.

At the start of the 2011/12 season, there was not a single ex-GDR club in the *Bundesliga*. Only five of the eighteen teams in Germany's second division hailed from the East. Many of the GDR's most successful clubs – the likes of Lok Leipzig, FC Magdeburg, and BFC – were also-rans, plying their trade in the fourth and fifth tiers of the football pyramid.[57] Thirty years earlier, these clubs played regularly in European competition, had first teams stocked with internationals, and drew respectable crowds. Now they played as true amateurs in front of hundreds rather than tens of thousands of fans, against unglamorous local opponents,

[56] Willmann, 'Wie alles anfing', pp. 106–7.

[57] For a summary of the post-*Wende* fate of GDR clubs, see Willmann, 'Wie alles anfing', pp. 103–7.

with teams consisting of journeymen, youngsters, and unheralded foreign imports.

During the first twenty years of the post-unification *Bundesliga*, only two East German clubs, Energie Cottbus and Hansa Rostock, survived in the top flight for any length of time. Hansa twice finished as high as sixth (1995/6 and 1997/8) and became, for a short time at least, the self-proclaimed 'club of the entire East'.[58] The validity of the title was questionable. But Hansa certainly benefited from the 'separatist East German cultural identity'[59] that emerged in the new *Bundesländer* (federal states) in response to the hardships and imbalances of unification. Neither Hansa nor Energie had been among the *Oberliga* elite. It was perhaps easier for fans of other clubs to welcome their long stays in the *Bundesliga* than would have been the case if BFC or Dynamo Dresden had enjoyed such success: Dynamo's promotion to the *2. Bundesliga* in 2011 was not a cause for celebration among Union Berlin fans interviewed for this book.[60] In the long run, though, neither club maintained its elevated status. In recent years, Hansa have flitted between the second and third divisions. Energie seem to be stuck in the *2. Bundesliga*, unable to compete financially even at that level.[61] As the NOFV president remarked in 2005, 'the economic potential [in the East] is simply absent and the major sponsors are all based in the West'.[62]

On-field struggles, as even the brighter examples from Rostock and Cottbus illustrate, have gone hand in hand with financial problems. Newly privatised clubs fell into the hands of incompetent, and in some cases corrupt, West German businessmen, many of whom took advantage of local inexperience and free-market opportunity. Sporting institutions protected by the state under communism were consequently, as Matthias Sammer complained, driven 'mercilessly' to the wall.[63] While the DFV's incorporation into the DFB proceeded relatively painlessly, business-oriented *Bundesliga* clubs rejected the idea of 'partnership agreements' with their East German counterparts, which were left to fend for themselves in a highly competitive environment.[64]

The transition to the market economy was especially painful at Sammer's former club, Dynamo Dresden. In a story with echoes of Andreas Thom's move from BFC to Bayer Leverkusen, part of the

58 Hesselmann and Rosentritt, *Hansa Rostock*, pp. 238–9, 306–7.
59 Betts, *Within Walls*, p. 228. 60 Interview with Tino C; interview with Theo Körner.
61 Raack, 'Was hat euch bloss so ruiniert?', 20.
62 Paul Joyce, 'Letter from Germany', *When Saturday Comes* 221 (July 2005): www.wsc.co.uk/content/view/1608/29/.
63 Raack, 'Was hat euch bloss so ruiniert?', 18.
64 Barsuhn, 'Die Wende und Vereinigung', pp. 413–14.

transfer agreement for the sale of Dresden's most prized asset to VfB Stuttgart in 1990 was a team bus. Three years later, to the astonishment of Dynamo officials, the bus was reclaimed by Stuttgart. 'None of us', as Jens Genschmar remarked in 2009, 'had ever heard of a lease contract'. Un-worldliness hampered the club in the areas essential to the development of modern football organisations in the 1990s. The nadir was reached with the appointment of West German construction magnate Rolf-Jürgen Otto as club chairman in 1993. Two years later, the GDR's most popular team was demoted to the third division after accruing debts of eight million Euros. The self-styled saviour of the club was later sentenced to three years in prison for various financial misdemeanours.[65] Dynamo's recovery from Otto's legacy has been slow and difficult. With an impressive new stadium complete and promotion to the second division achieved in 2011, there were at least more hopeful signs for the future.

Other East German clubs underwent similar experiences. At various points BFC, Union Berlin, Lok Leipzig, and Sachsen Leipzig all declared insolvency, Lok (1999 and 2004) and Sachsen (2003 and 2009) on two separate occasions. The DFB's removal of Union's playing licence for financial irregularities in 1993 prompted an unsuccessful protest campaign – and a banner at games that suggested the ways in which autonomous fan cultures found different political opponents. It read 'Union: loved by the people, feared by the *Stasi*, destroyed by the DFB???'[66] Such were the financial problems at BFC that the team withdrew from the northern division of the *Oberliga Nordost* (the fifth tier of German football) in 2001. Its results were annulled and the club was automatically relegated. The GDR's most successful team opened the 2002/3 season in the Berlin regional league. The head coach claimed that 'we are clearly playing to avoid relegation'.[67] Again, the scale of collapse – from the heights of European clashes against the likes of Liverpool, Roma, and Hamburg in the 1970s and 1980s to local derbies against Union Berlin's amateur team and Tennis Borussia's second XI at the start of the twenty-first century – must be emphasised. BFC, like most clubs in the East, faced a struggle for survival that lasted long after the curtain fell on the *Oberliga*.

In the mainstream media, post-unification football in East Germany was often reduced to hooliganism. The violence of the *Wende* period was

[65] Christoph Zimmer, 'Verbrannte Erde: Das lange Leiden der SG Dynamo Dresden', 3 *Ecken Ein Elfer* 6 (May 2009), 27–9.

[66] Luther and Willmann, *Eisern Union!*, pp. 178–82.

[67] Luther and Willmann, *BFC*, p. 265.

not easily overcome. The poor fare on the pitch and the financial catastrophes off it, not to mention mass unemployment, created a political and economic climate that neo-fascist groups readily exploited. Hanns Leske's comment on the lack of a 'civilised fan culture' in the East is greatly exaggerated.[68] But violent and racist tendencies among a minority of supporters at clubs such as FCM, Union Berlin, and BFC were and remain a cause for concern. The situation in Leipzig, a city where the transition to professional football was particularly inept, offered sobering insight into the wrong turns taken by football in the East. While rivals Lok and Sachsen were competitive only in terms of the number of insolvencies that they have faced (a 2–2 draw at the time of writing), elements within their fan base generated headlines for the wrong reasons. In December 2007 a group of fifty armed and masked Lok fans attacked a Christmas party organised by Sachsen ultras. The clubhouse where the party took place was badly damaged. Several Sachsen fans were hospitalised.[69] This was not an isolated incident. Lok's far-right fans, like their counterparts at BFC, became far better known to the German public than the team that they supported. The stigma of the 'wild East' was hard to escape, even for more successful clubs such as Hansa Rostock, widely and somewhat unjustly regarded as a 'club of the right' during the 1990s.[70]

Despite the manifest problems, there were success stories in the afterlife of GDR football. On a list of 'striking players' drawn up by the DFV in 1990 was a young midfielder from Chemnitzer FC (formerly FC Karl-Marx-Stadt) called Michael Ballack.[71] Born in Görlitz, Ballack's first football hero was a player from FCK, the club where he trained and played from a young age. He went on to become one of the leading players of his generation, captain and mainstay of the national team for the best part of a decade and a key component in successful Bayer Leverkusen, Bayern Munich, and Chelsea teams. Ballack was the tip of the iceberg. Just as key elements of the GDR sports system, from the elite schools model to the coaches, survived the *Wende* as transplants in countries such as Australia and Britain,[72] youth talent structures outlived the regime that founded them. Matthias Sammer captained

[68] Leske, 'Der Fußball-Osten'.

[69] Raack, 'Was hat euch bloss so ruiniert?', 20; Martin Thaler, 'Im Bermuda Triangle', 3 *Ecken Ein Elfer* 6 (May 2009), 36.

[70] Hesselmann and Rosentritt, *Hansa Rostock*, pp. 234–7.

[71] Archivgut des DFV, X/10, Auswertung der Spiele um den Länderpokale des DFV für Schüler- und Jugend-Landesauswahlmannschaften vom 13.–18.10.1990 in Parchim, 8 November 1990.

[72] See Dennis and Grix, *Sport under Communism*, pp. 178–9.

the German team that won the 1996 European Championship in England. Six years later, the German side that lost the World Cup final to Brazil in Japan contained three players – Ballack, Jens Jeremies (Dynamo Dresden), and Bernd Schneider (Carl Zeiss Jena) – who had come through the GDR system. Infrastructures to develop young footballers remain strong, even at clubs such as Magdeburg that are otherwise in poor shape.[73] Keeping hold of players, rather than producing them, was (and remains) the problem.[74]

Another shaft of light came from an area neglected by East German sports functionaries. As we saw in Chapter 12, women's football moved out of the margins in the GDR's dying days, with the creation of a national league and a national team, which contested its only game against Czechoslovakia in May 1990. The belated impetus carried over into the post-unification period. In contrast to its male counterparts, the GDR's most successful women's team, Turbine Potsdam, made a competitive transition to post-communist football. After difficult beginnings – conditioned by the financial constraints that affected all areas of the game in the new *Bundesländer* – the team from Brandenburg flourished.[75] Since 2003 it has won the German league title, one of the world's strongest women's leagues, five times; the German Cup three times; and (in 2010) the Champions' League, determining the best women's side in Europe.[76] Its best players have become integral parts of the German national team, one of the top sides in women's international football over the past two decades and World Cup winners in 2003 and 2007. Turbine illustrates that football and success are not incompatible terms in the post-*Wende* East.

Media focus on a minority of violent supporters has obscured the emergence of a more positive fan culture in East Germany, one that draws cleverly on the (sometimes new-found) underdog status of clubs. *Eigen-Sinn*, the practice of safeguarding cultural spaces from peers and higher-ups, has carried over into the post-communist era. In 2009, 2,000 Union Berlin supporters, echoing the self-help ethos that was a marked feature of GDR sport, put in 140,000 hours of volunteer work to ensure that renovations to the club's iconic stadium in Köpenick were completed in time for the team's debut in the second division.[77] A year earlier, fans of another beloved GDR team, Sachsen Leipzig – disillusioned by owners with little understanding of club traditions and even less financial competence – took matters into their own hands in a

[73] Leske, 'Der Fußball-Osten'. [74] Interview with Holger Fuchs.
[75] Linne, *Freigespielt*, pp. 226–7. [76] www.ffc-turbine.de/verein_erfolge.php.
[77] Luther and Willmann, *Eisern Union!*, pp. 333–42.

different way. They founded their own club, taking its original name (BSG Chemie Leipzig) and starting from scratch in the third division of the Leipzig district league.[78] This followed the 2004 decision by a group of Lok Leipzig fans to re-found their club, which began its new life playing in front of record crowds in the eleventh tier of German football.[79] Reappropriation of lost, or betrayed, identities was a common theme in post-1990s European football, as fans struggled to make their voices heard amid football's increased commercialisation. The reclamation projects of Lok and Chemie fans echoed fan-power initiatives in England. Supporters of South London-based AFC Wimbledon responded to the relocation of their club three hours north to Milton Keynes (and its renaming as MK Dons) by re-founding the club with its original name in its original location. In 2011, AFC Wimbledon gained promotion to the football league. It currently competes one division below the wealthier but unloved MK Dons. *Ostalgie* in football was never just uncritical nostalgia for a simpler, socialist past. It was also part of a transnational grassroots rejection of the game's reinvention as a money-spinning commodity that priced ordinary fans out of the market.

BSG Chemie are a long way from replicating Wimbledon's meteoric rise. But the club's rebirth illustrates that grassroots activism, a central feature of the autonomous enclaves that fans carved out in the GDR, remains important to East German football. In a rebuff to popular stereotypes of fans in the East, Chemie supporters have cultivated a progressive, anti-racist image. Close ties, what is known in German as 'fan friendship' (*Fanfreundschaft*), exist with Red Star Leipzig, founded in the south of the city in 1999 as a community-based organisation that, aside from its on-field activities, produces CDs by local artists, runs football teams for asylum seekers, and organises demonstrations against right-wing extremism. Five hundred spectators regularly show up for Red Star's games in the city league.[80]

The complexities of the post-*Wende* landscape are nowhere more pronounced than at BFC. Tainted by its connections to the *Stasi*, undone by financial mismanagement, and home to a small but nasty hooligan following, the GDR's serial champions are still to be found in the lower leagues, playing under their old name in front of 400 or 500 spectators. Some fans gave up the ghost long ago. 'BFC today', claimed one ex-supporter in 2003, 'is the club of *Wende* losers, active hooligans,

[78] Thaler, 'Im Bermuda Triangle', 37.

[79] Karsten Blaas, 'Lok, Rostock and Barrel', *When Saturday Comes* special on *Fußball* (2006), 12.

[80] Thaler, 'Im Bermuda Triangle', 38.

and a few dozen real fans who go to the ground to watch football'.[81] Others, though, have remained loyal. Indeed, many BFC fan clubs became more active after the *Wende*, adding bowling evenings and barbeques to their social calendars. Christmas parties were organised in the clubhouse that fans, imitating again the voluntarist ethos of East German sport, built for themselves. Without the security blanket of *Stasi* sponsorship, and in an unforgiving economic environment, they took more initiative and developed closer ties to the club leadership.[82]

Watching the team's matches at the Sportforum, once the heartland of the Dynamo sports empire but now a sleepy and somewhat decrepit place, in 2010 and 2011, there were reasons to feel disheartened: from the lumpy state of the pitch and often poor-quality football to the preponderance of shaven-headed males on the sparsely occupied terraces that, like the club itself, had seen better days. Graffiti scrawled on one of the railings offered a reminder of the inescapability of the past: it read simply 'FC *Stasi*'. But there were also encouraging signs. Fans took me for a beer in the stylish clubhouse behind the main stand. Women and children, while still in the minority, were in attendance, giving some credence to BFC's efforts to create a family atmosphere. The half-time sausage and beer, a staple of any German football experience, was cheap and good. The atmosphere was generally good-humoured, as shown when the crowd collapsed into laughter at the sight of the over-worked scoreboard attendant racing up and down a ladder with ever-larger numbers in a high-scoring match. Many of the banners on display took stubborn pride in the club's bad reputation, embracing the East German past in the same way that its ice hockey cousin, Dynamo Berlin, did in the new millennium.[83] *Ostalgie* was sometimes framed in severe-looking Sütterlin script. But one banner stood out from the rest. It was emblazoned with the title of a famous song by The Smiths: 'There is a light that never goes out'. It seemed a fitting motto for the desire of fans at BFC and other East German clubs to ensure that, whatever the changes in the world, football remains a game that they can call their own.

## The final whistle

Why, with a few notable exceptions, has East German football – and in particular the lives of fans and recreational players – hitherto received relatively little scholarly attention? After all, it was a more widespread shared experience among the people of Germany's first socialist state

[81] Luther and Willmann, *BFC*, p. 279. [82] Interview with BFC fans.
[83] Braun, '"Very nice, the enemies are gone!"', 181–2.

than *Republikflucht*, *Stasi* persecution, and organised religion. Within a purely sporting context, it was a more important part of the daily dynamics of the political and social system than the Olympic successes of the 1970s and 1980s. It is almost as if Manfred Ewald's line about the weakness of GDR football, which was taken up by many Western observers after 1990, has obscured its importance. Even many of those who played or watched the game in East Germany regarded it as a failure, a world turned in on itself in ways that were detrimental to everyone involved. 'The GDR *Oberliga*', wrote Christoph Dieckmann, 'was the most conservative league in the world'.[84] Reading in archives, often in painstaking detail, the numerous complaints about illegal transfers, ineligible players, or unfair points deductions, one is reminded of the narrow space in which officials, coaches, and players (often quite happily) operated.

Yet precisely because it could not be pinned down politically, football has generally mattered a great deal wherever it has been played. In Francoist Spain, the game was an integral part of what Raymond Carr called a 'culture of evasion', providing the opportunity to talk about something other than the largely taboo subjects of the civil war, the police state, and economic hardships.[85] A similar process evolved in the GDR. Subjects such as the Wall and *Stasi* surveillance were off limits in public and often in private discourse. Football provided safer ground for conversation, while allowing more sensitive political topics to be approached. Terrace chants in the 1980s included 'where's your Eigendorf then?' (in reference to the BFC star who defected in 1979) and even 'the Wall must go'.[86] At the same time, football was not simply a site of *Resistenz* to the (supposedly) totalitarian state. This was symbolised by the greatest moment in GDR football history, the win over West Germany at the 1974 World Cup finals, which distilled the wide-ranging, often ambiguous feelings of citizens about the socialist nation in which they lived and the German nation to which most still felt that they belonged. 'The popularity of the FRG team', as Dieckmann rightly concluded, 'in no way meant that the GDR team was hated. It fulfilled another function. It stood for homeland football and the charm of the outsider'.[87]

Deeply entwined in the social fabric of the GDR, football exercised the bodies and minds of hundreds of thousands of citizens on a daily or weekly basis. As such, the game tells us more about communist state and society than any other organised activity. It provided fans and players

[84] Dieckmann, '"Nur ein Leutzscher"', p. 319.

[85] Krüger, 'Strength through joy', pp. 81, 83.

[86] Willmann, 'Wie alles anfing', p. 99.

[87] Dieckmann, '"Nur ein Leutzscher"', p. 322.

alike with a means of preserving autonomy in their ways of being – in their leisure time choices, in their likes and dislikes, in where they chose to go, and in how they chose to behave. Protected by safety in numbers, young supporters found in football an outlet for exuberant behaviour that was anathema to the socialist classroom or FDJ rallies. Obscene and humorous terrace songs, the imbibing of large quantities of alcohol, and ticketless rail travel to away games in large, unruly groups were all characteristic of a quest for authentic experience that the state could not provide. In different ways, players – particularly recreational players – used the game to foster distinctive community identities that kept the socialist project at a distance. In BSGs such as Rotation Leipzig and Rotation Prenzlauer Berg, or in the women's section at Turbine Potsdam, the primary focus was always local, not national.

In the East German *Sportland*, football often had the appearance of an anarchic city-state where regular laws did not apply and secession appeared to be just around the corner. Communist officials, despite their best efforts, had astonishingly little influence on players or fans. Transfer rules were regularly flouted, as were directives on players' salaries and bonuses. Individual clubs, backed by ambitious local party bosses, supported the aims of the national team only if they did not clash with their own interests. Local rivalries were often entrenched and bitter. The game resolutely refused to follow the SED's script for Olympic sports. The more the authorities tried to bend the game to their will – by relocations, by tightening up rules on transfers or bonuses, or by infiltrating the fan scene – the more stubborn was the resistance into which they ran. The fact that many party functionaries, from local leaders to Erich Mielke, were football fans only made more difficult the task of bringing the game into line.

In the end, a stand-off prevailed. Football tolerated the SED. The SED, sometimes through gritted teeth, tolerated football. The boundaries between state and society were so porous that no simple delineation between 'regime' (denoting authority) and 'football' (denoting a possible site of resistance or dissent) can be posited. Fan-club leaders such as Theo Körner at Union Berlin could be FDJ activists. Heads of BSG football sections, champions of local patriotism, were often party comrades. Dynamo Dresden players were also members of the national police force. The blurring of the lines, typical of the framework for social relations in the GDR, made football both static (at a national level) and dynamic (at regional and local level). It offered an activity that served neither as a mouthpiece for socialism nor as a repressible platform for avowed opposition to it. The game's practitioners enjoyed only a constrained sense of freedom. *Schlachtenbummler* could travel across the GDR to watch their team in action, but trips to West Germany were the preserve of a select few. *Oberliga* players enjoyed, by GDR measures, a high living standard and unprecedented opportunities for travel abroad, but also had to reckon with the insidious presence of the *Stasi* in their dressing rooms. Recreational players, largely left to themselves, were ultimately reliant on the state for the financial subsidies that kept BSG football sections afloat. As in an unhealthy but functioning relationship, there was a co-dependence between football and communism that encouraged compromise rather than confrontation – and left neither side entirely satisfied.

East German football matters, finally, because it was part of an international story, one that speaks to football's role in the shared social and cultural history of European societies during the Cold War. The GDR was both part of, and apart from, the major developments in post-war football that led to its renewed popularity, and unparalleled commercial appeal, at the end of the twentieth century. The large crowds of the late 1940s and early 1950s, the role of television in reshaping spectatorship from the 1960s onwards, and the ugly spectre of hooliganism that gave football pariah status in many European countries by the mid 1980s, all featured in GDR football's narrative arc – just as they featured in the history of English football in the same period. Through participation in competitions and institutions, exposure to cutting-edge tactics (the Hungarians in the 1950s and the Dutch in the 1970s), and television, clubs, coaches, players, and fans were part of transnational dialogues.

At the same time, there were many fascinating pecularities about football under East German communism. Developments in the increasingly sophisticated marketing of football as a global brand, for example, arguably begun in earnest with the 1974 World Cup in West Germany, largely bypassed the GDR. As the last significant communist redoubt against the commercialisation of sport, the GDR remained suspicious of the capitalist spirit that underpinned much of football's internationalism – as illustrated by the rules imposed to ensure the immobility of its players, the homogeneity of its leagues, and the tight controls that governed every trip outside the Soviet bloc. In the words of Jens Genschmar, 'the *Wende* came a few years too late'.[88] By the early 1990s, top West German clubs, like their counterparts in other leading West European leagues, were cashing in on a revival in football's fortunes, occasioned by a reduced hooligan threat, safer stadia, and,

[88] Zimmer, 'Verbrannte Erde', 27–8.

above all, lucrative television deals. In this environment, East German clubs – raised in a world where shirt sponsors were a capitalist abomination and the only television deal was with the state provider – could not compete. Most of them were left behind after 1990 and are still catching up today.

East German communists were not the first, and are unlikely to be the last, to discover the difficulties inherent in exploiting football for political gain. In this sense, the history of East German football is part of not just a European, but a global narrative. Both Mussolini and Franco understood football's potential importance as a tool of social control. Neither could prevent the game from fostering what fascist ideologues vilified as *campanilismo* (provincialism).[89] In Spain football clubs played a major role in keeping alive Catalan and Basque nationalism, undermining the project for national unity embodied in the successes of Franco's favourite team, Real Madrid, during the 1950s and 1960s.[90] In apartheid South Africa, football was a means of crossing racial divides (just as it crossed national divides in Cold War Germany), but also an extraordinary force in giving agency to black South Africans, who built up institutions, clubs, and facilities that provided independent sporting spaces.[91] The game, as David Goldblatt notes, has always maintained an 'insufferable tendency to upset the smooth acclimation of power'.[92]

The tendency was also apparent in communist states. Even at the peak of Stalinist terror in the 1930s, the football stadium served as an autonomous enclave in the Soviet Union, a place where fans could direct chants against institutions of authority that would have had them arrested in the street or a bar. The popular Spartak Moscow club, in Robert Edelman's words, provided 'a safe way to resist'.[93] When the club's founder, the charismatic Nikolai Starostin, was sent to the gulag in 1943, football offered an avenue of escape open to few others. Starostin was enlisted by the commandant at the Ukhta camp to coach the local police team, which played in one of the lower divisions of the Soviet league.[94] Rules could be bent when it came to football. This allowed Starostin to survive. It allowed powerful men to make or remake teams in their own image. But it also gave supporters a degree of freedom that was hard to find in other parts of their lives.

89 Martin, *Football and Fascism*, pp. 166–70.

90 See e.g. Ball, *Morbo* (especially on Barcelona's contested role in Catalan resistance to Francoism).

91 See Peter Alegi, *Laduma! Soccer, Politics and Society in South Africa from its Origins to 2010* (Scottsville: University of KwaZulu-Natal Press, 2010), especially chs. 5–8.

92 Goldblatt, *The Ball Is Round*, pp. 310–12.

93 Edelman, *Spartak Moscow*, pp. 93–9, 134.

94 *Ibid.*, pp. 131–3.

Wherever one looks in Eastern Europe after 1945, variations on the same theme – football's otherness, its (unwitting) non-conformity – emerge with a brightness that stands in contrast to the stereotypical greyness of everyday life under communism: the riots that followed Hungary's loss to West Germany in the 1954 World Cup final, a display of public anger that some observers regard as the first spark of the 1956 Revolution; the mass brawl that followed the 1985 Bulgarian Cup final between Levski Sofia and CSKA Sofia; or the 1988 Romanian Cup final between Dinamo Bucharest and bitter rivals Steaua, at the conclusion of which the Dinamo defender Ioan Andone – protesting against Steaua's decision to walk off the pitch after the referee disallowed a late winning goal – walked over to the VIP box, dropped his shorts, and waved his penis at bemused communist leaders, including Valentin Ceauşescu, Steaua's president and the son of the country's dictator, Nicolae.[95]

Precisely because it is a broad-based force under nobody's direct or permanent control, football's dissenting role should not be overstated. Particularly through international success, it often provided an element of legitimacy for an incumbent regime, as was the case with Italy's World Cup triumphs of 1934 and 1938, Steaua's European Cup victory in 1986, and even (on a smaller scale) the GDR's win over West Germany in 1974. In Argentina, the brutal policies of Jorge Videla's military government were temporarily forgotten as the country hosted and won the 1978 World Cup.[96]

Nonetheless, football in East Germany tended to be more subversive than state-affirming. This was not sporting theatre stage-managed by an authoritarian government so that people could vent their frustrations on relatively inconsequential matters. If this were the case, the GDR would not have spent so much time and energy pondering the problems of hooliganism, for example, or placating citizens angered by BFC's dominance. In systems that aspired to totalitarian control, every crack in the façade was serious. Football created and exploited such cracks in abundance. The very fact that it was a contested terrain, a place of give and take between rulers and ruled, made football threatening. Kicking a ball around, or watching a ball being kicked around, was never likely to bring down communism by itself. But it was an essential part of keeping alive expressions of *Heimat*, *Resistenz*, and individualism that stubbornly resisted the SED's dictatorial goals.

[95] See Wilson, *Behind the Curtain*, pp. 83–4 (Hungary), pp. 185–90 (Bulgaria), pp. 203–5 (Romania).

[96] Goldblatt, *The Ball Is Round*, pp. 616–18.

In 1991, Joachim Streich, the most prolific goalscorer in GDR history, wrote that, 'Whatever people might think about our football in the East, it always provided a lot of entertainment'.[97] The game in East Germany was indeed fascinating, for the on-field stories alone: Chemie Leipzig's scarcely credible league title in 1964; FC Magdeburg's against-the-odds triumph against AC Milan in the European Cup Winners' Cup final ten years later; and the national team's dramatic tale of (apparent) under-achievement – redeemed, at least briefly, by its underdog victory in the match where communism needed it most, against West Germany in 1974. Even the smallest of football-related details can shed (often humorous) light on aspects of life in the GDR. In 1977, several Dynamo Dresden players were spotted leaving a cinema in Liverpool before the end of the feature. The reason for their departure, it transpired, was not thoughts of *Republikflucht*, but a queasiness induced by watching gory scenes from Steven Spielberg's then-current blockbuster *Jaws*, a film that was not widely available for viewing back home.[98]

As Eduardo Galeano put it, 'Tell me how you play and I'll tell you who you are'.[99] The ways in which East Germans played, and watched, football between 1945 and 1991 illustrate the complexities and ambiguities of the state and the society that shaped, and at least in part were shaped by, a game that refused to be ignored. For all of the constraints that it faced, and compromises that it made, football was often in the vanguard of popular resistance to communist rule. Whether it was the persistence of pan-German feelings in (and beyond) the reconstruction years, the local patriotism that flourished behind socialism's closed doors, or the loss of faith in the authorities in the 1980s that helped to spark the *Wende*, football was always the canary in the mine. This was the case because it was the one mass activity that took place (television aside) in public, while simultaneously being privately impervious to state control. Football – as the stories of *Oberliga* players, fan-club members, hooligans, and recreational players demonstrate – exemplified a stubborn working-class distance from the socialist project that the SED leadership, often more petty bourgeois than proletarian in its cultural tastes and values, never overcame. Equally, it was a game with cross-class appeal and, as the anti-BFC movement of the 1980s in particular indicated, genuine political clout.

At every stage of the GDR's history, football thus had a role (or, rather, many roles) to play, roles that were not confined to what went on in the stands or on the pitch. The game mattered because it was hugely

97 Dieckmann, '"Nur ein Leutzscher"', p. 328.
98 Hesse-Lichtenberger, *Tor!*, p. 231.
99 Galeano, *Soccer in Sun and Shadow*, p. 209.

popular. It was hugely popular because it mattered – whether as a political statement, a form of belonging, a means of exercise, a career, a window on the West, or an opportunity to socialise. It still matters as a vital perspective on East Germany now. Football gave its adherents a sense of *Eigen-Sinn* that communism could neither compete with nor control. The people's game proved far more durable than the people's state.

# Works cited

## INTERVIEWS

Tino C., Berlin, 25 May 2011 (Union Berlin fan)
Tim E., Berlin, 25 May 2011 (footballer at Empor Beelitz)
Holger Fuchs, Berlin, 23 May 2011 (DFV functionary)
Jens Genschmar, Dresden, 18 May 2011 (Dynamo Dresden fan)
Heiko H., Toronto, 13 October 2011 (Lokomotive Leipzig fan)
Thomas (Theo) Körner, Berlin, 26 May 2011 (Union Berlin fan)
Klaus L., Berlin, 12 May 2011 (football section leader at Rotation Prenzlauer Berg)
Frank L., Berlin, 25 May 2011 (Union Berlin fan)
Sven S., Berlin, 24 May 2011 (Union Berlin fan)
Heinz Werner, Berlin, 24 May 2011 (coach of Hansa Rostock, Union Berlin, Stahl Brandenburg, FC Karl-Marx-Stadt, and the national team)
Rainer, 29 May 2011* (BFC fan)
Toralf, 29 May 2011* (BFC fan)
Olaf S., 29 May 2011* (BFC fan)
Group interview with BFC fans, Berlin, 29 May 2011
(* Written response to questions sent by email)

## ARCHIVAL SOURCES

Archivgut des Deutschen Fußballverbandes der DDR (DFV)
Brandenburgisches Landeshauptarchiv (BLHA)
Bundesbeauftragte für die Unterlagen des Staatssicherheitsdienstes der ehemaligen Deutschen Demokratischen Republik (BStU)
Hauptstaatsarchiv (HStA) Dresden
Landeshauptarchiv Sachsen-Anhalt, Abteilung Merseburg (LHASA, MER)
Stiftung der Parteien und Massenorganisationen, Bundesarchiv (SAPMO-BArch)
- DC 4 (Amt für Jugendfragen)
- DO 1 (Ministerium des Innern)
- DO 101 (SV Dynamo)
- DP 3 (Generalstaatsanwalt der DDR)
- DR 5 (Staatliches Komitee für Körperkultur und Sport bzw. Staatssekretariat für Körperkultur und Sport)
- DR 8 (Staatliches Komitee für Fernsehen)
- DR 509 (Büro der Förderung des Sports in den Betrieben)

DY 12 (Deutscher Sportausschuß bzw. Deutscher Turn- und Sportverband)
DY 24 (Freie Deutsche Jugend)
DY 30 (Sozialistische Einheitspartei Deutschlands)
DY 34 (Freier Deutscher Gewerkschaftbund)
DY 41 (Gewerkschaften Medizin)
DY 46 (IG Metall)
Thüringisches Hauptstaatsarchiv Weimar (ThHStAW)
Union Berlin Archive

## NEWSPAPERS

*Deutsches Sport-Echo* (1947, 1953)
*Junge Welt (Berliner Ausgabe)* (1947, 1948)
*Die Neue Fußball-Woche* (1949, 1953–7, 1961, 1964, 1967, 1973–4, 1983–6, 1988)

## FILMS

*Frauen am Ball* (dir. Ted Tetzke, 1988)
*Nicht schummeln, Liebling!* (dir. Joachim Hasler, 1973)
*Und freitags in die 'Grüne Hölle'* (dir. Ernst Canzler, 1989)

## SECONDARY LITERATURE


Alegi, Peter, *African Soccerscapes: How a Continent Changed the World's Game* (Athens, OH: Ohio University Press, 2010).

*Laduma! Soccer, Politics and Society in South Africa from its Origins to 2010* (Scottsville: University of KwaZulu-Natal Press, 2010).

Allinson, Mark, '1977: The GDR's most normal year?', in Mary Fulbrook (ed.), *Power and Society in the GDR, 1961–1979: The 'Normalisation' of Rule?* (New York and Oxford: Berghahn, 2009), pp. 253–77.

*Politics and Popular Opinion in East Germany 1945–1968* (Manchester: Manchester University Press, 2000).

Anderson, Sheldon, 'Soccer and the failure of East German sports policy', *Soccer & Society* vol. 12, no. 5 (September 2011), 652–63.

Archetti, Eduardo, 'The spectacle of identities: football in Latin America', in Stephen Hart and Richard Young (eds.), *Contemporary Latin American Studies* (London: Arnold, 2003), pp. 116–26.

Baingo, Andreas and Michael Horn, *Die Geschichte der DDR-Oberliga* (Göttingen: Verlag Die Werkstatt, 2004).

Balbier, Uta, *Kalter Krieg auf der Aschenbahn: Der deutsch–deutsche Sport 1950–1972 – Eine politische Geschichte* (Paderborn: Schöningh, 2006).

Ball, Phil, *Morbo: The Story of Spanish Football* (London: WSC Books, 2001).

Barsuhn, Michael, 'Die Wende und Vereinigung im Fußball 1989/90,' in Jutta Braun and Hans Joachim Teichler (eds.), *Sportstadt Berlin im Kalten Krieg: Prestigekämpfe und Systemwettstreit* (Berlin: Ch. Links Verlag, 2006), pp. 376–415.

Barthes, Roland, *What is Sport?*, trans. Richard Howard (New Haven and London: Yale University Press, 2007).
Becker, Christian and Wolfgang Buss, 'Das "Wunder von Bern" und die DDR', *Deutschland Archiv* vol. 37, no. 3 (2004), 389–99.
Berdahl, Daphne, 'Re-presenting the socialist modern: museums and memory in the former GDR', in Katherine Pence and Paul Betts (eds.), *Socialist Modern: East German Everyday Culture and Politics* (Ann Arbor, MI: University of Michigan Press, 2008), pp. 345–66.
Beyer, Rolf, *Rotation Leipzig 1950: 50 Jahre* (Leipzig: Self-published, 2000).
Bitzer, Dirk and Bernd Wilting, *Stürmen für Deutschland: Die Geschichte des deutschen Fußballs von 1933 bis 1954* (Frankfurt/Main: Campus Verlag, 2003).
Blaas, Karsten, 'Lok, Rostock and Barrel', *When Saturday Comes* special on *Fußball* (2006), 10–12.
Blees, Thomas, *90 Minuten Klassenkampf: Das Länderspiel BRD–DDR 1974* (Frankfurt/Main: Fischer Taschenbuch Verlag, 1999).
Bolaño, Roberto, *The Third Reich*, trans. Natasha Wimmer (New York: Farrar, Strauss and Giroux, 2011).
Borowski, Tadeusz, *This Way for the Gas, Ladies and Gentlemen*, trans. Barbara Vedder (London: Penguin, 1976).
Braun, Jutta, 'The people's sport? Popular sport and fans in the later years of the German Democratic Republic', *German History* vol. 27, no. 3 (2009), 414–28.
'Sport frei! – Der Weg in die Sporteinheit', in Jutta Braun and Joachim Teichler (eds.), *Sportstadt Berlin* (Berlin: Ch. Links Verlag, 2006), pp. 351–75.
'"Very nice, the enemies are gone!" Coming to terms with GDR sports since 1989/90', *Historical Social Research* vol. 32, no. 1 (2007), 172–85.
Braun, Jutta and René Wiese, 'DDR-Fußball und gesamtdeutsche Identität im Kalten Krieg', *Historische Sozialforschung* vol. 4 (2005), 191–210.
Brooke, Jack-Pitt, 'A return to all riot on the east German front', *The Independent*, 30 November 2011: www.independent.co.uk/sport/football/news-and-comment/a-return-to-all-riot-on-the-east-german-front-6269683.html.
Broszat, Martin, *Nach Hitler: Der schwierige Umgang mit unserer Geschichte* (Munich: Oldenbourg Verlag, 1986).
Bruce, Gary, *The Firm: The Inside Story of the Stasi* (Oxford: Oxford University Press, 2010).
Brussig, Thomas *Helden wie wir* (Berlin: Verlag Volk und Welt, 1996).
*Leben bis Männer* (Frankfurt/Main: Fischer Taschenbuch Verlag, 2001).
Buford, Bill, *Among the Thugs* (London: Arrow, 1992).
Carrington, Ben, 'Sport without final guarantees: Cultural Studies/Marxism/sport', in Ben Carrington and Ian McDonald (eds.), *Marxism, Cultural Studies and Sport* (Abingdon: Routledge, 2007), pp. 15–31.
Childs, David and Richard Popplewell, *The Stasi: The East German Intelligence and Security Service* (London: MacMillan, 1996).
Davies, Sarah, *Popular Opinion in Stalinist Russia: Terror, Propaganda and Dissent, 1934–1941* (Cambridge: Cambridge University Press, 1997).

De Grazia, Victoria, *The Culture of Consent: Mass Organization of Leisure in Fascist Italy* (Cambridge: Cambridge University Press, 1981).

Dennis, Mike, 'Behind the wall: East German football between state and society', *GFL-Journal* no. 2 (2007), 46–73.

'Soccer hooliganism in the German Democratic Republic', in Alan Tomlinson and Christopher Young (eds.), *German Football: History, Culture, Society* (London: Routledge, 2006), pp. 52–72.

*The Stasi: Myth and Reality* (London: Pearson, 2003).

Dennis, Mike and Jonathan Grix, 'Behind the iron curtain: football as a site of contestation in the East German sports "miracle"', *Sport in History* vol. 30, no. 3 (September 2010), 447–74.

*Sport under Communism: Behind the East German 'Miracle'* (London: Palgrave Macmillan, 2012).

Dennis, Mike and Norman Laporte, *State and Minorities in Communist East Germany* (New York and Oxford: Berghahn, 2011).

Dieckmann, Christoph, '"Nur ein Leutzscher ist ein Deutscher"', in Wolfgang Niersbach (ed.), *100 Jahre DFB: Die Geschichte des Deutschen Fußball-Bundes* (Berlin: Sportverlag Berlin, 1999), pp. 311–36.

Downing, David, *Passovotchka: Moscow Dynamo in Britain, 1945* (London: Bloomsbury, 2000).

Dubois, Laurent, *Soccer Empire: The World Cup and the Future of France* (Berkeley, CA: University of California Press, 2010).

Duke, Vic, 'Going to the market: football in the societies of Eastern Europe', in Stephen Wagg (ed.), *Giving the Game Away: Football, Politics and Culture on Five Continents* (London: Leicester University Press, 1995), pp. 88–102.

Duke, Vic and Pavel Slepička, 'Bohemian rhapsody: football supporters in the Czech Republic', in Eric Dunning, Patrick Murphy, Ivan Waddington, and Antonios A. Astrinakis (eds.), *Fighting Fans: Football Hooliganism as a World Phenomenon* (Dublin: University College Dublin Press, 2002), pp. 49–61.

Dunning, Eric, *Sport Matters: Sociological Studies of Sport, Violence and Civilisation* (London: Routledge, 1999).

Dunning, Eric, Patrick Murphy, and Ivan Waddington, 'Towards a sociological understanding of football hooliganism as a world problem', in Eric Dunning, Patrick Murphy, Ivan Waddington, and Antonios A. Astrinakis (eds.), *Fighting Fans: Football Hooliganism as a World Phenomenon* (Dublin: University College Dublin Press, 2002), pp. 1–22.

Dwertmann, Hubert and Bero Rigauer, 'Football hooliganism in Germany: a developmental sociological study', in Eric Dunning, Patrick Murphy, Ivan Waddington, and Antonios A. Astrinakis (eds.), *Fighting Fans: Football Hooliganism as a World Phenomenon* (Dublin: University College Dublin Press, 2002), pp. 75–87.

Eco, Umberto, 'The World Cup and its pomps', in *Travels in Hyperreality*, trans. by William Weaver (New York: Harcourt, 1986), pp. 167–72.

Edelman, Robert, *Serious Fun: A History of Spectator Sports in the USSR* (Oxford: Oxford University Press, 1993).

'A small way of saying "no": Moscow working men, Spartak soccer, and the Communist Party, 1900–1945', *The American Historical Review* vol. 107, no. 5 (December 2002), 1441–74.

*Spartak Moscow: A History of the People's Team in the Workers' State* (Ithaca, NY: Cornell University Press, 2009).

Eisenberg, Christiane, 'Football in Germany: beginnings, 1890–1914', *International Journal of the History of Sport* vol. 8, no. 2 (1991), 205–20.

Ewald, Manfred, *Ich war der Sport* (Berlin: Elefanten Press, 1994).

Farin, Karin and Harald Hauswald, *Die dritte Halbzeit: Hooligans in Berlin-Ost* (Bad Tölz: Tilsner, 1998).

Fenemore, Mark, *Sex, Thugs and Rock'n'Roll: Teenage Rebels in Cold-War East Germany* (Oxford: Berghahn, 2007).

Fitzpatrick, Sheila, 'Supplicants and citizens: public letter-writing in Soviet Russia in the 1930s', *Slavic Review* vol. 55, no. 1 (Spring 1996), 78–105.

Freeman, Simon, *Baghdad FC: Iraq's Football Story* (London: John Murray, 2005).

Friedemann, Horst (ed.), *Sparwasser und Mauerblümchen: Die Geschichte des Fußballs in der DDR 1949–1991* (Essen: Klartext, 1991).

Friedrich, Jorg, Lothar Mikos, Hans-Jörg Stiehler, and Lutz Warnicke, 'Sports coverage on GDR television', *Historical Journal of Film, Radio and Television* vol. 24, no. 3 (2004), 411–25.

Fuge, Jens, *Leutzscher Legende: Von Britannia 1899 zum FC Sachsen* (Leipzig: Sachsenbuch Verlag, 1992).

*Der Rest von Leipzig: BSG Chemie Leipzig* (Kassel: Agon Sportverlag, 2009)

Fulbrook, Mary, *Anatomy of a Dictatorship: Inside the GDR 1949–1989* (Oxford: Oxford University Press, 1997).

*German National Identity after the Holocaust* (Cambridge: Polity Press, 1999).

*The People's State: East German Society from Hitler to Honecker* (New Haven: Yale University Press, 2005).

Funder, Anna, *Stasiland: Stories from behind the Berlin Wall* (London: Granta Books, 2003).

Galeano, Eduardo, *Soccer in Sun and Shadow*, trans. Mark Fried (London: Verso, 1998).

Gaus, Günter, *Wo Deutschland liegt: Eine Ortsbestimmung.* (Hamburg: Hoffmann & Campe, 1983).

Genschmar, Jens, *Mit Dynamo durch Europa: Die Europapokalspiele der SG Dynamo Dresden 1967–1991* (Dresden: Edition Sächsische Zeitung, 2011).

Gieseke, Jens, 'Ulbricht's secret police: the Ministry of State Security', in Patrick Major and Jonathan Osmond (eds.), *The Workers' and Peasants' State: Communism and Society in East Germany under Ulbricht 1945–71* (Manchester: Manchester University Press, 2002), pp. 41–58.

Gieselmann, Dirk and Philipp Köster, 'Ein Traum in Malimo', *11 Freunde Spezial: Die Siebziger* (2009), 50–5.

Gilbert, Doug, *The Miracle Machine* (New York: Coward, McCann & Geoghegan, 1980).

Gläser, Andreas, *Der BFC war schuld am Mauerbau: Ein stolzer Sohn des Proletariats erzählt* (Berlin: Aufbau Taschenbuch Verlag, 2003).

Goldblatt, David, *The Ball Is Round: A Global History of Football* (London: Penguin Books, 2006).

Grieder, Peter, *The East German Leadership, 1946–1973: Conflict and Crisis* (Manchester: Manchester University Press, 1999).

Grix, Jonathan, 'The decline of mass sport provision in the German Democratic Republic', *International Journey of the History of Sport* vol. 25, no. 4 (March 2008), 406–20.

Gröschner, Annett, *Sieben Tränen muß ein Club-Fan weinen: 1. FC Magdeburg – eine Fußballegende* (Leipzig: Gustav Kiepenhauer, 1999).

Guttmann, Allen, *Sports Spectators* (New York: Columbia University Press, 1986).

Handke, Peter, 'Die Welt im Fußball', in *Ich bin ein Bewohner des Elfenbeinturms* (Frankfurt/Main: Suhrkamp, 1972).

Hargreaves, John, *Sport, Power and Culture: A Social and Historical Analysis of Popular Sports in Britain* (Cambridge: Polity Press, 1986).

Harsch, Donna, 'Squaring the circle: the dilemmas and evolution of women's policy', in Patrick Major and Jonathan Osmond (ed.), *The Workers' and Peasants' State: Communism and Society in East Germany under Ulbricht 1945–71* (Manchester: Manchester University Press, 2002), pp. 151–70.

Havemann, Nils, *Fußball unterm Hakenkreuz: Der DFB zwischen Sport, Politik und Kommerz* (Frankfurt/Main: Campus Verlag, 2005).

Heinrich, Arthur, 'The 1954 Soccer World Cup and the Federal Republic of Germany's self-discovery', *American Behavioral Scientist* vol. 46, no. 11 (July 2003), 1491–1505.

Herbst, Andreas, Winfried Ranke, and Jürgen Winkler (eds.), *So funktionierte die DDR: Band 1* (Hamburg: Rowohlt Verlag, 1994).

Herzog, Markwart (ed.), *Fußball zur Zeit des Nationalsozialismus: Alltag – Medien – Künste – Stars* (Stuttgart: Kohlhammer, 2008).

Hesse-Lichtenberger, Ulrich, *Tor! The Story of German Football* (London: WSC Books, 2002).

Hesselmann, Markus and Robert Ide, 'A tale of two Germanys: football culture and national identity in the German Democratic Republic', in Alan Tomlinson and Christopher Young (eds.), *German Football: History, Culture, Society* (London: Routledge, 2006), pp. 36–51.

Hesselmann, Markus and Michael Rosentritt, *Hansa Rostock: Der Osten lebt* (Göttingen: Verlag Die Werkstatt, 2000).

Hill, Jeffrey, 'Sport and politics', *Journal of Contemporary History*, vol. 38, no. 3 (July 2003), 355–61.

Hinsching, Jochen (ed.), *Alltagssport in der DDR* (Aachen: Meyer & Meyer, 1998).

Hjelm, Jonny and Eva Oloffson, 'A breakthrough: women's football in Sweden', in Fan Hong and J. A. Mangan (eds.), *Soccer, Women, Sexual Liberation: Kicking Off a New Era* (London: Frank Cass, 2003), pp. 190–212.

Hobsbawm, Eric, *Age of Extremes: The Short Twentieth Century, 1914–1991* (London: Penguin, 1994).

Horn, Michael and Gottfried Weise, *Das große Lexikon des DDR-Fußballs* (Berlin: Schwarzkopf & Schwarzkopf, 2004).

Hornby, Nick, *Fever Pitch* (London: Victor Gollancz, 1992).

Inglis, David, 'Theodor Adorno on sport: the *jeu d'esprit* of despair', in Richard Giulianotti (ed.), *Sport and Modern Social Theorists* (London: Palgrave Macmillan, 2004), pp. 81–95.

Inglis, Simon, *The Football Grounds of Europe* (London: HarperCollinsWillow, 1990).

James, C. L. R., *Beyond a Boundary* (London: Yellow Jersey Press, 2005).

Jarausch, Konrad, 'Care and coercion: the GDR as welfare dictatorship', in Konrad Jarausch (ed.), *Dictatorship as Experience: Towards a Socio-cultural History of the GDR*, trans. Eve Duffy (New York and Oxford: Berghahn, 1999), pp. 47–69.

Jessen, Ralph, 'Mobility and blockage during the 1970s', in Konrad Jarausch (ed.), *Dictatorship as Experience: Towards a Socio-cultural History of the GDR*, trans. Eve Duffy (New York and Oxford: Berghahn, 1999), pp. 341–60.

Johnson, Molly Wilkinson, *Training Socialist Citizens: Sports and the State in East Germany* (Boston, MA: Brill, 2008).

Joyce, Paul, 'Letter from Germany,' *When Saturday Comes* 221 (July 2005): www.wsc.co.uk/content/view/1608/29/.

Jürgens, Tim and Alex Raack, 'Triumph des Vorkuhilas', *11 Freunde* 114 (May 2011), 60–5.

Karády, Viktor and Miklós Hadas, 'Soccer and Antisemitism in Hungary', in Michael Brenner and Gideon Reuveni (eds.), *Emancipation through Muscles: Jews and Sport in Europe* (Lincoln, NE: University of Nebraska Press, 2006), pp. 213–34.

Karte, Uwe and Jörg Röhrig, *Kabinengeflüster: Geschichten aus 40 Jahren DDR-Elf* (Kassel: Agon Sportverlag, 1997).

Kershaw, Ian, 'Hitler and the Nazi dictatorship', in Mary Fulbrook (ed.), *Twentieth-Century Germany: Politics, Culture and Society 1918–1990* (London: Hodder Arnold, 2001), pp. 99–120.

Keys, Barbara, *Globalizing Sport: National Rivalry and International Community in the 1930s* (Cambridge, MA: Harvard University Press, 2006).

Klaedtke, Uta, *Betriebssport in der DDR: Phänomene des Alltagssports* (Hamburg: Verlag Sport & Co, 2007).

Klemperer, Victor, *Ich will Zeugnis ablegen bis zum letzten: Tagebücher, 1942–1945* (Berlin: Aufbau Verlag, 1999).

Kluge, Volker, *Das Sportbuch DDR* (Berlin: Eulenspiegel Verlag, 2004).

Kopstein, Jeffrey, 'Chipping away at the state: workers' resistance and the demise of East Germany', *World Politics* no. 48 (April 1996), 391–423.

*The Politics of Economic Decline in East Germany* (Chapel Hill, NC: The University of North Carolina Press, 1997).

Körner, Axel, 'Culture', in Mary Fulbrook (ed.), *Europe since 1945* (Oxford: Oxford University Press, 2001), pp. 146–86.

Kowalski, Ronnie and Dilwyn Porter, 'Cold War football: British–European encounters in the 1940s and 1950s', in Stephen Wagg and David L. Andrews (eds.), *East Plays West: Sport and the Cold War* (London: Routledge, 2007), pp. 64–81.

Krüger, Arnd, 'Strength through joy: the culture of consent under fascism, Nazism and Francoism', in Arnd Krüger and Jim Riordan (eds.), *The International Politics of Sport in the Twentieth Century* (London: E & FN Spon, 1999), pp. 67–89.

Kunze, Reiner, *Die wunderbaren Jahren* (Frankfurt/Main: S. Fischer Verlag, 1976).

Kuper, Simon, *Football against the Enemy* (London: Orion, 1994).

Kuper, Simon and Stefan Szymanski, *Soccernomics: Why England Loses, Why Germany and Brazil Win, and Why the U.S., Japan, Australia, Turkey – and Even Iraq – Are Destined to Become the Kings of the World's Most Popular Sport* (New York: Nation Books, 2009).

Langenhan, Dagmar and Sabine Roß, 'The socialist glass ceiling: limits to female careers', in Konrad Jarausch (ed.), *Dictatorship as Experience: Towards a Socio-cultural History of the GDR*, trans. Eve Duffy (New York and Oxford: Berghahn, 1999), pp. 177–91.

Leske, Hanns, *Erich Mielke, die Stasi und das runde Leder: Der Einfluß der SED und des Ministeriums für Staatssicherheit auf dem Fußballsport in der DDR* (Göttingen: Verlag Die Werkstatt, 2004).

*Enzyklopädie des DDR-Fußballs* (Göttingen: Verlag Die Werkstatt, 2007).

Lindenberger, Thomas, 'Creating socialist governance: the case of the Deutsche Volkspolizei', in Konrad Jarausch (ed.), *Dictatorship as Experience: Towards a Socio-cultural History of the GDR*, trans. Eve Duffy (New York and Oxford: Berghahn, 1999), pp. 125–41.

(ed.), *Herrschaft und Eigen-Sinn in der Diktatur: Studien zur Gesellschaftsgeschichte der DDR* (Cologne: Böhlau Verlag, 1999).

Linne, Carina, *Freigespielt: Frauenfußball im geteilten Deutschland* (Berlin: be.bra verlag, 2011).

'Freigespielt – Frauenfußball zwischen der Ostsee und dem Erzgebirge zwischen 1960 und 1990', unpublished paper from the Schwabenakademie conference on 'The History of Women's Football in Germany', 5 February 2011, 1–20.

Loest, Erich, *Der elfte Mann* (Munich: Deutscher Taschenbuch Verlag, 2006).

Lüdtke, Alf, *Eigensinn: Fabrikalltag, Arbeitererfahrungen und Politik vom Kaisserreich bis in den Faschismus* (Hamburg: Ergebnisse, 1993).

'"Helden der Arbeit" – Mühen beim Arbeiten: Zur mißmutigen Loyalität von Industriearbeitern in der DDR', in Hartmut Kaelble, Jürgen Kocka, and Hartmut Zwahr (eds.), *Sozialgeschichte der DDR* (Stuttgart: Klett-Cotta, 1994), pp. 188–213.

(ed.), *The History of Everyday Life: Reconstructing Historical Experiences and Ways of Life*, trans. William Templer (Princeton, NJ: Princeton University Press, 1995).

Luther, Jorn and Frank Willmann, *BFC Dynamo: Der Meisterclub* (Berlin: Das Neue Berlin, 2003).

*Eisern Union!* (Berlin: BasisDruck Verlag, 2010).

Macrakis, Kristie, *Seduced by Secrets: Inside the Stasi's Spy-Tech World* (Cambridge: Cambridge University Press, 2008).

Madarász, Jeannette, 'Economic politics and company culture: the problem of routinisation', in Mary Fulbrook (ed.), *Power and Society in the GDR, 1961–1979: The 'Normalisation' of Rule?* (New York and Oxford, Berghahn, 2009), pp. 52–75.

Mählert, Ulrich, *Die Freie Deutsche Jugend 1945–1949: Von den 'Antifaschistischen Jugendauschüsse' zur SED-Massenorganisation* (Paderborn: Verlag Ferdinand Schöningh, 1995).

Major, Patrick, *Behind the Berlin Wall: East Germany and the Frontiers of Power* (Oxford: Oxford University Press, 2010).

'Going west: the open border and the problem of Republikflucht', in Patrick Major and Jonathan Osmond (eds.), *The Workers' and Peasants' State: Communism and Society in East Germany under Ulbricht 1945–71* (Manchester: Manchester University Press, 2002), pp. 190–208.

Martin, Simon, *Football and Fascism: The National Game under Mussolini* (London: Berg, 2004).

Mason, Tony, 'Football', in Tony Mason (ed.), *Sport in Britain: A Social History* (Cambridge: Cambridge University Press, 1989), pp. 146–85.

McDougall, Alan, 'A duty to forget? The 'Hitler Youth generation' and the transition from Nazism to communism in post-war East Germany, *c.* 1945–49', *German History* vol. 26, no. 1 (2008), 24–46.

'Playing the game: football and everyday life in the Honecker era', in Mary Fulbrook and Andrew Port (eds.), *Becoming East German: Socialist Structures and Sensibilities after Hitler* (New York and Oxford: Berghahn, 2013), pp. 257–76.

*Youth Politics in East Germany: The Free German Youth Movement 1946–68* (Oxford: Oxford University Press, 2004).

McLellan, Josie, '"Even under socialism, we don't want to do without love": East German erotica', *Bulletin of the German Historical Institute Supplement* 7 (2011), 49–65.

*Love in the Time of Communism: Intimacy and Sexuality in the GDR* (Cambridge: Cambridge University Press, 2011).

Meier, Doreen, 'Meine Gegnerin war eine wahre Kampfmaschine', *11 Freundinnen* (April 2010), 24–5.

Merkel, Ina, 'The GDR – a normal country in the centre of Europe', in Mary Fulbrook (ed.), *Power and Society in the GDR, 1961–1979: The 'Normalisation' of Rule?* (New York and Oxford, Berghahn, 2009), pp. 194–203.

(ed.), *"Wir sind doch nicht die Mecker-Ecke der Nation": Briefe an das DDR-Fernsehen* (Cologne: Böhlau Verlag, 1998).

Moog, Christa, *Die Fans von Union: Geschichten* (Düsseldorf: Claassen, 1986).

Moynihan, John, *Football Fever* (London: Quartet Books, 1974).

Naimark, Norman, *The Russians in Germany: A History of the Soviet Zone of Occupation, 1945–1949* (Cambridge, MA: Harvard University Press, 1995).

Niethammer, Lutz, 'Zeroing in on change: in search of popular experience in the industrial province in the German Democratic Republic', in Alf Lüdtke (ed.), *The History of Everyday Life: Reconstructing Historical*

*Experiences and Ways of Life*, trans. William Templer (Cambridge: Cambridge University Press, 1997), pp. 252–311.

O'Mahony, Mike, *Sport in the USSR: Physical Culture – Visual Culture* (London: Reaktion, 2006).

Ohse, Marc-Dietrich, *Jugend nach dem Mauerbau: Anpassung, Protest und Eigensinn* (Berlin: Ch. Links Verlag, 2003).

Oswald, Rudolf, *"Fußball-Volksgemeinschaft": Ideologie, Politik und Fanatismus im deutschen Fußball 1919–1964* (Frankfurt/Main: Campus Verlag, 2008).

Palmowski, Jan, 'Between conformity and *Eigen-Sinn*: new approaches to GDR history', *German History* vol. 20, no. 4 (2002), 494–502.

*Inventing a Socialist Nation: Heimat and the Politics of Everyday Life in the GDR 1945–90* (Cambridge: Cambridge University Press, 2009).

'Regional identities and the limits of democratic centralism in the GDR', *Journal of Contemporary History* vol. 41, no. 3 (July 2006), 503–26.

Patzüg, Veit, *Was wir niemals waren: Erinnerungen* (Dresden: Thelem Literatur, 2010).

Peel, Quentin, 'German unemployment falls below 3m', ft.com, 28 April 2011: www.ft.com/cms/s/0/23d92cda-7185-11e0-9b7a-00144feabdc0.html#axzz2d5AvXfQu.

Peiffer, Lorenz and Schulze-Marmeling, Dietrich (eds.), *Hakenkreuz und rundes Leder: Fußball im Nationalsozialismus* (Göttingen: Verlag Die Werkstatt, 2008).

Peukert, Detlev, *Inside Nazi Germany: Conformity, Opposition and Racism in Everyday Life*, trans. Richard Deveson (London: Batsford, 1987).

Pfister, Gertrud, 'The challenges of women's football in East and West Germany: a comparative study', *Soccer & Society*, vol. 4, no.2/3 (April/June 2003), 128–48.

*Frauensport in der DDR* (Cologne: Strauss, 2002).

Pittaway, Mark, *Eastern Europe 1939–2000* (London: Arnold, 2004).

Pleil, Ingolf, *Mielke, Macht und Meisterschaft: Die "Bearbeitung" der Sportgemeinschaft Dynamo Dresden durch das MfS 1978–1989* (Berlin: Ch. Links Verlag, 2001).

Pockart, Steffen, *Das Leuchten der Giraffe: Kotte ... Cocker ... Kaffee-Mix* (Norderstedt: Books on Demand, 2010).

Port, Andrew, *Conflict and Stability in the German Democratic Republic* (New York: Cambridge University Press, 2007).

Pyta, Wolfram, 'German football: a cultural history', in Alan Tomlinson and Christopher Young (eds.), *German Football: History, Culture, Society* (Abingdon: Routledge, 2006), pp. 1–22.

Quinn, Leon, 'The politics of pollution: government, environmentalism and mass opinion in East Germany, 1972–1990', unpublished Ph.D. thesis, University of Bristol (2002).

Raack, Alex, 'Was hat euch bloss so ruiniert? 20 Jahre nach dem Fall der Mauer, das Schicksal des Ostfussballs', *3 Ecken Ein Elfer* 6 (May 2009), 16–21.

Reng, Ronald, *A Life Too Short: The Tragedy of Robert Enke*, trans. Shaun Whiteside (London: Yellow Jersey Press, 2011).

Richthofen, Esther von, *Bringing Culture to the Masses: Control, Compromise and Participation in the GDR* (New York and Oxford: Berghahn, 2009).

Riordan, James, *Sport in Soviet Society: Development of Sport and Physical Education in Russia and the USSR* (Cambridge: Cambridge University Press, 1977).

Ross, Corey, *The East German Dictatorship: Problems and Perspectives in the Interpretation of the GDR* (London: Arnold, 2002).

Rybicki, Kristin, 'Sportler an einen Tisch! – Berlin und die "Westarbeit" des Deutschen Sportauschusses in den frühen 1950er Jahren', in Jutta Braun and Joachim Teichler (eds.), *Sportstadt Berlin* (Berlin: Ch. Links Verlag, 2006), pp. 66–95.

Schiller, Kay, 'Communism, youth and sport: the 1973 World Youth Festival in East Berlin', in Alan Tomlinson, Christopher Young, and Richard Holt (eds.), *Sport and the Transformation of Modern Europe: States, Media and Markets, 1950–2010* (Abingdon: Routledge, 2011), pp. 50–66.

Schiller, Kay and Christopher Young, 'The history and historiography of sport in Germany: social, cultural and political perspectives', *German History* vol. 27, no. 3 (2009), 313–30.

*The 1972 Munich Olympics and the Making of Modern Germany* (Berkeley, CA: University of California Press, 2010).

Schulze-Marmeling, Dietrich (ed.), *Davidstern und Lederball: Die Geschichte der Juden im deutschen und internationalen Fußball* (Göttingen: Verlag Die Werkstatt, 2003).

Schwan, Heribert, *"Tod dem Verräter!" Der lange Arm der Stasi und der Fall Lutz Eigendorf* (Munich: Knaur, 2000).

Sebald, W. G., *On the Natural History of Destruction* (Toronto: Knopf Canada, 2003).

Sheffer, Edith, 'On edge: building the border in East and West Germany', *Central European History* vol. 40, no. 2 (2007), 307–39.

Skyba, Peter, *Vom Hoffnungsträger zur Sicherheitsrisiko: Jugend in der DDR und Jugendpolitik der SED 1949–1960* (Cologne: Böhlau Verlag, 2000).

Spitzer, Giselher, *Fußball und Triathlon: Sportentwicklung in der DDR* (Aachen: Meyer & Meyer, 2004).

*Sicherungsvorgang Sport: Das Ministerium für Staatssicherheit und der DDR-Spitzensport* (Schorndorf: Verlag Hoffmann, 2005).

Spufford, Francis, *Red Plenty* (London: Faber and Faber, 2010).

Steege, Paul, Andrew Stuart Bergerson, Maureen Healy, and Pamela E. Swett, 'The history of everyday life: a second chapter', *Journal of Modern History* vol. 80, no. 2 (June 2008), 358–78.

Stieglitz, Olaf, Jürgen Martschukat, and Kirsten Heinsohn, 'Sportreportage: Sportgeschichte als Kultur- und Sozialgeschichte', *H-Soz-u-Kult*, 28 May 2009, 1–37: http://hsozkult.geschichte.hu-berlin.de/forum/2009-05-001.

Stitziel, Judd, 'Shopping, sewing, networking, complaining: consumer culture and the relationship between state and society in the GDR', in Katherine Pence and Paul Betts (eds.), *Socialist Modern: East German Everyday Culture and Politics* (Ann Arbor, MI: University of Michigan Press, 2008), pp. 253–86.

Stone, Chris, 'The role of football in everyday life', *Soccer & Society* vol. 8, no. 2/3 (April/July 2007), 169–84.

Stridde, Thomas, *Die Peter-Ducke-Story* (Jena: Glaux Verlag Christine Jäger, 2006).

Teichler, Hans Joachim, 'Fußball in der DDR', *Aus Politik und Zeitgeschichte. Beilage zur Wochenzeitung Das Parlament* vol. 56, no. 19 (2006), 26–33.

Thaler, Martin, 'Im Bermuda Triangle', *3 Ecken Ein Elfer* 6 (May 2009), 36–8.

Thiemann, Ellen, *Der Feind an meiner Seite: Die Spitzelkarriere eines Fussballers* (Munich: Herbig, 2005).

Trede, Bröder-Jürgen, 'Das vergessene Jahrhunderttor', *Spiegel-Online*, 6 October 2006: www.spiegel.de/sport/fussball/0,1518,440986,00.html.

Turner, Victor, *The Forest of Symbols: Aspects of Ndembu Ritual* (Ithaca, NY: Cornell University Press, 1967).

Van der Meer, Hans, *European Fields: The Landscape of Lower League Football* (Göttingen: SteidlMACK, 2006).

Wagg, Stephen, 'On the continent: football in the societies of North West Europe', in Stephen Wagg (ed.), *Giving the Game Away: Football, Politics and Culture on Five Continents* (London: Leicester University Press, 1995), pp. 103–24.

Wagner, Reinhard (ed.), *DDR-Witze Teil 2* (Berlin: Dietz Verlag, 1997).

Weitz, Eric, *Weimar Germany: Promise and Tragedy* (Princeton, NJ: Princeton University Press, 2007).

Wierling, Dorothee, 'The Hitler Youth generation in the GDR: insecurities, ambitions and dilemmas', in Konrad H. Jarausch (ed.), *Dictatorship as Experience: Towards a Socio-cultural History of the GDR* (New York: Berghahn, 1999), pp. 307–24.

'Die Jugend als innere Feind: Konflikte in der Erziehungsdiktatur der sechziger Jahre', in Hartmut Kaelble, Jürgen Kocka, and Hartmut Zwahr (eds.), *Sozialgeschichte der DDR* (Stuttgart: Klett-Cotta, 1994), pp. 404–25.

Wiese, René, 'Hertha BSC im Kalten Krieg (1945–1961)', in Jutta Braun and Joachim Teichler (eds.), *Sportstadt Berlin* (Berlin: Ch. Links Verlag, 2006), pp. 96–149.

'Wie der Fußball Löcher in die Mauer schoss – Die Ost–West-Alltagskultur des Fußballs in Berlin (1961–1990)', in Jutta Braun and Joachim Teichler (eds.), *Sportstadt Berlin* (Berlin: Ch. Links Verlag, 2006), pp. 239–84.

Williams, Jean, 'The fastest growing sport? Women's football in England', in Fan Hong and J. A. Mangan (eds.), *Soccer, Women, Sexual Liberation: Kicking Off a New Era* (London: Frank Cass, 2003), pp. 112–27.

Willmann, Frank (ed.), *Fußball-Land DDR: Anstoß, Abpfiff, Aus* (Berlin: Eulenspiel Verlag, 2004).

(ed.), *Stadionpartisanen: Fans und Hooligans in der DDR* (Berlin: Verlag Neues Leben, 2007).

(ed.), *Zonenfußball: Von Wismut Aue bis Rotes Banner Trinwillershagen* (Berlin: Verlag Neues Leben, 2011)

Wilson, Jonathan, *Behind the Curtain: Football in Eastern Europe* (London: Orion, 2006).

Wilton, Dan, 'Regime versus people? Public opinion and the development of sport and popular music in the GDR, 1961–1989', unpublished Ph.D. thesis, University College London (2005).

'The "societalisation" of the state: sport for the masses and popular music in the GDR', in Mary Fulbrook (ed.), *Power and Society in the GDR, 1961–1979: The 'Normalisation' of Rule?* (New York and Oxford, Berghahn, 2009), pp. 102–29.

Winner, David, *Brilliant Orange: The Neurotic Genius of Dutch Football* (London: Bloomsbury, 2000).

Wittich, Else (ed.), *Wo waren Sie, als das Sparwasser-Tor fiel?* (Hamburg: Konkret Literatur Verlag, 1998).

Wolle, Stefan, *Die heile Welt der Diktatur: Alltag und Herrschaft in der DDR 1971–1989* (Bonn: Bundeszentrale für politische Bildung, 1998).

Zatlin, Jonathan, *The Currency of Socialism: Money and Political Culture in East Germany* (Cambridge: Cambridge University Press, 2007).

Zimmer, Christoph, 'Verbrannte Erde: Das lange Leiden der SG Dynamo Dresden', *3 Ecken Ein Elfer* 6 (May 2009), 24–9.

# Index

Printed by Printforce, United Kingdom